Revolution

Martin Anderson

REVOLUTION

HARCOURT BRACE JOVANOVICH, PUBLISHERS

San Diego   New York   London

Requests for permission to make copies of any
part of the work should be mailed to:
Permissions, Harcourt Brace Jovanovich, Publishers,
Orlando, Florida 32887.

Library of Congress Cataloging-in-Publication Data
Anderson, Martin, 1936–
Revolution.
Bibliography: p.
Includes index.
1. Reagan, Ronald.   2. Anderson, Martin, 1936–
—Friends and associates.   3. United States—Politics
and government—1981–   . I. Title.
E877.A84   1988   973.927′092′4   87-33610
ISBN 0-15-177087-5

Designed by G. B. D. Smith

Printed in the United States of America

First edition

A B C D E

To Annelise:

My best friend, most valued collaborator,
wife—and the one who suggested *Revolution*
as the title for this book.

CONTENTS

FOREWORD

When I look back at the sweep of political events during the past twenty-five years it becomes clear that there is no way to begin to acknowledge all the important, critical contributions that were made by so many. Thousands of people—from the intellectual world, from the world of presidential campaigns, and from the policymaking world in Washington—made the revolution happen and without their individual contributions there would be no story to tell.

All studies in politics and economics owe deep intellectual debts to earlier works by economists and political scientists. This book is no exception. An equal debt is owed to the men and women who work in campaigns and help elect presidents, who accept appointments to public office, who struggle with the maddeningly complex reality of government, and who somehow craft the national policies that—for better or worse—we examine, criticize, and sometimes praise.

During the last seventeen years I have been a senior fellow at the Hoover Institution at Stanford University. With each passing year I become more convinced that it is the finest think tank in the world, unsurpassed in the brilliance, distinction, and collegiality of my colleagues; unmatched in the richness of its research resources; and located centrally on the campus of one of the finest universities in the world, Stanford, between the blue waters of the Pacific and the high Sierra Mountains.

New policy ideas do not materialize from the air and great intellectual institutions do not occur by chance. They come from individual thought and effort. A number of scholars at the Hoover Institution at Stanford University are at the cutting edge of the intellectual movement that swept Reagan to power, and at the heart of that think tank were two people who, more than any others, were responsible for building that California center of research and learning.

W. Glenn Campbell is the driving force. Born in Canada in 1924, a scion of the Campbell aristocrats who fought with Robert the Bruce, the king of Scotland, against the English in the 14th century, and the great, great grandson of an officer who fought with the Duke of Wellington at Waterloo, the brainy, hardfisted Campbell is probably closer in spirit to his forebears than he is to his former colleagues on the Harvard University faculty. Becoming director in 1960 at the urging of former president Herbert Hoover, Campbell set a standard of excellence, raised the funds that created the largest endowment of any comparable institution, selected the scholars, and managed its day-to-day operations.

Although Campbell has a long record of public service—appointed seven times to public office by five U.S. presidents—his greatest contribution has been building the Hoover Institution into a world-renowned think tank. Campbell is without peer, the premier intellectual entrepreneur of this century. His partner in this lifelong work is his wife, Rita Ricardo-Campbell, a direct descendent of David Ricardo, the 19th-century English economist. Better known for her work as a public policy scholar, she advised and counseled the director on everything from personnel to policy.

This book is the result of a two-hour conversation I had in June 1986 in San Diego with William Jovanovich and Peter Jovanovich, both of whom were introduced to me by Milton Friedman. They had sufficient confidence in the ideas and thoughts I expressed during our wide-ranging discussion to offer me a contract and then, later, to take the time to review the manuscript and provide me with some powerful suggestions for improving the book's structure.

Marie Arana-Ward, my editor at Harcourt Brace Jovanovich, helped greatly in shaping the manuscript into a coherent story. Her incisive questions forced me to rethink and rewrite a number of sections. It was she who suggested adding a discussion of the Iran-Contra affair, and she who spared the reader some less interesting stories that found their way into the original manuscript. Kathleen Bursley, HBJ attorney, gave the manuscript a careful legal review and provided a number of suggestions that helped my words say what they were supposed to say, accurately and precisely. Of course, as is customary, I will take responsibility and blame for the final organizational structure and for the writing.

A special thanks and acknowledgment go to Brenda McLean, my longtime assistant at Hoover. When the time came to write, she became the production manager and initial editor, transforming my rough drafts into miracles of print, and providing many helpful suggestions both in substance and grammar. Beyond that she performed seemingly endless research tasks, tracking down hundreds of pieces of information that stiffened the spine of the manuscript, and supervised a number of Stanford students—including Jason Matherly, Christopher J. de Rosa, James Erickson, and Michael C. Whitticar—who also contributed to the research and editing effort at various stages along the way. In the later stages, Margo Johnston was very helpful in typing and retyping draft after draft.

A special note of thanks to Margit and Russell Grigory, who produced a superb index under great time pressure; and to Michael J. Kuhlman, the IBM engineer who coaxed my word processor back to life after it died, entombing almost the entire manuscript.

Finally, I should like especially to thank the men and women who read parts or all of the manuscript. Their comments and criticisms improved it, and their words of encouragement inspired me. They are: Richard V. Allen, Annelise Anderson, Dennis L. Bark, Arnold Beichman, Mikhail Bernstam, Tom Bethell, W. Glenn Campbell, Angelo Codevilla, Gregory Fossedal, Vincent Gaudiani, Robert Hessen, Sidney Hook, Arthur Laffer, David McLean, William Niskanen, Rita Ricardo-Campbell, Paul Craig Roberts, William Safire, Gilbert Shelton, Judy Shelton, Kenneth Y. Tomlinson, Darrell M. Trent, Anne Wortham, and Dr. Julian Youmans.

PROLOGUE

It came like a rising tide—silently, inexorably, gently lapping forward. Only the political waves were noticeable, and these rushed in, then receded, only to rush in again and again—each time higher, stronger.

First came Barry Goldwater in 1964. The United States had not seen his like before. In his black, owl-like glasses, he burst upon the American political scene and seemed to speak for millions of Americans unsatisfied with the United States as it was. They wanted more individual liberty, less government, more national defense. And they wanted it now. The middle-of-the-road establishment sniffed and raised its eyebrows. The left was appalled.

Goldwater was attacked and vilified, first by the Left and then even by members of his own party as his political power grew. He won the Republican nomination for president in 1964 and pulled down almost 40 percent of the vote in the general election against Lyndon Baines Johnson. Goldwater was labeled an extremist and a radical, and his loss to the liberal Democrat Johnson was offered as proof that his presidential campaign was an aberration. Some even speculated that Goldwater's loss marked the end of the Republican party in the United States, that it locked in for good the political philosophy of liberalism. Goldwater was seen as a lonely phenomenon, a likeable, friendly man from the Southwest who somehow temporarily bewitched a surprisingly large number of Americans.

By the mid-1960s there was a general consensus that the Goldwater legions had passed from the political stage and the American establishment was secure and serene.

Then came Richard Nixon in 1968. Shy, brilliant, a man cursed with a five-o'clock-shadow beard, Nixon plotted his comeback from political exile with great cunning and skill. Defeated in his attempt to become governor of California in 1962, he returned, persuasively presenting the case for virtually all of Goldwater's policies and programs. And he was elected president in 1968 on the basis of those policies, very narrowly to be sure, with just a hair under 50 percent of the popular vote. It was the Goldwater campaign in 1964 and Nixon's victory in 1968 that established the political base of conservatism. Without Goldwater and Nixon there probably would have been no Reagan.

The Goldwater wave had been small and tentative. The Nixon wave was much stronger and more powerful. The policies that Nixon pursued, many of them the same policies that labeled Goldwater an extremist just four years earlier, proved so popular and effective that Richard Nixon was reelected in 1972 by one of the largest vote margins in U.S. history. The establishment was shocked. The Left was frightened. How could this man Nixon acquire so much political power? He was not a mesmerizing speaker. He looked dark and foreboding on television. He was not an affable personality like Barry Goldwater. Why?

While Nixon's political opponents desperately tried to solve this puzzle something happened that made the puzzle moot—Watergate. Scandal engulfed the Nixon administration and crushed it. Nixon was forced to resign his office in 1974; it was the first time that had ever happened to a president of the United States. Scandal, betrayal, and cover-ups accomplished what his political opponents on the Left had been powerless to do. Watergate stopped cold the major policy initiatives of the Nixon administration, and then led first to a caretaker president, Gerald Ford, and then to the left-wing administration of Jimmy Carter.

After Jimmy Carter's election, the Left breathed a collective sigh of relief. Nixon was gone, banished. Goldwater was an old man. A bright, smiling left-wing liberal was in the White House. The stake was driven into the heart of American conservatism. Happy days were here again.

The Right was distraught, depressed. Their first love, Goldwater, was soundly defeated. Nixon, it seemed, had disgraced and betrayed them. And now they lived in a country led by a president surrounded by left-wing yahoos.

By the end of the 1970s there was a general consensus that both the Goldwater fanatics and the Nixon cronies had passed from the political stage. The liberal establishment settled back again, secure and serene.

Then came 1980 and Ronald Reagan. A famous movie star who had twice been governor of the largest state in the United States, Reagan combined the personal appeal of Goldwater and the political skill of Nixon. And he believed in the same policies—more individual liberty, less government, and a stronger national defense. The Reagan wave that crashed down on the American political beach was much stronger and more powerful than those of Goldwater or Nixon. Once again the establishment was shocked. Even the corporate leaders of America did not support Reagan until they knew he was going to win, first supporting John Connally in the presidential primaries and then, after Reagan defeated Connally, switching to George Bush until he, too, lost to Reagan.

One of the unspoken secrets of Reagan's political success is that he is to a certain extent a populist—wary not only of big government, but also of big labor and big business. His powerful appeal to the average man in America terrified the Left. How could Reagan win the loyalty of so many working men and women? The Left dismissed the possibility that the working men and women of America subscribed to his policies. Instead, they concluded that it must be his personality, his handsome face, his winning smile, his clever staff, even his luck.

Reagan rolled on, piling up one policy revolution after another, winning his reelection with a resounding victory, until the same thing that did Nixon in did Reagan in—scandal. When the Iran-Contra affair exploded in the fall of 1986 the Reagan administration effectively came to a dead halt. For over a year, time stood still for Reagan as he fought the scandal. Unlike Nixon, Reagan survived. He was weaker, he lost precious time, but he continued on, achieving at least one major victory he had been aiming at for over ten years—

the mutual reduction of nuclear weapons by the Soviet Union and the United States.

Now, as Reagan's presidency draws to a close, there is once again a collective sigh going up in the United States. On the Left there is once again relief. At last Reagan is going back to California. And there are no more like him. Even if we don't get a Democrat in 1988, at least we will get a sensible Republican, not radical, perhaps a bit back to the left. On the Right, there is despair. Many conservatives see the Reagan revolution ending with Reagan, just as their opponents on the Left do. They are disillusioned, disheartened, once more fearing for the future of the United States.

Well, we shall see.

But in the meantime, perhaps we should look back at history for a moment, especially the last twenty-five years. Look at the rise of Barry Goldwater and Richard Nixon and Ronald Reagan. What linked these three men together? What threw them high on the rocky beach of American politics? What gave them the political power to change America and so change the world?

Was their power due to their overwhelming personalities, to personal characteristics that can never be duplicated? Or was it due to something independent of any one person, to intellectual and political currents that produced first Goldwater then Nixon then Reagan?

Some have and will continue to argue that personalities explain the political phenomenon of Goldwater, Nixon, and Reagan. But it is an unsatisfying explanation. The more you look at these people and what they did and what they represent, the more you are forced to conclude that much more is afoot here. Barry Goldwater's smile and Richard Nixon's jabbing forefinger and Ronald Reagan's friendly wave of the arm had virtually nothing to do with their rise to political power in the United States, and so far no one has attributed the move toward capitalism in China, and the Soviet Union, and New Zealand, and in dozens of other countries throughout the world to the power of these three personalities.

The more you look, the more you are forced to conclude that these three men did not cause the events in America during the last few decades. No, they were caused by them. The rising tide of a new capitalism, a powerful intellectual movement that is still rising created the political momentum that swept these men to political prominence and power. Neither Goldwater nor Nixon nor

Reagan caused or created the revolutionary movement that often carries their name, especially Reagan's. It was the other way around. They were part of the movement, they contributed mightily to the movement, but the movement gave them political life, not the reverse.

What this means is that when President Reagan retires, the set of policies known as the Reagan revolution will not retire with him, no more than Barry Goldwater's policies disappeared when he was defeated in 1964, no more than President Nixon's policies vanished when he was driven from office in 1974. The fundamental changes in national policy still occurring in the United States and in virtually every country of the world are the inevitable result of intellectual changes that have already occurred. This political movement—the new capitalism—transcends personality, transcends political party.

Perhaps President Reagan's retirement in 1989 will lead to a lull or even a brief recession to the left once again. Perhaps not. The only thing that seems unshakably clear is that an intellectual revolution has occurred worldwide. Communism, socialism, and any other form of dictatorship statism have proven to be intellectually bankrupt. The only vibrant, thriving political philosophy with a sound intellectual base remaining is capitalism. This appalls men and women of the Left. It delights men and women of the Right. But whether you are appalled or delighted, it may be important to know the nature of what you will be dealing with for the rest of this century and for much of the next.

As long as public policy and political change flow from the well of reigning, dominant intellectual beliefs, then the tide of the new capitalism will continue to rise. Only when and if there is a seismic shift to the Left in the intellectual world will we see a reversal of the political changes we are now witnessing.

Powerful political personalities can hasten those changes, or they can retard them, but they cannot stop them. The end of the Reagan presidency is near, but the end of the ideas that swept him to power is nowhere in sight. Before the twentieth century is over, we will likely see a new, stronger version of Reagan rise to take his place.

I have been thinking about this book for over twenty years. During those years I took notes, kept diaries, saved papers and documents, and watched and tried to understand why what was happening was happening. Several times when I believed events had run their course I turned to writing about them, and each time I was overtaken by fresh events, sometimes participating in them myself.

Historians do not like to write about things that have just happened or are still going on. They prefer the wise perspective that waiting two or three decades can give you. But I am not a historian. And we are in the midst of a profound revolution, so important that we cannot wait until it is over before we try to understand it. Better a rough, imperfect view of what is happening now, than a smooth, more perfect analysis of it all when it is over.

One thing I have observed and that has struck me over the years is how little seems to be known about the true nature of the intellectual and political revolution enveloping us these last two decades. Most people seem to believe that random forces are at work here, and many believe those forces are temporary, and a few seem to feel they radiate from the personality of one man. But when you examine the scope of what has happened in the United States and throughout much of the world during the last ten or fifteen years, it is hard to believe that what we see was caused by random, transient events or by any one person.

Just look at the United States in the 1980s. Ronald Reagan not only won the presidency but, after serving for four years, he was reelected president by one of the largest landslides in history. In spite of large federal deficits, huge trade imbalances, worrisome third world debt, and a speculative stock market crash, the United States managed to achieve, from 1982 to 1987, the greatest economic expansion in history, creating more wealth and more jobs during this five-year period than any other country at any time in the world.

And then, while Reagan was pouring more money ($1.5 trillion) into national defense than ever before and initiating a radical new missile defense system, the United States and the Soviet Union agreed to reduce their stockpiles of nuclear missiles. General Secretary Gorbachev and President Reagan agreed to eliminate short and intermediate range nuclear missiles from Europe, and President Reagan even began to talk openly of someday making nuclear missiles obsolete.

Today, it seems that everywhere we look in the world, we see the threads of a new liberty, based on more capitalism and greater prospects for peace. We may—remembering that unlike death and taxes nothing is sure in politics—be poised at the dawning of a new era. An era of peace and capitalism.

This is a time of profound revolution.

Perhaps the great underlying mystery in all of this is: How did it happen? How did an aging, ex-actor from Hollywood rise to power in the United States and preside over the greatest economic expansion in history? How, by spending more on military weapons than anyone ever had, did that bring us closer to eliminating the scourge of nuclear-tipped intercontinental ballistic missiles? How did Ronald Reagan, with a reputation for being lazy and not too bright, manage to stay in political power so long—and to succeed as well as he did?

This book is primarily a story about Ronald Reagan's rise to power in the United States, on what kind of man he is, the public policies he thought were important, and the main consequences of those policies. There is special emphasis on the worldwide intellectual movement that made Reagan's rise possible—the growth of the new capitalism.

The book is not a comprehensive treatise. It is a combination of stories and analyses of selected events and policies, many of which I participated in, that constitute the heart of what has become known as the Reagan revolution. The brushes, and the oils, and the canvas of the Reagan revolution are old. The painting is new. And the artists are still working on it.

This book is a story about the power of ideas, about how ideas come out of the intellectual world, are transformed by the world of presidential campaigns into items on the national policy agenda, and then how those ideas become law in Washington, D.C., and govern us and affect our daily lives.

The book is also a story about agonizing defeat and exhilarating victory, and about some of the people who suffered those defeats and savored those victories. It is largely a story of triumphs, but it is also a story of the ordeal of the Iran-Contra affair, of how avaricious men, desperate governments, and Americans who lied and misled their president may have combined to form the potent, deadly political cocktail that nearly felled Reagan.

It is a story about the rise of capitalism around the world and about the power of its principles.

It is a story about the intellectual and political revolution that has accompanied Reagan's ascent to the presidency, and the events and people that have influenced his tenure.

The revolution itself rolls on. It is by no means a complete story. There will be more to tell by other voices in other books.

Above all, this is a story that says little in politics happens by chance, that virtually everything is carefully done, carefully plotted, sometimes years in advance, that conspiracy properly defined is an American tradition as natural to us as breathing—and that it is good.

One

The Revolution

The ultimate irony of the twentieth century may be that lasting, worldwide political revolution was accomplished not by Trotsky and the communists but instead by Reagan and the capitalists.

Chapter One

UNITED STATES

Mikhail S. Gorbachev was indignant.

He didn't take off his shoe and pound it on the table as his predecessor, Nikita Khrushchev, once did when he became annoyed at a United Nations meeting. Gorbachev's reaction was of a more sophisticated kind.

He leaned forward, holding a massive three-and-one-half pound book in his hand, shaking it vigorously in the faces of the secretary of state and the White House national security adviser. "Don't tell me that! We know what you think!" Gorbachev shouted. "We have read this book and watched all its programs become adopted by the Reagan Administration."[1] George Shultz and Robert McFarlane were amazed. What was he talking about? Why was he so upset?

The first summit meeting between President Reagan and General Secretary Gorbachev was scheduled to take place the following week in Geneva, Switzerland. Shultz and McFarlane had flown to Moscow for preparatory talks directly with Gorbachev on November 5, 1985. As the discussion proceeded the Soviet ruler expressed obvious skepticism about American policies being represented to him by the emissaries from the United States. Suddenly, with the assured air of someone who knows he is right, he lashed out at Shultz and McFarlane asserting that the United States was an implacable foe of the Soviet Union, that the nuclear arms treaty had been undermined by right-wing forces, and that those same right-wing forces controlled all American policy. According to the report in the *New York Times*, "Mr. Gorbachev repeatedly cited a book published by the Hoover Institution, the research center in Palo Alto, California, as the *real blueprint* [italics added] for Reagan Administration policy."[2]

When I first read the accounts of Gorbachev's vision of America, and heard about it later from other sources, I was amazed. The blueprint he was waving at our secretary of state and national security adviser was a book I had initiated in 1977, almost eight years earlier.

By the late 1970s it was increasingly obvious that the United States had a number of very serious public policy problems. More and more people in the intellectual world plunged into research and writing about these issues, and some of them were coming up with innovative, effective solutions. The idea that I suggested to W. Glenn Campbell, director of the Hoover Institution, was to commission the best of these intellectuals to write short policy essays in their areas of expertise, including specific recommendations on what should be done.

The result was an 868-page anthology entitled *The United States in the 1980s*, a review and analysis of major domestic and international issues facing the United States as it entered the 1980s.[3] The book was published on January 29, 1980. A little over nine months later, on November 4, 1980, Ronald Reagan was elected the fortieth president of the United States. Much of the policy recommended in the book soon became the policy of the United States government. Many of the people associated with the book later became associated with the Reagan administration.

At last count, seventeen of the people who contributed to or advised on the book held important positions in the Reagan administration, including secretary of state, chairman of the Federal Reserve, domestic policy adviser to the president, undersecretary of defense, and the chairman of the Council of Economic Advisers.

It certainly looked suspicious. As Sidney Blumenthal, a reporter for the *Washington Post*, wrote, "Gorbachev seemed to regard the anthology by the conservative think tank as the product of an

American equivalent of the Soviet Politburo, a document with the force of an official directive."[4]

Of course it was not that. The anthology was published by the Hoover Institution Press, but the scholars who wrote the policy essays were associated with many universities and institutions other than Hoover. My first reaction was not to deny the story. After all, how often does one get credited with crafting the entire policy blueprint of the United States?

Many American observers had no better understanding of what was going on than Gorbachev or his vaunted KGB did. And the true story is much more complicated than a few people conspiring successfully to determine the policies of the United States government. The Hoover book was just one part of an intellectual revolution that has been building and growing stronger—in the United States and throughout the world—for decades. Those who wrote the policy essays and the ones who served in the United States government were just a fraction of those involved in the powerful intellectual and political movement that rose to power in the 1980s.

When Ronald Wilson Reagan was elected president, many people in the United States were surprised, some were shocked, and a few were stunned. Most of the world was puzzled. But their surprise and puzzlement soon turned into astonishment as President Reagan's policies began to take effect.

Not everyone was surprised or puzzled, though. There were a few who had been working to accomplish this for most of their lives. Perhaps none of them anticipated the magnitude and swiftness of the change. But for them what happened during the 1980s in the United States was the product of a lifetime of effort—an effort to forge an intellectual revolution that would lead to massive political change. The events of 1980 were a political expression of powerful forces that have been growing and deepening in the United States for many years.

First came major changes in national economic policy as America moved away from the economics of the Left and sped toward a freer, more capitalistic economy. Soon to become known throughout the world as Reaganomics, these policies released a burst of productive energy that created millions of new jobs, cut taxes, and drove down both inflation and interest rates to their lowest points in decades. The stock market boomed to record levels.

Next came major changes in national defense policy. Confident that the economy was strong enough to support it, the American people began a massive rebuilding of military power, adding hundreds of billions of dollars to defense spending. And then came major changes in nuclear weapons policy. Abandoning the old and flawed doctrine of mutually assured destruction, a concept that dominated much of U.S. military thinking since the coming of nuclear missiles that could fly from one country to another, America suddenly set forth on a new path of missile defense, and began pouring billions of dollars and the thinking of many of its most brilliant scientists into the development of new weapons that could destroy nuclear missiles in flight long before they ever touched our soil.

If we accept *Webster's Third New International Dictionary* definition that revolution is "a fundamental change in political organization; especially: the overthrow or renunciation of one government or ruler and the substitution of another by the governed," then by any reasonable standard, what was happening in America was a revolution, not a violent physical revolution driven by guns, but a revolution of political thought, a revolution of ideas.

When Reagan was reelected in 1984 by the largest electoral vote margin in history,[5] it became clear that something serious and fundamental was happening. It was no longer possible to dismiss his presence and political victories as some mysterious, unexplainable accident of nature, or to blame it on his charm, good looks, and sense of humor. No, it was now clear that what was happening went far beyond one man, that it was something in scope and power equivalent to an intellectual earthquake that would shake the political establishment of the United States—and the world—for some time to come.

The intellectual and political revolution occurring in the United States is known throughout the world as conservative. But if by conservative we mean a disposition to maintain existing views, traditions, or institutions, then in many ways it is profoundly nonconservative.

Most of those who helped fan its flames and drive it forward sensed its true character—radical and revolutionary—for it was aimed at sweeping out the status quo. It was radical because, in the true meaning of the word, it grappled with the roots of the political, economic, and social problems that were before it. It was revolutionary because its aim was fundamental change in the existing political, economic and social order. And perhaps it was ultrarevolutionary because it attempted, and succeeded, in accomplishing this change without the use of guns or violence—an ordinary event in the United States, but still unusual in today's world.

There have been numerous attempts to explain these dramatic political changes. Most of these explanations have focused on the role of the neoconservatives and the New Right, including the religious-political movement called the Moral Majority. While these groups did contribute significantly to the recent dramatic political changes in the United States, explanations that feature their role have been unsatisfying and unconvincing, largely because they have overlooked the main thrust of the movement they are attempting to explain. In order for there to be a New Right, there must have been an Old Right. In order for someone to be a neoconservative, there has to have been a conservative movement that one can be neo to.

The election of Ronald Reagan in 1980 and many of the events that followed were the political results of an intellectual movement building for many years in the United States and, to a lesser extent, throughout the world. But what has been called the Reagan revolution is not completely, or even mostly, due to Ronald Reagan. He was an extremely important contributor to the intellectual and political movement that swept him to the presidency in 1980. He gave that movement focus and leadership. But Reagan did not give it life.

That movement was no accident, but rather the logical outgrowth of policy ideas and political forces set in motion during the 1950s and 1960s, ideas and forces that gathered strength and speed during the 1970s, then achieved political power in the 1980s, and promise to dominate national policy in the United States for the remainder of the twentieth century. There have been many contributors to this movement: the traditional Republicans and the old conservatives who formed its core; the libertarians who gave it consistency and sharply defined goals, at the same time widening the boundaries of intellectual debate; the neoconservatives whose desertion from the Left seemed to confirm the validity of the movement and who infused that movement with new intellectual vigor; the New Right with their political enthusiasm and persistence; and the Moral Majority with their large numbers and moral certitude. They were all necessary, though none by itself sufficient, to have achieved the kind of intellectual and political change that occurred in so short a time.

By 1980, liberalism, the dominant political philosophy of the United States, was intellectually bankrupt. A new American political philosophy, not yet fully formed, but built on the framework of conservative and libertarian ideas of the last several decades, was beginning to dominate and control the national policy agenda. The ideas of statism and collectivism were crumbling before the ideas of individualism and liberty.

American liberalism is but a pale cousin of real socialism, and a very distant relation to the real thing, communism. And throughout the world the philosophy of socialism and communism have been discredited, as country after country watches the glittering dream of socialist theory turn to ash.

The major policy changes recently realized in the United States did not happen by accident. They were undertaken purposely.

In the United States policy changes are designed and shaped in turn by three different worlds. The original ideas generally spring from the intellectual world, move on into the world of presidential campaigns and, if they are successful, end up in the policymaking world in Washington.

The intellectual world in the United States consists of the universities, think tanks, publishing houses, and the media. This is where almost all new policy ideas come from. And it is these ideas, strategies, and plans that represent real power in policymaking. In the final analysis it is the intellectuals who really determine the policy agenda of the United States. There may be long delays— five, ten, or more years—before the ideas of the intellectuals, sometimes mangled beyond easy recognition, emerge on the national policy scene. But when they do appear they have enormous impact. In the long run the intellectual world has the most powerful and continuing impact on the making of national policy.

Then there is the world of the presidential campaign, a phenomenon whose importance is unique to the United States. The presidential campaign plays an unusual role in the development of national policy. Every four years, as the presidential candidates organize themselves to engage in one of the most physically and mentally exhausting pursuits known, policy ideas suddenly take on a special importance. One or two years before the actual campaign begins, it usually dawns on the candidate that he or she must have a cogent, vote-getting position on virtually every major issue (and many minor ones) that face the country. The candidates will also soon develop a keen desire for one or two new, bold ideas that will set them apart from their opponents. That terribly urgent need for ideas touches off a diligent search by the candidate and staff aides. And their search begins in the intellectual world.

Thus, for both Democrats and Republicans, American presidential campaigns act as policy catalysts. The ideas they take from the intellectual world are tested in the white-hot crucible of the presidential campaign. There they are laid out in party platforms and campaign promises for the voting public's ultimate judgment.

Finally, there is the policymaking world of Washington. After the campaign is over, and the promises and pledges are made, there comes the time for settling the bill. Contrary to conventional wisdom, most party platform planks and campaign pledges do inspire and determine policy in Washington. This truth is often obscured by the broken pledges and promises—the exceptions—that usually dominate the news. But when the time comes for our top policymakers in the White House or Congress to make the final choices on policy changes, their range of action is quite limited. The power of national policymakers is constrained, channeled, and limited by the prevailing intellectual and political forces.

These three very different worlds—the arcane discourse of the intellectual, the circus crusade of the presidential campaign, and the power-jostling of policymakers in Washington—are all vital links in the chain that creates the policies and laws that govern our lives.

The people with deeply held convictions who operate in these worlds play significant roles in the major changes that have occurred in America in the latter part of the twentieth century. None of them is indispensable, none of them could do it alone. Without their collective efforts, the changes would not have occurred. And perhaps more important than the policy changes they helped bring about, is what they prove about the power of ideas and the efficacy of a free society.

Chapter Two

CHINA

I was actually looking forward to tea with Deng Xiaoping, the man who ruled China, the most communist country in the world. "Who," I thought to myself, "could have figured that being a policy adviser to Richard Nixon and Ronald Reagan, the arch enemies of communism, would lead to an invitation to an intimate meeting in the Great Hall of the People, in Beijing, China, with the archcommunist, himself?" Now I knew how those left-wing Democrats felt when they accepted President Reagan's invitation to a state dinner at the White House. We knew we shouldn't go, but nothing was going to stop us from satisfying a lively desire to see for ourselves. Curiosity can be a powerful force.

It was December 1981 and winter was well under way in northern China. I was a member of a small delegation from the United States, representing the U.S.-Chinese Joint Economic Committee. The purpose of the committee was to work out the tax, investment, and trade details of some general economic agreements undertaken earlier between the two countries. Donald Regan, then secretary of the treasury, was head of the U.S. delegation. When we walked off the plane in Beijing it was very cold. Light snow flurries drifted down.

My first surprise came as our motorcade approached the city limits of the capital. The smog in Beijing was dense and heavy, an almost evil-looking cloak of soot and fumes draping itself over the low buildings. It was far worse than the worst day I have ever seen in Los Angeles, and almost as bad as the poisonous cloud that perpetually hangs over Mexico City. Some of the first Chinese I saw were dressed in dark blue, riding bicycles, their faces covered with the white surgical masks only seen in the United States in hospital operating rooms. But in Beijing the white masks are used to keep airborne dirt and chemicals out of your lungs, and are also worn as a matter of course by anyone who has a cold—to prevent infecting others.

Another thing that surprised me was the total absence of political signs and posters and political slogans on the walls. Even though it was late 1981, I expected a profusion of boldly colored examples of ideological brainwashing by a communist regime that knew what it was doing. It's what I had seen on American network television news for the better part of twenty years and I was looking forward to seeing it personally. Instead, all we saw was block after block of dull tan and gray buildings, and concrete walls—all blank.

By the time we met with Deng Xiaoping a few days later I was forced to review my impression of what China was and where it was going. With Mao's death and the Gang of Four's ouster in the 1978 coup, there were signs that the monolithic facade of communism in China was cracking, ever so slightly. During the past two or three years I was so completely preoccupied with Reagan's presidential campaign and the establishment of a new government that I paid little attention to what was being written and said about China. But what I saw was a lot different than what I thought it would be. People were not all dressed drably in blue Mao jackets, and those who still wore them sported bright flashes of color, too. There were people selling things on the streets, very much like street vendors in the United States, a very capitalistic activity. There were even a few rickshaws prowling slowly along the street looking for fares. It was a long way from New York City, but it was significantly different from the picture of Red China that I had drawn in my mind from reading newspapers and watching television.

Our meeting with Deng Xiaoping was held in a large, plain room in the Great Hall. I was somewhat relieved to see that he was wearing his Mao jacket and pants. Deng is a small man, just a little over five feet tall and slender, a startling physical contrast to the immense political power he wields over one billion Chinese people, four times the population of the United States.

Deng Xiaoping was smoking a cigarette. For an instant he looked almost like a child—a very mean, tough child. When he began to speak, however, that illusion vanished. This was an intelligent, determined man who somehow had elbowed and clawed his way to absolute power in a hardfisted, totalitarian country. And now that he had control he meant to astound the world. He was beginning to move surely and smoothly to tear down the pillars of communism that Mao and his henchmen worked so hard and killed so many to erect.

The U.S. delegation—Donald Regan, Arthur W. Hummel, Jr., the U.S. ambassador to China, and I, in that order—sat with Deng in a row of four lightly stuffed armchairs framed with varnished blond wood. Three small tables, draped with heavy white cloth, were wedged between the chairs, and we were served light green tea in delicate white porcelain cups. Even though we were alone, except for three Chinese interpreters who hovered behind Deng, the chairs all faced forward, as if we were on a stage. Next to Deng's left foot on the floor was a beautiful white porcelain spittoon, which he did not use.

The discussion ranged over a wide variety of topics, from polite small talk to tax and trade policy to insistent demands from Deng that the United States sell him powerful computers he wanted to spur economic growth. Nobody mentioned the Great Leap Forward or the Cultural Revolution. There was no reference to communist philosophy or theory, only an intense, purposeful interest in very practical matters of economics and technology. For a hardline Republican working in the Reagan White House it was puzzling, and fascinating.

Later in the trip, one night during the cocktail period before an elaborate banquet in our honor, things became much clearer. I was talking to Bo Yibo, a courtly man in his seventies who was one of Deng's top economic advisers. Looking at his calm face and friendly eyes you would never guess he had recently been released from prison. He had been there for ten years. Both he and his wife were convicted at the height of the Cultural Revolution when Mao was riding high and Bo Yibo had the misfortune of being one of the chief financial people in China. His wife died in that prison one year later. And now he was out, and enormously powerful. My only thought was, "God help the people that put him and his wife in jail once he gets settled and starts looking for them."

His English was very good, much better than my nonexistent Chinese, so I asked him directly, "I have observed a number of things during our visit that seem to indicate a substantial change from the way you used to do things. What is your economic policy now, and what do you intend to do?"

"You see," he replied, "for many years in China we were following a policy whereby everyone put everything into one big iron bowl. And then everyone took from the bowl what they needed." Bo Yibo paused and I thought, "Well, that's the neatest summary of communist economic theory I've ever heard." After a pause the expression on his face became more serious and he quietly and firmly said, "It didn't work."

"It didn't work?" Did he realize what he had said? For one of the highest ranking economists in China to flatly state that the economic theory of communism did not work was flabbergasting. The closest thing to it in the United States would have been if Murray Weidenbaum, the first chairman of the Council of Economic Advisers under President Reagan, had stood up and said that a free market economy didn't work.

Later that night, in the plush quarters provided for us, I thought again and again about what I had been told. The guest house was located on the enclosed grounds that the Gang of Four appropriated for their own dwellings, and somehow that made it even more difficult to believe that the new communist leaders had come to a decision that communist economic theory did not work. I was skeptical.

But if it were true, the consequences would be great and incalculable because the political philosophy of communism is built on the foundation of communist economic theory. A free economy is incompatible with political dictatorship. How far would the Chinese go—could they go—before the rumblings of economic freedom threatened their political control?

One of their first and most fundamental changes was to reintroduce economic incentives to the Chinese economy. For thirty long years, from 1949 to 1979, there was no clear connection between performance and compensation in China. The productivity of a work team was judged by the total value of the points its members received, but every worker got points for just showing up every day. He could either work hard or loaf. Many chose to loaf, and production suffered. The problem was most acute in the agricultural communes. The Chinese people could not grow enough food to feed themselves.

What the new Chinese government did was to institute a supply-side tax policy with a vengeance. They told the peasants, about 80 percent of the population, that the rules were changed. From now on they were free to keep for themselves all the agricultural produce they raised—after they met the quota they owed to the state. In effect, this was a 100 percent tax on the first part of the peasant's crop, and no tax at all on what he grew or raised beyond that. The marginal tax rate was zero.

The results came fast and were spectacular.

In the late 1970s China was stalked by drought and famine. Within a few short years she was self-sufficient in food. By the middle of the 1980s she was a net exporter of food to the rest of the world.

We spent a week in China, and the bits and pieces of evidence we saw and heard all pointed to the coming of an intellectual earthquake there. For over thirty years China was the ideological leader of the communist world. The Soviet Union was a much greater military force, but its Stalin-style communism made it a difficult role model. Communist Cuba was warmer, smaller, and closer to the United States, but even Castro never matched up to the purity of communist principle embodied in Mao Tse-tung. And the sheer size of China added one billion practicing communists, most of them reluctant and sullen, to the worldwide rolls of communism.

China had once been the holy temple of communism. And now she was becoming an apostate. Instead of hearing communist ideology and ethical commandments from Mao's red book, *Quotations from Chairman Mao Tse-tung*, we were told proudly that China had three new proverbs that served as guiding principles for their society.

The first proverb was "shi shi qiu shi," which translated means "seek truth from facts." It was a rejection of ideological dogma in favor of deductive reasoning.

The second proverb was "yi shijian wei zhenli di weiyi biao-zhum," which means simply that "practice is the sole criterion of truth." A far cry from the thoughts of Mao, it meant that the ideological correctness of public policy is to be judged solely by whether or not the policy works.

The third proverb was "jiefang sixiang," or "emancipate the mind from dogma." This was meant as a call for experimentation, urging the people to try new things even when the moral and political guidelines of the past would have condemned such experiments (and the person who tried them).

From the viewpoint of any communist, or any good statist ideologue for that matter, these three proverbs were intellectual heresy. To seek the truth from the facts of reality, to judge the rightness of a national policy by how well the policy works, and not to be bound by the past—this was an Aristotelian invitation to embrace capitalism.

China's ideological defection is a striking symbol of the new revolution of capitalist ideas that has grown and matured in the United States and is now beginning to sweep the world. When China turned toward capitalism, alarm bells went off in the minds of good socialists and communists all over the world.

Of course, the Chinese were not so shameless as to admit to anything so much at odds with their political practice of the last thirty years. Deng went to great lengths to argue that the changes were necessary to improve and preserve the socialist system, and that there were no contradictions between a market economy and a socialist economy. But he hardly ever, if at all, mentioned the word communism.

The Chinese governor of the province of Canton was less circumspect. He had his own proverb, which was, "everybody must get richer faster." Now that really made my Republican heart beat a little faster.

A few days later our U.S. Air Force jet roared up into the blue China sky, across the Yellow Sea, the Peninsula of Korea, and the Sea of Japan, then slowly descended to the Tokyo airport in Japan. The contrast was stunning. A little over a thousand miles away we left behind a poor, backward, agricultural country and now we were descending into Tokyo, a modern, powerful capitalist metropolis that gleamed and glistened in the morning sun. It must make the Chinese shiver every time they see Tokyo or Kyoto, or any of the new, powerful cities of Japan, given the past record of what the Japanese did to the Chinese when they had the military upper hand. All was peaceful now, and the Japanese military forces were dormant. But who knew what the future might bring? In wealth and technological know-how, the Japanese were light years ahead of the Chinese, and if they should ever channel that economic power and technological skill into weapons of war, China could be at their mercy.

The Chinese people have always looked far ahead, and far back. Perhaps the answer to why they suddenly reneged on their profound commitment to the political philosophy of communism can be found more in the national security area than in economics. If China had continued with communism, with periodic cultural revolutions, and slavish adherence to old dogma and slogans, they would have condemned themselves to being a poorer and poorer country in a richer and richer world. That might have been tolerable if the rulers could maintain their reins of power; and given the vast size of the Chinese mainland and its huge population, it was, for many years, a viable option. But the swift advances in the economic power and the military power of other countries changed that.

Since the early 1980s the Chinese people have tasted a few of the fruits of capitalism, and their appetite seems barely whetted. They have embarked on a course from which there is no easy turning back, and if their success continues, they will never turn back. China will not become another United States, but we may see the day when Chinese capitalism emerges as one of the three or four major powers in the world.

They may even now be thinking about that. In 1985 Deng Xiaoping was asked whether he had any advice for President Reagan or Premier Gorbachev and he replied, "No. I am not qualified. China is a backward country." But then he added slyly, "Perhaps 50 years from now, China would have a larger say." And then he laughed heartily.[1]

Chapter Three

THE COLLAPSE OF THE SOCIALIST IDEA

The 1980s has been a decade of stunning change. The world is now in the midst of a profound intellectual and political revolution that may rival in scope and importance the transition from the Dark Ages to the Enlightenment. In this transition the United States has led the way. American capitalism has been the model for the rest of the world. Its intellectuals have spun most of the theoretical foundations. Its politicians have turned those ideas into a modern, high-powered capitalistic nation. Its businessmen and professionals have created wealth, new technology, and art far beyond the wildest dreams of our ancestors. And its armed forces have successfully protected not only the United States, but most of the free world, from conquest by the military machines of fascist and communist dictatorships.

One by one, in country after country, political forces leaning toward more individual rights, private property, and less government intervention in the economy have taken power. In Great Britain, a brilliant, powerful woman led the Conservative party to victory in 1979, reversing the socialist tide that swamped England for decades. Prime Minister Margaret Thatcher is still in power in the late 1980s. In Canada, the charismatic leftist Pierre Trudeau and his Liberal party were overthrown, and replaced by the Progressive Conservative party led by Prime Minister Brian Mulroney. These changes, taken by themselves, are not exciting or radical. After all, Canada and Great Britain are probably more like the United States than any other countries of the world.

Yet as we look for evidence of a possible worldwide trend toward capitalism it is interesting to note that the move to the right in both Canada and Great Britain occurred at about the same time as the move to the right in the United States. The revolutionary change in China was so sudden and dramatic, even though it occurred at the same time, that few, if any, drew any connection between its political upheaval and those in North America and Europe. But this was not all that has happened in the 1980s: in fact, in terms of intellectual and political upheaval, the world has become a busy place.

France is one of the most powerful countries of the free world, exemplified by the size of its economy, its strong intellectual and political traditions, and the explosive power of its nuclear weapons. So it was of more than passing interest that 1981 was a major turning point in the political history of modern France. François Mitterrand became the first socialist president to be elected, and he did it with strong backing from the Communist party of France. For the first time in modern history the Left had control. It was a stunning contrast to the direction of political movements in other countries. Just as England and Canada moved to the right, just as China was moving away from communism, and just a few months after Ronald Reagan took power in the United States, the socialists came to power, finally, in France.

Without anyone having planned it, the political events of 1981 established a dramatic rivalry between two competing political philosophies in two large, powerful industrial societies. Within the space of a few months, France turned left and the United States turned right.

France was led by a tough, brilliant intellectual of the Left, a noted writer, a politician with keen political senses. The sixty-four-year-old Mitterrand was the pick of the leftist litter. The American leader, six years older than Mitterrand, was also a politician with keen political sense. As the leader of the political Right in America for many years, Reagan was committed to a program of more capitalism. It was a rare opportunity to set the new socialism against the new capitalism.

Within five years the contest was over. Reagan was reelected by a huge margin in 1984 and the United States was stronger than ever. In France, there was economic disaster, and the socialist government was routed in early 1986 by a conservative landslide. In the clearest test case of the twentieth century, capitalism triumphed in the United States, and socialism failed in France.

Of all the commentary around the world about what is happening in America, and what President Reagan's role has been, and what America means to other nations, one of the most incisive was expressed in the 1986 interview that François Mitterrand gave the writer Marguerite Duras. Only a socialist of Mitterrand's intellect could perceive what he sees, and only a fellow citizen could have coaxed it out of him:

DURAS: What if we talked about America?

MITTERRAND: If you want to.

DURAS: You know Reagan. Tell us who he is.

MITTERRAND: He is a man of common sense, gracious and pleasant. He communicates through jokes, by telling ultra-California stories, by speaking mainly about California and the Bible. He has two religions: free enterprise and God—the Christian God. . . . He is not a man who dwells on concepts, yet he has ideas and clings to them.

DURAS: One cannot conceive of Reagan as the leader of any country but America.

MITTERRAND: It is no small achievement to lead a country of 250 million. The American people are vibrant, powerful, full of energy, imagination, and character. Their continent is rich with extraordinary resources. They have an excellent university system. Put all these elements together and you have a great nation. . . . What first strikes me about the United States is the immensity of the territory it still has to explore, to develop, to farm. When you fly from New York to Los Angeles, you spend more than an hour over the red and white sands of the desert, cut here and there by the blue lines of rivers. You feel that the journey west has just begun, that we are still at the dawn of time. For the people below, each step is like a conquest.

DURAS: I hope that Americans will preserve this emptiness, that they will never build on the deserts. I used to be bored when I was in America, because you could talk about everything but politics. It was often deadly. Starting with the Vietnam War, Americans began, little by little, to change.

MITTERRAND: I made several trips to America around that time. In the universities, in 1967 and 1968, I met some very progressive young people. Their rhetoric was extremist and out of touch with reality—idealistic. They were reproachful toward Europeans like us—including socialists—who seemed to them timid, not sufficiently engaged in the battles from which they imagined revolution would emerge.

Once again, liberty had fired their spirit. Freedom, liberation— an ancient music to which young hearts respond. The journey, the adventure, the departure. . . . It is a metaphysical quest, and politics provides no answers of this kind. Although no system will ever be able to satisfy those who harbor such a desire, I think that American democracy guarantees that the greatest number will enjoy a liberty that is genuine, lived, practical. This isn't so bad, even if it remains imperfect—very imperfect.

DURAS: I think America is the country I feel closest to, even though I've never lived there. . . . I love America, myself. I am a Reaganite. Would you have believed that?

MITTERRAND: I think I have found that out! I feel sympathy for Reagan as a man, less sympathy for his policies.

DURAS: I think he is the incarnation of a kind of primal, almost archaic, power. He governs less with his intellect than with common sense. But I approve of this. And he doesn't look for anything more than the approval of the American people.

MITTERRAND: But Ronald Reagan is not only President of the United States. He is head of the most powerful empire in the world.

DURAS: Good for us! Thanks be to God! It is funny, he displays the same defiance toward the Soviet Union as would an old member of a European Communist party. All of a sudden, he recognized what kind of people the Russians are, and he will never turn his back on this knowledge. That's it—the great virtue of simplicity. You may be slow, but when you learn something, it's forever.

MITTERRAND: I am, like you, a friend of the Americans, and even though my political views are very different from those of their current leaders, we maintain good relations. Not just for the sake of diplomatic good manners. I recognize the critical role played by the United States—whatever its flaws and fantasies—in safeguarding a certain way of life for which, all in all, I care."[1]

Not very long ago you would have been thought somewhat crazy if you predicted that an ardent French socialist leader would not only praise the United States and express enormous admiration for Ronald Reagan, but would also acknowledge that American capitalism, more than any other political system, guarantees a genuine, practical liberty for the greatest number of people and that its role in the world is critical to protecting that way of life for the other democracies.

But the stirrings of capitalism were not confined to the continents of Europe and Asia. Even on the other side of the earth, down under, far from the normal routes of traffic, similar changes were occurring.

New Zealand is a country composed of two islands, each about the size of England, lying approximately halfway between Antarctica and Australia. It was discovered by the Western world in 1642 when some Dutchmen happened upon it and went ashore. The Maori warriors who inhabited the islands killed a few of the Dutchmen and the Maori were left alone again for over one hundred years. Then in 1769 the Englishman James Cook explored the islands and paved the way for eventual colonization by the British.

The land was taken over by a flood of English immigrants. Today it is largely a replica of Great Britain, although on a much smaller scale. The total population is slightly over 3 million, and about 90 percent of it is European, mostly from England and Scotland.

When the British came they brought with them the idea of socialism and created there about as perfect a socialist state as ever was constructed. And for many years it seemed to work. The standard of living was fairly high and the country seemed to prosper.

But by the late 1970s it was becoming obvious that, like so many other socialist countries, New Zealand was succeeding to the extent that it was in spite of, rather than because of, its oppressive form of government. The great natural resources of New Zealand and the ingenuity and intelligence of its settlers overcame, for a time, the fetters of government intervention. But finally, the inherent weaknesses of the socialist economy emerged.

By the 1980s more than 30,000 New Zealanders were leaving

the country every year, inflation was soaring, 130,000 people were jobless, economic growth was low, and the national debt was dangerously high. The economy was in a terrible mess. In the 1984 elections the more conservative National party was swept out of office and the left-wing Labour party took over.

Following the recommendations of his finance minister, David Lange, the new government head, proceeded to wipe out wage and price controls, to let the New Zealand dollar float on the international markets, and to start cutting back on dozens of government subsidy programs. By 1986 they managed to cut the top income tax rate from 66 percent to 48 percent. Nothing was said about socialism or capitalism. It was called a "comprehensive strategy" to put New Zealand "on the road to permanently higher standards of living, faster growth with full employment, and low inflation."[2] The New Zealanders were dumping some of the key pillars of socialism with the same dispatch and deftness as their Chinese colleagues.

The origins of New Zealand's surprising and sudden turn towards capitalism can be traced to a remarkable little book published in 1980. Entitled *There's Got To Be A Better Way*, and only 79 pages long, it was the first serious political and economic statement of what was wrong with the New Zealand economy (government intervention) and what should be done to correct it (a significant dose of capitalistic economics). When the book first came out the author, Roger Douglas, was just another member of the opposition party out of power, and the ideas were considered just theory. But a few years later Mr. Douglas became the minister of finance and theory started to become practice.

The political moves toward capitalism that occurred in China, France, and New Zealand are perhaps the most dramatic and clearcut examples of the new intellectual revolution. The changes are irregular, some of them will be reversed, and the process is slow, but little by little the intrusive fist of the state is being replaced by the invisible hand of the free economy.

In 1985 the prime minister of India, Rajiv Gandhi, broke sharply with entrenched socialist economic policies and proposed new economic policies that seemed to mirror those of President Reagan. The sweeping program of reduced tax rates for both business and individuals, and reduced government regulations for important areas of the economy, were aimed at restoring the incentive of people to save, to invest, and to produce.

In early 1985 the socialist prime minister of Italy, Bettino Craxi, said that the economic policies of President Reagan were so successful as to "make not only Italy but the whole of Europe think."[3] A few weeks later a fellow named Alfredo Reichlin, the chief economic spokesman of the Italian Communist party, acknowledged that "the old ideas of socialism are in crisis. It is the problem of statism, a program that doesn't take into account individual needs and values."[4]

By the fall of 1986 two other European countries were seriously considering major tax reform along the lines of what had just taken place in the United States. The finance minister of Belgium, Mark Eyskens, said that "U.S.-style tax reform will be a priority for the Belgian government in the months ahead,"[5] and the finance minister of West Germany, Gerhard Stoltenberg, outlined plans for major changes in Germany's tax system. Again, following the example of the United States, the main target of the changes was "the system of steep progressive taxation" on individuals.[6]

In Latin America the new president of Ecuador, Leon Febres Cordero, was elected on a platform of "bread, roofs, and jobs." Abandoning the leftist economics of his predecessor, he talks openly of the miracle of the market, and works vigorously to reduce state controls of the economy and to expand the private sector. According to the Latin American expert, Roger Fontaine, "Ecuador, with its full throttle free enterprise economy, is the only democratic regime in the region determined to make capitalism work."[7]

As 1988 began, the rush to capitalism continued. Angola, one of Africa's foremost communist-style governments, announced that it was moving away from its current economic policy, copied from the Soviet model, and towards free markets. Angola's move came after enduring what the *New York Times* said rivaled "the experience of Mozambique as the most spectacular failure of Africa's many attempts at socialism."[8] That same day, the *New York Times* also reported that Vietnam had embraced "a sweeping new domestic economic policy that in effect abandons centralized planning."[9]

When countries such as Angola and Vietnam begin to turn away from communism there is not much left—save for a few anachronisms that continue to resist any move toward the ideological nemesis, capitalism. Countries such as Burma, Albania, Cuba, Rumania, Mozambique, Nicaragua, North Korea, Ethiopia, and East Germany have insisted on perpetuating the socialist state. They have paid dearly for it.

It is as if their economies, like Rip Van Winkle, have been asleep for decades. Their people are poor, life is austere. All have slavishly followed the model of the Soviet Union, and their communist economies stand as tragic symbols of a failing political philosophy.

But what about the Soviet Union, the granddaddy of communist countries? It is the oldest. It has the most powerful military force. And it has the largest economy, second in size only to the United States. Unlike some of its smaller followers, however, even the Soviet Union is now beginning to flirt with capitalism, not out of desire, but out of naked necessity.

The Soviet Union's superpower status in the world cannot be attributed to the moral power of its political system or the efficacy of its economic system. It is a superpower only because of the absolute size of its military forces and its willingness to use them. The Soviet Union, without nuclear missiles, warships, and tanks would be an underdeveloped and poor country, more pitied than feared. And Soviet military power, as in other countries, is heavily dependent on the size and strength of its economy.

As other superpowers in the world—the United States, Japan, France, Great Britain, and now China—introduce more and more capitalism into their economies, and those economies grow more powerful and productive, the relative strength of the Soviet Union is weakening. The Soviet economy is generally considered to be one of the most inefficient in the world. It is a textbook example of a centrally planned and centrally controlled economy, but unlike the theory, it doesn't work very well in practice.

Soviet productive achievements, particularly in the fields of military and space technology, have been substantial. But they were achieved in spite of, not because of, the Soviet economy. Only the sheer size of the Soviet Union, its vast natural resources, and its millions of intelligent, capable people have made it possible to produce as much as the Soviets have.

But the Soviets are worried. Their military might is dependent on the productivity of the economy, and they realize that when the economy falters their military power is threatened. And their economy is in trouble, big trouble. Economic collapse is not likely, but it is having increasing difficulty keeping up with the rest of the world. The Soviet economic mess, building now for years, has been exacerbated by three major developments: the drop in world oil prices, sharply reducing the value of one of its major natural resources; the introduction of capitalistic elements in China that are greatly increasing the productive power of China's economy and posing a direct competitive threat; and America's accelerating missile defense program, which, if the Soviets try to match or counter it, will severely drain their economy.

The Soviets now seem to be damned if they do and damned if they don't. It they don't take urgent, effective steps to dramatically improve their economy, their relative status and power in the world will decline and they don't want that. Unfortunately for communism, the step that will most likely work—implementing elements of capitalism—poses a serious internal political threat. When an economy is freed, restraints on individuals are loosened so, as *Pravda* warned in 1985, "the expansion of the private sector is fraught with serious economic, social, and ideological consequences." [10]

These consequences go far beyond the acute embarrassment of confessing the failure of communism. They pose a direct threat to the ruling classes of the Soviet Union.

Mikhail Gorbachev, the new ruler of the Soviet Union, seems to clearly understand the depth of the difficulties. In 1985 he launched a major effort aimed at getting the Soviet economy moving again. Borrowing a page from the Chinese book, he insists there is nothing wrong with Soviet ideology while, at the same time, urging change. On June 11, 1985, Gorbachev delivered a speech entitled, "A Fundamental Issue of the Party's Economic Policy" to the central committee of the Communist party, calling on them to find "ways and the reserves for accelerating scientific and technical progress and the growth of the Soviet economy." Early in his speech he insisted that the "Soviet economy has always been characterized by a high level of dynamism . . . the enormous advantages of socialism and of its planned economy have made themselves clear. Our successes are beyond contention; they are generally recognized." [11]

And then he plunged into the main theme of his speech, emphasizing the critical importance of a strong economy, pointing out that "we are compelled to invest immense funds in defense," and then criticizing in great detail the current state of the Soviet economy. Suddenly, close to the end of his speech, he started to list the actions needed to reform the economy. Gorbachev's vocabulary was curiously familiar: "managing independence . . . economic levers . . . incentives . . . the best, most competitive goods . . . price setting . . . profitability . . . financial autonomy . . . freedom . . . flexibility." And then he closed with the following remarks:

> "Our system of material incentives is extremely confused, cumbersome, and inefficient . . . bonuses are frequently regarded as some kind of mechanical addition to wages paid to everybody without exception, regardless of the contribution made by a specific employee to the results achieved. . . .
> "Everything that is out-of-date must be boldly eliminated so that a, so to speak, cost-conscious economic mechanism can begin operating at full capacity, an economic mechanism that will stimulate economic development and literally rap the knuckles of sloppy economic planners. . . .
> "Times have changed. . . ."[12]

That was in 1985. On November 18, 1986 the Soviet parliament adopted a new law that may not have made Karl Marx roll over in his grave, but probably made him twitch a bit. The new Soviet law provided that twenty-nine different types of individual private enterprise could begin operation in May of 1987, including the "manufacture of clothes, shoes, furniture, toys and fishing tackle." Soviet citizens are now allowed to "repair houses, cars, television sets and radios," and the lucky ones who own automobiles may use them as private taxicabs.[13]

This is creeping capitalism with a vengeance.

But so far the Soviet rulers have moved slowly and carefully to implement Gorbachev's 1985 blueprint for adopting certain basic elements of capitalism. Instead they have blamed the Soviet economic failures on the fact that Soviets drink too much (they do), that Soviet workers don't work very hard (why should they?), and that there is too much corruption (some experts believe that without the black market the Soviet economy would have collapsed years ago).

But sooner or later, the Soviets are either going to admit, tacitly if not openly, that communism is a failure, and introduce revolutionary changes as the Chinese are doing, or consign themselves to the role of a fading economic power.

Almost a decade after their communist brothers and sisters in China abandoned key elements of the communist philosophy, the Soviets have begun to follow. The steps are modest and tentative, but the degree and scope of change is not what is important. What is critically important is that they have violated some of the most sacred principles of communism.

And there may be more coming. A lot more.

In 1987 General Secretary Mikhail Gorbachev published an extraordinary book in the United States entitled *Perestroika*. Translated narrowly and literally, perestroika is the Russian word for "restructuring." But in Gorbachev's view the word has a more profound meaning. "Perestroika is a word with many meanings," he writes, "but if we are to choose from its many possible synonyms the key one which expresses its essence most accurately, then we can say thus: *perestroika is a revolution*." [Italics added][14]

Indeed, Gorbachev's book is revolutionary. Even if one does not take all his words at face value, just the fact that the Soviet ruler would publish a book in the United States purporting to be a detailed explanation of his future plans for the Soviet Union is extraordinary. And to baldly admit that "perestroika is an urgent necessity arising from the profound excesses of development in our socialist society[15] is truly extraordinary.

To deal with the failure of the communist economy, Gorbachev urges "radical reforms for revolutionary change[16] . . . there is no reasonable alternative to a dynamic, revolutionary perestroika. Its alternative is continued stagnation.[17] To make sure no one misses his point, he emphasizes that "the Soviet people are convinced that as a result of perestroika and democratization the country will become richer and stronger . . . we will not retreat from perestroika but will carry it through".[18]

If someone from outer space were to read a copy of *Perestroika* they would never realize that the Soviet Union is a communist country. Gorbachev barely mentions communism. Instead he refers constantly to "socialism," effectively consigning the word communism to the same dustbin that holds the Soviet memory of Stalin.

At one point, Gorbachev goes to great pains to disassociate himself from one of the major philosophical underpinnings of communism, saying:

> "On this point we want to be perfectly clear: socialism has nothing to do with equalizing. Socialism cannot ensure conditions of life and consumption in accordance with the principle 'From each according to his ability, to each according to his needs.' This will be under communism. Socialism has a different criterion for distributing social benefits: 'From each according to his ability, to each according to his work.' "[19]

Wow. The way Gorbachev defines socialism it sounds a lot like capitalism. It is as if President Reagan were to write a book, have it translated into Russian, publish and distribute it in the Soviet Union, and in the book declare that "our economy and society is in deep trouble" and that we need "new thinking for our country and the world and we are going to have revolutionary economic and political change in the United States based on the idea that every person must contribute to the society according to his or her ability, but they can only have for their own use what they need. This must be the basis of a new social order in the United States. The idea that people will be rewarded according to what they produce, that private property is inviolate, that individual liberty must reign supreme—that will all have to wait for capitalism."

If Reagan were to do this would one conclude that he believed deeply in the efficacy of capitalism?

Now there is every reason to be heartily skeptical of Gorbachev's words. Lenin himself, back in 1921 when early communism wasn't working too well, introduced a New Economic Policy that introduced elements of capitalism into the Soviet economy, and that was quickly followed by the development of one of the most brutal and dangerous dictatorships in the world. Many Soviet leaders still hunger for world domination. The word of Soviet rulers has never been especially trustworthy, a fact that Gorbachev shamelessly admits when he pledges the Soviet Union to a new policy even in the field of truth, saying "we want to return to the true, original meaning of the words we use in international contacts. In declaring our commitment to honest and open politics, we do mean honesty, decency and sincerity."[20] It is also true that no Soviet leadership ever had a high regard for individual liberty.

But on the other hand, just the publication of *Perestroika* is a remarkable event in the gray darkness of the Soviet empire. What the words say, to be believed or not, is stunning to an extent that is perhaps only surpassed by what Mikhail Gorbachev's Chinese communist brothers have actually been doing to their economy since 1979.

Indeed, Gorbachev's book is a blueprint for change, radical change.

Will it happen? As in all things political, no one knows. But the Soviets *are* going to unusual lengths to assure us that nothing fundamental will change as they pursue revolutionary changes. For a moment let us ignore the logical contradiction and try to follow their words. Gorbachev writes,

> "There are people in the West who would like to tell us that socialism is in a deep crisis and has brought our society to a dead end . . .
>
> "We have only one way out, they say: to adopt capitalist methods of economic management and social patterns, to drift toward capitalism . . .
>
> "To put an end to all the rumors and speculations that abound in the West about this, I would like to point out once again that we are conducting all our reforms in accordance with the socialist choice.
>
> "We will proceed toward better socialism rather than away from it. We are saying this honestly, without trying to fool our own people or the world . . .
>
> "Those in the West who expect us to give up socialism will be disappointed. It is high time they understood this.
>
> "We want more socialism . . ."[21]

I don't know why, but when I read the urgent words of Gorbachev, I am reminded of two things: first, the famous line from Shakespeare's *Hamlet* that says "the lady doth protest too much methinks"; and, second, the late Senator Aiken's solution for the Vietnam War—"declare victory and withdraw."

So, no matter what the Soviets say, we would all be perhaps

well advised to paraphrase the advice that former Attorney General John Mitchell once gave Americans on how to judge the Nixon administration—"Watch what they do, not what they say."

The meaning of Gorbachev's words, if he does what he says he will do, belie the claim that we will see more socialism. Unless the Soviet ruler has discovered a new economics, some way of making down up, some new way of adding two and two, then the changes he proposes for the Soviet economy must and will lead inevitably to more capitalism.

The Soviets, like the Chinese, will call it socialism, perhaps advanced socialism, but the rest of the world will know what they are doing if they do it. In the same spirit as the old admonition that advises us to call a bird that quacks, and swims, and dives, and looks like a duck—a duck, so we will soon call what Gorbachev has proposed—if he does it—an abandonment of the economic principles of communism and an acceptance of capitalism.

What Gorbachev and the Soviets are doing is, I think, quite understandable. Put yourself in their place. Their communist economy—like every other statist economy in history—is, besides being intrinsically immoral, excruciatingly inefficient. Centrally controlled economies simply cannot produce the quantity and quality of goods and services that free capitalist economies can. Gorbachev laments that the Soviet "consumer found himself totally at the mercy of the producer and had to make do with what the latter chose to give him."[22] Well, we know that the only political system that makes the consumer king is capitalism.

Gorbachev even falls back on asserting that one of Lenin's tenets was "the need for taking into account the requirements of objective economic laws."[23] But objective economic laws, if followed, dictate capitalism.

According to Gorbachev, "Perestroika also means a resolute and radical elimination of obstacles hindering social and economic development, of outdated methods of managing the economy."[24] Obstacles? Outdated methods? If these have been the essence of the Soviet economy for most of the past seventy years, the essential elements of communist economic policy, then what will replace them. The tribal methods of old Africa? The establishment of a royal family? The communism of Albania or Cuba? Unlikely. The only economic method we know of today that works effectively is the method at the heart of the economic success and progress in the United States, Canada, western Europe, and Japan—capitalism.

If, and this is a big if, the Soviets have concluded that, in order to make their economy work and their country strong, they must introduce fundamental elements of capitalism into their society, then they are faced with a monumental dilemma.

The Soviet military superiority to every other country in the world, save the United States, is crucial to their status as a world power. Without military might the Soviet Union would today be a third-rate nation, struggling and stumbling along like the other centrally planned economies of the world.

If I were a high-ranking Soviet official, I would be terribly concerned about the rising military power of the United States, the potential military power of a resurgent China, and the possibility of a fully armed Japanese economic colossus in the next century.

All military power is relative. As the other great powers in the world grow in military power, so must the Soviet Union or their place in the world pecking order will decline. A Soviet Union in some future world where the military power of the United States, and China, and Japan was greater than theirs would be a Soviet Union that was largely irrelevant to the sweep of history. There is nothing the Soviet Union now produces that could not be found better and cheaper elsewhere—except fear. The Soviets are probably not so paranoid as to think that a situation in which they were militarily weaker would lead to an invasion from the United States, but they might not be so sure about what a heavily armed China or Japan might do.

If, and this is also a big if, the Soviets have concluded that they cannot sustain their military power in the world without a stronger economy, and if they have also concluded that their military edge is absolutely necessary, then it would certainly be sensible to do what that logic dictates—to take the political risk of adopting whatever elements of capitalism are necessary. We would understand their reluctance to openly admit to what they were doing, for to do so would be to admit that seventy years of communism had failed.

The Soviet leaders, like many other people I know, will do the right thing if they have to. Today the inevitable sweep of historical forces is compelling the Soviet Union to seriously consider elements of capitalism. They do not want to do it, they do not like it, they will fight its inevitability every step of the way. But if they intend to succeed, if they intend to realize the full economic potential of their huge country and large population, they will have to do it.

If they succeed it will be a mixed blessing. A stronger, freer, more prosperous Soviet Union can only mean good for the vast majority of Soviet citizens, but there is also the danger that a stronger Soviet Union will lead to greater military power and a greater threat to the security of the United States—and to world peace.

The Reagan revolution refined United States capitalism. The Gorbachev revolution may destroy communism—and it may one day destroy the United States if we are not careful, if we do not take it seriously, and if it succeeds.

There is also the possibility that the naked necessity of moving toward more economic freedom may lead the Soviet Union up the path to more political freedom, to a less "evil" empire. If that happens then the optimists among us will hope that perestroika will one day transform the greatest prison-state in the world into a model of modern capitalism, complete with true liberty for all its people.

Chapter Four

THE NEW CAPITALISM

What is going on? Is it just coincidence that the conservatives were returned to power in England and Canada? That Ronald Reagan is president of the United States? That socialism failed miserably in France? That China blithely announced it was no longer doing business with communist economic theory? That the economy of the Soviet Union is staggering?

No, it is not coincidence. If you step back and take a look at the changes in the ideological thinking of the nations of the world, patterns emerge.

For all of the twentieth century and stretching back into the nineteenth century, a tremendous intellectual and political battle has been fought over the question: What political system will bring to a nation the greatest amount of happiness for the greatest number of its citizens? What political system will ensure their safety, give them the opportunity for material prosperity, and the freedom to develop and express their full potential in their personal interests, such as art, literature, sports, leisure, and work? During this period two major ideologies have dominated, and driven, the major political changes in the world. One is communism and the other is capitalism. They are in direct competition with each other for the loyalties of people all over the world, and capitalism is winning.

At first the contest was unfair, because the early practice of a fledgling capitalism was compared to the dreamy ideals of a communism that had never been tried. The early practice of capitalism was often seen to be imperfect. In fact, many of the social and economic ills, especially poverty, that were in the process of being cured by capitalism were often attributed, erroneously, to it. The actual practice of capitalism was not fault-free, but it did work and it accomplished a great deal.

So it was no contest at the beginning. The results of practical capitalism—no matter how spectacular—could not compete with the promised prowess of communism. Communism seemed to appeal particularly to intellectuals who, unlike their less talented brothers and sisters, could conceptually conjure what an ideal society might be like and what it would accomplish.

As capitalism began to grab hold in the societies of the old world, especially in England, and in the United States, enormous progress was made. But the incipient practice of capitalism did not create ideal societies overnight. What was left undone was the subject of growing, bitter criticism, especially by those who held up the idealistic communist goals.

As time went on there were two major historical developments. First, more nations actually embraced communism, or—to put it more accurately—had it fastened upon them by revolutionaries with guns. And so the world began to accumulate communist experience. As some intellectuals, though not many, had predicted, communism in the flesh was a disaster. It oppressed brutally, was a poor producer of wealth, and fostered great disparities in the distribution of the wealth it did produce; it suppressed liberty and smothered human initiative and achievement.

At the same time a more mature, modern capitalism, exemplified by the American system, showed what a powerful vehicle capitalism was for enhancing individual liberty, generating economic prosperity, and providing for strong national defense.

Now communism and socialism have been tried and tested for many years. Indeed, the last seventy years have given us a massive social experiment unequaled in the history of the world. It has been incredibly costly in terms of human suffering and wasted resources, but terribly important in teaching us a most valuable lesson.

The theories of communism and socialism may sound good, but in real life they don't work. In practice they have had awful results, and a careful reexamination of their theories shows that the theories themselves aren't so good either. Consequently, during the last ten years a striking transformation has taken place in political philosophy worldwide. It is becoming increasingly clear that a mature capitalism is superior in every way to mature communism. Capitalism's resurgence has been slow, but it has been powerful. Its strength is that it has worked.

The new intellectual force of capitalism has not proceeded swiftly or smoothly. Bits and pieces of it have been introduced into socialist societies in anxious attempts to reap its benefits without having to admit the failures of their earlier statism. The socialist and communist leaders have wanted the economic power of capitalism, but they have also wanted to preserve their cultural heritage and, most especially, to hang on to their political power. As a result the course of the new capitalism has resembled that of a giant glacier—apparently quiet for years, now imperceptibly on the move again, flowing with unstoppable power.

As professor Peter L. Berger said in his 1986 book, *The Capitalist Revolution*, "Capitalism has become a global phenomenon. . . . Capitalism has been one of the most dynamic forces in human history, transforming one society after another, and today it has become established as an international system determining the economic fate of most of mankind and, at least indirectly, its social, political, and cultural fate, as well."[1]

The evidence is overwhelming. The greater the degree to which a nation has practiced capitalism, the greater the degree to which it has achieved economic prosperity, ensured its national security, and increased the freedom of its citizens. On the other hand, the greater the degree to which a nation has practiced statism, whether it was fascism or a military dictatorship or communism, the worse it has fared. The fact that some communist dictatorships, such as the Soviet Union, are in the aggregate, larger or more powerful than a smaller, freer country is not an advertisement for communism. The question to ask is: What might have been?

There is not a *single* example of a successful collectivist state, if you use the twin criteria of prosperity and freedom to measure them. Every statist society is fundamentally a slave society, a society in which the many do the bidding of a few. The average citizen of a collectivist state lives in fear of the government, and the government thrives on the fear of its citizens.

Today, in the year 1988, we know that if socialist countries have prospered it has been in spite of their socialism. To prosper, extraordinary efforts are made on the part of the people to subvert and circumvent the system. The results have been devastating. The greater the degree to which a society is governed by the iron hand of the state, the greater the degree of failure.

One of America's most eloquent Democrats, Daniel Patrick Moynihan, said in a commencement address at New York University in 1984, "The truth is that the Soviet idea is spent. It commands some influence in the world; and fear. But it summons no loyalty. History is moving away from it with astounding speed. I would not press the image, but it is as if the whole Marxist-Leninist ethos is hurtling off into a black hole in the universe. They will be remembered for what? The death of Andrei Sakharov? Yelena Bonner? Are there Marxist-Leninists here and about in the world? Yes: especially when the West allows communism to identify with nationalism. But in truth, when they do succeed, how well do they do? And for how long?"

Tomorrow will demonstrate beyond any doubt that a capitalist society will increase in power relative to the alternatives of communism, dictatorship, and other forms of statism. Capitalism is the promise of tomorrow for the world, for those who will be able to take it.

Capitalism has demonstrated in actual practice, not theory, that it is a more moral society, giving men and women a degree of freedom and liberty almost unthinkable in a noncapitalistic society; that it is a more productive society; that it allows people to earn a level of material prosperity only kings enjoyed not too long ago; and finally, that it produces a more powerful society, with the productive capacity and technological skills to fashion a defense force second to none in the world.

The idea of capitalism, now literally sweeping across the surface of the earth, is stronger, and more vibrant and vital, than it has ever been. The rush to capitalism is a phenomenon of the 1980s, born of frustration with failed statist economies, born of the burning envy of the power and success of capitalist economies, born of the fear of being left in the dust of the revolution.

There is one curious phenomenon of note in the ongoing struggle between capitalism and communism. Citizens of communist countries are not only referred to as communists, they *call* themselves communists. This is not true in the capitalist world. Often called capitalists in a pejorative way by others, those who live in capitalist countries rarely, if ever, call themselves capitalists. It is even true in America, where almost nobody refers to himself as an American capitalist. But that may begin to change as the power of capitalism grows and becomes more widely appreciated. Then perhaps more people will proudly say, "I am a capitalist." We have French communists and Soviet communists and even American communists. It may not be long before we shall hear some say, "I am a French capitalist. I am an English capitalist. I am a Chinese capitalist. I am an Indian capitalist. I am an Italian capitalist. And perhaps some day there will be those who will say without fear, "I am a Russian capitalist."

The international capitalist community is growing steadily and rapidly. Today its strength is somewhat masked because of all the euphemisms used to describe it. But if these trends continue the day will come when someone will say, "We are all capitalists now."

The ultimate irony of the twentieth century may be that lasting, worldwide political revolution was accomplished not by Trotsky and the communists but instead by Reagan and the capitalists.

Two

Reagan
the Candidate

In Washington this is called "going to the mat."
It means that if you start something you will finish
it. No matter how certain losing becomes, no matter how difficult the battle, no matter how much
it costs you—you will fight on to the end.

Chapter Five

GOING TO THE MAT

Reagan was through. You could see it on the faces of some of his closest advisers: the blank sad looks, the quick, darting eyes, the overpoliteness. They sat motionless in the old hotel room, furnished elegantly with heavy, dark red velvet-covered chairs and a sofa, and dimly lit by several old lamps that should have been on an antique dealer's shelf. There was no air conditioning. The cream-colored gauze drapes moved silently as an unseasonably warm breeze came through the half-opened window.

It was Tuesday, March 23, 1976, 4:25 P.M. in the afternoon. About thirty-five minutes earlier Reagan's 727 jet dropped from a gray, misty sky and landed at La Crosse Municipal Airport in Wisconsin, and we were now huddled in the living room of the Reagans' suite in the turn-of-the-century Hotel Stoddard.

Five months earlier I agreed to join Reagan's presidential campaign, to be in charge of policy development, to travel with him. So far it was a disaster. Reagan was attempting the almost impossible task of wresting the party's nomination from incumbent President Gerald R. Ford. Ford had trounced Reagan in the first five critical primary elections. After squeaking past Reagan in the first election on February 24 in New Hampshire, Ford began to roll. During the next three weeks he won four more decisive victories over Reagan, sometimes by huge margins, in Massachusetts, Vermont, Florida and Illinois. It was five straight, stinging defeats for Reagan, a man who never lost anything of consequence in his whole life, who had breezed to wealth, love, and fame.

By March 23, a week after Reagan's fifth loss, and the day of his expected loss in North Carolina (public opinion polls showed him running ten full points behind President Ford), I began to understand the meaning of the word despair. I was beginning to lose all hope. The campaign was flat broke. We were roughly two million dollars in debt.[1] No one would sell or rent us anything— no airplane, no automobiles, no advertising, no hotel rooms, no food unless we paid in advance, in cash. None of the senior staff had been paid for weeks. The head of Reagan's campaign, John Sears, secretly met with Ford's campaign chairman, Rogers Morton, to discuss Reagan's withdrawal from the race.[2] And the power structure of the Republican party totally abandoned him. Except for Senator Paul Laxalt and a few congressmen, there wasn't anyone of consequence in the Republican party supporting Reagan.

In 1976 there were twelve former chairmen of the Republican National Committee who were still living and breathing. On February 27, eleven of them endorsed President Ford's "bid to defeat Ronald Reagan for the GOP presidential nomination." Only George Bush, who could not be politically active because he was then director of the Central Intelligence Agency, abstained.[3] On March 17 the National Republican Conference of Mayors called on Reagan "to withdraw from the presidential race."[4] The editorial pages of newspapers picked up the scent and soon were baying for Reagan's blood. On March 18, the *Los Angeles Times* declared with confident finality: "For Reagan, the real question ought not to be *whether* to bow out, but *when*."[5]

And then, while Reagan was being slammed to his knees by the relentless onslaught of his more moderate political rivals, his former colleagues, the Republican governors, tried to administer the coup de grace. On March 20, 1976, seven Republican governors issued a statement "calling on Ronald Reagan to quit the GOP nomination race."[6]

So there we sat that dreary afternoon, in a strange hotel room in a strange city, beaten and humiliated. I did not know Reagan very well then, and had only been traveling with him regularly for a few weeks. The others in the room, most of them, had been with him for many years. His wife, Nancy, sat near him looking silently at his face. The others in the room that I remember were John Sears, Michael Deaver, Lyn Nofziger, and Peter Hannaford. The unasked question that hung over the room was, "When are you going to quit?" But no one would ask. We all knew.

Suddenly Sears broached a new idea. "Governor," he said, "one of your more ardent supporters down in Texas, Jimmy Lyon, has offered to lend the campaign $100,000 immediately if we use the money to buy national television time and show that speech of you giving President Ford and Henry Kissinger hell on national defense." Jimmy Lyon was already a legend in the campaign. A Texas tycoon, movie-actor handsome with dark wavy hair, he was a wealthy man with a fondness for wearing open-necked silk shirts that revealed the long, heavy gold chain lying on his hairy chest. He was a believer's believer, and he always matched his strongly-voiced political opinions with large contributions. "What we can do, Governor," Sears continued, "is basically forget everything that has happened up to now, borrow the $100,000 from Jimmy, and gamble everything on one last appeal to the voters. But you should understand, it's very much of a long shot."

Reagan was quiet—the whole room was quiet, for what seemed like endless minutes—before he spoke. "OK, we'll do it. Borrow the $100,000. And run the national defense piece on national television. I'm taking this all the way to the convention in Kansas City, and I'm going even if I lose every damn primary between now and then."

Ooof. There were twenty-one more primaries to go, from Pennsylvania to California, from Montana to Tennessee. A few minutes ago I thought I'd be going home in a couple of days and now I was signed on to a kamikaze cross-country presidential campaign. We were all slightly stunned, and secretly delighted.

We decided to put out a press release announcing Reagan's forthcoming speech to the nation before the North Carolina primary results were announced that night. Lyn Nofziger pulled out his very old, rather dilapidated portable typewriter and quickly tapped out a draft of a press release. Peter Hannaford and I reviewed it and gave it to the press before Reagan went downstairs for his evening speech.

That evening in the woods of Wisconsin, Reagan was speaking to a meeting of Ducks Unlimited, an organization of conservationists dedicated to preserving and protecting the duck population of America. Perhaps five hundred members were crowded into the main ballroom of the hotel for dinner and to hear Reagan. About 7 P.M. Hannaford and I left our rooms and drifted downstairs to check out the crowd and also to see if the national press corps had picked up any early returns from North Carolina.

Hannaford and I stood quietly in the press area watching Reagan fascinate and excite his audience. They loved him. But apparently not enough of them loved him to give him the presidential primaries. He was the most attractive loser I had ever seen. We waited aimlessly, scuffing our toes on the carpet, looking every now and then at the faces of the press corps for the gleeful grin that would tell us the North Carolinian sword had fallen.

Suddenly I felt a sharp tug on my left coat sleeve. I looked over and there was Frank Reynolds of ABC, one of the most respected and liked television commentators in the country. "Look at this," he said excitedly, as he pushed a small, crumpled scrap of yellow paper at me. I took the paper and looked at two numbers scrawled in pencil: 45—55. "Well," I thought to myself, "we're losing by ten points." But what was Reynolds so excited about? Completely exasperated now, Reynolds leaned over and whispered loudly, jamming his forefinger on the penciled 55. "No, no, you guys got the fifty-five. Reagan is winning!"

It didn't hit right away. Sort of like being in shock after a bad accident. By that time Reynolds repeated his story to Peter Hannaford who blithely commented, "Oh, interesting. What percent of the vote is in?"

Of course, I thought, that would explain it. An early return.

Reynolds replied, "Five percent."

And Hannaford said, poker-faced, "Well, it's early yet."

Hannaford and I kept our faces straight until Reynolds left and then I turned to him and said, "Let's get out of here." We walked rapidly over to the bar and ordered a Coca Cola.

"Wouldn't it be something if we won?" Pete asked.

To which I replied, "It would be fantastic."

It was. It was the most satisfying political victory I have ever experienced. Not because it was the first (it wasn't), not because it was the most important (it wasn't), but because it was the best. It was the distance we all went that night from the depths of certain defeat to the high hill where all things were once again possible. Reagan's victory was made doubly sweet by the fact that he announced his decision not to quit to the press well before the North Carolina results came in.

In Washington this is called "going to the mat." It means that if you start something you will finish it. No matter how certain losing becomes, no matter how difficult the battle, no matter how much it costs you—you will fight on to the end. Going to the mat is a quality especially admired by politicians, and particularly prized by their supporters. There is little that is more disconcerting than to watch someone you have worked years for suddenly change his or her mind and withdraw from a political race. Politics is riddled by enough uncertainty. It is critical to have someone you can count on.

On the plane back to California, the staff, the press, and the Secret Service agents sang and talked and partied, a few got quietly drunk (not the Secret Service), and the Reagans celebrated his astonishing victory with a special treat—a big dish of vanilla ice cream and a small plastic cup of champagne.

To this day no one really knows why the public opinion polls were off by about seventeen points (Reagan won 53 to 46), although the power of Jesse Helms' political organization in North Carolina, headed by his chief political counsellor Tom Ellis, was obviously underestimated. The North Carolina victory marked the beginning of Reagan's second try for the presidency, as Reagan arose slowly, phoenix-like, from the ashes of the early primaries and drove once again toward the 1976 presidential nomination.

The second try went right down to the wire. He fought, as he said he would, in every primary from then to the convention in August at Kansas City, Missouri. By the time Reagan walked into that convention hall the nomination was a toss-up. It was so close nobody knew who would win. The machinations and wheeling and dealing that went on behind the scenes (and some right out in the open) in Kansas City is a book in itself. The result, as we all know, is that Ronald Reagan lost to President Ford.

But it was so close. Even at the end, 47.4 percent of the total number of delegates stayed with Reagan and acknowledged defeat rather than desert to the winning side, as they easily could have done. It was, in effect, Reagan's second defeat for the presidency in less than a year, and the closeness of the vote made it more poignant and painful. Everyone could replay in his or her mind the "what if?" game dozens of times, knowing, in fact, that if we had done one or two things differently, perhaps he would have won. But he didn't win. He lost.

August 19, 1976, was the last day of the Republican National Convention. That night President Ford would give his acceptance speech for the nomination. That morning Ronald Reagan met privately with his campaign staff at the convention. Tears ran down not a few faces as he spoke.

> "The cause goes on. It's just one battle in a long war and it will go on as long as we all live. Nancy and I, we aren't going to go back and sit in a rocking chair on the front porch and say that's all for us.
>
> "You just stay in there and you stay there with the same beliefs and the same faith that made you do what you're doing here. The individuals on the stage may change. The cause is there and the cause will prevail because it is right.
>
> "Don't give up your ideals. Don't compromise. Don't turn to expediency. And don't for heaven's sake, having seen the innerworkings of the watch, don't get cynical.
>
> "No, don't get cynical. Don't get cynical because look at yourselves and what you were willing to do and recognize that there are millions and millions of Americans out there who want what you want. Who want it to be that way. Who want it to be a shining city on a hill."

The next day, August 20, we all flew back to California on our chartered United Airlines 727 jet. During the flight, like others on the staff, I sat with the Reagans and we talked briefly. He was disappointed, but not depressed. Even then he spoke of what was to come, not of what had been.

At the end of our talk I asked them to sign my tickets to the floor of the convention as a souvenir. Nancy wrote, "With so much appreciation & love," and signed it "Nancy &." To which Reagan added his own signature, in a neat display of husband-wife cooperation.

Reagan looked out the plane's window for a few seconds and

then wrote on the second ticket, "We dreamed—we fought & the dream is still with us. Thanks."

The dream is still with us. In those six words Reagan summed up what he was going to do, and expressed what many of us on the airplane felt that day. It may have been the end of the 1976 presidential campaign, but it was also the beginning of the 1980 campaign. On August 20, 1976, Ronald Reagan in effect began his third drive for the presidency.

On the third try he made it. On July 17, 1980, in Detroit, Michigan, four years after his narrow defeat by President Ford, he won the Republican nomination by an overwhelming vote. One hundred and ten days later he won the general election. And eleven weeks after that, on January 20, 1981, Ronald Wilson Reagan became the fortieth president of the United States of America.

Theodore White, the chronicler of American presidential campaigns, once wrote that there is "an iron rule of politics: the higher the office, the more important the candidate. . . . at the supreme level of Presidential politics, the candidate and his behavior outweigh all other elements of his campaign. . . . He is the individual bayonet point of a mighty movement." As the campaign intensifies, the movement, like a powerful wedge, gets larger and larger and goes faster and faster. And as it does, the point of the wedge, where the candidate sits, gets white-hot from the blinding speed and pressure. The fiery heat tempers some candidates, while others are charred and destroyed. Reagan's character was one that was tempered by the fire of a campaign. Adversity seemed to strengthen him, criticism toughened him, defeat deepened his resolve.

I worked for Ronald Reagan off and on over a period of seven years: almost three years in presidential campaigns, traveling with him to two Republican conventions, in the 1980 transition, and slightly over a year in the White House. How he reacted to extreme pressure those two times in 1976—in March just before the North Carolina primary, and then in August, after he lost the nomination by a whisker—tells you more, I think, about the nature of his character and the intensity of his commitment than anything else I have ever heard him say or seen him do.

Chapter Six

THE ACTOR-INVENTOR

When you meet Ronald Reagan, the first thing you notice about him is how big he is. He is half a foot taller than most people, weighs over two hundred pounds, and is lean and muscular. He still looks and moves very much like the lifeguard he was for seven years in the 1920s, when he saved seventy-seven people from drowning in the Illinois Rock River.[1]

One of the most lasting and widespread myths about Ronald Reagan is that he uses small index cards to cue him as to what to say. The implication of the 3×5 inch card stories is that Reagan has no clear views of his own and is dense to the degree that he must refer constantly to cue cards, especially during a speech, to keep his thoughts on track.

The truth of the matter is that Reagan has never used 3×5 cards. The cards he used during the presidential campaigns were actually four inches wide and six inches long. And the cards were rarely used for notes of any kind. Instead they held the full text of Reagan's speeches, which he often wrote himself.

Over the years Reagan invented a unique system to prepare, edit, and deliver speeches. He hated drafts of speeches typewritten on thin letter paper. They were annoying to carry and bothersome to read from, especially when standing behind an outside lectern on a windy day. On the other hand, the 4×6 cards filled his requirements neatly. They were small enough to fit into his suitcoat pocket, yet large enough to accommodate the full text of a major speech on twenty-five to thirty of the cards. They are like large playing cards, thick enough to sort and control easily while giving a speech.

But the space on a 4×6 card is very limited. You can't write very much on it. And that space limitation becomes even more critical when the words have to be large enough to read in swift glances from a distance of two feet or so. Reagan solved that problem by inventing his own shorthand. Some words he left out. Other words he compressed or shortened by dropping letters or using abbreviations. Every now and then he would make up a word. Using his shorthand system he could condense a full typewritten page onto one side of a single 4×6 card. The result, crystal clear to Reagan's eyes, looks like secret code to anyone else.

To further refine his system, and to pack more text on a card, Reagan eliminated all indentations and paragraphs. One sentence follows right after the other, separated only by thick black lines. To make sure he can read the cards easily, he painstakingly printed each shorthand word in bold, block letters, usually in black ink, sometimes in dark blue. Each card is numbered in the upper right-hand corner so he can keep track of them and, finally, the finished pack of cards is bound together with a thick elastic band.

The result is a simple and effective speech system. People who speak on important issues take great care to ensure that what they say is accurate and cogent and complete. The reason is simple: what you say is recorded by the press for posterity, and can be dragged up later to embarrass and confute you. But the truth is that nothing bores and irritates the listener more than a speaker carefully reading the text of a prepared speech. All spontaneity and rapport with the audience is lost. So this is the conflict. Speak extemporaneously and you run the risk of misspeaking; but read your text carefully and you run the risk of boring your audience stiff.

Reagan's speech system allows him to be precise and lively. As he walks across the stage to the lectern to address his audience, both arms swing back and forth; there is no sign anywhere of a prepared speech. Only those seated on the stage behind him no-

SANITY ·· BLNCNG · BUD, & (12
LNDNG ·· INFLAT. WCH. ROBs ···OF
OUR EARNING + MORTGAGES··FUT.
·· TELL THM. ·· BLV. ·· NAT. ·· DO
WHTEVR HS. ·· BE DONE ·· BE
SO STRONG — NO OTHR NAT.
WL. EVR ·· TEMPTD ·· BRK. ·· PC. &
TEST CHLNG ·· STRNGTH.

+ LET US TELL THM. THT AE
MUR AGN — Y.As. ·· ASKD · FITE · DIE
·· CO. — THY — BE ALLOWD ··WIN.
AE DIDNT BSV >UNLESS — CAUSE
·· INTND ·· WIN. ·· SIGNRs ··c DEC· IND.
·· WCH. —— LIB. — ·· INTND · IT. CHOSN
· GROW UP — SAME KND ·· FROM·· KNEW
·· GROWING UP. ·· VIC ·· IF · DIDNT ·—

One of Ronald Reagan's handwritten speech cards using the shorthand system he invented (actual size).

tice, if they watch closely, that his left hand drops into his suitcoat pocket and pulls out a neat, small packet of 4×6 cards, each one packed with tightly written shorthand.

Holding the cards before him, with the top of the lectern blocking the audience's view, he slips off the elastic band with his right hand and sets the cards down. As he speaks, scarcely anyone notices him glance down at the cards, which he deftly sorts every few seconds, slipping the top card to the bottom of the deck. When he's through speaking he scoops the cards together, quickly stacks them and slides them back into the side pocket of his suitcoat. Even on a very warm day, tieless and coatless, he can still slip the cards into the hip pocket of his trousers.

Reagan has a couple of personal attributes that further enhance the illusion that he does not read from a formally prepared text. First, he has a literal, photographic memory. He, like others with the gift, can look briefly at a page and later recall the image of that page in his mind, and actually see and read what is on the page. He could glance down at a 4×6 card lying on the lectern before him and then, looking directly at the audience, read the shorthand printed on the card. Usually one glance per card is enough.

Second, he has a special way of using his hard contact lenses. He does not like to wear reading glasses while giving a speech. He solved this problem in an unusual way. Just before he would give a speech, while still on the airplane or in the car, he would lean forward, bring both hands to his face, and then with his forefinger and thumb pluck out the lens in his right eye. After popping it into his mouth for a quick wash he delicately placed the lens into its small plastic case and dropped it into his pocket.

Now Reagan has one long-vision eye and one short-vision eye. With his naked right eye he reads the hand-printed shorthand on the white 4×6 cards. Then, looking up, he focuses on the faces of the audience with the lens-clad left eye. Throughout the entire speech, his eyes flick up and down, focusing and refocusing, left eye, right eye, left, right, left, right. Most of us could never do it. It is difficult enough to wear contact lenses, let alone train your eyes to act independently. But Reagan worked on it over the years and, by the time of his presidential campaigns, had refined the technique to perfection.

This skill with his eyes, plus his photographic memory, plus his unique shorthand hand-printed on those stiff 4×6 white cards makes it possible for him to read complicated, detailed policy speeches without anyone knowing that he is reading from a text. In the audience all you see is Reagan, not wearing eyeglasses, looking directly at you and speaking clearly and knowledgeably about complicated issues with hardly a hesitation. Even the all-seeing eye of the television camera does not detect the cards. A few of the national news people who traveled regularly with Reagan on his campaign were aware that he used cards, but they do not seem to have suspected the extent of his speechmaking system.

Another major advantage of his speech system is the ease with which you can edit and rewrite speeches. To cut a section, all you do is remove some cards. To add a section you write new cards and insert them. You can move the front part of the speech to the back, or the middle to the front, just by shuffling the cards. The system is as flexible as a smooth gold chain.

In the preparation of new speeches the system is unrivaled. On the presidential campaign trail when Reagan sat down and opened his briefcase to work, what you saw inside were twenty-five or thirty packs of 4×6 cards, each bound tightly by an elastic band. Most of the packs were complete speeches on different topics. Some packs contained cards culled from old speeches or cards with specific thoughts. Reagan would pore over the packs of cards, then pluck a few cards from one pack, more cards from another, and combine them. In a matter of minutes, he could create an entirely new speech.

The only drawback to Reagan's system is that it is very personal and time-consuming. During his campaigns, he spent a lot of time on it. His major speeches were written out first in longhand, in ink, on lined, legal-size yellow pads. Once he was satisfied with the speech, he would "card" it by translating it into his shorthand onto 4×6 cards. Usually he did it all by himself, although by the time the presidential campaigns ended there were one or two secretaries and a speechwriter, Peter Hannaford, who learned enough of his shorthand to take the handwritten text and prepare cards well enough for him to use. But he always preferred to use cards he printed himself.

He worked at it constantly. Within minutes of taking off on the campaign plane, Reagan would be deeply immersed in the contents of the briefcase he always had with him. Most of the time, when he wasn't reading, he would be printing cards or drafting new speeches, statements, or letters. During the early days of his campaigning, he spent hour after hour speechwriting.

But it was not all work on the campaign plane. I soon realized I was not the only person who picked up the newspaper and turned to the comics and read them first. Every day of the campaign, Reagan would eagerly look forward to a moment in the morning to read the latest installment of his favorite comics. He read them fairly seriously, following the actions of the characters as their adventures unfolded day after day, remembering what they had done. Part of my job during the campaign was to prepare a digest of the national and international news for him, as well as local newspapers. I quickly made it a point to include, when I could find them, the day's comics.

After he became president, Reagan no longer had time to handcraft his speeches. As president, and to some degree during the closing, hectic days of the presidential campaign, he was forced to use a Teleprompter. It is a complex system that projects the text of a speech onto two small one-way glass panes about one-foot square which are mounted several feet in front of him to his left and to his right. As he speaks, the text is scrolled across the glass by a projector and read like the rolling credits of a movie. This technique is expensive and requires a small, well-trained support staff in addition to the technical equipment. The speech must be prepared in advance and typed onto a special tape that can be projected. The glass panes must be positioned just so, and the operator who controls the speed of the scrolling must be perfectly attuned to the speaker's speed and speaking rhythm. As president, Reagan has no time to personally translate speeches into the shorthand he invented. The Teleprompter is more awkward and expensive than small decks of 4×6 cards, but it does make it possible to give lively speeches with the appearance of spontaneity, without the intense preparation required by Reagan's personal speechmaking system.

There are some final touches Reagan adds to his speeches. Sometimes circumstances force him to stand in full view of his audience, with no lectern to lean on, no chair to sit in. In early 1980 there was a series of debates with the other major candidates for the Republican nomination for president. One evening, after one of these debates, we sat in his hotel suite watching a rebroadcast of the debate on television, and Reagan critiqued the performance of the other candidates. With the enthusiasm of a drama coach he said, "Notice that none of them knows what to do with their arms and hands. It's one of the hardest things to do right when you're making a speech."

As I recall it, he then pointed to Senator Howard Baker who had his hands buried deep in the side pockets of his baggy trousers, one hand apparently jingling a bunch of coins. George Bush stood with his arms folded across his chest. Congressman John Anderson stood with his hands clasped behind his back. They all looked uncomfortable.

"The only way to look natural on a stage is to hold your hands and arms in a way that does not feel natural." And then Reagan got to his feet and demonstrated.

"What you have to do is just let your arms hang by your side, straight down. Then you curl your fingers so that they just cup your thumb. It feels uncomfortable, but you look relaxed and at ease. It's something I learned a long time ago in Hollywood from an expert on public speaking."

The major weapon in Reagan's political arsenal is the speech. He discovered his ability to move large audiences as a freshman at Eureka College in Illinois in 1928, when he was selected to be the chief spokesman for a massive student strike against the college administration. The night he addressed the student strikers he was astonished to find that they "came to their feet with a roar." As Reagan said later, "It was heady wine." [2]

The strike was successful, and he never forgot it. Reagan steadily honed his skill of persuading large numbers of people to listen, to agree, and then to act on his words. He became especially skillful at taking complex, difficult policy issues, extracting the essence of the idea, and then translating that essence into clear, vivid language that almost everyone could understand.

Not everyone agreed, but everyone understood.

During the presidential campaigns of 1976 and 1980 I spent many months traveling with Reagan, on airplanes, on busses, in cars, and in hotel rooms. I watched him use that gift of speech like an F-14 Tomcat fighter plane, wreaking havoc on his political enemies and blasting new policy paths where others had failed. I also sat next to him while he prepared many of those powerful speeches. Everyone—the traveling press corps, the public, even his own staff—

concentrated exclusively on his message. No one seemed to be concerned at all with how he did it.

Reagan's ability to speak, to inspire, and move those who watched and listened to him, was critical to his success as a political figure. From afar it appeared effortless. It was almost as if he had some special gift that enabled him to talk to his audience clearly and simply about complex public policy issues in a way that personally touched them.

But it wasn't effortless and it wasn't easy. Part of it Reagan was born with: the mellow voice, the photographic memory, the body of a tackle on a pro football team. But most of it was simply intense, long hours of work and ingenuity.

If there is a moral in this story of the 4 × 6 cards it is that things often appear to be what they are not. This is especially true in politics and in the making of national policy, where events are often believed to be the result of chance, with no sound reasoning, careful planning, or purposeful action. Sometimes, of course, events are a matter of chance, but most often, almost always, they are not. Major changes in national policies seldom occur by chance or by themselves. When they seem to, it is usually because we do not fully understand what lies behind the changes that have occurred.

Much of what appears to be in American politics is not, and much of what is, does not appear.

Chapter Seven

PRIORITIES

There are three fundamental issues in American politics—peace, prosperity, and individual liberty. There are dozens of other major sub-issues as well, all vitally important, many affecting millions of people and involving billions of dollars. But the big issues for most Americans are whether or not they feel secure against any serious foreign threat, whether or not they are economically prosperous, and whether or not they feel their individual freedoms are being protected and expanded.

Individual liberty is the ultimate goal, the freedom for people to follow their own paths, to make their own decisions, to live up to their potential, to control their own lives, and to pursue their own happiness. But this goal is not possible without peace and prosperity—the two legs on which liberty stands.

I remember one time during the closing days of Ronald Reagan's 1980 drive to wrest political power from Jimmy Carter and the Democrats when Reagan was thinking out loud about President Carter's disastrous performance during the preceding four years.

"The problem with Carter," said Reagan, "is that he tries to do everything at once and he tries to do too much of it himself. If we win we are going to set priorities and do things one at a time."

And that is exactly what Reagan did when he was elected, and it was probably the wisest thing he did as president. He established two top priorities. The first was to rebuild America's military strength. The second was to rebuild America's economic strength. All other issues, important as they might be, were rigorously relegated to the sidelines. Those policy priorities set, he handpicked key people to implement them, and delegated the authority and responsibility to get the job done. He seemed to do it easily, without any apparent soul-searching or intellectual struggle, almost as if by instinct.

Many, including some on his own staff, were critical of the rigid priorities and the massive delegation of authority. They wanted him to move on a dozen fronts at once. They wanted him personally involved in their pet projects, to know all the details, and the problems and the nuances that they knew. They wanted his time. Reagan knew this, but he also understood the nature of the modern presidency in a way that few have grasped. The keys to being a successful president today are priorities and time; setting priorities and managing personal time so that your work is focused on those priorities.

If you add up the things that the American public expects the president to do personally—develop policy solutions to complex domestic and international problems, give press conferences, meet with foreign heads of state, meet with countless special interest groups, make innumerable public speeches, be commander-in-chief of the armed forces, deal with 435 congressmen and 100 senators and 50 governors, give elegant White House dinners, answer mail and return phone calls—the total number of hours required to do what he should do far exceed the number of hours in the day. And if you allow him eight hours to sleep, a couple of hours to eat, an hour with his family, and perhaps a few minutes by himself to think, the impossibility of the task is even greater. Delegation of authority in the modern presidency is not a choice. The reality of the overwhelming demands on a president's time makes it a necessity.

In practice this delegation means that many people, perhaps as many as forty or fifty, act daily in the name of the president. There is no way the president can avoid this. The only choice he has is whether or not he focuses the time he has on the most important, most critical issues. If he does, he has a fighting chance. If he does not, the job is impossible.

After a president sets the priorities, the challenge is to keep them. Every day is like walking on rapidly spinning logs floating down a surging river. The president is constantly bombarded with crisis after crisis, decision after decision, each one urgent and important. The impact of this unrelenting pressure can blur the priorities of even the most dedicated, and he must constantly resurface his most important priorities or they will be submerged in a sea of less important but more urgent detail.

The hardest thing for a president to do is to let go of something that is *very* important and urgent so that he can attend to something that is *vitally* important. It is a rare management skill, and there is no job in the world that even comes close to preparing a person for the pressures of the presidency. Shuffling priorities seems to be an innate skill that, like an ear for music or an eye for painting, one is born with. Ronald Reagan has the skill in spades. He set a few top priorities and then controlled the day's events so that he could work on those priorities.

When it comes to the making of national policy, two major issues dominate: defense policy and economic policy. Since World War II these two issues have been of overriding importance on our national policy agenda. During campaigns it is the candidate's position on national defense and the economy that determines who will be elected president. This phenomenon is true of many other countries besides America. Even in the land of the dictators the question of military might and economic productivity occupy the central thoughts of the rulers.

There are good reasons for this.

A powerful defense and a strong economy are vital to the survival of any large nation. Without either one there is a real question as to whether or not the United States could survive in today's hostile, competitive world.

Each is necessary for the other. We cannot maintain a strong defense unless we have a healthy economy. And without a strong defense, we may not have any economy to worry about.

The future of liberty throughout the world depends largely on the future of liberty in America. Just imagine a world in which the United States did not exist, and a world in which Nazi Germany or

1941 Japan or the Soviet Union of today did exist. And the future of liberty in America depends on our having a powerful military force and a strong, growing economy,

Essentially, it comes down to a simple proposition: if we can stay alive and free, and if we can become prosperous, then we can probably cope with anything.

National defense and economic policy are big, sprawling issues that, at least in America during the past several decades, have dwarfed all others. And during the 1980s we have gone through fundamental, some might even say revolutionary, changes in these paramount issues. In economics we have embarked on a strong reaffirmation of capitalism. In defense we have fundamentally altered the very way we think about national defense in a nuclear age, moving away from the concept of holding ourselves mutually hostage through a pact of mutually assured destruction, and moving toward the concept of defending ourselves by destroying nuclear missiles before they can strike their targets.

The two major problems that face the United States during its third century as a republic are the same two issues that have been at the top of Reagan's public priority list since the earliest days of his candidacy—the threat of nuclear annihilation and the challenge of maintaining a strong, growing economy. He chose his priorities well.

Three

Reagan's Vision

"Those who would read this letter a hundred years
from now will know whether those missiles were
fired. They will know whether we met our challenge. Whether they have the freedoms that we
have known up until now will depend on what we
do here."
—from a speech by Ronald Reagan to the
Republican Convention in 1976.

Chapter Eight

NUCLEAR MISSILES

Reagan set his priority on nuclear missiles early. It was late at night on the last day of the 1976 Republican convention in Kansas City, Missouri. We were standing in Reagan's skybox, peering tensely over the thick, waist-high glass panel separating us from the rest of the convention hall down below. Over two hundred feet away, President Gerald Ford was moving into the last minutes of his speech accepting the nomination. He was unusually animated, clearly savoring the close victory of the night before. The delegates were quiet and attentive, half of them ready to rise, applaud and shout "We want Ford" when he ended. As far as anyone could tell, the convention was all over.

Or almost over.

Twenty-five minutes earlier, as vice presidential nominee Senator Robert Dole of Kansas wound up his speech to set the stage for President Ford's triumphant entry, the doorkeeper of Reagan's skybox tapped me gently on the shoulder.

"There's a man outside," he whispered. "Says he has to talk to you now. His name is Harlow."

Skyboxes ring the upper levels of Kemper Arena in Kansas City.

Designed for those who can afford and are willing to pay to watch live sports events in semi-isolation and clubroom comfort, they now served as observation booths and holding rooms for the major television networks and candidates. The one we occupied had wood paneling, a couple of dozen heavily upholstered seats, a food buffet, bar, and a bathroom. Ford's box was at the north end of the arena, and directly opposite, at the south end, was Reagan's.

Reagan's skybox was packed. Besides the candidate, his wife, and family, there were dozens of friends and senior staff, including most of those who, for the last three nights, operated far below in the candidate's heavily guarded command trailer outside, tucked into the shadows of Kemper Arena.

Earlier that same evening a spontaneous demonstration happened on the convention floor. As the Reagans entered the hall and took their seats, a low murmur rose from the delegates, growing louder and louder until the insistent pleas could be clearly heard anywhere in the hall. The chant of "SPEECH . . . SPEECH . . . SPEECH" drowned out every attempt of the convention chairman, Congressman John Rhodes of Arizona, to keep order. The program schedule fell further and further behind, making it impossible for Ford to accept his nomination on prime time television.

Finally, the drumbeat cadence of "SPEECH . . . SPEECH" died down. Then slowly, first by ones and twos, then in whole sections of delegations, people stood looking at Reagan, and waved their arms in a slow overhand motion, shouting, "COME ON DOWN . . . COME ON DOWN."

Most of us in the skybox witnessed enough moving events in the campaign to have become somewhat jaded at demonstrations of political affection. But watching and hearing this, our sophistication slipped a bit; and some throat muscles tightened.

Reagan, too, was deeply moved. He felt an enormous obligation to his delegates standing below him, a few hundred feet away, pleading with him to come down. They worked for months for him, some for years, had sacrificed time and money, and stood against the Republican establishment politicians in their home states. Crushed by his loss, yet somehow curiously defiant, they now wanted him to come and speak to them.

As Reagan sat watching, a look of unhappiness deepened on his face. Finally, in exasperation, he rose slowly. Leaning over the glass panel, he reached out his right arm, waving, and knowing that the delegates down on the floor couldn't possibly hear him, shouted, "All right, I'll try."

Reagan also knew he had no control over whether he spoke to them from the podium. The convention was controlled by the Republican National Committee, and they in turn by President Ford's campaign committee. Reagan had not asked to address the convention, even though half the delegates were his. Of course, he could try to force the issue and demand to speak. But this was not his style. He felt strongly that it was Ford's show now and he should not impose himself; yet he was frustrated by being unable to respond to the hundreds of cries of his loyal supporters far below on the convention floor.

I worked my way from the bar in the back of the skybox over to the door. I was puzzled. What could Harlow want?

Bryce Harlow was one of the most extraordinary political figures in the country. Barely known outside of Washington, D.C., soft-spoken, and just over five feet tall, he was among the most respected men in Washington and had been at the top of the Republican power pyramid for over twenty-five years: as Eisenhower's top speechwriter, as Nixon's congressional liaison and counsellor, and, most recently, as a member of Ford's own kitchen cabinet.

Bryce Harlow was the kind of man who could give politics a good name. Never elected to any public office, he served four U.S. presidents with great distinction, providing them with more advice, most of which they accepted, on more important public issues than perhaps any man in the history of the United States. His impact on public policy since World War II has been immense, and largely unheralded save for a few knowledgeable people in Washington.

Months earlier, hoping to entice him into supporting Ronald Reagan, I set up a dinner meeting between Harlow and Reagan at the Metropolitan Club in Washington. They enjoyed meeting each other but Harlow stayed loyal to President Ford, and for the last four days he was in Ford's command trailer, using all the political skill and knowledge at his command to defeat Reagan.

Over a hundred people were packed tightly together outside the door, ten to twelve deep, watched by the scanning eyes of the Secret Service agents on duty. I cracked open the door, spotted Bryce, vouched for him to the agents, and brought him into the skybox.

Once inside, in the quiet, unobtrusive manner that was his

trademark, Harlow explained. "We have all been talking down-stairs and feel it would be a terrible thing for the Republican party if Ronald Reagan left this convention hall without speaking to the delegates. Will he come down and speak to them?"

I couldn't be sure. Reagan had not prepared a formal accep-tance speech. He felt uncomfortable doing so until he knew for certain he was going to be nominated. The night before, overtures were made for him to appear on the platform to demonstrate party unity after Ford won the nomination. But he refused. It was one thing to support the man he battled for ten months in preference to Carter; it was another to embrace him and pretend no differ-ences existed.

He had given little thought to what kind of remarks would be appropriate in such a situation. In spite of the fact that Reagan is probably the most capable and confident political speaker in the country, it was asking a lot to expect him to deliver an extempo-raneous speech before this roiling convention, after the president had spoken, to tens of millions of Americans watching on tele-vision. The people watching would assume it was arranged far in advance and would expect a superlative performance, a speech that would be inspiring, that would unify the party, that would be re-membered.

It could also easily determine whether Ronald Reagan would ever run for president again.

Off to one side of the skybox Reagan's campaign manager John Sears was talking with Lyn Nofziger, a longtime Reagan adviser and his convention director. I looked at Harlow and said, "Let's see what the other fellows think."

As we walked over, another of Reagan's senior aides, Michael Deaver, joined us.

Senator Dole had now finished his speech, and the delegates on the floor—half of them—were clapping and shouting as Presi-dent Ford moved toward the microphone. At the front of the sky-box the Reagans watched Ford intently, their concentration broken only when delegates leaned in over the heavy glass enclosure and asked them for autographs on their admission tickets.

Bryce Harlow watched the Reagans silently for a few minutes, then turned back to us and became more insistent.

"Reagan has to speak to this convention. Those delegates down there have picked two candidates. Now they want to hear from him. If he doesn't, it will split the Republican party in two."

Several seconds went by. Then Deaver broke the silence.

"Does the president want the governor to speak?"

Harlow hesitated, then nodded yes. "I'm sure he does."

Deaver is in many ways like Harlow—quiet, unassuming, with a quick, incisive political intelligence.

"If the president would ask the governor, from the speaker's platform, to speak to the convention, it might be possible."

Harlow looked intently at Deaver. "I'm sure he will do that."

Deaver turned and eased his way through the family and friends who surrounded Reagan.

"Governor," said Deaver, "President Ford wants to ask you to come down and speak after he is finished."

Reagan looked surprised and lines of concern deepened across his face.

"But what will I say?"

"Don't worry," said Deaver, "You'll think of something."

Reagan nodded his head silently, somewhat ruefully, and Deaver returned to our group.

"O.K. If the president will ask him personally to come down from the speaker's stand, he will."

Harlow nodded and said, "Let me go back down and confirm it."

After Harlow left we again looked down at the convention floor. President Ford had begun to speak. Except for a few who wanted to beat the crowd and were already moving toward the exits, the delegates looked relaxed and attentive. Reagan kept his eyes on Ford, occasionally turning to Nancy or rising to autograph another ticket.

A few minutes later Harlow returned. We gathered in a small, tight circle at the back of the skybox, and Harlow, bent over like a quarterback calling signals in a football game, said, "It's all set. As soon as President Ford is through speaking and the demonstration begins, Senator Dole will go up to him on the platform and tell him that Reagan is willing to come down if he will ask him over the microphone."

Deaver went over to tell Reagan that Ford would soon be issuing a unique invitation and Harlow returned to the convention floor. Ford's speech was almost over. We could only wait. Would the president agree to give Reagan the honor of being the last person to address the 1976 convention? Or would he worry that Reagan might use the opportunity to set half of the delegates, and ultimately half of the Republican party, against him with a burst of the eloquent oratory of which he was so capable? Or would Ford sense that he had to invite him, that, rattling across the deck of the country, there was a political force out there he had to contend with, a force that if ignored, would seriously endanger his own chances of being elected in the fall?

I doubt that any of us in the skybox heard the last few minutes of Ford's speech. Every thought was focused on whether or not the president would issue the invitation. As Ford ended his speech, a demonstration burst forth from half the delegates. Many delegations, like those from Texas, California, and North Carolina, responded with only light, perfunctory applause. But in the swirling sea of white and blue FORD/DOLE signs their apostasy went unnoticed.

Ford raised his hands in a victory salute, soon joined by Betty Ford, Dole, Nelson Rockefeller, and others. The cheering continued for a minute or so.

Then Ford moved toward the podium. He reached for the heavy, chrome plated microphone and leaned into it, but did not speak. He paused a moment and then turned to the left and looked up at Reagan.

The wild cheering and applause for Ford continued to thunder from the convention floor.

"He's not going to ask him," I remember thinking. "There's no way he can. The delegates are cheering and clapping so loud Reagan won't be able to hear him."

Then Ford smiled. He stepped back from the podium and, raising his long arms high over his head, beckoned to Reagan with wide, sweeping thrusts and said in pantomime, "Come on down."

As Ford swung his arms, the searchlights at the other end of the hall swept across the arena and focused on the Reagans. Every eye in the arena turned up to Reagan, and some delegates began to rise from their chairs.

Ronald Reagan looked genuinely startled. He turned back to a small group of us standing behind him and said, "Does that mean I've been asked?"

Someone said yes, and he and Nancy stood. With one deft thrust of his hand Reagan pushed an unruly lock of dark brown hair into place, buttoned his coat, and he and Nancy started for the door.

As Reagan left the skybox to join Ford on the platform, Richard Whalen, one of Reagan's campaign advisers, leaned over to Darrell Trent, Reagan's deputy campaign manager, and said quietly, "Ford has just given the future of the party to Reagan."

The Secret Service were alerted earlier to the possibility we might be going down to the platform. Quickly, they formed a cocoon around the Reagans, moving them through the door and the solid wall of people waiting outside to catch a glimpse of them. As the small entourage moved by me on the way to the convention floor, I followed in its wake. I suppose I should have remained in the skybox, but it was the final night of the convention, and very likely Reagan's last hurrah, so I went.

Normally restrained and polite, the Secret Service agents in front of us used short body blocks and discreetly placed elbows until the wall of people outside the door gave way and we raced through, across the hall, down several flights of stairs, along the ground floor corridors, winding up and around in the labyrinth of corridors and stairs under the platform until suddenly we were standing on the platform, bathed in the warm, bright television lights before the entire convention.

When Reagan approached the podium every person in the hall was standing. The shouting and applause thundered as he placed both hands on the wooden stand and leaned slightly toward them. Off to the left, barely three feet away, in the surrealism that seems to permeate so much of American politics, Nelson Rockefeller stood grinning, clapping his hands wildly. Standing next to Betty Ford and Rockefeller was President Ford, beaming. An air of frenzied relief and excitement swept over the floor and the platform.

Reagan had come down.

As he began to speak, every person in the arena was standing, and the moment so caught them all that they continued to stand as he spoke—some out of respect, some because others were, some in awe. Never in anyone's memory had the delegates to a Republican national convention stood for an entire speech.

Reagan's speech to the standing delegates that August night was short. Conceived under great time pressure and with the knowledge that millions of Americans would be watching and listening, his remarks seemed to prove that great pressures can concentrate the mind wonderfully. He spoke without a prepared text—no notes, no cards. The essential policy themes that he drove home that night were the fundamental ones that strike a chord in us all—the themes of peace, prosperity, and individual liberty.

But the most notable aspect of his short speech was what Reagan thought was *the* most important issue facing the United States. It wasn't the size of the federal government, or fraud and abuse in welfare programs, or the growing tax burden. It was simply the issue of whether or not we would be wise enough to prevent a nuclear war that could literally destroy our civilization.

Here is what he said.

"Mr. President, Mrs. Ford, Mr. Vice President, Mr. Vice President-to-be, the distinguished guests here, and you ladies and gentlemen. I'm going to say fellow Republicans here, but those who are watching from a distance, with all those millions of Democrats and Independents who I know are looking for a cause around which to rally and which I believe we can give them . . .

"There are cynics who say that a party platform is something no one bothers to read and doesn't very often amount to much. Whether it is different this time than it has ever been before, I believe the Republican party has a platform that is a banner of bold, unmistakable colors with no pale, pastel shades.

"We have just heard a call to arms, based on that platform, and a call to us to really be successful in communicating, and reveal to the American people the difference between this platform and the platform of the opposing party which is nothing but revamp and a reissue and a running of the late, late show of the thing that we've been hearing from them for the last forty years.

"If I could just take a moment . . . I had an assignment the other day. Someone asked me to write a letter for a time capsule that is going to be opened in Los Angeles a hundred years from now, on our tercentennial. It sounded like an easy assignment. They suggested I write something about the problems and issues of the day and I set out to do so, riding down the coast in an automobile looking at the blue Pacific out on one side and the Santa Ynez mountains on the other, and I couldn't help but wonder if it was going to be that beautiful a hundred years from now as it was on that summer day.

"And then, as I tried to write . . . let your own minds turn to that task. You're going to write for people a hundred years from now who know all about us. We know nothing about them. We don't know what kind of a world they'll be living in.

"And suddenly I thought to myself, if I write of problems they'll be domestic problems, of which the president spoke here tonight, the challenges confronting us, erosion of freedom that has taken place under Democrat rule in this country, the invasion of private rights, the controls and restrictions on the vitality of the great free economy that we enjoy. These are the challenges that we must meet.

"And then again there is the challenge of which he spoke, that we live in a world in which the great powers have poised and aimed at each other horrible missiles of destruction, that can, in a matter of minutes, arrive in each others' country and destroy virtually the civilized world we live in.

"And suddenly it dawned on me.

"Those who would read this letter a hundred years from now will know whether those missiles were fired. They will know whether we met our challenge. Whether they have the freedoms that we have known up until now will depend on what we do here.

"Will they look back with appreciation and say, 'Thank God for those people in 1976 who headed off that loss of freedom, who kept our world from nuclear destruction?'

"And if we fail, they probably won't get to read the letter at all because it spoke of individual freedom and they won't be allowed to talk of that or read of it.

"This is our challenge. And this is why, here in this hall tonight, better than we've ever done before, we have got to quit talking to each other and about each other, and go out and communicate to the world that we may be fewer in numbers than we've ever been but we carry the message they're waiting for.

"We must go forth from here united, determined, that what a great general said a few years ago is true, 'There's no substitute for victory.' "[1]

It was a political fantasy. In less than six minutes the man whom the delegates rejected only twenty-four hours before now inspired them and united them. A few delegates were to later admit that as he spoke, they began to have second thoughts.

"We may have picked the wrong man," one said.

Reagan's preoccupation with the threat of nuclear war, so evident in his emotional address that night, did not go away. All during the next ten years—the years of political eclipse after his defeat in 1976, the hectic, chaotic years when he campaigned again for the presidency, the transition after he won, and the years of his presidency as he grappled with dozens of complex issues—the concern about nuclear war, and the challenge to diminish the threat of that war was always foremost in his mind.

It was not something he talked about a lot in public. But he had strong feelings, and strong convictions about what could and should be done. He had a grand strategy, never fully articulated, that he relentlessly pursued. The strategy was simple and elegant, and quite radical.

He began with certain basic premises.

First, that a nuclear war between the United States and the Soviet Union would have devastating consequences for both sides. It wasn't a question of surviving a nuclear war. Both countries could survive in the literal sense—some buildings, some people—but civilization as we know it, especially the free, powerful prosperity of the United States, would be gone, perhaps forever, replaced by a new Dark Age.

Second, he was committed to the *reduction* of nuclear weapons, not a limitation in their rate of increase, or freezing them at their current levels. This was truly a radical idea when Reagan first proposed it in the 1970s. The first time I recall him mentioning the idea was on the campaign plane in 1976 while he was discussing his position on the Strategic Arms Limitation Talks (SALT) with Richard V. Allen, his chief foreign and defense policy adviser.

"You know," Reagan said, "I've always liked the idea of START instead of SALT." Both Allen and I looked puzzled. "What we should be trying to do is reduce the number of nuclear weapons, not just limit their growth. Instead of talks to limit the growth of nuclear weapons we should be having STrategic Arms Reduction Talks—START."

Nobody on the campaign staff raised any serious objections to his idea of reducing the stockpiles of nuclear weapons, but on the other hand, and it's difficult as a former campaign staffer to admit this, nobody believed there was the slightest possibility it could ever happen. And when Reagan began to talk privately of a dream he had when someday we might live in a world free of all nuclear missiles, well, we just smiled.

After all, the conventional wisdom on nuclear weapons was very clear during the late 1970s. Even the combined foreign policy wizardry of Richard Nixon and Henry Kissinger only managed to produce a controlled but fairly high rate of growth in the nuclear weapons arsenals of the two superpowers. Virtually no one at the time thought seriously that there was a chance of any reduction in nuclear missiles. In fact, during the late 1970s and early 1980s, the most radical proposal put forth was a freeze on existing nuclear stockpiles. Strongly supported by communist countries and left-wing politicians all over the Western world, who were apparently convinced that we could do no better, the freeze idea was—a little ironically—the ultimate in reactionary politics. Those who advocated a nuclear weapons freeze, while pursuing a course they seemed to think was on the cutting edge of nuclear politics, were really giving up and surrendering to a future built on the trusting bond of mutually assured destruction.

Third, Reagan was morally appalled at the doctrine of mutually assured destruction (MAD) that had been our national nuclear weapons defense policy for some twenty years. As he edged closer and closer to the presidency he became increasingly aware that some day he might have to decide whether or not to give an order to launch a retaliatory attack on the Soviet Union that would surely kill tens of millions of innocent civilians. He did not believe it was wise to allow ourselves to get into a position where our only option would be to retaliate by annihilation of another society. As he said in 1983, "I've become more and more deeply convinced that the human spirit must be capable of rising above dealing with other nations and human beings by threatening their existence . . . to rely on the specter of retaliation, on mutual threat (is) a sad commentary on the human condition. Wouldn't it be better to save lives than to avenge them?"[2]

Fourth, he believed that the Soviet Union was an implacable foe, an evil empire as he once indelicately put it. He had no illusions about the Soviet leadership. Like all those who rely on brute force to achieve power, the Soviets, he believed, would only respond to implacable determination, backed up by military power equal or superior to theirs. But he did not believe the Soviets were crazy or irrational.

Reagan was convinced they would act in their own best interests, that the Soviets would always do the right thing if they had to. He believed the trick was in getting them to recognize what was in their best interests, and demonstrating clearly to them that they had no other alternatives.

Fifth, he was convinced that the productive power of the United States economy was vastly superior to the Soviet economy, that if we began a drive to upgrade the power and scope of our military forces, the Soviets would not be able to keep pace. On numerous occasions during the presidential campaigns when he was talking privately to his policy advisers he would say, "The only way the Soviets will stop their drive for military superiority is when they realize that we are willing to go all out in an arms race. Right now people say there is an arms race, but the Soviets are the only ones racing. If we release the forces of our economy to produce the weapons we need the Soviets will never be able to keep up. And then, and only then, will they become reasonable and willing to seriously consider reductions in nuclear weapons."

Sixth, he was very skeptical about the effectiveness of arms control treaties. One day, on the airplane during a campaign trip, I noticed that he was intensely absorbed in a book. Later that day he handed it to me and said, "This is an interesting book written by an old friend of mine, Larry Beilenson. He shows that countries always break their treaties."

The name of the book was *The Treaty Trap: A History of the Performance of Political Treaties by the United States and European Nations*. It was written in 1969 by Laurence W. Beilenson, a distinguished Los Angeles lawyer who had served as counsel for the Screen Actors Guild, the union that Reagan once headed. The book was an exhaustive, detailed account of the history of the performance and breach of treaties by the United States and European nations during the past 300 years. The message of the book was that all major nations, without exception, have been habitual treaty breakers, abiding by the treaty terms only as long as it continued to be in their national interests to do so. The conclusion was that it was dangerous to rely literally on any treaty, no matter how solemn or binding.

Reagan did believe that treaties were useful and had a purpose, but that their usefulness was limited. A treaty expressed the nations' interests at the time of the signing, and was a useful way to codify their mutual concerns at that time. But national interest changed over time, especially with the rapid advances in technology that continually gave rise to newer, more powerful weapons. And treaties became obsolete.

But turning the elements of Reagan's six-point strategy into a comprehensive program that would work was difficult. How could we get away from a policy of mutually assured destruction? How could you convince the Soviets to act responsibly? Of what value was a treaty that simply ratified ever-increasing stockpiles of nuclear missiles? For some time after he became president, Reagan followed the only course he saw open to him, a massive rebuilding of our entire defense establishment—everything from new missiles and planes to improved recruiting to a refurbishing of our intelligence and counterintelligence capabilities. But even that did not appear to be enough. The Soviets were as intractable as ever, building thousands of new intercontinental ballistic missiles, more accurate, more powerful, more mobile, and more deadly than ever.

And then Ronald Reagan used the key that would unlock the gates between him and his dream of a missile-free world. It was the idea of missile defense.

The idea of missile defense is not new. It has been with us at least as long as we have had missiles that could attack. Both the United States and the Soviet Union have spent billions of dollars since the 1950s in a quest for a way to destroy missiles in flight. The United States effort peaked in 1971 and then for a number of reasons—the signing of the ABM (Anti-Ballistic Missile) treaty with the Soviet Union in 1972, the heavy cost, and a mounting sense of futility of ever developing the technology that could cope with the rapid expansion of Soviet offensive nuclear power—we gave up on the idea. In 1975 we even tore down one hundred interceptor missiles we had deployed in North Dakota. The idea of missile defense faded away.

But missile defense intrigued Reagan, and when he learned in late 1979 that stunning technological advances made such a defense now feasible, he eagerly pushed ahead. It became possible to construct a defensive shield against nuclear missiles, and the implications were breathtaking. Even an imperfect shield would drastically reduce the potential firepower of a hostile nation. We would no longer have to worry about an accidental firing of a missile. And the key to it was new technology, technology that the Soviet Union would have difficulty matching.

Our defense would no longer depend on the sanity of the Soviet rulers; it would be in our own hands. And most importantly, it would enable us to move away from relying totally on the idea of mutually assured destruction and the building of more and more offensive nuclear missiles. As Aleksei Kosygin, the prime minister of the Soviet Union, said back in 1967, "A defensive system, which prevents attack, is not a cause of the arms race but represents a factor preventing the death of people . . . An anti-missile system may cost more than an offensive one, but it is intended not for killing people but for saving human lives."[3]

For years Reagan studied the idea of missile defense, talked to experts, and asked questions. And then on March 23, 1983, in a nationally televised address to the American people, he changed the way we fundamentally think about national defense in a world of nuclear weapons. From that day on America was committed to building a defense shield to protect us from incoming missiles.

Rarely does political rhetoric match substance, but what President Reagan did that cold winter night of March 23, 1983, changed the course of human history. In one grand, sweeping political move he seized the moral high ground in the international issue of nuclear missiles. He offered the hope that we might one day remove the terror of nuclear warfare that hangs over the world.

The initial reaction to the speech was vehement and furious. The worlds of many people were turned upside down. The Soviets were stunned and angry, and fearful. Soon Reagan's missile defense program became their number one political target. Many American scientists said it couldn't be done, and one was reminded of the scientists who once confidently proclaimed that the atomic bomb would not work and an accurate intercontinental ballistic missile was impossible. There was much caterwauling from the liberal Democratic political opposition in the United States, and Senator Edward Kennedy immediately dubbed the program "Star Wars."

But it was all to no avail. Those who thought to damage the effort by calling it by the apparently pejorative name Star Wars forgot the moral of the famous movie from whence the name came. In the movie *Star Wars*, the forces of evil are arranged against the forces of good. And, in the end, the forces of good prevail, armed with the latest and swiftest new space technology.

After a few years there were so many new and unexpected technological breakthroughs that many of the scientific doubting Thomases fell silent. The Soviets remained angry and fearful, but within three years they began to seriously discuss nuclear arms reduction, just as Reagan predicted. Reagan finally had the catalyst that could give shape and form to his nuclear weapons defense strategy.

In 1986, just ten years after Reagan first went public with his vision of keeping our world free from nuclear destruction, in what some observers thought was his political farewell speech to the Republican National Convention in Kansas City in 1976, agreement was reached between the two superpowers that there should be at least a 50 percent reduction in the nuclear arms of both the Soviet Union and the United States. At Iceland, and then again in Washington in 1987, Mikhail Gorbachev and Ronald Reagan seriously discussed the eventual elimination of all nuclear weapons.

A 50 percent reduction. The eventual elimination of all nuclear missiles. It makes your eyes blink. Would anyone have thought it possible five years earlier? Can you think of anyone, any expert on nuclear affairs, any politician, any national opinion-maker who would have dared predict the possibility of a Soviet ruler trying to co-opt President Reagan's dream of no nuclear missiles and proclaiming his desire to eliminate all of them? To be sure, it is not yet a reality and there is much intense, detailed negotiations that must take place before it could become a reality. But that lone vision of reducing the number of nuclear weapons and driving toward a world free of nuclear missiles is a lot closer and much, much more widely shared now than it was when Reagan took office.

If you step back and look at the sweep of events during the 1980s it is hard to believe what happened. How in the world did President Reagan get the Soviets to agree to pursue a thoroughly reasonable, but truly radical, goal of reducing the number of nuclear missiles in the world? What kind of spell did he weave over

General Secretary Gorbachev that would produce a Soviet call for massive nuclear arms reductions? How did Reagan succeed where everyone else had failed?

Well, there are some people who think he was lucky. But nobody is that lucky.

The way he did it—looking back at it—was quite simple. There were two critical steps that he took. First, he steadfastly pursued a buildup of our overall military strength that was necessary to counter the Soviet military threat and to restore a margin of safety. Second, and perhaps more important, he staked out a clear path to a protective missile defense system. He understood what is truly important to the Soviet leadership, and the Soviets seem to have understood clearly what is at stake; that they cannot ever expect to gain an overwhelming military superiority over the United States, and to even try would place unacceptable strains on their economy. Therefore, the only course left to them is serious arms reduction negotiations.

And that is why the Soviets are now willing to negotiate seriously about the reduction of nuclear weapons. If the United States had not (1) poured hundreds of billions of dollars into increased defense spending and (2) raced forward with research and development of a state-of-the-art missile defense system, there would have been no summit between Reagan and Gorbachev in Geneva in 1985, no summit in Iceland in 1986, no summit in the United States in 1987, no Soviet agreement to the U.S. goal of reducing the numbers of nuclear weapons, no agreement in 1987 to eliminate all medium and short-range nuclear missiles from Europe, and no prospects for further historic agreements on the reduction of nuclear weapons.

The most concrete result of Reagan's commitment to reducing the number of nuclear weapons in the world was the treaty that he and Mikhail Gorbachev signed on December 10, 1987, in Washington, D.C. It was one of those few occasions that will be marked by the history books. As the *New York Times* reported, "there were few in the capital who failed to feel a frisson of excitement as Mikhail S. Gorbachev stepped from his limousine and grasped Ronald Reagan's hand."[4]

The treaty, if approved by the United States Senate, would require the dismantling of 1,752 Soviet missiles and 859 American missiles, removing their nuclear warheads. In all, some 2,611 nuclear missiles will be destroyed. It is a stunning achievement. "For the first time in history," said Reagan, "the language of arms control was replaced by arms reduction—in this case the complete elimination of an entire class of U.S. and Soviet nuclear missiles."[5] And Gorbachev responded that "the signing of the first-ever agreement eliminating nuclear weapons—has a universal significance for mankind."[6]

There are bound to be powerful political ramifications in the future. For the last forty years the burning policy issue of the Left has been how to control the growth of nuclear weapons. When President Reagan signed the 1987 nuclear arms reduction treaty with the Soviet Union, he effectively stole the policy crown jewels of the Democrats in America and leftists everywhere.

In 1988 Reagan was scheduled to fly, for the first time, to the Soviet Union for another summit meeting with Gorbachev to discuss reducing Soviet and U.S. intercontinental ballistic missile forces by 50 percent or more. What has happened is so unthinkable that it is difficult to wrap one's mind around the idea of bilateral nuclear disarmament—but that's what it is.

The pitfalls are many. Even if both parties do agree on an unprecedented, historic reduction in nuclear weapons, both sides would for the foreseeable future still retain the power literally to destroy the other. Without effective on-site verification we can never be completely sure the Soviets will do what they say they will do. So an effective missile defense system is as essential as ever. It could be the most important insurance we ever had.

The dramatic results of Reagan's nuclear weapons strategy, confirmed by the Soviet Union's response, should be a constant reminder to us all that the only course promising peace and security to the United States is sufficient military strength, a military strength that contains strategic defense as well as offense. Reagan's strategy is right.

In the years to come there will be more summit meetings and countless discussions on arms reduction. There are grounds for optimism, but we must proceed very carefully. For the United States there is great potential danger, as well as great opportunity, in the upcoming negotiations. The future will tell us if our negotiators have the skill and the patience to fashion an arms reduction agreement that is in our national interest.

Chapter Nine

STAR WARS

July 31, 1979. A little over a year before the Republicans would pick their nominee for president. It was Tuesday and the weather at the Los Angeles airport was going to be warm and sticky again. But that morning I didn't care; I was going to the cool mountains of Colorado. Ronald Reagan had decided to visit the North American Aerospace Defense Command (NORAD) and asked me to go with him.

The visit was set up by a fellow named Douglas Morrow, a screenwriter who was an old Hollywood acquaintance of Reagan's. Morrow knew the current commander of NORAD, a four-star Air Force general named James Hill. General Hill told Morrow he would be happy to give Reagan a special tour of the nuclear warning facilities, and Morrow conveyed the invitation.

Reagan had never had the opportunity to see firsthand the military base responsible for warning the United States of a pending nuclear attack. Given his future job possibility, he was intrigued and accepted immediately. I hadn't seen it either and was curious to see what we had out there. The three of us, Reagan, Morrow, and I flew early that morning by commercial jet to Denver and drove from there south to NORAD headquarters, located in the mountains near Colorado Springs.

The North American Aerospace Defense Command is a critical part of the American defense system. It is the nerve center of the far-flung, worldwide network of radar detectors that alerts us to any surprise attack. If a Soviet nuclear missile should rise from its launcher and head toward the United States, sensitive radar would immediately feed signals back to the large, powerful NORAD computers which can, in a matter of seconds, calculate the speed and direction of the incoming missile and quickly tell what part of America is about to be annihilated. Its computers will provide the basic facts that a president will rely on while deciding whether to launch a retaliatory nuclear attack, which would probably mark the beginning of World War III. Reagan was keenly interested in finding out how this system worked and what information it could provide.

The NORAD command post is a vast underground city, a multilevel maze of rooms and corridors carved deep into the solid granite core of Cheyenne Mountain. As we drove up to the entrance it did not look very impressive from the outside. Only a few minutes later, as we stood in front of a massive steel door several feet thick and watched it swing open, did we begin to sense the awesome scope of this underground base. Most of the day was spent going from briefing to briefing, each one conducted by high-ranking uniformed officers in small conference rooms that looked just like other military briefing rooms except that none had windows. The briefings focused on the relative nuclear capabilities of the United States and the Soviet Union, and on our means for detecting a nuclear attack.

Toward the end of the day we were ushered into the command room, the center where all the information comes together. It is a very large room, several stories high, and it looks just like such command centers do in the movies. Completely covering one end of the room is a huge display screen showing an outline map of the United States and the surrounding airspace. Seated in front of the screen, each one facing a video display console complete with dozens of switches and lights, were the young men and women who constantly monitor these displays for the first sign of a sudden nuclear attack. There were papers scattered about, ashtrays half filled with twisted cigarette butts, and white styrofoam cups of coffee that they slowly sipped. If you ignored the display screen it had much the same atmosphere as a business office.

The officers showing us around pointed out that attacking nuclear missiles would show up as tiny, bright, blinking lights slowly moving across the screen. Just as they finished giving us this information, I noticed several bright blinking lights moving across the display screen on the part that traced out the southwestern borders of the United States. Nobody seemed to notice. Finally after ten or fifteen seconds, I cleared my throat a little and said, "Say, what are those lights down there?" I couldn't believe that this base had been operational for more than twenty years and nothing had happened until today. The officers with us seemed a little embarrassed and hesitated. Finally, one of them smiled and said, "Oh, the radar picks up small planes too. Those lights are some of the drug smugglers starting their early evening runs across the border."

Well, at least it wasn't a nuclear attack. I never did find out if they were joking or not, but it did persuade us that the system was very sensitive.

At the end of our tour we were taken back to the commanding general's office for an informal discussion before we left to fly back to Los Angeles. As the general and Reagan talked I kept wondering about a question that was bothering me most of the day but I had been reluctant to ask because it might seem stupid or silly. At an earlier briefing on the capabilities of Soviet nuclear weapons the briefing officers talked about a new monster nuclear missile that the Soviets now had.

Called the SS-18, it dwarfed any of our missiles. According to our latest count, the Soviets had 308 of them. During a lull in the conversation I decided to ask the question and turned to General Hill and said, "What would happen if the Soviets were to fire, say, just one of those heavy SS-18 missiles at NORAD and it hit, let's say, within a few hundred yards of that heavy steel front door."

Without a flicker of emotion he quickly answered, "It would blow us away." He went on to explain, "You see, this base was designed back in the 1960s when missiles like that did not exist. That size nuclear missile makes the design obsolete."

A look of disbelief came over Reagan's face. The discussion continued, and we pressed the issue of what would really happen if the Soviets were to fire just one nuclear missile at a U.S. city. "Well," the general replied carefully, "we would pick it up right after it was launched, but by the time the officials of the city could be alerted that a nuclear bomb would hit them, there would be only ten or fifteen minutes left. That's all we can do. We can't stop it." We didn't ask the general what would happen if the Soviet Union fired hundreds or even thousands of nuclear missiles at us.

That pretty much ended our conversation for the day. On the flight back to Los Angeles that night it was obvious that Reagan was deeply concerned about what he learned. He couldn't believe the United States had no defense against Soviet missiles. He slowly shook his head and said, "We have spent all that money and have all that equipment, and there is nothing we can do to prevent a nuclear missile from hitting us."

The United States has spent hundreds of billions of dollars for national security since World War II. We have the best, most technologically advanced equipment in the world, but we are powerless to protect our country and its people. In 1796 Charles C. Pinckney, minister to France, declared to C. M. Talleyrand that we would spend "millions for defense, sir, but not a cent for tribute." In the 1980s we seem to have spent billions for defense, but not one cent for protection.

As we neared the end of our flight Reagan reflected on the terrible dilemma that would face a U.S. president if, for whatever reason, nuclear missiles were fired at the United States. "The only options he would have," Reagan said, "would be to press the button or do nothing. They're both bad. We should have some way of defending ourselves against nuclear missiles."

I reminded Reagan of the ABM debate that occurred early in President Nixon's first term of office, of how we pursued the idea of missile defense and then, inexplicably, abandoned it. I suggested that we should see what technological advances had developed since then and reexamine the idea once again. He agreed.

Almost four years later, on March 23, 1983, when President Reagan suddenly announced that the United States was going to develop a strategic defense against nuclear missiles, the world was stunned and surprised. So were most people in the United States. So was the Department of Defense. And so were most of the White House staff and the national news media. Because of the extraordinary secrecy surrounding the announcement of this radical and fundamental change in U.S. nuclear weapons policy, and the relatively small number of people who knew of and participated in the decision, it was soon widely accepted that this was a rash action Reagan had taken, taken without serious consultation with nuclear weapons experts, taken on the spur of the moment, taken without serious reflection on what he was doing and what its consequences might be.

But it did not happen that way.

A few days after our visit to NORAD in Colorado, in the summer of 1979, I was talking to John Sears, who was then in charge of Reagan's presidential campaign. Sears is an extraordinary man. While still in his late twenties he was the top delegate hunter for Richard Nixon in his successful run for the Republican presidential nomination in 1968. He was the key person, the driving force, in persuading Reagan to run for the presidency in 1976 and again in 1980.

Sears was quiet, with a rounded, owlish face masking a calculating political mind that thought boldly about things few people ever presumed to think about at all. Later on, for very good reasons, he was summarily fired by Reagan. But in the summer of 1979 he was the leader of Reagan's presidential campaign.

Earlier that year I took a leave of absence from the Hoover Institution and moved to Los Angeles, where we set up the presidential campaign headquarters next to the Los Angeles International Airport. I was in charge of our policy development efforts and up to that point had concentrated on two major domestic issues: economic policy and energy policy. We worked out the essentials of a comprehensive economic program and the broad outlines of a new national energy policy by early summer and I produced two internal policy memoranda spelling out these policies for review by Reagan and key members of his campaign staff.

We were in good shape on the domestic policy side, but Sears became increasingly nervous about Reagan's political vulnerability on the foreign policy side, especially the areas of national defense, nuclear weapons, and arms control. The problem was particularly worrisome because there was no full-time member of the campaign staff who was an acknowledged expert in foreign affairs and defense. Later, Richard V. Allen would join the staff and fill that role, but at the time he and a few other foreign policy and defense policy experts were advising us on a part-time basis from various cities around the country. Sears and I were discussing this problem and what to do about it when he said, "Look, we're getting vulnerable on this. Why don't you call together some of our defense experts and see what they can come up with?"

I agreed, with one caveat. The problem with asking outside policy experts what to do in a presidential campaign is that they will often tell you only what they think can be done politically. They will censor things that may be technically possible but not, in their judgment, politically possible. So I told Sears I would do what he suggested, but first I would like to take a day or two to write out a foreign and defense policy strategy from the viewpoint of what I thought the American people would like if they could have their wishes come true.

"Let me write down what I think a good program would be, and then let's talk to our experts to find out how we can do it, rather than ask them what should be done and then have us try to figure out how to do it." Sears nodded his assent and I went back to my apartment and wrote Policy Memorandum No. 3 the same night. That was in early August 1979.

Most of the memorandum dealt with general principles of national defense, foreign policy, and arms control. But toward the end, I recalled Reagan's powerful reaction to our NORAD visit, and the discussions I later had with Ed Meese, Dick Allen, John Sears, and Peter Hannaford on the virtues of an anti-ballistic missile system, the implications of the 1972 ABM treaty, and the lengthy national debate on missile defense that occurred in 1969. I decided to include a proposal for a new, updated missile defense system. That section of Policy Memorandum No. 3 said:

> *Develop a Protective Missile System.* During the early 1970s there was a great debate about whether or not this country should build an anti-ballistic missile system. The ABM lost, and is now prohibited by SALT agreements. But perhaps it is now time to seriously reconsider the concept.
>
> To begin with, such a system concentrates on defense, on making sure that enemy missiles never strike U.S. soil. And that idea is probably fundamentally far more appealing to the American people than the questionable satisfaction of knowing that those who initiated an attack against us were also blown away. Moreover, the installation of an effective protective missile system would also prevent even an accidental missile from

landing. Of course, there is the question of reliability, especially with the development of multiple entry warheads, but
there have apparently been striking advances in missile technology during the past decade or so that would make such a
system technically possible.

If it could be done, it would be a major step toward redress-
ing the military balance of power, and it would be a purely
defensive step.

Taken in conjunction with a reasonable buildup in our conventional forces, and an acceleration in development of cruise
missiles, laser beam technology, and conventional nuclear missiles like the MX, the development of an effective protective
missile system might go a long way toward establishing the kind
of national security that will be necessary in the 1980s.

The question of technical feasibility and cost are critical,
but we should be able to get a good evaluation of the concept
from the group of national defense experts we have working
with us.

Copies of the foreign policy and national security memorandum
were distributed to Reagan and the key staff people. The idea of
a protective missile defense system was never questioned. Reagan
embraced the principle of missile defense wholeheartedly. The only
real question he raised was, "Can we do it? Is the technology available?" And later, "How soon can we do it? How much will it cost?"
Several months later, Dick Allen joined the campaign on more or
less a full-time basis and continued to strongly support the idea of
missile defense. All the other key people in the campaign, especially Ed Meese, also supported the idea.

But missile defense was never raised by Reagan during the 1980
presidential campaign. The reason was one of political strategy. I
felt that Reagan should use it during the campaign, but his main
political advisers, especially Michael Deaver, argued against it. They
liked the substance of the idea but judged that there was no way
Reagan could discuss radical changes in traditional nuclear weapons
policy without leaving himself wide open to demagogic attacks from
his Democratic opponent. They were right, and this was confirmed
when, as a sitting president three years into his first term—not as
a candidate running against a sitting president—Reagan proposed
his strategic defense initiative and was subjected to massive, in-

tense criticism which continues to this day. In 1980 it was clearly an idea whose time had not yet come politically.

The idea of missile defense began to spread. In the Senate, Senator Wallop, a Republican from Wyoming, together with one of his top aides, Angelo Codevilla, were quietly exploring the feasibility of reviving the ABM system put to sleep in the mid-1970s. In 1980 Senator Wallop was one of the lonely voices urging Reagan to support missile defense efforts.

The fortunes of missile defense took a long step forward when the Republican party endorsed the concept in its 1980 platform. Richard Allen and I were the chief representatives of the Reagan campaign to the platform committee of the Republican National Convention when it met in Detroit, Michigan during the hot, early weeks of July. This was the fourth convention platform that Dick and I worked on together since 1968 and, as usual, he took defense and foreign policy matters and I concentrated on domestic and economic policy, although I did take a strong interest in the military manpower section.

Allen, who later became Reagan's first national security adviser, had extensive influence on the language and policies adopted in that platform. One of the most important defense policy pledges that the Republican party took that year was little noted at the time. But, as he had done so many times in the past, Allen was looking ahead and laying the foundation of the future missile defense edifice. As events were to prove less than three years later, the party's endorsement of missile defense was critical to the ultimate success of the strategic missile defense initiative.

It was July 14, 1980. The temperature in Detroit was in the 90s, and the humidity was high enough to make it feel like an outdoor sauna. Inside the brand new convention hall in the Renaissance Center, the Republican delegates, sitting in cool comfort on padded seats, adopted a platform that stated flatly, "We reject the mutual-assured-destruction (MAD) strategy of the Carter Administration which limits the President during crises to a Hobson's choice between mass mutual suicide and surrender," and contained the following plank: "[W]e will proceed with vigorous research and development of an effective anti-ballistic missile system, such as is already at hand in the Soviet Union, as well as more modern ABM technologies."

With this single sentence the political party that was to win control of the White House 113 days later committed itself to developing an effective protective missile defense system for the United States. And the wording carefully and precisely went far beyond the conventional techniques of missile defense. "More modern ABM technologies" embraced new infrared sensing devices and laser beams and whatever else we might invent.

Six months later, when Ronald Reagan became president, he brought with him, in key positions, most of the small group of people who were deeply committed to building missile defenses. There were many others appointed to important policy positions in the defense and foreign policy areas who were not missionaries of missile defense, but it is also true that nobody who opposed the idea was knowingly placed in any of those positions.

Following the custom of many years, Reagan's senior White House staff gathered in the Roosevelt Room in the west wing of the White House every morning from Monday to Friday for the daily staff meeting. This was the nerve center of White House operations, where policy and legislative strategy, and personnel and press relations were thrashed out for thirty or forty minutes. The Roosevelt Room is perhaps the most powerful room in the United States, at least if you measure its influence by the number and importance of the recommendations made and decisions taken there.

The Roosevelt Room is just across a narrow, red carpeted corridor from the Oval Office, where a couple of well-dressed, sometimes smiling, secret service agents stand just outside the door whenever the president is there. The agents look disarmingly friendly, but they are armed to the teeth.

The walls of the Roosevelt Room are a soft salmon pink, framed by carved white molding. The doors, and the conference table which seats twenty people comfortably, are mahogany. The chairs are heavily padded in dark green leather—like the ones in the reading rooms of exclusive men's clubs. Seven floodlights, recessed in the ceiling directly over the table, provide almost shadowless light. And on the wall closest to the Oval Office hangs a large oil portrait of Teddy Roosevelt.

Every morning, a few minutes before 8 o'clock, the heads of the major White House sections strolled in through the back doors. Every staff member knew his or her place at the conference table. There were no nameplates, and nobody had ever been told where to sit. In theory, you could sit wherever you wanted to. In practice, the unspoken pecking order of the White House directed each person to the proper place with precision and order. At exactly 8 A.M., never more than plus or minus a minute or two, the chief of staff, James Baker, would enter, smile, say good morning to everyone, and immediately take the last empty chair, the one at the head of the table just in front of the old grandfather clock.

Quickly, deftly, the action moved around the table, from Baker's left to his right. One by one the staff reported on the issues and events they felt were important enough to bring to the attention of the others. Some items were for information only, some were strictly questions, but most were problems that would have to be dealt with and they asked for advice and support. The clock was always running and there were only thirty minutes or so to review the day's agenda for the United States.

The senior staff meeting is a routine way of running the largest government in the world and has been used by all modern presidents. But in the early Reagan White House there were other meetings. A half hour before the senior staff meeting, the three senior members of the staff—James Baker, Ed Meese, and Michael Deaver—met for a hasty breakfast downstairs in the White House mess to discuss the major events of the last 24 hours, and to suggest items that should be placed on the agenda of the morning senior staff meeting. Then, after the senior staff meeting, these three men would meet briefly with the president to discuss the most important, most urgent items that had been netted from the earlier meetings.

There was also a special meeting on national policy issues. Ed Meese was counsellor to the president with overall responsibility for the development of national policy. Dick Allen was assistant to the president for national security affairs, with responsibility for the development of foreign and national defense policy. My title was assistant to the president for policy development and I was responsible for economic policy and other domestic policies. The daily senior staff meeting was not very good for discussing most policy issues. There were too many people, too many nonpolicy issues to discuss and act upon, and too little time. And the earlier meeting of Baker, Meese, and Deaver was too small to consider the many issues that required more expert, more detailed knowledge.

So we set up a special policy meeting. Every morning, right after the senior staff meeting, a few of us walked out of the Roosevelt Room down the hall into the spacious corner office occupied by Ed Meese. There, at a small, dining-room-size table that sat eight comfortably—and ten uncomfortably—the policy agenda of the Reagan administration was debated and crafted.

The policy meeting was chaired by Ed Meese. The other participants included Richard Allen, myself, Edwin Harper, who held the twin titles of deputy director of the Office of Management and Budget and assistant to the president, and was the White House liaison for all budget and spending matters, George Keyworth, the science adviser to the president, and the top members of Meese's staff, who helped him coordinate the sprawling, immensely complicated policy process of the federal government.

The Meese policy meetings focused on what ought to be done. Another group in the White House focused on how it could be done; namely, the Legislative Strategy Group, which met in the afternoon. This meeting was chaired by Jim Baker, whose unenviable task was to determine how to convince a Congress—including a House of Representatives securely controlled by Democrats—to pass the conservative, often radical programs of President Reagan.

It was at those morning policy meetings in Ed Meese's office that the idea of missile defense was resurrected. During the first year there was a policy troika in the White House—Ed Meese, Dick Allen, and myself. While we had many diverse interests and responsibilities, we all shared a strong commitment to missile defense and used every opportunity to further the concept. Keyworth, the president's science adviser, was quietly recruited to this initial group of three.

George Keyworth was a relatively unknown scientist who was working at the Los Alamos Laboratory in New Mexico when Edward Teller, the famous nuclear scientist, recommended him to us as science adviser. During the untidy first months of the new administration the responsibility for finding a good science adviser fell to the Office of Policy Development, and much of the initial screening work was done by my deputy, Edward Gray. During my years on Nixon's White House staff in the late 1960s I watched the role of the science adviser move away from being a representative of the president to the scientific community and a provider of the best scientific advice available, to being the representative of the scientific community as just one more powerful special interest group, whose eyes were fixed on the growing pots of money in Washington. I strongly urged that we return to the concept of science adviser that worked so well for Jack Kennedy when he was president, that we do away with the formal Office of Science and Technology Policy, cut the staff drastically, and find an eminent scientist who liked the idea of being the science adviser to the president, not the envoy of the scientific community to the president.

Keyworth fit those specifications precisely and, as a bonus, he came from a weapons laboratory and was not hostile to using science to help defend the country. But when the scientists of America found out what we were up to they were furious, apparently indignant that anyone could be so presumptuous as to select a scientist who was not first blessed by the reigning mandarins of science. For weeks they mounted an increasingly virulent campaign of abuse and vilification against Keyworth. The anti-Keyworth letters poured in. At one point they even managed to persuade William Buckley, one of the most important and influential conservatives in America, to weigh in against Keyworth.

Keyworth was troubled by the mounting opposition and questioned the wisdom of proceeding with his appointment. But none of the mounting criticism dented our original premise, that Keyworth was an outstanding scientist, a fine person, and one who shared the president's beliefs. Ed Gray and I talked it over and redoubled our commitment to Keyworth. I recall saying that "when this is over and Keyworth is the science adviser, those scientists will fall all over themselves praising his virtues." Keyworth was finally appointed and, sure enough, within months the scientific community made peace and began to praise him.

Keyworth was asked to attend the morning national policy meetings in Ed Meese's office. Since Keyworth regarded Edward Teller—the most distinguished, well-known proponent of missile defense outside of government—with awe, we were not surprised to find Keyworth generally supportive of missile defense.

During this time, interest in some sort of missile defense program was growing in other places. In Congress, Senator Wallop was actively promoting strategic missile defense. General Daniel Graham, the former head of the Defense Intelligence Agency, who eventually became one of the best known and most effective proponents of missile defense, began to put together a major missile defense program called High Frontier.

And a group of Reagan's older friends, part of his so-called kitchen cabinet, banded together to use their influence with him on behalf of moving the nation toward missile defense. This latter group was headed by Karl R. Bendetsen, a conservative Democrat and one of the country's top national security experts, who had once been the undersecretary of the Army for President Truman. There were three others. Jaquelin Hume was a tall, slender whitehaired businessman from San Francisco with quiet, courtly manners. Hume was little known outside of Reagan's inner circle, but he was one of the most effective political people in California, backing Reagan for governor in the early 1960s. William A. Wilson was a businessman from southern California, and he and his wife had been friends of the Reagans for years. It was easy to see why he and Reagan were close friends. Wilson shared Reagan's basic outlook on life, his political views, was about the same age, and even looked a lot like him. Joseph Coors was an old conservative political warrior from Colorado who, beginning with the Goldwater campaign in 1964, played an increasingly influential role in national Republican politics. He was also the Coors of Coors beer, which gave him a special prestige. These four people, plus General Graham and Edward Teller, soon became a source of influential outside advice for Reagan on missile defense.

During the first eight or nine months of Reagan's first term we were totally occupied with the avalanche of work that normally falls on any new administration and, in addition, the development of Reagan's new comprehensive economic program. There just wasn't any time to seriously consider many other new policy initiatives.

Then, as we moved into the fall of 1981, and it became clearer that Reagan's new economic program was largely in place, other policy ideas began moving up on the priority list. One of those ideas was a protective missile defense system, an idea that was steadily gaining converts and momentum. General Graham's High Frontier project was rapidly expanding, and the number of supporters in Congress was growing. The small group of people in the White House interested in missile defense were aware of this growing support, as well as the continuing efforts of an ad hoc subcommittee of his kitchen cabinet, composed of Dr. Edward Teller and others. We all knew that President Reagan strongly believed in the philosophy of missile defense and that the only questions he had were technical and political ones.

The political questions did not trouble us. We knew Reagan

would make those decisions at the appropriate time, and anything that could successfully protect the United States from the devastation of a nuclear missile attack was likely to be very popular with the American people. On the other hand, the technical questions of missile defense could only be resolved by missile experts. Our earlier discussions with advisers such as Edward Teller, William Van Cleave, and General Graham convinced us that a nuclear missile defense was technically possible. But now that case had to be made directly to the president.

We had an unusual problem. The decision to be made by the president was not whether he should or should not begin to build a missile defense system. Rather, the decision was whether or not there was enough justification to reinvigorate our missile defense efforts, and resurrect the missile defense research and development that virtually shut down in the early 1970s after the ABM treaty with the Soviet Union was signed. The question of if and when to build and deploy missile defenses was much farther down the road and would largely depend on whether we stepped up our research and development efforts immediately, and how successful those efforts would be.

The normal way to proceed would have been to talk to the Defense Department, have them study the problem, and give the president their recommendations. That option was never suggested, perhaps because we all knew it would not work. Twelve years before, there was a bruising battle on an anti-ballistic missile system only narrowly won by President Nixon. But by 1975 those ABM missile launchers that were deployed in northern North Dakota near the Canadian border were torn down, and most of the defense establishment became, shall we say, gun shy of any serious talk of missile defense. Moreover, the Defense Department, being the largest bureaucracy in the United States, is the perfect example of the worst of bureaucracy.

To begin with, missile defense would be seen as a new idea, and nothing threatens an entrenched bureaucracy like a new idea, especially an idea they have not thought of themselves. Second, the military budget was, as usual, very tight, and you could smell the fear that missile defense money would have to come out of other pet defense programs. If we asked the Defense Department to study the issue, even knowing that Caspar Weinberger, the secretary of defense, would almost certainly support the idea enthusiastically, we were pretty sure what the outcome would be—nothing.

So we did something that, by the book, we should not have done. Without ever formally acknowledging it, even to ourselves, a small, informal group on strategic missile defense was formed within the White House. It was a quadriad with Ed Meese as chairman. All of us—Meese, Allen, Keyworth, and myself—were committed to providing a missile defense shield for the country. But we had to do two things. First, we had to find out much more about the technical feasibility and the cost. We had to know a lot more before we dared expose the idea to the harsh glare of the national media and the certain, scathing attacks that would come from the Democrats, to say nothing of the steadfast opposition that could be expected for some time from the bureaucracy of the Defense Department. And second, we had to provide the president with an objective rundown of the pros and cons so that he would have a sound basis for making a decision.

Things started to roll in early September with a series of phone calls involving Karl Bendetsen, General Graham, Ed Meese, and myself. From those calls came a decision to hold a meeting to discuss the general concept of missile defense and its technical and economic feasibility.

The first White House meeting on the missile defense system, which President Reagan called his Strategic Defense Initiative, and that the rest of the world called Star Wars, took place on the first floor of the west wing in Ed Meese's corner office at 11:15 a.m. on Monday, September 14, 1981. There were seven people at the meeting. Meese, as chairman, sat at the head of the table, his back toward the large, paned glass windows facing Pennsylvania Avenue. As Meese looked down the length of the table, to his right sat Karl Bendetsen, General Daniel Graham, and George Keyworth; to his left sat Edward Teller, myself, and Edwin W. Thomas, Jr., the assistant counsellor to the president and Meese's top administrative aide. Edward Teller and George Keyworth were highly regarded scientists who were specialists in defense technology. General Graham and Karl Bendetsen were noted military experts who had devoted much time and study to space technology.

As the discussion progressed, I felt a rising sense of excitement when it became clear that not only did everyone feel we should pursue the idea of missile defense, but they also deeply believed it could be done. There was a general agreement that we should shift our nuclear defense strategy from reliance on total offense, called for by the policy of mutually assured destruction, to a policy that relied on *both* offense and defense to deter a nuclear war. There was also general agreement that a major part of a missile defense effort would probably be based in space, far above the earth's surface, and that an effective missile defense effort could defend not only our population and cities, but also our offensive nuclear missiles. The outside advisers agreed to prepare a detailed report and recommendations on missile defense by the end of November, six weeks hence.

A second meeting with these outside missile defense experts took place in the White House four weeks later, on Monday, October 12, 1981, at 10:25 A.M. Again, the meeting was in Ed Meese's office. It was a smaller group: Ed Meese and his aide, Edwin Thomas, myself, General Graham, and Karl Bendetsen. Graham and Bendetsen reported on the status of their efforts and indicated a growing amount of support and interest from people they had been talking to in Congress, the NASA, the CIA, the Air Force, and the Department of Defense. Their status report was glowing and encouraging. Toward the end of the meeting we even considered calling the program a Global Ballistic Missile Defense (GBMD), but the name never caught on. I still think that either Protective Missile Defense or Global Ballistic Missile Defense are better names than Strategic Defense Initiative, but that battle has been lost forever, I fear.

Early in 1982 the outside advisers were ready with their report for President Reagan on the feasibility of missile defense. They met with the president privately at 2 P.M. on Friday, January 8, 1982, in the Roosevelt Room. The meeting was originally scheduled for the Oval Office, but given the number of people involved and the nature of the briefing, it was moved to the room with a large conference table. The meeting was not listed on the president's official schedule. Those attending included outside advisers Karl Bendetsen, Jaquelin Hume, William Wilson, Edward Teller, and Joseph Coors. Among the White House staff attending were Ed Meese, William Clark, George Keyworth, and myself. President Reagan walked in, greeted all his old friends, then sat down and began to listen and ask questions about missile defense. It was a lively, animated discussion. The meeting, originally scheduled to last 15 minutes, stretched on to almost an hour.

President Reagan did not have to be convinced that building a missile defense was the right thing to do. His only concern was whether or not it was possible and affordable, and most of his questions were directed to the technical feasibility of the proposal. When the meeting concluded, he seemed to be satisfied. He didn't say he was going ahead, but it was clear from his demeanor that he was convinced it could be done. There was a lot of research and development to do, but there had been such technological strides in the few short years since the United States virtually abandoned our old missile defense efforts that the future looked promising.

That January 8, 1982, meeting was a critical turning point. As I left the Roosevelt Room I was personally convinced that President Reagan was going ahead with missile defense. How and when I did not know. But I did know that whenever he decided to move forward on such an important policy path he rarely looked back or changed his mind.

The next year was a quiet one for Star Wars. It was a time of rapid turnover and some turmoil on the senior White House staff. In November 1981 Richard V. Allen had been investigated by the FBI concerning $1,000 in cash a Japanese reporter tried to give Nancy Reagan, and three inexpensive watches Allen received as a gift from a longtime friend, Professor Tomotsu Takase. In the ensuing political uproar, Allen was charged, tried, and convicted in the court of the national media. Although later exonerated of any wrongdoing, he was forced by the worldwide publicity to resign on January 4, 1982.

President Reagan named William P. Clark, then deputy secretary of state, to replace Allen as his national security adviser. Bill Clark was one of Reagan's most trusted advisers, an old associate who served as chief of staff when Reagan was governor of California in the 1960s. Although Clark was an able lawyer and a distinguished judge, he was not the strategic, geopolitical thinker Allen was, and except for his one-year stint as deputy secretary of state, he was a novice in the field of national security. But he was an excellent administrator, a good conciliator of opposing views and factions, and a man of sound judgment.

Clark cut an imposing figure in the White House. Usually impeccably dressed in a dark blue three-piece suit, pin-striped in faint bluish white, he strode the red carpeted halls of the west wing shod in very expensive, hand-tooled, black cowboy boots. His gold cufflinks, the button-down white shirt, the dark English club tie with bright red and silver stripes, and the gold-rimmed half glasses for reading, all combined to give him a touch of elegance.

Leaving the State Department and joining Clark as his deputy at the White House was Robert C. McFarlane. These two men soon became essential links in the missile defense chain. The early months of Clark's tenure were spent dealing with more urgent issues than missile defense and it was not until late in the year that the idea surfaced once again—this time from President Reagan.

In December 1982 William Clark arranged for the members of the Joint Chiefs of Staff to meet privately with President Reagan in the White House. Part of a regular monthly meeting suggested by Clark, the president and the joint chiefs met without the potentially inhibiting presence of the secretary of defense or the secretary of state. At one point in the December 1982 meeting, President Reagan waited until he had the full attention of his joint chiefs and then asked, "What if . . . what if we began to move away from our total reliance on offense to deter a nuclear attack and moved toward a relatively greater reliance on defense?"

As the president continued to press the issue, small lights and bells began to go off in the minds of the joint chiefs and shortly after they were chauffeured back home, across the Potomac River to the Pentagon, one of them telephoned Clark and asked, "Did we just get instructions to take a hard look at missile defense?"

Clark said, "Yes," and the joint chiefs now had their marching orders.

Clark then asked his deputy, McFarlane, to get deeply involved in the question of missile defense; to explore it, study it, to become fully aware of every nuance of its pros and cons. Soon McFarlane had a small team on the national security staff actively at work.

Less than six weeks into the new year (February 11, 1983) the joint chiefs met with President Reagan and recommended to him that the United States abandon its complete dependence on the old doctrine of mutually assured destruction and move ahead with the research and development of a missile defense system. The joint chiefs thus confirmed the validity of an idea that Reagan had been thinking about for almost four years. Now things began to happen quickly.

Reagan knew it was time to go, politically speaking. It was not the perfect time, but it was likely to be the best time he would ever have. He was settled in his job, his respect at home and abroad was growing, and his power as a sitting president about to run for reelection was nearing its peak.

His deputy national security adviser, Robert McFarlane, although a relative newcomer to the Reagan inner circle, knew exactly what his commander-in-chief wanted done. So in early March 1983, McFarlane, using the ultimate means of secrecy, his own typewriter, sat down and composed a draft of the strategic missile defense statement, which was later shared with and edited by Dr. Keyworth.

The specific plan was held very, very closely, as it had to be. If it hadn't been, missile defense would have been strangled in its crib. But because it was held so tightly it also produced surprise and embarrassment for many important people in the administration.

The secretary of state, George Shultz, was not consulted on the speech until just two days beforehand. Neither was the secretary of defense, Caspar Weinberger, nor members of the Joint Chiefs of Staff, nor the undersecretary of defense, Richard DeLauer. Our top arms control adviser, Paul Nitze, was not told until late in the morning on the day of the speech. The secret was so tightly held in the White House that the communications director, David Gergen, only found out about it just before the president was to speak.

When Reagan addressed the nation on March 23, 1983, he set forth what was probably the most important new policy of his administration. The intensity of his commitment to this new course was clearly demonstrated by the personal handwritten changes he made in the speech draft that was prepared for him. His main concern was the threat of nuclear war, and when he came to the end of a paragraph that spelled out his end goal of building a strategic missile defense—an agreement with the Soviet Union that would bring about a mutual reduction of nuclear weapons—he added one line in his bold, jagged script. "But let me just say I am totally committed to this course."

The idea of a defense against nuclear missiles is almost as old as nuclear missiles. From the first day that men began constructing a nuclear warhead of almost unimaginable explosive power to be sent by remote control to the farthest corners of the earth, other men have worked to find a way to stop that nuclear arrow in flight—

to destroy it long before it ever comes near its intended target. Since the 1950s that effort has continued unabated in the Soviet Union. Today they own the only operational limited missile defense system in the world, and their search for ever more effective missile defense goes on. Our efforts peaked in the early 1970s, and then in 1975 we destroyed what little missile defense capability we had built, although we continued a small research program. That small research program kept the idea alive and flickering until 1983 when President Reagan fanned the flame.

At first glance, Star Wars appeared to be an impulsive, possibly dangerous gesture, a whim indulged in by an ignorant politician, irresponsibly taken without even cursory consultation with expert advisers.

In fact, it is almost a classic case of the slow, steady development of an idea with power and logic and moral strength. There is a long history of spirited discussion and debate among intellectuals and policymakers on the issue of missile defense that stretches back well into the 1950s. But somehow the spirit of detente with the Soviet Union, their huge and growing stockpile of nuclear missiles, and the signing of the ABM treaty all combined to kill our interest in missile defense in the early 1970s. In fact, during the decade from 1970 to 1980 the idea of missile defense became a nonissue— it just wasn't discussed very much.

The 1980 presidential campaign was the critical catalyst that stirred the old idea of missile defense and brought it back to life. The campaign stimulated the desire and provided the opportunity for Reagan to visit NORAD and to see for himself what the state of our missile defenses were. The campaign brought together a small, effective group of people committed to missile defense. And the campaign caused the Republican party to include missile defense as a major plank in its defense platform.

Star Wars was a carefully thought out proposal, developed over many years, with the advice and consultation of some of the best nuclear weapons experts in the world. Reagan saw it as a moral alternative to mutually assured destruction; he waited until he was sure it was technically possible, sure we could afford it, and then, exercising exquisite political timing, fundamentally changed how we in America and most of the world think about national defense.

Chapter Ten

ACCIDENT

It is 11 o'clock Monday morning in Siberia. The Soviet missile base is nestled in a dense part of the forest, just northeast of Lake Baikal, the largest and deepest freshwater lake in the world. The sky is bright and overcast with thick gray clouds preventing the U.S. spy satellite from seeing the heavy steel horizontal doors slide apart, exposing the large black cylinder that lurks deep in the earth, surrounded by thick walls of concrete. The Soviets have waited weeks for a rainless cloudy day so they can run their periodic test-firing of one of the 308 SS-18 nuclear missiles aimed at the continental United States. This one is targeted on Washington, D.C. A few minutes into the test one of the young Soviet fire control officers, still hung over and slightly sick from two large tumblers of vodka he drank the night before to put himself to sleep, hears a low roar and sees a puff of smoke float from the top of the launching silo. "Christ," he swears to himself, "Can't these new mechanics even do a test right?"

Then, to his shock and horror, the low roar becomes a shrieking blast and the black nuclear-tipped monster begins to rise slowly into the morning sky. The launch is an accident and we may never know why it happened, like the nuclear reactor disaster at Chernobyl. Or we may someday find out, as we did after our Challenger space shuttle exploded before millions of television viewers in 1986. But it doesn't make any difference now.

For a few seconds the Soviet missile officer and his comrades stand frozen as they try to comprehend what is happening. Then the young officer reaches down and picks up the bright green phone that connects him to nuclear command headquarters near Moscow. When the other end answers he says evenly, "We have had a terrible accident."

Six thousand miles away, across the North Pole on the other side of the earth, in Washington, D.C., it is pitch black—3 o'clock in the morning of the next day. President Reagan has been in bed four hours, happy and satisfied with a state dinner that went well. Almost everyone is asleep in the United States, except for those with night jobs and a few still partying on the West Coast.

In Moscow, phones begin to ring frantically in the offices of key Soviet rulers. Luckily, General Secretary Gorbachev is in town, and six minutes later, after pounding his fist on his desk and cursing softly, he orders the hot line used to alert the United States. His last words are, "Make sure they understand we did not intend to do this."

Just about the same time the hot line phone goes off with a piercing wail in a very special room in the Pentagon, startling the young man on duty, the first flickers of bright white lights appear on the main screen at NORAD headquarters in Colorado. The soldier who first sees it reaches over and crushes the cigarette burning in the small ashtray before him and thinks, "Damn, of all the nights the system can pick to go haywire it picks my night." For several minutes he watches the light flicker and move across the screen. Other equipment confirms what he is seeing and suddenly red lights start flashing and alarm bells begin ringing. "Oh my God," he says out loud to no one in particular. "It's a goddamn attack."

By the time the telephone rings in the president's bedroom the Soviet missile has been flying for twelve minutes.

The Situation Room in the west wing of the White House is quiet. The few people on duty late that night are subdued and stunned. They know a Soviet missile is coming at them. The president's national security adviser has been notified and is driving in from the suburbs of Maryland. He should be there in twenty-five or thirty minutes. The secretary of defense is in California. The secretary of state is in Bangkok. The president hurriedly dresses. His bedroom is in the mansion part of the White House and he knows that, after he is finished dressing, it will take him at least five minutes, walking fast, to move through the long corridors to the Situation Room in the west wing.

It takes about twenty-eight minutes for one of the Soviet monster missiles to fly the 6,000 miles from Siberia to Washington, D.C. It takes so long because it does not fly in a straight line. Instead, it soars along a very high, graceful arc that carries it some 800 miles up into outer space, over the polar ice caps of the Arctic, before it begins to plunge back down toward earth. It comes down on its target at a steep angle of 22.5 degrees, racing ahead of its own sound. The Soviet SS-18 missile carries at least ten nuclear warheads. At the designated time each warhead leaves its nest in the nose of the missile and flies on its own course. When the nuclear warheads fly true there are more than enough of them on one Soviet missile to annihilate the White House, the Capitol, and the Pentagon.

The president takes two minutes to slip on a robe, find his eyeglasses, and put on his slippers, and five more minutes to walk over to the Situation Room. When he arrives, there are about nine minutes remaining before the missile comes. The president enters the small room accompanied by two Secret Service agents and sits down at the small conference table, glaring at the blank television screen sunk in the wall. He just looks at the men sitting across from him. He doesn't have to say anything.

The officer in charge quickly briefs him, and then he glances down at his watch. "Mr. President," he says in a tight, controlled voice, "a Soviet nuclear missile, one of their big ones, an SS-18, will strike Washington in about eight minutes. It is a multiple warhead missile and we are pretty sure most of the nuclear warheads are targeted on the White House complex. The Soviets have called on the hotline, and they say it was an accident, but there is nothing they can do now. They are begging us not to do anything."

"Well," the president asks, "shouldn't we all go down in the shelter?"

One of the older soldiers on duty shakes his head, "It won't make any difference. The blast will just bury us."

The telephone hanging off the end of the conference table rings. It is the secretary of defense. Six minutes left now. "Mr. President," he says urgently, "this is awful. I know the Soviets claim it was an accident, but I don't believe them. This is that 'decapitation strike' scenario we ran through last year. It's a trick. If you don't retaliate now our country is going to be leaderless and we're going to be at the Soviet's mercy. We must respond."

The president knows he is going to die in about five minutes, but before he dies he will have to make the most important decision of his life. Should he launch a nuclear counterattack against the Soviet Union backed with the full force of America's might, or should he let most of Washington be destroyed and hope it really was just a terrible accident?

That story has not happened yet, but it could, and today there is nothing we can do about it.

While we move ahead with negotiations on nuclear arms reductions and with the development of a protective missile defense system, there is something that we have almost completely overlooked—and that is the possibility of an accidental launch of a nuclear-tipped ICBM.

Today, two armadas of ICBMs stand poised to lift off in minutes—the Soviet Union's, loaded with upwards of 6,000 powerful nuclear warheads, and ours with some 2,000—gracefully lofting their deadly cargoes toward one another if someone decides to trigger our pact of mutually assured destruction.

Fortunately, the likelihood of a planned nuclear attack by one superpower upon the other is very remote. The awesome consequences for both sides are so horrible that such an event could only occur if collective insanity should strike the leadership of one of the countries. In the surrealistic nuclear world we all live in, the possession of these devastating weapons has probably reduced the chance of a major war in our time.

But at the same time, the existence of great numbers of nuclear missiles has increased the chance of a terrible accident with unprecedented consequences. As these huge nuclear weapons stockpiles increase, the possibility of a nuclear missile being launched accidentally also increases.

The increase in the sheer number of missiles, and the need for thousands of highly trained young men and women to operate and control them, leads inexorably to a greater chance of human error.

And then there is the always present problem of mechanical or electrical failure. The United States has put a great effort into making them as foolproof as we can, but the mechanism of an intercontinental ballistic missile is awesomely complex, and some of them are getting fairly old.

I think it is fair to say that the size of the Soviet and U.S. missile forces, combined with the effects of age, increases the chance of an accident with each passing day. As Detroit has proven to us over the years, if you produce enough automobiles, no matter how carefully, and let enough people drive them for a long time, no matter how carefully, sooner or later you will have accidents.

From the viewpoint of the United States there is probably a greater chance that a Soviet missile could be fired accidentally at us than there is that we could fire one accidentally at them. There are a number of reasons for this. First, they have more missiles than we do. Second, while we have exercised extreme care on the command and control of our missiles to safeguard against an accidental launch, we may not be justified in assuming the Soviets have done likewise. Their past record of accidents in their military weapons systems is, shall we say, somewhat unsettling. Finally, the Soviets have recently begun a major effort to place a large number of their nuclear missiles on mobile launchers, in order to prevent us from determining where they are located. The new SS-25 mobile missiles that can be moved around in the forests of Siberia create some very interesting command and control problems. How many Soviets does it take to fire such a missile? How do you transmit the command to launch? Who has the authority to fire the missile?

There may be some people who don't believe a nuclear missile could be launched accidentally, or that a few people could squirm free of the command structure and perhaps fire an outlaw missile or two. But most of us believe something like that, although highly unlikely, could occur.

And then, in addition to an accidental firing, there are other situations that could lead to a limited, but deadly nuclear missile attack on the United States. Nuclear weaponry is spreading slowly and steadily beyond the superpowers. While a small nation could not threaten us with an overwhelming nuclear attack, the ability of any nation to fire even one nuclear missile at us should be considered a serious threat.

The knowledge of how to build a nuclear bomb is widespread. Today we even have private companies launching missiles into space. And we have learned from events in the Middle East that determined fanatics, absolutely convinced of the rightness of their cause, will not hesitate to drive a truckload of explosives into a building filled with hundreds of U.S. Marines, or to murder innocent civilians. Will they hesitate to fire a nuclear missile if they have one? It may not be long before we find out.

And they wouldn't even have to fire the missile. They could simply threaten to and perhaps hold, not a few Americans, but an entire U.S. city hostage to their demands.

As Henry Kissinger noted, "Calculations and restraints that are highly plausible to advanced industrial societies are not necessarily equally persuasive to leaders of the Qaddafi variety."

In the past we concentrated, and rightly so, on how to prevent an all-out nuclear war. But in doing so we have tended to overlook the growing possibility that someday, for whatever reason, a missile or two will be fired at the United States.

If that happened today we would be helpless.

And this is one kind of nuclear terror that we should not have to live with any longer. While we continue to move ahead with the big issues of arms control and reduction, and developing a strategic defense system capable of coping with the threat of an all-out nuclear war, shouldn't we build a limited defense system that could insure us against the catastrophic impact of even one nuclear missile?

We need to build an insurance missile defense.

Not many people throughout the world know that the Soviet Union has had such a system in place for years. Under the terms of the ABM treaty signed in 1972, both the United States and the Soviet Union have the right to build a limited missile defense system consisting of up to one hundred interceptor missile launchers. Each nation is limited to one system and they have the choice of placing it near their capital or one of their major missile sites.

The Soviets chose to deploy their interceptor missiles around

Moscow. Today they have the only operational missile defense system in the world, with nearly 100 interceptor missiles in place, many of them brand new SH-08s, replacing the older missiles. These Soviet interceptor missiles, tipped with nuclear warheads, stand ready to blast off at a moment's notice.

They are very fast missiles, and because they intercept their targets high above the earth's surface, they can effectively protect a very large part of the Soviet Union from a small missile attack. They cannot protect the Soviet Union from the combined assault of hundreds or thousands of nuclear missiles, but they do guarantee Soviet rulers that they need never fear the chilling assault of a nuclear missile launched accidentally, or being held hostage to a threat from a third world power that has somehow managed to get their hands on a few nuclear ICBMs.

In the years since we signed the ABM treaty, the Soviets have moved quickly and decisively to deploy a missile defense system, and they continue to research and build and improve on their defenses against strategic missiles.

What have we done in the United States?

Well, in the early 1970s we began to build a defensive missile system near one of our nuclear missile bases located way up in Grand Forks, North Dakota, close to the Canadian border. By 1975 we had pretty well finished it. But that same year we stopped and tore down what we built.

That's right. While the Soviet Union continued to move ahead with their defensive missile site near Moscow, we took ours down. We did continue to conduct research on missile defense, but today we have nothing that actually works.

If a nuclear missile or two, for whatever reason, were launched toward the United States today, we would be helpless.

What would you do if that happened and you were president?

The answer is that we should not even have to contemplate such a question and all its ramifications. The Soviets don't. If we mistakenly fired a nuclear missile at Moscow, they could tell us not to worry and blast it harmlessly out of the sky with one of their interceptors.

The tragedy of our situation today is that we cannot do the same. And yet we could if we wanted to.

It isn't a question of technology; it isn't a question of money.

The technology is already here, on the shelf, waiting to be used. And the cost is easily affordable.

On June 10, 1984, the U.S. Army conducted a trailblazing experiment. An old Minuteman missile with a dummy nuclear warhead was launched toward a target more than 4,000 miles away. Before it arrived at its target the Army fired a new interceptor missile they built with currently available parts and technology. That new interceptor proved to be incredibly accurate. It located the incoming Minuteman with its sensors and put itself on a course that enabled it to intercept more than one hundred miles above the earth's surface. Just before the intercept collision occurred, a 15-foot wide umbrella-shaped steel mesh sprang from the interceptor's nose, hitting the Minuteman like a huge flyswatter. There was a tremendous impact, but no nuclear explosion.

Most of us have a pretty good idea what would happen if two automobiles traveling 60 miles per hour hit head-on. With an effective collision speed of 120 miles per hour there isn't much left. When that interceptor missile smashed into the Minuteman the estimated collision speed was more than 20,000 miles per hour. That's more than 165 times faster than the head-on automobile collision. One hundred miles up in space it is very, very cold, so when the interceptor missile smashed into the Minuteman, the two disintegrated into harmless debris.

That is what would happen to a real nuclear warhead. There would be no nuclear explosion. The radioactive plutonium in the warhead is a metal and it would, like any other metal, smash into little pieces that would burn up in the atmosphere as they fell toward earth. Just like a lot of small meteorites.

What happened that early summer day in 1984 was momentous. The Army test demonstrated that a nuclear warhead can, in fact, be disintegrated in outer space, with no nuclear explosion, without even using conventional explosives.

And that was the old interceptor missile. By early 1986 the U.S. Army had completed plans for a better one. It's called ERIS, which stands for Exoatmospheric Reentry-vehicle Interceptor Subsystem. The new interceptor missile is extremely accurate, carries no explosives in its nose cone, and is only 20 inches in diameter and less than 14 feet long. Utilizing our existing radar system with some upgrading, we could build a complete limited missile defense system (with one hundred missiles) for approximately $150 million a year, or a total cost of $1.5 billion spread over ten years. If we started in 1988, the first missiles would be standing guard, ready to fire, in the early 1990s.

We know that a full-scale strategic missile defense is years away, and we may never be able to fully protect the United States from an all-out attack by thousands of Soviet missiles. But we have proven that a limited missile defense system, designed to intercept and destroy a handful of nuclear missiles, could be built today with existing technology, and that it could guarantee complete protection from either the accidental firing of a single nuclear missile or from deliberate attack or threat by a few missiles. And we can do it without using nuclear warheads, which is something the Soviets cannot yet do.

For several years we have had sufficient technology to enable us to build an effective limited missile defense system, one clearly permitted under the ABM treaty, one that could insure that the United States would never face the possibility of having the most terrible accident in history.

The fact that we have not built any missile defenses must be incomprehensible to the Soviets. Building and deploying a limited missile defense system now would place us on a par with the Soviet Union in terms of operational missile defenses. But more importantly, it would give the American people an opportunity to live in a nuclear world where we could at least protect ourselves from an accidental nuclear attack.[1]

Four

Reaganomics

It was the greatest economic expansion in history. Wealth poured from the factories of the United States, and Americans got richer and richer. During the five years between November 1982 and November 1987 more wealth and services were produced than in any like period in history.

Chapter Eleven

POLICY MEMORANDUM NO. 1

In March 1979 I left the Hoover Institution on an indefinite leave of absence to join the Reagan campaign. I packed a few bags, said good-bye to my wife, Annelise, and moved four hundred miles south to a small oceanfront apartment in Marina del Rey, near Reagan's national campaign headquarters in Los Angeles. Almost two years before the election, the Reagan campaign was already running full blast, staffed by a growing group of people from all parts of the United States.

The headquarters was located in a fairly new, quite ordinary office building a few hundred yards from one of the largest airports in the world, Los Angeles International. The unusual location was chosen for three major reasons. The first was symbolic. We decided that rather than run the campaign from New York City or Washington, D.C., we would do the unexpected and run from the West Coast, driving home the message that Reagan was an outsider, a Californian, a man who was coming east across the country to Washington. Once we decided to go from West to East, it was natural to make our base next to the Los Angeles airport. Los Angeles is the de facto capital of the western U.S., and being right next to the airport we would save a great deal of our time and the time of those who swirled in and out of campaign headquarters for the next two years. Also, the Reagans lived in Los Angeles, and most of his aides and advisers lived in California. It was convenient.

My main responsibility was to formulate and coordinate policy positions on the issues Reagan would deal with in the months ahead. The first and overriding concern was economic policy, for several reasons: (1) it was the most urgently important problem facing the country, (2) Reagan was convinced that unless we restored our economic health we could not effectively handle all the other problems facing us, especially national defense, and (3) it could make or break his campaign.

One of the peculiar things about America is the sharp disparity between what its intellectuals think about and what is important to the Republic's survival and prosperity. If you survey the last ten years of the top scholarly economic journals in America—the *Journal of Political Economy* and the *American Economic Review*—you would look in vain for comprehensive economic programs. There will be dozens of sophisticated articles (laced with arcane mathematical formulae) on aspects of taxation, fiscal policy, or labor policy. But you won't see anything that attempts to wrestle with an overall national policy. Yet when someone decides to run for president, one of the first questions a reporter will put to him or her is, "Can you please tell us what your economic policy is going to be?" And the distinguished economists who have never had the audacity to write about this themselves will be the first ones to look up from their newspapers to see how this wretch of a politician will respond to the question on the evening network television news.

When we set to work developing an economic policy, we started with a great advantage over the other candidates. Ronald Reagan had a very clear sense of what should be done. Over the years he studied and took positions on most major economic issues. He had not proposed any overall economic plan for the country, but he was convinced that tax rates, particularly those on people's earnings, were too high, that a lot of government spending was wasteful and extravagant, and that many government regulations were of minimal benefit and hurt the economy. He felt our monetary policy was erratic and our currency unsound, and finally, believed the constant change of government economic policy itself was a major cause of business uncertainty, which in turn had a powerful impact on the economy. This was something John Maynard Keynes, the noted English economist, emphasized almost fifty years earlier.

From my discussions with Reagan I knew he thought long and hard about these economic issues and felt comfortable with the positions he took. He developed his positions a piece at a time; in speeches, radio commentaries, and private discussions over a period of fifteen or more years. The good news was that he knew what he was talking about; the bad news was that his economic policies had never been presented as a comprehensive approach and acquired what one might call an intellectual critical mass that the public could identify.

The same was true in many other issue areas. Dozens of times Reagan had confronted major policy issues, studied and analyzed them, and drawn conclusions. But he had never attempted—to that point in time—to weave these policy positions into a more cohesive whole, presenting a focused, comprehensive solution to complicated public policy issues.

During the early months of the campaign, I concluded that the most significant policy weakness we had was a lack of clearly focused themes. We needed statements of principle, some theoretical documents for the campaign that would serve as internal guides for the rapidly growing campaign staff and as tools of explanation to drive home Reagan's policy positions to the national press and the voters.

After a lot more discussion with Reagan and other staff members I wrote three policy memoranda in August 1979. They dealt with what I thought were the three most important issues to face us the next year in the presidential campaign. One was on economic policy, one on energy policy, and one on foreign and defense policy.

Policy Memorandum No. 1, as it was called, covered economic policy. We really had two problems here. First, we had to come up with an economically sound plan, something that would work, and work soon. Second, we had to show convincingly that what was being offered made sense and that the voters should support it, and Reagan's candidacy.

The memorandum drew heavily on what I knew of Reagan's personal views and on my own background and experience.

The document was never made public. Reagan and perhaps a

dozen top campaign staff members saw it, and later many of the economic advisers who joined Reagan's team. Looking back now, I think it demonstrated that Reagan did, in fact, have a multifaceted, comprehensive approach to resolving the nation's economic problems. It showed clearly, too, that economic policy is not tax policy alone, or spending control alone, or regulatory reform, or monetary policy. It showed that it is all four of these together, at the same time, plus a few other things.

None of the elements of the proposed plan were new. They had been around since economics became a defined field of study. The only novel thing was that we looked at all the various economic problems and solutions at the same time, showing the interrelationship of these solutions to one another, and most importantly, calling it Reagan's comprehensive economic program.

This is that memorandum.

Policy Memorandum No. 1
Reagan for President
Los Angeles, California
August, 1979

ECONOMIC POLICY

Problem

By a wide margin the most important issue in the minds of voters today is inflation. If we add other economic related issues—such as the fear of becoming unemployed, the energy shortage, and high taxation—it is clear that national economic policy is of critical importance.

Compounding the problem for any presidential candidate is the public's pessimism. They believe that there is little that the President, any President, can do about it.

Thus, the economic policy problem is twofold:

(1) The development of a valid plan. Our economic problems are deep-rooted and complex. To resolve them will require an economic program that is capable of dealing with a wide range of complex issues. It must be comprehensive, economically sound, and timely. In other words, we must come up with a program that, if applied, will work.

(2) Convincing the public of its validity. Because of the

voter's deep skepticism about the ability of any President to deal with the economy, it is important to show conclusively, that if Reagan is elected president in 1980, he can and will carry out the specific actions necessary to restore economic health—to reduce and eliminate inflation, to increase employment, and to stimulate economic growth.

The Myth of the Economic Bellyache

For many years it has been an article of faith among academic economists, and especially so among Republican politicians, that any attempt to increase employment would lead to more inflation, and that any attempt to reduce inflation would result in more unemployment. Their faith in this reverse linkage between unemployment and inflation has now been communicated to a large part of the public.

The consequence has been political paralysis in regard to the development of a powerful economic policy by Republicans during the past decade or two. The Democrats, being naturally less responsible, have pushed policies which they believed created jobs, even though at the expense of higher inflation. Unfortunately for them the day of reckoning is now at hand. The day has come when inflation has become so bad that many voters are more concerned about it than possible unemployment.

These lingering doubts about the "iron law" of the reverse relationship between unemployment and inflation has now blossomed into rampant skepticism and full disbelief, even among economists.

If we look carefully at the experience of the last two decades—from 1960 to now—we can see that there has been no trade-off between inflation and unemployment. What everyone believed was happening simply was not happening.

As the 1978 report of the Federal Reserve Bank of Minneapolis succinctly stated:

". . . Many believe that even a modest cut in the government budget deficit or in money growth would cause massive unemployment or long periods of slow economic growth and high unemployment. Such beliefs are based on a confusion.

". . . In the United States from 1960 to 1978 . . . there appears to be *no trade-off.*

". . . *Higher inflation tends to be associated with higher, not lower, unemployment* . . . in the late 1960s and early 1970s when inflation rose, unemployment generally rose.

". . . If history is any guide, this means that if more stimulative policies are expected, then we should get more inflation and more unemployment. Consequently, if tighter policies are expected, we should get less of each. *Gains can thus be made against inflation without incurring the high costs of increased unemployment.*"

It is thus possible to reduce inflation and stimulate economic growth without having an economic bellyache, recession, or depression.

The challenge is to break free from the discredited economic beliefs of the past and to craft a realistic economic policy powerful enough to halt our slide into economic chaos.

The Plan

Inflation is the main domestic problem facing the United States today, not only for its pure economic effects, but also because of its negative social and political consequences.

And the main cause of inflation is the massive, continuing budget deficit of the federal government.

The budget deficit must be reduced and eventually eliminated, but in doing so it is important to remember that every deficit is a function of both revenue and expenditures. The most effective way to eliminate the deficit is to reduce the rate of growth of federal expenditures and to simultaneously stimulate the economy so as to increase revenues in such a way that the private share grows proportionately more than the government share.

The basic components of such an economic policy are:

(1) We must speed up economic growth to increase the take-home pay of workers and to provide more jobs.
   It is time the United States began moving forward again—with new inventions, new products, greater

productivity, more jobs, and a rapidly rising standard of living that means more goods and services for all of us. This can be done if we:

(a) Reduce federal tax rates.

The level of taxation in the United States has now become so high that it is stifling the incentive for individuals to earn, save, and invest. We must have a program—of at least three years duration—of across-the-board tax cuts. The personal income tax rate must be cut by a specific percentage every year for three years, especially the higher, incentive-destroying marginal rates. The capital gains tax, and the corporate income tax must be cut a commensurate amount. Tax rates that are too high destroy incentives to earn, cripple productivity, lead to deficit financing and inflation, and create unemployment. We can go a long way toward restoring the economic health of this country by moving toward reasonable, more fair levels of taxation.

(b) Index federal income tax brackets.

The most insidious tax increase is the one we must pay when inflation pushes us into higher tax brackets. While inflation is with us, taxes should be based on real incomes, not government inflated ones. Federal tax rate brackets, as well as the amount of exemptions, deductions, and credits, should be adjusted to compensate for inflation.

(c) Reduce and eliminate counterproductive federal government regulation of business, education, and the professions.

The recent example of the deregulation of the airline industry has demonstrated that the removal of outdated, overly restrictive government regulations can result in better products and services for consumers, lower prices, more jobs, more profits for business, and more tax revenues for government. Deregulation should be pursued vigorously on a broad front—in the trucking industry, et al. The aggregate cost to business of complying with federal regulation in 1977 was over $75 billion

(Weidenbaum), and these costs are passed on to the consumer in the form of higher prices—higher prices of homes, of food, of gasoline, of virtually everything we buy. This does not mean we should eliminate all regulation now, but it does mean that we should forcefully trim back government interference in the private economy.

(2) **Federal spending must be controlled.**

It is not necessary to cut federal spending from its current levels, but it is necessary to reduce the rate of increase in federal spending. This would include the following actions:

(a) **Reduce and eliminate waste and extravagance in federal spending.**

The amount of fraud, waste and extravagance in federal programs is legendary. According to an August 8, 1978 report of the Senate Governmental Affairs Committee, "recent evidence makes it clear that fraud, abuse, and waste in the operations of federal departments and agencies and in federally funded programs are reaching epidemic proportions." And the Office of Management and Budget now estimates the amount of annual waste could reach as high as *$50 billion*. To facilitate the identification and elimination of this waste *citizen task forces* (similar to the ones Reagan pioneered while Governor of California) should be established for all major government programs.

(b) **Establish effective controls on federal spending.**

To re-establish control over the federal spending machine we should require a two-thirds majority vote in the Congress to approve every major appropriations bill, and building on Reagan's pioneering effort with Proposition 1 in California in 1973, seek a constitutional limitation on the percentage of the people's earnings that can be taken and spent by the federal government.

(c) **Give the President line-item veto power over the budget.**

This is a budget control device that Reagan used very effectively in California. The President would submit his budget to Congress. Congress could then add or subtract from this budget, but the President would have the authority to delete line budget items that had been added.

(d) **Transfer certain federal programs, along with the tax resources that finance them, back to state and local governments.**

By transferring the operation of certain federal programs, such as welfare and education, to state and local governments the effectiveness of these programs can be increased and we can eliminate the cost of the federal bureaucracy and the "traffic charge" of sending tax money to Washington to be doled out to state and local governments under federal regulations.

(3) **Balance the federal budget.**

If all the other steps mentioned above are taken the federal budget will move rapidly toward balance. To ensure that it stays in balance, we should add a *balanced budget amendment* to the Constitution. This would best be done by Congress, but if Congress should fail to act the President should take the case to the people and call for a constitutional convention to enact such an amendment.

(4) **Economic policy must be consistent, dependable, with no abrupt changes.**

One of the fundamental causes of inflation, low productivity, and high unemployment is uncertainty. The decision makers in a free, private economy simply cannot operate effectively if the economic rules are subject to sudden, capricious change. As the 1978 report of the Federal Reserve Bank of Minneapolis states: "What policy makers must do to fight inflation is to eliminate, whenever possible, surprises in monetary and fiscal policies . . . the only way to make policy credible is to announce it, implement it faithfully, and avoid shifting it abruptly." The most powerful cause of business uncertainty is the capability of the federal government to suddenly impose wage and price controls on the economy. There is almost unanimous agreement among economists and politicians that such controls do far more damage than good. Yet the political pressures are often such as to preclude rational action. We need a *constitutional amendment to prohibit the imposition of wage and price controls* except in case of war or national emergency.

(5) Propose an "Economic Bill of Rights."
There are a number of elements of economic policy that are so crucial and fundamental to the proper functioning of a free economy that they should not be subject to the political whims of any particular Congress or Administration. Certain guarantees of economic freedom should be embodied into our Constitution in the same way that certain personal freedoms are guaranteed by the Bill of Rights. These economic guarantees should be set forth in a single amendment, with appropriate sections. Such an amendment might include:

Section 1. Limit the amount the federal government can spend.
Section 2. Require the federal budget to be balanced.
Section 3. Prohibit the imposition of wage and price controls.
Section 4. Establish line-item veto power for the President.
Section 5. Require a two-thirds vote of Congress on all major spending bills.

During the course of the campaign a blue-ribbon drafting group should be established and charged with the task of producing the specific language of such an amendment.

Summary
The goal of economic policy should be more and better material progress for all Americans, and for their children. It must be future-oriented, optimistic, and sound.

The program itself must inspire confidence from the voters, and respect from economic experts.

It must give the people valid hope for their personal economic future.

And it must begin to provide concrete results in 1981, not a decade or two hence.

That was the initial economic plan. The basic economic strategy that President Reagan pursued was agreed upon in August 1979, fully seventeen months before he became president. He never deviated from the basic strategy, although elements of the plan were modified and tempered as Reagan moved from being a private citizen in California to the most powerful public person in the world. Again and again, in the campaign, during the transition, and all during his tenure as president, he adjusted his economic plan to accommodate changes in the economy and political opposition in the Congress, but he did not adjust the blueprint.

Chapter Twelve

REAGAN'S ECONOMIC PLAN

On the morning of September 8, 1980, the campaign tour left Philadelphia. We were about halfway to Chicago and I was sitting at the conference table in the front of the plane when the telephone rang. It was James Baker calling from our national campaign headquarters. He had just talked with William Casey and Ed Meese about the final draft of the economic speech Reagan was scheduled to give at noon the next day in Chicago. "Damn it, Marty," he complained, "we can't have the governor propose a deficit of $50 billion a year. The press will kill us."

Baker was talking on our ground-to-air communications link, an electronic marvel that allowed us to reach over and grab one of the phones hanging on the wall of the airplane just as if we were in a public telephone booth. The conversations were always a little scratchy, but remarkably clear considering we were zipping along at 545 m.p.h. in a United 727 jet at an altitude over 35,000 feet. At that moment I almost wished we didn't have a phone. Baker's point was right, but there wasn't anything I could do.

For several months we had struggled to superimpose Reagan's grand economic strategy onto the reality of the economy and make all the parts fit together. Everyone in the campaign agreed with the basic thrust of the strategy, but there was a lot of disagreement about how to put the comprehensive plan together.

Three days earlier I thought it was finally settled. I produced a policy paper outlining in some detail the basic principles of Reagan's plan, including a detailed five-year forecast on its effect on the federal budget, and our speechwriters drafted a campaign speech spelling out the economics in more mellow language. Late on the morning of September 6, 1980, Ed Meese, Reagan's most trusted general policy adviser, called me to say he thought the economic speech package was excellent. Caspar Weinberger called a little later to say he was delighted with the speech, calling it "good stuff." The economic policy package—the speech, a more detailed policy paper we called a fact sheet, and a detailed budget forecast—had been circulated to and approved by Reagan and all of his important policy advisers, including Ed Meese, William Casey, George Bush, Alan Greenspan, George Shultz, Caspar Weinberger, William Timmons, Jack Kemp, Bryce Harlow, Richard Wirthlin, James Lynn, Charls Walker, Richard Whalen, William Gavin, Annelise Anderson, Robert Boyd, and two top members of my own staff, Kevin Hopkins and Douglas Bandow.

They all liked it.

Well, almost all. William Timmons, a highly regarded political strategist who ran President Ford's 1976 presidential campaign against Jimmy Carter, was in charge of our political operations. Robert Garrick, a retired admiral who was the chief administrator at campaign headquarters, was responsible for sending out draft policy statements for review and getting the comments back to the authors. Timmons sent a blistering memorandum to Garrick denouncing the proposed speech as "disjointed, poorly organized, and not well written." Then, to make sure I would not miss his point, he telephoned my assistant and left the following message for me on a pink phone slip, "Mr. Timmons thinks speech is a piece of shit."

A memorandum to me later that afternoon from William Casey, chairman of the campaign, settled the matter. His message got to the point quickly:

> The economic speech will be scrutinized very closely and should follow very closely what we are prepared to defend, as spelled

out on the fact sheet. I believe the fact sheet should be pretty much converted into the speech. The present speech draft has too many preliminaries, too much of a wind up, too much digression and too much time spent on criticizing Carter's economic policy. . . . This will not be a definitive economic speech unless you stay very close to the fact sheet. . . . Let me say again, I think the only way to revise this satisfactorily in the time available is to stay pretty close in scope and content to the fact sheet.

Fortunately, presidential campaigns do not require unanimous consent. Bill Gavin and I, and about a half dozen staff members, worked until about 2 a.m. the next morning to revise the speech along the lines of the more substantive fact sheet. We were satisfied with the result that rolled off the typewriters the next day.

The approach was straightforward. The first step was to decide what we wanted to do, and we, including Reagan and all his key economic and political advisers, all agreed that we wanted to cut individual and business tax rates, slow the growth of domestic spending, increase defense spending, and balance the budget as soon as possible. Yet everything was connected to everything else. If we cut tax rates, we would have less money to spend on defense. If we increased defense spending, it would be more difficult to balance the budget. If we could slow the increase in domestic spending, it would be easier to cut tax rates. The real trick was deciding how much to do of each, and put together a combination of tax cuts, spending control, and defense increases that would lead us along the shortest, most effective path to revitalizing the economy.

Doing this meant we had to take an important second step, one that went beyond philosophical principles and optimistic words. To figure out what the effects of our policy changes would be, year by year, we had to analyze the best economic forecasts available— ones that predicted for each year into the next five years (assuming no changes in future national policy), how much the federal government would receive in tax revenues, how much the government would spend on domestic programs and national defense, and whether there would be a deficit or a surplus for each particular year. The effects of the policy changes were the bottom line. All the nice theories and fancy rhetoric would count for nothing if the numbers did not work out.

These economic forecasts play a major role in determining economic policy, because they define the general limits. For example, if the forecasts show that future tax revenues will be greater than future spending and there is money left over, it means that money could be used to reduce tax rates, increase spending on existing programs, or perhaps even create new government programs. If forecasts show revenues running short and future deficits in store, it is much more difficult. Any additional spending or tax cuts almost surely will increase the deficit further.

The economic forecasts we used that summer were prepared by the Congressional Budget Office (CBO). There are some forty or fifty major private forecasts, but the CBO forecasts have an unequaled reputation for objectivity. One could argue that other forecasts might be more accurate, but we had political as well as economic concerns. The forecasts we used had to be beyond any criticism by professional economists and the national news media. If we concocted our own forecasts or used those furnished by someone with any lesser reputation for objectivity, the next day every major paper in the country would have run stories about the funny numbers we used. We had no choice. If we were going to use forecasts, we had to use the CBO forecasts.

The economic policy speech was prepared in two parts. The section Reagan would deliver was called "A Strategy for Growth: The American Economy in the 1980s. A separate fact sheet entitled "Ronald Reagan's Strategy for Economic Growth and Stability in the 1980s" would be handed out to the national press along with the text of the prepared speech. The speech would set forth the basic economic strategy, outline the major elements of the program, and explain to the general public why it was a good idea. The fact sheet, which was about twice as long, was a more detailed presentation using the latest economic forecasts to show the expected effect of the program on key elements of taxing and spending. The speech itself was aimed at the vast television audience that would watch it. The fact sheet was aimed at answering questions the press, and financial and business community, would have.

I had prepared a draft of the fact sheet as a memorandum to Reagan almost three weeks earlier. Since then, the fact sheet was carefully reviewed by Reagan and twenty top advisers, including George Shultz, Ed Meese, Alan Greenspan, Bill Casey, Dick Wirthlin, Art Laffer, and Caspar Weinberger.

Working from the fact sheet, William Gavin and I wrote the first draft of Reagan's speech. Gavin was one of the best speechwriters in America; I first worked with him in the Nixon presidential campaign in 1968. In 1967, as a young schoolteacher in New Jersey who was never in a political campaign before, he wrote a letter to Richard Nixon encouraging him to run for president. The letter caught the eye of one of Nixon's law firm partners, Leonard Garment, who on impulse invited Gavin to drop by for lunch at his law offices on Wall Street. Gavin did come by for lunch, and he went on to write some of Nixon's most powerful rhetoric. Gavin got better over the years and could write Reagan's words almost as well as Reagan.

The Gavin-Anderson draft was reviewed and edited by Lyn Nofziger, one of Reagan's oldest advisers, who previously had been a newspaper reporter. The completed draft of the speech was given to Reagan on the morning of September 7, 1980. By 4:30 p.m. that same day Reagan reviewed it, made a number of small changes, and gave it his OK.

Some advisers in the campaign argued that we shouldn't use any numbers at all, that we should just lay out the general economic principles and ride it through. But the chances of getting away with that became less likely with each passing day. Reagan's opponents were slamming him harder and harder on his economic program. The national press traveling with us insisted increasingly on seeing the details. Reagan could not continue to respond in generalities to questions that demanded specifics. It became crucially important to provide details when the press began openly to question whether Reagan's economic program would work.

His political opponents were not that charitable. John Anderson, running on an independent political ticket, implicitly labeled Reagan a liar as he asserted repeatedly that "the only way Reagan is going to cut taxes, increase defense spending, and balance the budget at the same time is to use blue smoke and mirrors." It was a nicely honed political attack, and it had the Reagan campaign on the defensive. "How will he do that?" people began to wonder. George Bush mocked the program by calling it voodoo economics, a catchy phrase that seemed to stick in people's memories.

The problem was that all the things Reagan wanted to do didn't fit completely into any of the current economic forecasts. Each element of his economic policy, taken by itself, made sense and was a good thing to do. But the real art of making national economic policy is finding the best blend of all the elements, then cutting back each one by just enough so they will all fit reality. By late August 1980, we began to sweat for more reasons than the summer's heat.

On the other hand, the CBO forecasts we used were very encouraging. They showed government revenues increasing faster than government spending, year after year.

Let's dwell for a moment on this point. In early August 1980, the consensus view of the most reputable forecasters was that tax revenues would increase so much faster than government spending that the country would be faced with very large, rapidly growing *surpluses* within three years. This is something the economic forecasting experts know well, but there are less than 100 of these experts in the United States, and perhaps less than 1,000 in the entire world. I have never met anyone other than an economic forecasting expert who was aware of this phenomenon.

In the summer of 1980 the CBO forecast was predicting a deficit of $44 billion for 1981, which then declined sharply to a much smaller $15 billion deficit for 1982. But by 1983, the CBO predicted, there would be a healthy budget *surplus* of $37 billion, and that surplus would grow to $96 billion in 1984, and then to an almost unbelievable surplus of $175 billion by 1985. And that was *after* taking into account a planned increase in defense spending from $152 billion in 1981 to $214 billion in 1985.

The federal government was going to be rolling in money. The only problem was how to spend it. If Democrats were reelected we were sure they would propose dozens of new social programs costing tens of billions of dollars. Reagan, however, was determined to spend that surplus in an unusual way. He wanted to give the money back to the taxpayers via a major tax rate cut, just as he once did as governor of California, when he discovered he was running a huge state budget surplus.

In view of what actually happened to the economy, much of this euphoria may seem a little silly. But at the time it was real. Even the most cautious, prudent economic experts were predicting large, increasing government surpluses as far as the eye could see. Any proposed economic program had to conform to those forecasts to be valid. One can argue that any economic forecast, especially one that goes beyond a year, is so uncertain that one should be careful about relying on it too much. I agree. In fact, from time to time I have suggested that if the Congress passed a law requiring some government agency to predict the final scores of the Super Bowl football games for the next five years, it would be easier to do accurately than forecasting government tax revenues and spending for the same period.

Any time we evaluate proposed changes in government policy, we must estimate what its effect will be in one year, in five years, and sometimes even longer. The fact that we cannot do it well does not mean we should not do it at all. In fact, we cannot really avoid making a forecast. If we said we would not use economic forecasts we would, in effect, simply be predicting that there would be no changes, and that in itself is a forecast. Making no forecast could be worse than working with an imprecise forecast, no matter how fuzzy. Those who make the forecasts understand their real limitations. But once they write down their best estimate, no matter how they qualify it, those numbers take on a life of their own. And as they are repeated in newspapers, on television, and in conversation, they are imbued more and more with the qualities of certainty and precision, until finally they become concrete guides for policy actions. They may not be perfect, they may not even be very good, but, as is true of so many things in the making of public policy, we use the best we have and do the best we can with it.

The good news for Governor Reagan in those economic forecasts of the summer of 1980 were the large predicted surpluses. Once he was elected and got beyond the 1981 budget (for which few would hold him responsible), 1982 showed a virtually balanced budget, and then—over the next three years—a combined surplus of $308 billion. With $308 billion you could do a lot of tax cutting and a lot of defense spending and still balance the budget easily, while hardly touching domestic spending. John Anderson was wrong when he said Reagan would have to do it with blue smoke and mirrors. We were going to do it with economic forecasts.

The bad news for Governor Reagan in those same economic forecasts was that the predicted record-breaking surpluses still were not large enough to accommodate all of the ambitious programs he wanted. Something had to go. If we kept our current plans for cutting taxes and increasing defense spending, there wouldn't be enough of a surplus in future years to bring the federal budget back into balance in a short period of time. After months of discussion among the campaign staff and our economic advisers we decided that the importance of increasing defense spending and going ahead with the full tax cut program was more important than balancing the federal budget quickly. We reasoned that if this was not done it would be much more difficult for the economy to recover and our national security position would be further weakened. Unfortunately, the country was already running a sizeable deficit. If these necessary steps were taken to prevent things from getting worse, there would be a short-term price to pay—$11 billion would be added to the deficit in the next year, and another $38 billion the following year. The result was a projected deficit of $55 billion in 1981 and $53 billion in 1982. In future years that would decline sharply, and by 1985 we could expect a $45 billion surplus.

It all made good economic sense and good defense sense, but politically it was a problem, a real problem. The part of the program the political opposition would seize on was that Reagan would be proposing, for the next two years, larger budget deficits than President Carter. We couldn't expect to get a fair hearing on all aspects of the plan in the heat of a presidential campaign. Carter would simply charge that Reagan's economics would produce bigger deficits than his. But by the time we explained the economic wisdom of doing just that in the short run, the political damage would be done, and the campaign would be over. President Carter would very likely be reelected and that, I was convinced, would mean a weaker economy and less money for defense.

The economic program we devised was in our judgment the best thing to do for the economy. But as the campaign plane flew on to Chicago that day in early September 1980, and I continued the telephone conversation with our national headquarters in Virginia, (where we had earlier moved to from Los Angeles) it became very clear that the economic program had terrible political problems.

Jim Baker's final words to me were, "We just can't go with these $50 billion deficits. There must be something you can do." I hung up and slipped the telephone receiver back into its wall holder. Within twenty-four hours Reagan was scheduled to give his long-awaited economic speech. If we stayed with what we had he would be attacked unmercifully for those large proposed deficits in the next two years. We couldn't touch the defense spending plans. That left the tax cut. The only way to cut the deficit back was to delay the tax cut for a year or two or reduce its size sharply. And if we did that the entire economic program would be weakened and the hopes for a rapid economic recovery would evaporate. We were damned if we did and damned if we didn't.

Sometimes the intense pressures of a campaign can make you think of things you never would think of otherwise. My mind was racing over the various possibilities open to us when I recalled something my wife, Annelise, mentioned to me a few days earlier. She was now traveling with George Bush, our new vice presidential running mate, and spending a lot of time briefing him and his staff on Reagan's economic plans. In discussions with the staff of the Senate Budget Committee, she heard about a new economic forecast they just made and told me it looked even better than the one we were working with. I was getting a little desperate by now, without too much hope. So when we got to Chicago, I called her for the name and phone number of the Senate Budget Committee's top expert, Robert Boyd.

As I talked to Boyd later, I could hardly believe what he was telling me. Their latest revised numbers showed a major increase in federal tax receipts during the next five years and a major decline in government spending on domestic programs. Over the five-year period tax receipts were going to be $102 billion more, and federal domestic spending was going to be $122 billion less. Taken together it meant we had $224 billion of additional money to play with. Maybe we could stick with the original tax cut and defense spending increases after all, and still balance the budget within a reasonable period of time.

I got out my Hewlett-Packard calculator and our current economic forecasts. About ten minutes later I knew we had it. We could go for the full tax cut, the full increase in defense spending, and still balance the budget by 1983, maybe even by 1982. Most importantly, the new estimates slashed those $50 billion deficits dramatically in the next two years. Even with the full implementation of the program we could confidently predict that the deficits for 1981 and 1982 would fall into the $20 billion range. The political problem was gone.

But now there was another problem. Nobody knew this but me. Except for Alan Greenspan and William Van Cleave, all the other economic advisers and policy people in the campaign were either back at headquarters or scattered about the country. We were in Chicago staying at the Palmer House, one of the last old distinguished hotels in the country. At 8:00 p.m. that evening I was scheduled, along with Greenspan and Van Cleave, to brief the national press corps on the economic speech Reagan was giving the next morning. There were eighty-six reporters traveling with us, representing the three major television networks, *Time, Newsweek,* the *Wall Street Journal,* the *New York Times,* the *Washington Post,* and dozens of other media outlets. We also had eight foreign reporters with us from Germany, Australia, Switzerland, Canada, and England. They had been anticipating this speech for weeks and we could expect some very close questioning on the details of Reagan's economic plan.

I was staying in room 2363. Late that afternoon four of us met there to decide how we would handle the press briefing. Alan Greenspan was our economic expert. Bill Van Cleave was the defense expert. The fourth person was Kevin Hopkins, one of my top assistants, a very bright young economist who was quick with numbers. They were excited by the new forecast and after carefully reviewing the numbers began to recalculate the expected impact of Reagan's economic program. While Greenspan, Van Cleave, and I discussed the numbers, Hopkins' fingers were flying on his calculator. We soon decided to use most of the economic forecast manna from the Senate Budget Committee to reduce the projected budget deficit in Reagan's economic program. Almost three-fourths of the newly found money went into deficit reduction. The 1981 deficit dropped from $55 billion to $27 billion. The 1982 deficit decreased from $53 billion to $21 billion. The budget was balanced for 1983, and by the time we got to 1985 we were looking at a surplus of $93 billion.

We could have increased the budget surplus even more for the 1983–1985 period, but instead decided to reduce our estimate of how much improved economic growth would add to tax revenues. From the beginning Greenspan was concerned that we were being too optimistic about how much additional tax revenue we could expect from the extra anticipated growth. He reluctantly went along before but with the new economic forecast and the imminent prospect of having to explain this estimate to the national press corps, he suggested once again that we cut it back. I asked him what estimate he felt comfortable and confident with and he specified changes that would use up $47 billion of the $224 billion the new estimates just gave us. I readily agreed. Greenspan was one of the few economists in the country who enjoyed almost universal respect among the press. A happy Greenspan, fully confident about the program, was crucial to a successful press briefing that night.

The result was a proposed tax cut of $531 billion over five years, exactly what Reagan wanted; $457 billion of this was earmarked for individuals, and $74 billion for businesses. Greenspan's new growth estimate showed the tax cut would generate $92 billion of additional tax revenue over the same five-year period.

Reagan and his advisers have been falsely charged with believing that the tax cut would almost instantly produce large increases in tax revenues that would wipe out the tax losses due to the reduction in tax rates. In fact, Reagan conservatively estimated that only a little over 17 percent of the tax cut would be recovered over the five-year period. Privately, he and many of his advisers believed it could easily be more. But we decided to err on the side of caution. As it later turned out, we did substantially underestimate the impact of economic growth on tax revenue.

As Greenspan, Van Cleave, Hopkins, and I worked on the fact sheet budget numbers, we got closer and closer to final agreement. But there were two major sticking points. It was now a little after 6 p.m., less than two hours away from our scheduled press briefing. Greenspan still doubted the wisdom of using any numbers at all. As the country's premier economic forecaster, he knew better than anyone how uncertain any economic forecast was, particularly when it went further ahead than a year or two. He was also skittish about locking us into specific dollar estimates because he knew they would be subject to intense scrutiny and if we made any mistakes, no matter how unlikely, the consequences could be disastrous.

I agreed with Alan's reasoning but argued that the alternative was worse. If we didn't give the press some real numbers that they could analyze and inspect for themselves, their skepticism would rise to new heights. On Monday of the preceding week, a column by Jack W. Germond and Jules Witcover in hundreds of newspapers across the country charged that "Reagan has yet to produce an alternative plan of his own that is likely to be convincing as an improvement. Whether he is finally able to do that sometime over the next nine weeks will tell us a great deal about his prospects for winning the election Nov. 4. . . . Reagan's managers, or at least some of them, recognize this: for months they have been promising a definitive exposition of Reagan's economic policy. All they have produced so far, however, is essentially a mouse."[1] Germond and Witcover, both committed liberals, were two of the most highly respected political reporters in the country.

And then on Friday of that same week, the *Washington Post* ran a story headlined, "REAGAN PLAN FIGURES CALLED WAY OFF BASE." The lead paragraph of the story stated, "Carter Administration officials, in what is *likely to become a major theme* [italics added] of the presidential election campaign, yesterday attacked as unworkable the economic proposals made by Republican presidential candidate Ronald Reagan. 'They just simply do not add up,' a key official said of the tax and spending measures endorsed by Reagan."[2]

With sixty days to go in the campaign, the Carter people and the liberal media smelled a little blood. Before long the attack was in full cry.

We would have to give them actual budget numbers, I reasoned. Greenspan asked Hopkins for the sheet of paper that held the working draft of our budget numbers, settled back on the one big soft chair in the room, and withdrew into a private reverie of intense concentration.

Then Van Cleave announced he didn't think we should use numbers either, but for a very different reason. The Senate Budget Committee economic forecasts we were using for our base had built in real (after inflation) defense spending increases that averaged 5 percent a year for the next five years. In regular dollars this meant a doubling of defense spending to $270 billion by 1985. Most of us thought this was a whopping good increase. It also had the added political attraction that we could say that others—namely a bipartisan group of senior senators—shared Reagan's defense spending plans.

Van Cleave was nervous. He was afraid that Reagan would be committing himself to a level of defense spending increases that might turn out to be too low and act as a ceiling. He argued for complete flexibility. Let Reagan get elected without any commitments to specific dollar figures for defense, then he would be free to do whatever he wanted. Van Cleave is one of the most astute and knowledgeable defense policy intellectuals in the United States, and he had very, very good reasons for wanting defense spending increased as much as possible. He was one of Reagan's first defense advisers during the early days of the 1976 campaign, and he knew how strongly Reagan felt about this issue. I agreed with him on wanting to maximize defense spending, but argued that first Reagan had to be elected. If we didn't make actual dollar predictions, we couldn't predict total spending. And if we couldn't do that, we couldn't predict the net impact of Reagan's overall economic policy on the budget. "And there goes the economic program," I said, "and probably the election."

But Van Cleave was adamant, as stubborn as he was brilliant. He just shook his head and said, "No, I don't like it." Alan Greenspan was still looking at the numbers when I realized we were about out of time. Our briefing was one hour away. If there were going to be specific numbers in the fact sheet, the budget table had to be typed, and xeroxed, and then stapled to the fact sheet. I asked Alan one more time if he felt he could go with real numbers. He looked up with an expression indicating he was willing, but he sure wasn't enthusiastic.

Before he could change his mind I took the marked up budget table with Hopkins's scribbled calculations, and hurried downstairs to our press room. The press room always had banks of typewriters for use by the reporters who traveled with us. I sat down at one of the free typewriters, an old Royal office manual, very similar to the one I had learned to type on as a high school student. In a few places the paint on the typewriter was worn down and the metal shone through, but the typing action was smooth and easy. Fifteen minutes later I finished translating Reagan's economic program into specific dollar estimates for the next five years. I carefully handed that single sheet to one of our secretaries, and then went back upstairs while it was xeroxed and stapled to the fact sheet.

That set of numbers is reproduced in Table 1 exactly as we handed it out to the press corps that night. It contains the essence of the original Reaganomics program, and it also illustrates how you go about making changes in national economic policy. If you go through it, line by line, you can see for yourself what was done, and decide if you might have done it differently at that time.

The first line, Gross National Product, represents the economic experts' best estimate of the economy's size for those next five years. And that, by and large, determined how much money would be there for the federal government to tax. Line two contains the estimate of tax receipts derived from line one. This is the esti-

Table 1

Budgetary Goals: FY 1981 to FY 1985
(annual amounts in billions of dollars)

Senate Budget Committee Estimates: Second Concurrent Resolution August 27, 1980	Fiscal Year				
	1981	1982	1983	1984	1985
Gross National Product	2793	3152	3555	3983	4446
Federal Tax Receipts ("Current Law")	610	712	828	951	1102
Federal Spending	633	710	778	845	920
Defense spending	159	187	212	239	270
Nondefense spending	474	523	566	606	650
Proposed Policy Changes					
a) control growth of federal spending	+13	+28	+39	+51	+64
b) across-the-board reduction of personal income tax rates and subsequent indexing	−18	−48	−89	−130	−172
c) accelerated depreciation to stimulate investment	−4	−13	−18	−19	−20
d) additional economic growth	+5	+10	+18	+20	+39
*estimated (deficit) or surplus	(27)	(21)	—	28	93
*as percent of total spending	(4.3%)	(3.0%)	*	3.3%	10.1%
e) full achievement of spending reduction goals: additional savings	+6	+15	+23	+34	+28
*estimated (deficit) or surplus	(21)	(6)	23	62	121
*as percent of total spending	(3.3%)	*	3.0%	7.3%	13.2%

*less than 1 percent

mated amount the federal government would have available to spend, assuming the tax rates did not change. Line three estimates federal expenditures, again assuming no changes in government programs. Lines four and five show how total government spending was expected to be divided between defense and all other nondefense spending. Essentially, lines one through five show what would probably happen if you didn't change the tax rates, or fiddle with existing government programs, or propose new ones. Of course, everyone always does.

The bottom half of the table shows the changes in economic policy that Reagan wanted and the estimated impact of those changes. Line six indicates how much Reagan wanted to cut back the increases in the currently planned government spending. The percent reductions ranged from 2 percent in 1981 to 7 percent by 1985. Because the planned increases in spending were much larger than that, the net effect was to simply *slow* the planned growth in spending. Instead of a $287 billion increase over the next five years, he was thinking that a $224 billion increase ought to be sufficient.

Line seven shows the estimated gross cost of the tax cut for individuals. In Reagan's judgment this was the most important thing he could do to strengthen the economy, and the amount of money he allocated to it confirms his sincerity. Line eight, accelerated depreciation to stimulate investment, indicates the business tax cut. The tax rates would stay the same, but business would be allowed to take more generous depreciation allowances on the investments they made. As you can see, most of the money spent on Reagan's economic program was for tax reduction, either for individuals or business. In fact, fully 86 percent of Reagan's planned tax cut over the five years went to individuals; only 14 percent went to business.

Line nine, additional economic growth, is the estimate of the additional federal tax revenues that would result from the increased size of the economy caused by the tax cut. The five-year projection used here came directly from Alan Greenspan; these were his estimates and we accepted them. Their message was that a little over 17 percent of the tax receipts lost because of the tax cut would be made up for by additional economic growth. The estimate was deliberately made on the low side to refute the growing belief that Reagan thought his tax cuts would immediately produce more, not less, revenue.

The net result of all the policy changes in lines six through nine is shown on line 10, the estimated (deficit) or surplus. After taking into account the effect of a major effort to control the growth of federal spending, a large tax cut for individuals and business, and the impact of new economic growth, we came up with the following results. The predicted deficit was $27 billion for 1981 and $21 billion for 1982. In 1983, using the then current economic forecasts, the budget would be balanced. By 1985 the budget surplus was expected to be $93 billion. (Line eleven shows the predicted deficit or surplus as a percentage of total government spending.)

Line twelve shows what might happen if Reagan were successful in achieving his full spending reduction goals, which ranged from a 3 percent reduction in 1981 to 10 percent in 1985. Line thirteen shows that if he were to reach those spending reduction goals, he could get the budget very close to balancing one full year earlier, in 1982.

The deep background briefing took place that night in the Crystal Room on the third floor of the Palmer House. Deep background means the press can print whatever you say but they won't use your name as the source. To my relief we picked up some extra time when the press requested that the briefing be delayed. Former President Ford was scheduled to have dinner with Governor Reagan at 7:50 p.m. in his hotel suite, and Ford wanted to meet with the press corps for a short press conference before dinner. All agreed, the dinner was held, and the briefing finally started around 8:15 p.m. Van Cleave wasn't very happy and there were furrows of concern on Greenspan's forehead, but when we stepped out on the briefing stage we certainly looked happy and confident. I began the briefing by joking that "we had originally planned to do this briefing using blue smoke and mirrors, but we couldn't find any smoke or mirrors and decided to use facts instead." The briefing went very well. Greenspan and Van Cleave easily answered the tough, searching questions with accurate, clear answers.

After it ended the reporters headed for their typewriters, armed with the text of the speech Reagan would give the next day, the fact sheet, and their notes from the briefing. Most of them would be working, writing, and then sending or dictating their stories back to their home newspapers long after we went to sleep. The speech and the fact sheet were embargoed for release until 12:25 p.m. the next day, which meant that the reporters traveling with us could write their stories that night, but nobody could actually print or say anything about it until Reagan finished speaking the following day.

September 9, 1980, was going to be another hectic day of campaigning for Reagan. He was scheduled to deliver what was perhaps the most crucial speech of his campaign to the International Business Council of Chicago at 11:25 a.m. In the afternoon we would fly to Milwaukee, Wisconsin, and then on to Cleveland, Ohio, that night.

Four months before he was to take office, Reagan spelled out his detailed blueprint for the economy. The speech he delivered that morning in Chicago was an unusual speech in American politics. It was specific and highly detailed. In the speech, and in the fact sheet that accompanied it, Reagan laid out a comprehensive economic program that viewed the economy as a whole, not one category at a time.

His plan had five basic parts:

(1) Controlling the rate of growth of government spending to reasonable, prudent levels.
(2) Reducing personal income tax rates and accelerating and simplifying depreciation schedules in an orderly, systematic way to remove the increasing disincentives to work, to save, to invest, and to produce.
(3) A thorough review of regulations that affect the economy, and prompt action to change them to encourage economic growth.
(4) The establishment of a stable and sound monetary policy.
(5) The restoration of confidence by following a consistent national economic policy that does not change from month to month.

As Reagan spoke the next morning the message of his economic program spread across the land on the front pages of the morning newspapers. It was a controversial program. The Democrats, as expected, attacked it with abandon. Representatives of big business, including the National Association of Manufacturers, criticized it because they didn't think the tax cut for business was big enough.

Two days later, on Thursday, September 11, the lead editorial

America's presidents of the past twenty years (1968–1988). [White House photo, Bill Fitz-Patrick]

Ronald Reagan in 1939 starring as Lieutenant Brass Bancroft in *Secret Service of the Air*. [Photo courtesy Ronald Reagan]

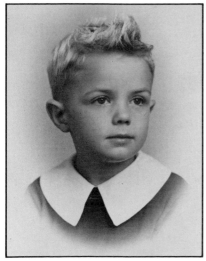

Me in 1939.

Annelise Graebner Anderson in her California office in 1974 after returning from Washington. She was senior policy adviser in both the Nixon and Reagan presidential campaigns; Associate Director of OMB, 1981–83; and now is Senior Research Fellow at the Hoover Institution. [Photo by Martin Anderson]

As Special Assistant to President Nixon—1969.

One of the people I leaned on in both the Nixon and Reagan presidential campaigns—Darrell M. Trent. [White House photo]

Frank Whetstone of Cutbank, Montana. Master delegate-gatherer for Barry Goldwater, Richard Nixon, and Ronald Reagan. [Photo courtesy Frank Whetstone]

Bryce Harlow, the guru of the modern Republican party and adviser to presidents Eisenhower, Nixon, Ford, and Reagan. [Photo by Martin Anderson]

Discussing policy issues with Reagan in his hotel suite during the trip in November 1979 when he announced he would run for the presidency. [Photo by Roger Sandler]

Flying with Reagan in a small private jet during the pre-presidential primary days of late 1975. [Photo by Michael Evans, courtesy Reagan Presidential Foundation]

The 1976 presidential campaign team. Left to right: Lyn Nofziger, Richard Wirthlin, Peter Hannaford, Martin Anderson, Michael Deaver, and Ronald Reagan. Seated next to Reagan is John Sears, then campaign manager. [Photo by Dennis Brack/Black Star]

Reagan discussing final details of his economic program with Alan Greenspan and me on the campaign plane in September 1980. [Photo by Michael Evans, courtesy Reagan Presidential Foundation]

Michael K. Deaver, in happier days, when he was Reagan's chief of staff on the campaign trail. [Photo by Martin Anderson]

Discussing the text of Reagan's announcement speech, in his Pacific Palisades home in California in November 1979. Left to right: Edwin Meese, Ronald Reagan, Martin Anderson, and James Lake. [Photo by Roger Sandler]

The Reagans are each other's best friend and most valued adviser. [Photo courtesy Ronald Reagan]

Ronald Reagan is fundamentally a loner, a man perfectly
content to be with himself. He is a closet workaholic,
constantly reading, thinking, and writing. The briefcase
on the floor guarding the seat next to him is mine.
[Photo by Martin Anderson]

During the presidential campaigns Reagan spent hundreds of
hours drafting speeches and policy statements, as he is doing
here during a flight in the fall of 1979.
[Photo by Martin Anderson]

Ronald Reagan did not take naps on the campaign plane in 1980,
but occasionally Nancy did. [Photo by Martin Anderson]

Reagan's secret 1980 preparations for debate with President Carter. Held in
converted garage of a large Virginia estate, Wexford, President Kennedy's
former home. David Stockman takes Carter's part in mock debate with Reagan,
as campaign staff pretend to be reporters. [Photo by Martin Anderson]

Tea with Deng Xiaoping inside the Great Hall in Beijing, China, in December 1981 to discuss new economic arrangements between the United States and China (Deng Xiaoping, Donald Regan, Ambassador Arthur H. Hummel, Martin Anderson).

Discussing budget deficit in the Oval Office on January 28, 1981. Left to right: President Reagan, David Stockman, Donald Regan, Murray Weidenbaum, Martin Anderson. [White House photo, Michael Evans]

in the *Wall Street Journal* summed up the reaction to the first comprehensive explanation of Reagan's economic program:

> Ronald Reagan finally found some number crunchers to churn out an answer to the question of how he could cut taxes, increase defense spending and balance the budget all at once . . . if there are no tax cuts, taxes will increase sharply. . . . These built-in tax increases generate huge leverage—for increasing spending, reducing taxes or reducing the government deficit. All you need to do is project the numbers out a few years, and combine the rising tax rate with modest fiscal restraint, and the supposedly impossible challenge to Mr. Reagan becomes child's play. . . . The supply-side analysis remains in Mr. Reagan's economic package, but has obviously been muted by the Nixon/Ford economic advisers who could provide numbers that could withstand attack. His military budget increases are not huge, though a bit more is promised. His spending cuts are cautious. . . . Mr. Reagan has, in short, spelled out a prudent, gradual, responsible reordering of economic priorities, not much different from the kind of thing Republicans have always offered.[3]

The credibility of Reagan's economic program turned out to be bulletproof. He could be criticized for wanting to cut taxes and increase defense spending. He could be criticized for wanting to balance the budget and slow the growth of domestic programs. But he couldn't be criticized for not being *able* to do what he wanted to do. He now had the numbers to prove he could do it if the electorate gave him the chance.

On the campaign plane, the morning after Reagan's economic speech, Marty Schramm, one of the reporters traveling with us, walked over to me and said, "Well, how does it feel now that the baby is born?" It felt good; perhaps the right word is relieved. My real concern was whether the baby would live and grow up to do all the things it had the potential to do.

Chapter Thirteen

LEGEND OF THE SUPPLY-SIDERS

One of the most durable legends in recent history concerns the rise and power of the supply-siders and the ideas they represent. This is the legend:

"Once upon a time, in a faraway land called California, there lived a friendly cowboy who decided to run for president of the United States. During his leisurely campaign, in which he took many long afternoon naps and generally seemed to enjoy himself, he came across the notion that you could increase government revenue immediately by cutting taxes. He got that notion from a young, bubbly economist who scribbled his ideas down on napkins in restaurants and from a few others who had absolutely no training in economics. But never mind. He liked the idea and told everyone he met that if you cut taxes by a whopping amount you would instantly get more money for the government, and then you could sharply increase defense spending and balance the budget at the same time.

One of his opponents was unkind enough to label this sort of thing 'voodoo economics.' Another opponent declared derisively that maybe he was going to do it with 'blue smoke and mirrors.' Everyone smiled a lot and had a good time at the cowboy's expense.

"But then, to the astonishment of half the United States, and virtually all of the world, Ronald Reagan got himself elected president of the United States of America. He immediately set out to do what he said he would do. Within months he had bewitched the Congress and they went along with his crazy tax cut. He also got them to agree to a massive, multibillion dollar increase in defense spending.

"After a few years, to nobody's surprise, tax revenues fell sharply and the budget deficit grew bigger and bigger. But Reagan and his supply-side advisers remained unconcerned and calm. 'Just wait,' they said, 'it will all work out and the deficit will go away.' And we are still waiting."

That is the legend.

Like all good legends, this one strongly reinforces the interests and prejudices of many people. It makes a good story, but it is not true. Fortunately, the true story is perhaps even better.

The term "supply side" means that part of economic policy that deals with the effect of tax rates on economic activity, and how changes in these rates affect people's incentives to work, to earn money, to produce goods and services, to invest, and to save. By and large, supply-side economics has to do with government tax policy, although some have used the term in a broader sense, embracing monetary policy and the proper size of government. But essentially, supply-side economics is concerned with the impact of tax rates on individual effort.

The idea is a simple one. As a government raises tax rates, the amount of earnings that taxpayers get to keep for themselves declines. If the government raises tax rates high enough, people respond by not working as hard, and they hide more of their earnings from the government. The result is that there is less money available for the government to tax. At some point increases in the tax rate become counterproductive as far as tax revenue is concerned. Higher tax rates simply produce less tax revenue. When that point is reached tax revenues can be increased, paradoxically, by cutting tax rates.

The supply-side effect is an idea as old as the science of economics itself. It was part of the economics of Adam Smith, Jean-Baptiste Say, John Stuart Mill, David Hume, and the other classical economists right up through the beginning of the twentieth century. Over two hundred years ago, in 1776, Adam Smith wrote, "High taxes, sometimes by diminishing the consumption of the taxed commodities, and sometimes by encouraging smuggling, frequently afford a smaller revenue to government than what might be drawn from more moderate taxes. When the diminution of revenue is the effect of the diminution of consumption, there can be but one remedy, and that is the lowering of the tax."[1]

It was the cornerstone of William Gladstone's tax policy in Britain during the late 1880s. It was a key element of President Coolidge's economic policy in the 1920s in the United States. Coolidge's secretary of the treasury, Andrew Mellon, pressed successfully for tax rate reductions, arguing, "It seems difficult for some to understand that high rates of taxation do not necessarily mean large revenues to the Government, and that more revenue may often be obtained by lower rates."[2]

And if one should be so stuffy as to define a Keynesian economist as one who follows any of the precepts of what John Maynard Keynes believed and wrote, then, by that narrow definition, those who came to be known as supply-siders in the 1980s in the United States would have to be considered at least part Keynesian. In 1933, Harcourt, Brace and Company published a thirty-seven page pamphlet by Keynes, bound in a bright orange cover. It was called *The Means to Prosperity*, a rather prophetic title considering what was done under Reagan some fifty-odd years later. According to Keynes,

"Nor should the argument seem strange that taxation may be so high as to defeat its object, and that, given sufficient time to gather the fruits, a reduction of taxation will run a better chance, than an increase, of balancing the Budget. For to take the opposite view today is to resemble a manufacturer who, running at a loss, decides to raise his price, and when his declining sales increase the loss, wrapping himself in the rectitude of plain arithmetic, decides that prudence requires him to raise the price still more;—and who, when at last his account is balanced with nought on both sides, is still found righteously

declaring that it would have been the act of a gambler to reduce the price when you were already making a loss."[3]

Ronald Reagan couldn't have said it better.

For the next fifty years, following the onset of the Great
Depression, the crucial role that tax rates played in national economic policy seemed to take a back seat on the economic bus.
While it remained firmly in place as an important element of economics, the effect of tax rates seemed to suffer from benign neglect when economists applied their theories to the real world of
commerce. Perhaps they were preoccupied with the devastating effects of the depression, the onset of World War II, and their increasing fascination with socialist schemes that could only be
implemented with lots of tax revenue. Whatever the reasons, most
tended to ignore the crippling results of a high tax burden. And tax
rates rose steadily in country after country around the world.

As we entered the 1970s the tax burden of the United States
reached record postwar highs and was headed even higher. President Kennedy briefly, and quite effectively, used a 25 percent tax
cut in the early 1960s to fulfill his campaign pledge of "getting the
country moving again." But its significance was noticed by few.

One phenomenon of a rising tax burden is that as the tax rate
gets higher any further increase has a relatively greater negative
impact on economic activity. By the middle of the 1970s the negative effect of those high tax rates started to become more obvious.
The old, old idea of supply-side tax effects slowly began to surface,
and people extolling its importance started to pop up like exploding kernels of popcorn.

The first person to introduce me to the essence of supply-side
economic policy was Arthur F. Burns. In early 1969 Burns was
President Nixon's top domestic policy adviser. Besides being a professor of economics at Columbia University, he had accumulated
vast experience in economic policy as President Eisenhower's chief
economic adviser during the 1950s.

Of the people I have known in my life—the scholars, the politicians, the wealthy, and the famous—less than a half-dozen or so
could be called great men. Arthur F. Burns was one. He was a
person of immense intellect. When you first met Burns he struck
you as the embodiment of a nineteeneth century patrician, white-

haired Austrian professor. His manner was dignified, deliberate, and he spoke softly and slowly. But beneath that white-thatched dome, perfectly parted down the middle in complete and utter defiance of conventional hairstyle standards in America, lay a brain with the power and speed of a large computer.

Burns' role in the Reagan years had its roots in the Nixon administration. During the 1968 presidential campaign, Burns was Richard Nixon's top economic adviser. Nixon had enormous respect for him, and Burns was genuinely fond of Nixon, although he treated him as a "young man who was coming along nicely." That attitude of slight condescension, no matter how justified, combined with his slowness of coming to the point in policy discussions, resulted in a special assignment for me. I was to spend as much time with Burns as necessary, to get the full extent of his economic advice and counsel, and then I was to give the essence of this to Nixon directly, minus all the developing argument and with no condescension.

Burns was one of the first to join President Nixon's White House staff in 1969. He was given general responsibility for policy development in domestic and economic affairs. But finding a title for him was a problem. His title couldn't clash with that of Paul McCracken, the chairman of the Council of Economic Advisers, or with the title for the new urban affairs adviser to the president, Daniel Patrick Moynihan, and the chief administrative people were to have the title of assistant. Finally, I suggested we use "counsellor to the president."

Everyone liked it, it appealed to Arthur, and he accepted the position, although what he really wanted, and what Nixon really wanted to give him, was the chairmanship of the Federal Reserve. But McChesney Martin was not about to resign until his full term was up. As Arthur once put it, "Martin will be sitting in that chair right up to midnight, Hawaii time, of his last day in office." That turned out to be true and Burns had to wait for slightly over a year to achieve his long-sought dream in 1971 of chairing the Federal Reserve Board, the most powerful financial post in the world.

Sometimes, late at night when we were working in his huge, stately office on the first floor of the Old Executive Office Building, Burns would lay down his pipe and, with a vaguely conspiratorial look on his face, turn in his chair to reach behind him to a lower drawer in the wooden cabinet. When his hand emerged it held a large bottle of aged 100 proof bourbon, emblazoned with an ornate gold and green seal bearing the name of Very, Very Old Fitzgerald. He would ceremoniously pour a half-inch or so into a couple of heavy, clear glasses, and we would slowly sip bourbon until the problem was solved or it was too late to continue. As it happened, they stopped bottling that fine old bourbon in 1971, and it is no longer available.

One night, after he came back to our offices following a meeting with the president, he told me about the economic program he had just urged Nixon to follow. Burns had made two major recommendations. First, and most importantly, he counseled Nixon to control and restrain the growth in federal spending to achieve and maintain a balanced budget. Second, he strongly urged Nixon to consider a major, sustained reduction in individual income tax rates. As he sat in his office, slowly puffing on his pipe, Burns relayed to me what he just told Nixon.

"I said to him, 'Mr. President, I think you should seriously consider reducing the individual income tax rate five percent across-the-board this year, and then again next year, and then again in the third year. It would greatly strengthen the economy.' "

The economic policy Burns suggested to Nixon in 1969 contained the essentials of the economic program President Reagan proposed some twelve years later: (1) control spending and seek a balanced budget, and (2) reduce tax rates systematically and simultaneously. In 1969 the problem of federal spending was minor compared to what Reagan faced in 1981, and the tax cut Burns suggested was only half of what Reagan proposed. But the principle was the same.

President Nixon did not follow Arthur Burns' economic advice. Federal spending gradually increased by bits and pieces, each time for urgent, political reasons. The tax rate reduction program was never seriously considered, never even studied. But it was supply-side economics, as it came to be called in the 1980s, and Arthur Burns recommended it.

That is why in 1979 I was not at all surprised that Burns, now one of Ronald Reagan's economic advisers, wholeheartedly embraced my suggestion to Reagan that he make spending control and systematic tax-cutting the centerpieces of his comprehensive economic program. Burns also fully endorsed Reagan's goal of a balanced budget, his plans for regulatory reform, and his advocacy of a sound, predictable monetary policy. Arthur Burns never did waver in his belief that large amounts of sustained deficit spending were wrong and ultimately harmful to a free economy, but then, neither has Ronald Reagan.

The godfather of modern supply-side economics emphasizing tax policy is generally acknowledged to be Robert Mundell, a quiet, low-key Canadian citizen who is an economics professor at Columbia University. Mundell has written surprisingly little on the subject and virtually the entire extent of his notoriety stems from his long association with a young economist named Arthur Laffer. Laffer graduated from Yale University in 1963 and then pursued his doctorate in economics at Stanford University, where he was one of the brightest students they ever had. Laffer joined the economics faculty of the University of Chicago in 1967 and spent several years working closely with Professor Mundell, who was then also at Chicago. The young Laffer thought of it as "the most fruitful period of his life."[4] It was there that Laffer and Mundell began their reexamination of the incentive effects of taxation and began to apply their thinking to the current problems of the economy.

Mundell and Laffer, in one sense, were an odd couple. Mundell was considerably older, retiring to the point of being reclusive, while Laffer was young, bristling with energy, without a shy bone in his body. At the time they came together in that big, brawny midwestern city, much of academic economics was dry and rigid, a highly orthodox intellectualism devoting an excessive amount of time to creating complex mathematical models with less and less direct relevance to the economic issues people were struggling with daily.

The thinking of Mundell and Laffer was way, way outside the mainstream of the current economic thinking. But they both seemed blissfully immune to the sniffs of their colleagues and proceeded to dust off an important aspect of economic theory that lay on the shelves neglected and unappreciated by establishment economists for so many years. Mundell was considered to be somewhat of an eccentric and Laffer was very young, and for some time the academic establishment happily ignored both of them.

But not for too long. Laffer turned out to be an irrepressible propagandist, and soon he became the chief advocate of the virtues of tax rate reduction. After serving a stint as an economist in the

Office of Management and Budget under George Shultz in 1970, Laffer began to lecture and write about the taxation policy he and Mundell discussed during their days together at the University of Chicago.

According to supply-side lore, one day in 1974 while sitting at a restaurant table in Washington, D.C., Laffer grabbed a pencil and hastily sketched a single curve on his napkin that showed how government tax revenue would change as the tax rate went from zero percent to 100 percent. As one might expect, government revenue increased when the tax rate went up, finally leveled off, and when the tax rate continued to climb toward the upper limit of 100 percent of peoples' income, tax revenues plunged back down toward zero. In the years that followed, that simple line drawing became well known, and Professor Laffer achieved worldwide fame as the author of the Laffer Curve. The fame was well deserved because he was, as far as we know, the first person who took the simple idea of supply-side tax effects that has been around since the dawn of economics and painted a picture of it.

One small footnote. The curve was not first drawn on a restaurant napkin. That whimsical story was an apparent invention of one of Laffer's first protégés, Jude Wanniski. I have talked to Laffer directly about this and he has "no recollection whatsoever of drawing on a napkin." It's just as well he doesn't. The restaurant involved was the Two Continents, formerly located in the Washington Hotel across the street from the Treasury Department. It was a quality restaurant and is reported to have used only expensive linen napkins.

Professor Laffer never received much applause from his colleagues in the academic world. In fact, some of their criticism of his work has been unmerciful, and, in at least one instance, downright mean. From the very beginning of his academic career, Laffer was treated almost as an outcast. One low in personal nastiness occurred early in Laffer's career, in 1971, when Nobel laureate Paul Samuelson, the most distinguished member of the economics faculty of MIT, presented a lecture at the University of Chicago, "Why They Are Laughing at Laffer." The mockery was aimed at an economic forecast Laffer made while serving in the government, a forecast that initially looked wide off the mark, but was later proved by actual events to be unusually accurate. Samuelson's lecture, especially its title, was cruel and reckless, and could cripple and destroy the intellectual reputation of a young scholar. And it was an uneven match.

I knew Paul Samuelson well. He was my professor of economics when I attended graduate school at MIT from 1959 to 1962. One of the heavyweights of the field, he was the first man to convince me, via a complex mathematical model, that a free economy was practical. Samuelson's brilliant mind and knack for razor sharp analysis was hidden behind a homely face. His small, pointed ears gave him an extraterrestrial look, a look enhanced by his short, slender body. He was small, and he was mean. But what he did to Laffer that day in Chicago, even by academic standards of morality, was an extraordinary example of intellectual bullying.

In the academic world of economists one of the rarest, most treasured honors is to have your name associated with a curve. There are very few. Perhaps Laffer made a mistake by getting his name on a curve, by luck or design, at a very young age. It must have been especially galling to other economists when they realized how easy it would have been for them to do it themselves, if only they had thought of it.

One of Laffer's first converts was Jude Wanniski. Wanniski was an especially zealous convert, perhaps because his starting point was so far from Laffer's. A registered Democrat at least until 1977, he boasted that as a youth he "campaigned for Adlai Stevenson in 1952 and 1956, voted for John Kennedy in 1960 and Lyndon Johnson in 1964, split tickets for Richard Nixon in 1968 and 1972, and almost, but not quite, voted for Jimmy Carter in 1976."[5] Wanniski did not study economics at UCLA where he graduated in 1959, but he was drawn to the politics of the far Left, attending weekly Tuesday night meetings on campus of the Young Peoples' Socialist League, the Socialist party youth group. When he was twenty years old he considered himself a Fabian socialist, but didn't seem to fit in too well with the Marxists he met with on Tuesday nights, and he gradually drifted to the right.[6]

Wanniski met Laffer in Washington in 1971 when he was a reporter for *The National Observer*. He soon became Laffer's eager student. The next year Wanniski moved to New York City and joined the editorial page staff of the *Wall Street Journal*, brimming over with the nuggets of economic theory that Laffer fed him. There in New York, from the mighty pulpit of the *Journal*, Wanniski began his campaign to sell a supply-side tax cut to America. With the dash and boldness of a modern Samuel Adams, he wrote the powerful message of tax rate reduction. His first major piece, entitled "It's Time to Cut Taxes," was published on December 11, 1974. Wanniski quoted Robert Mundell as saying that, "The level of U.S. taxes has become a drag on economic growth in the United States. The national economy is being choked by taxes—asphyxiated."

And then he boldly declared, "A tax cut not only increases demand, but increases the incentive to produce. . . . With lower taxes, it is more attractive to invest and more attractive to work; demand is increased but so is supply. . . . The $30 billion tax cut is needed immediately." [7]

Robert Bartley, the editor of the *Wall Street Journal*, opened its powerful editorial pages to writing on supply-side tax policy. What was a very closely held idea was suddenly being shared with millions of readers, not only in the United States, but in dozens of other countries throughout the world. Wanniski was the one who pounded on the supply-side door, but it was Bartley who chose to open it; and he opened it wide, to Wanniski, and to others, including the highly respected intellectual, Irving Kristol.

The term supply-side was coined by Herbert Stein, a persistent critic of Laffer and his friends, in a paper delivered to a meeting of economists in April 1976. The would-be taxcutters were identified as supply-side fiscalists. Stein's term had a whiff of an intellectual sneer about it, although he later denied any attempt to use the phrase derisively. [8] But Wanniski liked the label when he came across it, ignored the insult, and abandoned the fiscalist part as he gleefully applied the supply-side adjective to everything in sight.

Wanniski had no formal economic training, but that did not inhibit him. He was intelligent and intrepid and barreled straight ahead. I first became aware of his efforts in 1976 when I was asked by Leslie Lenkowsky, then director of a small but influential foundation in New York City called the Richardson Foundation, if I would review an application for a major grant they just received. I agreed, and a few days later received a copy of Jude Wanniski's proposal to write a book on economic policy. The proposal was well written and promised to deal with some important areas, especially in tax policy, but Wanniski didn't even have a bachelor's degree in economics.

But I thought, "Well, Adam Smith didn't have a degree in economics either." So I told Lenkowsky that although it was a risky project, the author was an intelligent and talented writer. If he succeeded the results could be very worthwhile, and I strongly urged them to fund it. In 1976 the Richardson Foundation gave Wanniski a $40,000 grant and he left the *Wall Street Journal* to write his powerful book on supply-side taxation. With characteristic boldness he entitled it, *The Way the World Works.* The book was published in 1978 and gave another push to the growing interest in a supply-side tax cut.

Meanwhile, other people were working on the supply-side idea in Congress. A year before Wanniski's book was published Congressman Jack Kemp and Senator William Roth introduced a bill to cut personal income tax rates by 30 percent over a period of three years. The idea was now on the national agenda, and the Kemp-Roth bill began its journey toward becoming a household word.

In a not unusual occurrence, the intellectual beginnings of the Kemp-Roth legislation stirred long before Wanniski and Laffer met Kemp. In 1975 Paul Craig Roberts, a young economist who had recently spent two years (1971–73) at the Hoover Institution, joined Kemp's congressional staff. In collaboration with a well-regarded economic consultant, Norman Ture, he started writing economic policy material for Kemp with a decided supply-side slant. Late in 1976 Roberts became the chief economist for the Republican staff of the House Budget Committee and from that vantage point masterminded the drafting of the now famous Kemp-Roth tax cut proposal first introduced in the Congress in 1977.

After serving as assistant secretary of the treasury for economic policy from 1981 to 1982, Roberts joined the staff of the Center for Strategic and International Studies in Washington, D.C. Like his former academic colleague, Laffer, he was ignored by much of the academic community of economists in the United States. But he was one of the first people in the 1970s to reexamine the critical importance of tax rates, and to help fashion legislation featuring lower tax rates as a crucial element of economic policy. Roberts may receive little recognition in the United States, but at least one country abroad has noticed him. On April 8, 1987, he was awarded the *Légion D'Honneur,* one of the highest honors the French government can bestow, and hailed as "the artisan of a renewal in eco-

nomic science and policy, after half-a-century of state inter-
ventionism."⁹

One thing is clear: When an idea's time has come, whether it's
a new one or an old one polished up a bit, it's apt to occur to a lot
of people at about the same time. Robert Mundell, Arthur Laffer,
Paul Craig Roberts, Robert Bartley, and Jude Wanniski all played
important roles in spreading the essential idea that tax rates matter,
that they can and do affect economic growth. There were others
who also helped, writing and arguing the case—Jack Kemp, Norman Ture, Bruce Bartlett, Irving Kristol, Steve Entin, and Alan
Reynolds. All together there were probably about a dozen or so
people who propelled the effect of tax rates into a major plank of
economic policy. All but Kemp were intellectuals, and Kemp was
very close to being a politico-intellectual. They were like a many-
linked chain. Perhaps the chain would have held without any one
of them, or two of them, but we know it would not have been
without all of them.

There is one other fellow who ought to be included in the
family tree rundown of the supply-side idea. That's Ronald Reagan. On October 8, 1976, at the height of the presidential campaign between Jimmy Carter and Gerald Ford, and almost a year
before the Kemp-Roth tax cut legislation was introduced, Reagan
authored a national newspaper column entitled, "Tax Cuts and Increased Revenue." The lead in Reagan's column that day read,
"Warren Harding did it. John Kennedy did it. But Jimmy Carter
and President Ford aren't talking about it. That 'it' that Harding
and Kennedy had in common was to cut the income tax. In both
cases, federal revenues went up instead of down . . . the presidential candidates would do us all a service if they would discuss the
pros and cons of the concept. Since the idea worked under both
Democratic and Republican administrations before, who's to say it
couldn't work again?"

As far as I know, Reagan's 1976 call to examine the record of
the tax rate cuts under Presidents Harding and Kennedy is as close
as anyone associated with Reagan ever came to claiming that a tax
rate cut would instantly yield more government revenue. Yet the
myth persisted—the myth that Reagan and his key economic advisers believed that large tax cuts would produce more revenue.
And even when dozens of the finest economists in the land exam-

ined and blessed Reagan's comprehensive economic program, and even though neither they, nor Reagan, nor any of Reagan's senior aides ever made any such outlandish claim, the myth continued, year after year.

What Reagan and his advisers did believe, and what they said repeatedly, was that, given the high level of taxation, a tax rate cut would *not lose as much revenue as one might expect*. People would work harder, and their incomes would rise over time to offset a substantial part of the revenue loss due to the tax rate cut. In fact, this is what happened—in spades. Reagan's very cautious 1980 campaign estimate of the effects of the supply-side tax cut on government revenue—that 17 percent of the lost revenue would be recouped by increased economic growth—proved far too conservative.

By 1988 we had a pretty clear idea of the impact of Reagan's tax rate reductions. A series of studies by Lawrence B. Lindsey, a Harvard economist and professor, that were done for the highly respected National Bureau of Economic Research, proved conclusively that much—perhaps half—of the tax revenue lost because of the tax rate cuts was made up for by increased revenue, revenue increases that would *not* have taken place without the cuts.[10]

Moreover, to the surprise of almost everyone, including Reagan's economic advisers, the amount of taxes paid by one special group of taxpayers—those with adjusted gross incomes over $200,000 a year—increased rather sharply. By 1985, the amount of revenue raised from these high-income taxpayers was about 25 percent *higher* than it would have been without the rate reduction.[11]

In the final analysis, the Reagan tax rate cuts resulted in the wealthy carrying a larger share of the total tax burden. Under the new tax rates, the rich paid more and the poor paid less. That should be enough to make even the Left reconsider some of their ideas about economic justice.

One curious thing about the myth of Reagan's believing he could gain instant increases in tax revenue by cutting tax rates is that it seems to continue most strongly in exactly the place where you would think it would be weakest—in the heart of the economic academic community, among the intellectuals who pride themselves on distinguishing fact from myth. Some examples:

On December 29, 1985, Martin Feldstein, professor of economics at Harvard University, presented a paper at the annual meeting of the American Economic Association. The paper was

entitled, "Supply-Side Economics: Old Truths and New Claims."
Feldstein has a reputation as one of the finest scholars in the world.
Besides being a Harvard professor, he is the president of the National Bureau of Economic Research and was one of President Reagan's chairmen of the Council of Economic Advisers.

Feldstein's paper was a devastating attack on the supply-siders, or at least it seemed so. He concluded his paper by writing, "The experience since 1981 has not been kind to the claims of the new supply side extremists that an across-the-board reduction in tax rates would spur unprecedented growth, reduce inflation painlessly, increase tax revenue and stimulate a spectacular rise in personal saving. Each of those predictions has proven to be wrong."

I was fascinated. As far as I knew, Ronald Reagan had not claimed that a reduction in tax rates would increase tax revenue, nor had any of his economic advisers. I wrote Feldstein a letter and asked him to send me the names and citations that he used as a basis for his article. Nothing unusual about that. Scholars are always happy to exchange information that may be too detailed even for footnotes.

Five weeks went by before I got his reply. No wonder. He didn't have any sources for that part of his article. Feldstein simply *assumed* the charge he made against the supply-siders was correct, and built his entire thesis on the basis of an assumption snatched from the air. In his letter he explained lamely, "I doubt that any individual said all of the things I referred to. But I think that a combination of the *Wall Street Journal*, Art Laffer, Norman Ture, and Paul Craig Roberts must have said all of them. I don't have specific situations but I think a research assistant reading the editorial pages of the *Wall Street Journal* and the news stories on comments by those individuals would find ample examples."[12]

Astounding. That kind of casual research would earn a failing grade for any student in the country.

A little over a year later, I was glancing through an essay on supply-side economic theory. It was written by Walter S. Salant, a senior economist with an impeccable reputation for scholarly research, who since 1954, had been a fellow at the Brookings Institution. At the end of his essay Salant concluded, "What such policies cannot do and could never have been reasonably expected to do is to increase output and reduce inflationary pressures in a few years by more than trivial fractions. . . . The argument that such policies can do this in any short period—let alone *immediately* [italics added], as was claimed by some supply-siders—is not wrong in merely one link in the chain of reasoning connecting the premises and the conclusions but is wrong or questionable in almost every link." [13]

Hmmm. That was essentially one of the same basic arguments Feldstein had used over a year before. Maybe Dr. Salant could tell me who made that claim and when and what the exact words were. So I wrote a letter to him asking pretty much the same question I asked Feldstein. In less than two weeks I had the reply.

Dr. Salant didn't have any foundation for his work either. He wrote, apparently somewhat embarrassed, that "when I looked in my files for specific citations of statements that adoption of supply side policies would increase output very quickly, I was not able to find them. I probably discarded them." [14]

In 1987 Herbert Stein, then a senior fellow at the American Enterprise Institute in Washington, D.C., wrote a brief foreword for a book on Reagan's economic policies written by Michael Boskin of Stanford University. He stated that "in 1980 the Reagan campaign team was saying, or implying, that a large tax cut would raise the revenue." [15] Stein knew better. Back in 1984 he had written a book, *Presidential Economics,* in which he noted that Reagan had been advised by a distinguished group of economists in the 1980 campaign, and that they and Reagan clearly understood that lowering tax rates would not immediately raise government revenue. In Stein's own words, "the Reagan estimators . . . added an amount of revenue due to the additional growth to be caused by the Reagan tax cuts, which would rise to about 20 percent of the tax cut." [16]

Curious about his lapse of memory just three years later, I wrote Stein a letter and asked if he could tell me who the members of Reagan's 1980 campaign team were who had said something different and exactly what it was they had said. Stein replied promptly, avoiding the direct question I had put to him, and instead proffered a copy of a letter to the editor of the *Wall Street Journal*—from Jack Kemp in March 1980—that purportedly supported Stein's contention.

I read Kemp's letter. It said just the opposite, "Under some circumstances, cutting tax rates will increase revenue; under others, reduce it." [17] Herbert Stein couldn't have said it better.

Now I was really curious. Had some sort of collective irresponsibility crept into academic economists? Where was their normal passion for truth, where was their questioning, their probing, careful research? I began to read more carefully, looking for other evidence of false statements about Reagan's economic policy. It was everywhere.

On October 24, 1987 the august English magazine, *The Economist*, in a lengthy article on "Conservative Economics" stated bluntly (and wrongly) that "Mr. Reagan and the thinkers who influenced him . . . said that lower tax rates would cause not just a rise in output, but a rise so large that tax revenues would be higher than before."[18]

In early November, 1987, I came across a new book on economic policy by Alan S. Blinder, a professor of economics at Princeton University. For the scholarly, left-wing economist, his attack on the supply-siders was unexpectedly brutal and reckless. Referring to them as "a small, well-financed, and highly polemical group of politicians, journalists, and economists," he asserted that the "supply-siders armed themselves with neither theory nor evidence, just boldfaced assertions."[19] Sneering at the strawmen he concocted, Blinder wrote, "Concerned that large tax cuts will lead to huge budget deficits? Not to worry, said supply-siders. With income growing so rapidly, the expanding tax base will bring more money into the government coffers even at lower tax rates. Where taxes are concerned, down is up!"[20]

That is pretty humorous writing for an economist. It is also untrue. The scholar Blinder seems to be guilty of the very sin he falsely attributed to the supply-siders' "boldfaced assertions."

Feeling somewhat like Diogenes searching with a lantern in broad daylight for an honest man, I wrote my now familiar letter to Professor Blinder requesting the evidence on which he based his scholarly writings.

Within a few days I received a long reply. While admitting to "a certain amount of rhetorical flourish," he stubbornly insisted that he thought his "message is accurate nonetheless," and provided me with eight "examples" of "nonsense uttered by (my) associates." They ranged in quality from a 1980 quote by the social commentator George Gilder (who apparently did make such claims, but which unfortunately don't count because Gilder is neither an economist, nor did he ever advise Reagan on economic policy) to some unspecified references "to something by Jack Kemp in the Congressional Record back in 1977," which Blinder "confess(ed) to have never read."[21]

I corresponded and discussed this matter with him further and it soon became clear that he sincerely believed what he had written, in spite of the fact that he had never read any of the 1980 campaign documents, and could not provide any specific citations supporting his claims concerning either Reagan or his main economic advisers.

In November 1987 the proceedings of a European forum on the economic policy of the conservation revolution was published in London. Princeton University professor of economics, William Branson, flatly stated: "The Reagan policy was based on the theory that cutting tax *rates* would increase tax *revenue* thereby creating a budget surplus."[22] After making his false statement he concluded triumphantly that "The Reagan fiscal program . . . was not based on a clever political ploy; its foundation was incorrect economic analysis."[23]

Branson was not alone in his ignorance at the forum. Even his distinguished colleague, Robert Solow, a professor at the Massachusetts Institute of Technology and the winner of the 1987 Nobel Prize in Economics ($330,000), backed up the essence of what Branson said.

I was surprised because I knew Solow. I had studied under him at MIT in the early 1960s and, although he occasionally let his extreme left-wing political views interfere with his teaching, he was normally very careful. But not in Paris. Professor Solow, speaking with scathing contempt about "the Reagan people and other conservatives," asserted: "It is hardly credible that serious people believed those things, and I don't think they did. I think they said and say things like that in the same spirit that manufacturers make wildly vague claims for their products. It was PR from the word Go and remains PR."[24]

I decided not to write to Solow and Branson.

When eminent scholars from Harvard, Princeton, MIT, AEI, and Brookings make such consistently false charges, openly, to large audiences of their professional peers and not a peep is raised, there may be something more at work here than careless or shabby scholarship on the part of an individual professor or two.

One has to seriously entertain the possibility that academic economists as a group, a group which is heavily left-wing in the political proclivities of its members, has been driven into such an envious and resentful fury by Reaganomics, that they have, for a time, put aside their professional standards—and attacked Reagan's economic policies maliciously and deliberately with false and misleading statements. Perhaps there is a nicer explanation for this intellectual malpractice, perhaps they all meant well, but were just careless. Unfortunately, in the world of scholarship the result of both carelessness and lying is the same.

No wonder the national press got basic parts of the supply-side story wrong. Maybe someday, someone will unearth the definitive statements showing that the supply-siders made illogical, untrue statements regarding the effect of changes in tax rates. But until that happens, we will have to conclude that their critics have unfairly and carelessly maligned them.

The great myth of the supply-siders is that a handful of people, with few economic credentials, single-handedly persuaded Ronald Reagan to embrace a radical theory opposed by the economic establishment. It was touched off by an article on April 7, 1980, in the *Village Voice*, the weekly newspaper of the Left in New York City. Entitled "Worlds in Collision: The Battle for Reagan's Mind," it was written by two left-wing writers named Alexander Cockburn and James Ridgeway. The article was largely based on an interview with Jude Wanniski.

The thesis of the article was simple and wrong. According to Cockburn and Ridgeway,

"[The] battle for Reagan's mind is now on. On the one side are the forces of Jude Wanniski; Congressman Jack Kemp, Reagan's policy coordinator; and Professor Arthur Laffer, the theorist behind the 30 percent tax cut which Reagan is currently presenting as a campaign plank and which is the most seductive element in his appeal to the working class and middle class Democrats who could well propel the governor to victory in November.

"Opposed to this group are ranked such mainstream conservative Reagan supporters as Arthur Burns, Milton Friedman, Alan Greenspan, George Schultz [*sic*], and—more elusively—former Treasury Secretary William Simon. Along with many in Reagan's entourage such as Martin Anderson, domestic issues adviser, they see Reagan captured by zealots, or 'hard-line ideologues,' as *Business Week* terms the Wanniski group in a calculated onslaught this week. . . .

"The battle is substantive. Its most articulate spokesman-strategist among the wild men is Jude Wanniski. Wanniski, formerly of the *Wall Street Journal* and author of *The Way the World Works*, has been the most adroit propagandist for the ideas of Laffer and Professor Robert Mundell of Columbia. Wanniski was the guiding hand behind the Kemp-Roth tax-cut bill. He has advised Reagan. . . .

"The struggle rages—Reagan's old-time Sacramento gang and heavyweight pundits slugging it out with the hotheads."

This was all silly nonsense. Jack Kemp was not Reagan's policy coordinator; he was one of many valued part-time advisers. There was no battle for Reagan's mind on economic policy. Reagan's view had been formulated over a period of many, many years and by April 1980 he had long since drawn his own conclusions about the economy. Most importantly, his economic policy positions were strongly endorsed and supported by his key economic advisers— including Arthur F. Burns, Milton Friedman, Alan Greenspan, Paul McCracken, George Shultz, William Simon, and Murray Weidenbaum, as well as all of his senior campaign advisers.

To be sure, a significant part of Reagan's economic policy was the same policy view being touted by Wanniski, Kemp, Laffer, Mundell, Roberts, and others who focused the attention of economists on the tax aspect of that policy. And Wanniski, Kemp, and Laffer were among the hundreds of policy advisers Reagan accumulated during the course of his campaign. But there was no battle for Reagan's mind over economic policy.

Much of Wanniski's story was fiction. It set up an imaginary opposition to the economic policies Reagan already settled on, and held out the prospect of a great victory for this small band of renegade economists if Reagan should decide to follow their advice against the opposing advice coming from the large number of internationally distinguished economists who were advising him. The story was apparently designed to give full credit for Reagan's economic policies to people who could be dismissed by the establishment press as unqualified and inexperienced, to make it look as if

Reagan drew his economic policies from wild men who could be labeled as crazies.

It was a brilliant piece of journalism. It fit an old pattern that the left-wing press had used countless times before to discredit the policies of the growing right-wing forces in the United States. The strategy was simple. Pick the least credible representatives of policy views you oppose and then portray that person, and his or her views, as the essence of the policy position. What is reported may be accurate, but out of context it completely distorts the nature of the policy and the reputations of the people who support it.

In the long interview that was the heart of the article, the following exchange took place.

VILLAGE VOICE: Does Reagan really believe in supply side economics?

WANNISKI: Yes. Reagan loves the stuff. John Sears, before he left (he was fired by Reagan several months earlier), kept telling Kemp that he should spend more time on the campaign trail with Reagan, because whenever he spent a day or two with Reagan, Reagan came alive. When Kemp leaves, Reagan subsides. He is now at the point where he is getting better and better all the time.

VILLAGE VOICE: On economic policy then, it's basically you and Kemp?

WANNISKI: And Laffer.

VILLAGE VOICE: Is there an opposing camp?

WANNISKI: The opposing camp is an official board of advisers. It includes Arthur Burns, Milton Friedman, Casper *[sic]* Weinberger, George Schultz *[sic]*, Alan Greenspan. It's a force that has to be reckoned with. They are more or less in a position of arguing caution.

VILLAGE VOICE: You are the wild men?

WANNISKI: We are the wild men.

The *Village Voice* article was greeted by Reagan and his campaign aides with astonishment. It read like something out of a scandal sheet, not a fairly responsible left-wing newspaper. Nobody responded to its charges publicly. It all seemed too absurd to comment on. Even Wanniski's friends were appalled. Some months after the article appeared a close ally of Wanniski, Bruce Bartlett, a smart, young economist on the staff of the Congressional Joint Economic Committee wrote, "For months, Wanniski has been filling his newspaper columns with stories about the ongoing battle for Reagan's mind. Unfortunately, in early April he went too far in a long personal interview in the *Village Voice*. In this interview, Wanniski seemed to take credit for inventing the Laffer Curve, inventing the Kemp-Roth Bill, and taking Jack Kemp, an obscure Buffalo congressman, and making him a major national spokesman for tax reduction. He also made some amazing claims for what an across-the-board tax reduction would accomplish, saying it would reduce prostitution, pornography, drug use, and even abortion." [25] Arthur Laffer just shook his head and said he was "offended beyond belief." [26]

But bizarre as the Cockburn and Ridgeway article was, it did have two practical consequences.

First, Reagan and his campaign staff immediately dropped Wanniski. And, to the best of my knowledge, Wanniski never spoke to Reagan again, never again participated in the large groups of policy experts that Reagan met with regularly, and never played any role in the development and implementation of national economic policy after Reagan was elected president. It was too bad, because Wanniski had contributed to the economic part of the intellectual revolution that was beginning to sweep over the United States and much of the world. He should and could have continued to be a significant player, but he overreached. Instead of taking great satisfaction in what he contributed, he tried to take credit for things he had not done. Instead of accepting the fact that many of the finest economists in the world were supporting policies he agreed with, he conjured up a strawman opposition designed to make him look good at the expense of others. The net result was to injure himself with those who should have been his most loyal friends and strongest admirers.

Second, the myth of a great battle for Reagan's mind on the matter of economic policy took root and grew. The *Village Voice* article may have been false, but it had an enormous appeal for people who disliked and feared Reagan's political philosophy. The national media swallowed the story whole, and for many years small flashes and glimpses of the story were repeated and repeated. For a short time during the campaign I tried to privately disabuse reporters of the story's validity, but they liked the story, and many of them just smiled and repeated it anyway. Perhaps we should have put out a formal statement disavowing it, but the pressures of the presidential campaign soon overwhelmed that instinct and we went on to what we thought were more important things.

So the legend of the supply-siders grew. There were strong vested interests in keeping the myth alive. The stories that appeared in the national and international press describing Reagan's so-called infatuation with radical economic theories were damaging politically. A good part of the reason why the myth grew and continued was that those maligned by the myth, the group of economists and campaign advisers Reagan was listening to, were loathe to engage in a non-constructive debate over who was due credit for the new economic ideas.

On the other hand, those identified by the press as supply-siders, in particular, Wanniski, Laffer, and Kemp, benefited enormously from the blazing publicity. Wanniski and Laffer both ran private economic consulting firms and made a great deal of money from their notoriety, as dozens of clients signed up to get private advice and newsletters from the wild men who had, reportedly against total opposition from the economic establishment, created a new economics and then persuaded Ronald Reagan to accept it. Congressman Kemp rode his new reputation as one of the original supply-siders into a viable candidacy for the Republican presidential nomination.

Much of Jack Kemp's fame as a supply-sider was well deserved. He was the earliest and strongest political leader for tax cuts. But Kemp did not then have an overall economic program, and Reagan did not follow Kemp's advice over that of his other economic advisers. Part of the reason it appeared that Reagan was endorsing Kemp's economic policies, rather than agreeing with some of them, was the result of a political deal.

During the fall of 1979, as we were assembling Reagan's team of economic advisers, the political people in the campaign, led by John Sears, became increasingly concerned about the budding political campaign of Jack Kemp for the presidency. Kemp was only a congressman from the northern part of New York state. But he was an articulate conservative, nationally famous for having been the quarterback of a professional football team, the Buffalo Bills.

He was young and aggressive. He was gaining increasing support from the same bloc of voters that we were counting on to nominate Reagan. So he was a political threat to Reagan.

At that time Kemp and some of his key presidential campaign advisers—Jude Wanniski, Paul Craig Roberts, Arthur Laffer, and Irving Kristol—were becoming more and more enthusiastic about the virtues of a tax cut. Though fairly recent converts to the delights of tax rate reductions, they quickly grasped that not only was it good for the economy, it was also terrific politics. Kemp in particular realized that he needed a big, bold issue to propel him from the relative obscurity of Congress to the forefront of the national political stage. A major tax cut package was not only his best political opportunity, it was his only opportunity.

On the other hand, few thought that Kemp had a significant chance of winning the Republican party nomination in 1980. But he could have taken precious conservative votes away from Reagan, perhaps enough votes to ensure the nomination of Reagan's most serious rival, George Bush. Kemp couldn't win, but he could contribute to Reagan's defeat. Because of this political danger, John Sears, then chairman of Reagan's presidential campaign, began a series of meetings and negotiations with Kemp and his political advisers to persuade Kemp to drop his futile race and not jeopardize Reagan's chance of becoming the presidential nominee.

Kemp knew he couldn't win, but he also knew he had a semi-veto over Reagan's campaign, and he was not about to give that up. If Kemp could gain increased national exposure in return for his support of Reagan, it could be very valuable to him in a future run at the presidency. Kemp had a price for supporting Reagan, and the price was that Reagan endorse the specific tax plan he and his advisers embraced.

When Reagan and his political advisers heard the terms of the deal, they shrugged and essentially said, "Why not?" Reagan had already indicated support for a series of annual tax rate reductions as a part of his comprehensive economic plan. Why not give Jack Kemp's political future a boost by endorsing the Kemp-Roth tax proposal? After all, Reagan himself said many times that "there was no limit to what a man could achieve as long as he did not care who got the credit." And there was one final consideration. With Kemp's full political support behind him, Reagan immensely strengthened his own bid for the nomination.

So it all worked out. Reagan endorsed Kemp's tax proposal as part of a political deal and got Kemp's support. And Kemp gained tremendous public exposure that put him on the short list of Republican presidential hopefuls for 1988.

The simple idea that was supply-side economics, and that was an important part of President Reagan's economic program, proved to be lasting and durable. As the 1980s draw to a close, it has become part of the conventional economic wisdom in the United States, at least outside of the academic community, and is rapidly picking up new converts all over the globe.

Chapter Fourteen

REAGAN'S ADVISERS

The most important player on Ronald Reagan's economic team is Ronald Reagan. The person most responsible for creating the economic program that came to be known as Reaganomics is Reagan himself. For over twenty years he observed the American economy, read and studied the writings of some of the best economists in the world, including the giants of the free market economy— Ludwig von Mises, Friedrich Hayek and Milton Friedman—and he spoke and wrote on the economy, going through the rigorous mental discipline of explaining his thoughts to others.

Over the years he made all the key decisions on the economic strategies he finally embraced. He always felt comfortable with his knowledge of the field and he was in command all the way. As the only full-time economic adviser to Reagan during the presidential campaigns of 1976 and 1980, I was in a unique position. I could suggest economists to Reagan and he would meet with them. I could give him memoranda and articles and books and he would read them. I could give him facts and reasoning, and he would use them and act on them. But he rarely, if ever, relied solely on my personal judgments on economic policy. And for good reasons.

First, he had increasing access to an expanding group of the world's finest economists, the most profound economic theorists, including Nobel Prize winners, the best practicing business economists, the kind that commanded $10,000 and more for their daily consulting fees, and some of the most experienced people from the real world of national economic policy. There were former secretaries of the treasury, chairmen of the Council of Economic Advisers, and directors of the Office of Management and Budget.

I recall the first time he met with the full complement of his distinguished group of economic advisers in 1980. After a few introductory comments to them he said, "I'd like you to tell me what has to be done to restore the health of the economy. Don't worry about the politics of what has to be done. That's my job. I'll take care of that."

But as comfortable as he felt with the policy positions he developed over the years, he wanted to make sure he was right, and he understood the political importance of having the personal support of influential economists for those policies. So, as early as 1975, after I agreed to join his presidential campaign, I started a systematic effort to introduce the nation's best economists to Reagan. Most of them were selected from my personal file of leading policy experts I began collecting during Nixon's campaign in 1967. This was part of a more general effort to recruit an army of intellectuals to advise and counsel Reagan on the entire range of policy issues.

Reagan's first formal meeting with a group of economic experts took place on December 16, 1975, in Los Angeles. I called a number of leading economists at various universities and asked them if they would be willing to meet with him to discuss some of the important economic issues facing us. Ten were asked, nine agreed to advise him, and five attended the first meeting.

The nine charter members of Reagan's economic team were Milton Friedman (University of Chicago), C. Lowell Harriss (Columbia University), Hendrik Houthakker (Harvard University), Arthur Laffer (University of Chicago), J. Clayburn La Force (UCLA), Richard Muth (Stanford University), William Niskanen (Ford Motor Company), Ezra Solomon (Stanford University), and Murray Weidenbaum (Washington University).

The only one who declined my invitation was Marina von Neumann Whitman, a professor at the University of Pittsburgh who formerly served as a member of the Council of Economic Advisers under President Nixon. She told me she was probably going to be totally apolitical in 1976. Later, in 1976, I was told she did manage to find time to fly to Plains, Georgia, to consult with the Democratic presidential candidate, Jimmy Carter.

The five who came were Harriss, Laffer, La Force, Muth, and Niskanen. The meeting began at 10 A.M. in a small conference room of the Beverly Wilshire Hotel. Reagan sat at the head of a small, rectangular table. Down the left side of the table sat Muth, Laffer, and I. On the other side were Harriss, Niskanen, and La Force. Joining us in the small room were five other senior members of Reagan's growing campaign staff: Edwin Meese, Peter Hannaford, Lyn Nofziger, Richard Wirthlin, and Jeffrey Bell. The discussion lasted for the better part of two hours and covered a broad range of topics from inflation to deficits to a gold standard and taxes.

In my ten pages of handwritten notes, there is one brief reference to a point made by Arthur Laffer. "If you cut tax rates, revenues may go up. If you raise tax rates too much, income goes down." This is probably the first time Reagan was braced directly with the supply-side tax rate reduction idea.

During the 1968 presidential campaign, when I was in charge of policy research for Richard Nixon, I learned that policy advisers from the intellectual world could be a tremendous asset to a campaign. Organized into task forces, with a chairman responsible for writing and submitting a formal report of their collective recommendations, they did much more than provide general policy advice. The individual members of the task forces were usually willing to be consulted when necessary, day and night, by the candidate and his staff. Often, as questions suddenly developed on special issues, a quick phone call to one of the country's top experts would yield a reasonable answer in a few minutes. Much of their value lay hidden from the press as time after time they were able to provide small nuggets of information that stopped small policy problems from growing into major political embarrassments. Later, after Nixon won the election, we discovered that the cadre of policy advisers was a primary pool of talent for appointments to high-level government jobs. And finally, the very existence of a large group of distinguished intellectuals gave a powerful boost to the credibility of the candidate. In effect, those intellectuals were co-signing the ideas of the candidate.

In 1980 we drew on all that we learned from the use of issue task forces in past campaigns. The result was the largest and most distinguished group of intellectuals ever assembled for an American political campaign. Richard Allen organized the foreign and defense policy groups and I did the economic and domestic policy ones. While I was traveling on the campaign airplane, my deputy, Darrell M. Trent, who was a senior policy adviser, managed the economic and domestic policy task force effort at national headquarters.

Darrell Trent was one of the few people who played a significant role in both the Reagan and Nixon presidential campaigns. One of those people who always managed to get the job done on time, he was born in Kansas, went West to school and graduated from Stanford University. From 1981 to 1983 he served as the Deputy Secretary of Transportation. Besides being one of the country's leading political activists he was a Senior Research Fellow at the Hoover Institution, where he co-authored a book on international terrorism, and now runs a large corporation engaged in the disposal of toxic wastes. Trent is one of those rare Americans who has taken large bits of time from his business career, from making money, to write and engage in politics and serve in Washington.

The official press release on October 23, 1980, documented the extent of these policy task forces, "Governor Ronald Reagan today announced the completion of 23 domestic and economic policy task forces with 329 advisers who have been asked to address the important issues that will have to be faced by a new administration.

"These task forces join 25 foreign policy and defense working groups with 132 advisers that are examining, in detail, the major questions that relate to these two important areas." By the time the 1980 presidential campaign was over Reagan had 461 of America's top intellectuals advising him.

The forty-eight policy task forces each produced detailed reports on what a new administration should do on everything from welfare reform to missile defense, from economic policy to foreign relations. When Reagan took power in 1981, the battle plan for what to do with that power was largely written.

The American press scarcely noticed. Out on the campaign trail, press releases announcing the membership of Reagan's policy task forces were received with high, good humor. Most of the press didn't understand or care about them. They were not alone; most of Reagan's political staff didn't pay much attention to them either.

There was an air of bemused tolerance about all these intellectuals running around in a political campaign.

The press in other countries did not catch on at all. As a result, people around the world, some of them intensely interested in what might happen in the United States, were totally uninformed on a critical passage in American politics. A Frenchman or an Italian or a German, and certainly a Russian, got the clear impression from their local press that Reagan was running alone, perhaps supported by a small staff of right-wing reactionaries. It is no wonder that later, when Reagan began to act on his policy agenda, they were very surprised. "How is he doing this? He laughs, he smiles, and all this happens. He must be a very lucky man."

As the task forces were being set up, economic policy was given special attention. I broke down economic policy into six major areas: (1) tax policy, (2) spending control, (3) regulatory reform, (4) international monetary policy, (5) inflation, and (6) the federal budget. A separate policy task force was established for each area.

To get people to serve, I telephoned most of them personally. A few had been advising Reagan for years, but most had not. When I called them, the first thing I told them was that I was not asking for their political support. I just wanted to know if they would be willing to give their advice and counsel on economic policy to Reagan and provide him with suggestions on what he should do if elected. To many, this may seem like a fine distinction and de facto political support anyway, but it was important to many of the potential advisers. Most of them adopted a policy of providing advice freely to any political candidate who asked. Some of them, I suspect, would have willingly joined other candidates' policy task forces, if they were asked. But the other candidates did not seem to care about expert advice as much as Reagan did, and few were ever asked.

The six economic policy task forces were deliberately organized around the basic elements of Reagan's developing comprehensive economic program. Each one represented an important aspect of that policy. Then, to emphasize the comprehensive character of the new economic policy, I suggested we establish a premier campaign advisory group, which we named the Economic Policy Coordinating Committee, to advise Reagan on the formulation of an *overall* economic program, drawing on the work and advice of the six separate task forces. Its final goal was a new national economic strategy for the 1980s. There were thirteen members of that committee, including the chairman of all six task forces and some of the best known economists in the world.

The chairman of the coordinating committee was George Shultz. Shultz was one of the most respected economists in the country, with vast and varied experience in government. A former dean of the business school of the University of Chicago, Arthur Burns recommended him to Richard Nixon for secretary of labor in 1968. He then went on to become the director of the Office of Management and Budget and finally ended up serving as secretary of the treasury. Largely as a result of his fine work at the treasury, he was one of the few living Americans who enjoyed a great deal of respect from the government leaders and economists of other countries. At the time the Reagan campaign began he was teaching at the graduate school of business at Stanford and was well on his way to becoming a millionaire as the president of Bechtel, one of the world's largest construction companies.

Over the years Shultz had not been a great fan of Ronald Reagan's, and he supported Ford against Reagan during the primaries in 1976. In 1978 Shultz had not yet committed himself to any presidential candidate, so I suggested that Reagan meet with him. The years that I spent with Reagan convinced me that the best way to persuade someone of his virtues was to let that person talk to Reagan. It always seemed to work. Reagan was willing, so I telephoned Shultz.

"Sure," Shultz said, "I'd like to meet him. Do you think if he comes up here there's any chance that he would have dinner at my house. My wife and I would be honored to have him."

So, on the night of July 19, 1978, Reagan came to dinner at George Shultz's house, a stately, old, two-story wooden frame, white house in the faculty housing area of the Stanford campus. Shultz's guests included the Bechtels of the Bechtel Corporation, W. Glenn Campbell, the director of the Hoover Institution, Rita Ricardo-Campbell, Alan Greenspan, and a few economics professors from Stanford. Ed Meese, Peter Hannaford, my wife Annelise, and I accompanied Reagan. After dinner we gathered in the Shultz's spacious living room and for several hours had a wide-ranging, rather spirited discussion on national policy issues. Shultz was deeply impressed with Reagan and, though he did not support him publicly until 1980, during the months that followed we heard reports from influential people all over the country, and especially in the East, that Shultz was speaking very favorably of Reagan in private.

Several years later Shultz became Reagan's Secretary of State and was still serving in 1988. George Shultz will probably be most remembered for his role in engineering the nuclear arms reduction agreements with the Soviet Union that Reagan searched for so long, but he was also a key player in the 1986 tax reforms that reduced personal income tax rates to less than half of what they were when Reagan was elected.

There were twelve other members of Reagan's top economic advisory group in the presidential campaign of 1980. Six chaired issue task forces in various areas of economic policy: Arthur F. Burns (task force on international monetary policy), Alan Greenspan (task force on budget policy), Paul McCracken, former chairman of the Council of Economic Advisers (task force on inflation), Charles E. Walker, former deputy secretary of the treasury (task force on tax policy), Murray L. Weidenbaum (task force on regulatory reform), and Caspar Weinberger (task force on spending control). The other six members of the coordinating committee were: Milton Friedman, Michel T. Halbouty, former president of the American Association of Petroleum Geologists and chairman of our task force on energy policy, Jack Kemp, James T. Lynn, former director of the Office of Management and Budget, William E. Simon, former secretary of the treasury, and Walter Wriston, chairman of Citibank/Citicorp.

Counting all the economists on the task forces and the coordinating committee, Reagan had a grand total of 74 advisers on economic policy alone for the 1980 presidential campaign. It was quite a group. Their educational backgrounds included Harvard, Princeton, Dartmouth, Yale, Berkeley, Stanford, MIT, and the University of Chicago. In size, in the economic reputation and government experience of its members, it was unmatched.

Together, the 74 advisers played an important role in helping Reagan develop his economic policy during the campaign. Later, many were appointed to high government positions where they helped implement that policy. These appointments included the chairman of the board of governors of the Federal Reserve (Alan Greenspan), a justice of the Supreme Court (Antonin Scalia), a secretary of state (George Shultz), a secretary of defense (Caspar Weinberger), a deputy secretary of defense (William Howard Taft,

IV), a director of the Office of Management and Budget (James Miller), a deputy director of OMB (Edwin Harper), two chairmen of the Council of Economic Advisers (Murray Weidenbaum and Beryl Sprinkel), two members of the CEA (William Niskanen and Thomas Moore), an undersecretary and the assistant secretary for economic policy in the Department of the Treasury (Norman Ture and Paul Craig Roberts), an ambassador to Germany (Arthur F. Burns), and the head of the Congressional Budget Office (Rudolph Penner). One campaign task force member, Professor James Buchanan, was awarded the Nobel Prize for economics in 1986.

Reagan himself had majored in economics at Eureka College in Illinois. And while he never had any illusions of knowing more about economics than his growing band of advisers, he felt very confident about his own knowledge of the basics. Anne Edwards, Reagan's biographer, said of his college career, "His memory and his ear for words got him through English, French, and history. But economics was an instinctive science for him. He understood the more complicated theses without a great deal of studying."[1]

Watching and listening to him in meeting after meeting with some of the economic greats of our time reminded me of a small piece of advice given to me by my own doctoral thesis adviser, Professor Eli Shapiro, as I prepared for my final examinations in economic theory at MIT in 1962. Several weeks before examinations he said, "If I were you I wouldn't review any more journal articles or notes from your advanced courses. Go home and find the economic textbook you used for your first course in economics when you were a college freshman, and read that. You will be forgiven if you don't know some fine point of the latest twist in the theory, but you won't pass if you make any mistake on the basics." I took his advice, and he was right.

Reagan did not know the latest nuances of economic theory, but he had his basics down as well as any of his economic advisers. Reagan graduated from college in 1932, president of his senior class.[2] The economics he was taught was the old classical variety, straight from the works of Adam Smith, Alfred Marshall, Irving Fisher, Eugene Boem-Barwek, David Ricardo, and Jean Baptiste Say. John Maynard Keynes had not yet written the *General Theory*. Few complicated mathematical models were used for the exposition of economic theory; instead, the old economists relied on words, using the English language to explain basic principles.

The essence of the comprehensive economic program Reagan has pursued in the 1980s is derived from the classical economic principles he learned almost sixty years ago as a young man. He refined and honed his ideas into a modern, national economic policy with the assistance of his advisers.

As he shaped his program during the 1980 campaign and in the transition after he won, Reagan talked to many people and sought their views. And many, many more people sought to impose their economic views on Reagan as he came closer and closer to becoming the fortieth president of the United States, and especially after his election. But of all these advisers and would-be advisers, there were eight people who, I observed, he seemed to rely on most heavily when it came to economic advice.

Perhaps those with the most influence were Milton Friedman, Alan Greenspan, and William Simon. Friedman lived in California, Reagan's home state, and Greenspan and Simon were both New Yorkers, from Wall Street. Reagan was especially taken with Milton Friedman. He just could not resist Friedman's infectious enthusiasm and Reagan's eyes sparkled with delight every time he engaged in a dialogue with him.

Of the thousands of people who have helped shape the new intellectual forces sweeping around the world, Milton Friedman probably has had the greatest influence. By his articles, lectures, books co-authored with his brilliant wife, Rose, and television series, Friedman has had an enormous impact on the people's changing view of the nature of a free society. The breadth and depth of this influence cannot be explained by just the words he wrote and spoke. A lot of it can only be explained by his extraordinary personality.

To meet Friedman is to encounter a ball of controlled energy. The alert, quick eyes are friendly. At first he listens quietly, intensely. As long as he totally agrees he listens, but that usually isn't for long. At the first sign of the slightest break in your logic, or your facts, he pounces with a bewildering array of questions, statements, and relentless logic. And it's all done in such a friendly, earnest way that even the intellectually shredded thoroughly enjoy the encounter. Friedman is the intellectual's intellectual. He makes people think, and he almost always does it in such a way that it gives them pleasure.

It is a rare skill. There are many people who are contemptuous of those less intelligent than themselves. He is not. There are others with finely honed critical skills that can devastate a colleague in minutes, and create an enemy for life. He does not. There are many intellectuals who care only for the abstractions they glory in, not the people the abstractions represent. Friedman is driven more by what ideas and policies do to and for people than by the theoretical beauty of an argument.

Alan Greenspan has probably been a key player in more Republican presidential campaigns, and Republican party platforms, and Republican administrations than any other economist in the country. During his campaign days he was a private economic consultant in New York City, one of the highest paid in the country. A tall bachelor in his early sixties, with as few gray hairs as Ronald Reagan, he first became involved in national politics during the 1968 Nixon campaign. A professional musician (clarinet) before he began to practice economics, he is widely known and respected for his grasp of current economic conditions as well as economic theory. He has a special knack for translating economic theory into crisp, clean ideas that can be used in political campaigns. Alan was always the first one I called to join me on the campaign plane when I needed help, and he always came, and provided invaluable advice. Now, as chairman of the board of governors of the federal reserve system, he must eschew politics.

William E. Simon is a blunt talking man who believes passionately in economic and political freedom. As secretary of the treasury from 1974 to 1977 he always seemed to be two steps in front of his colleagues, urging them on to greater efforts to control federal spending, reduce taxation, and relax government regulations. Perhaps his most notable achievement was his 1978 book, *A Time for Truth*, essentially a call to arms to "avert the threatening collapse of our political and economic order."[3] Few books on economics sell well, and the first printing of Simon's book was only 10,000 copies. But it caught the imagination of the American public and soon had sold 150,000 copies in hardcover and 2.4 million copies in paperback. Simon was one of those few economists who were to the right of Reagan, and Reagan valued his advice and counsel.

The remaining five of Reagan's big eight economic advisers were Arthur F. Burns, Paul McCracken, George Shultz, Murray Weidenbaum, and Caspar Weinberger. As he prepared for the presidency, Reagan relied on a wide range of economic advisers where specific facts and particular programs were concerned, but when it came to receiving counsel on general economic policy strategy, he invariably turned to the big eight.

What later became known as Reaganomics came directly out of the heart of the Republican economic establishment of the United States. It represented the thinking of some of the best economic minds in the world.

Chapter Fifteen

THE GREAT EXPANSION. . . . . . AND THE UNFINISHED BUSINESS

It was the greatest economic expansion in history. Wealth poured from the factories of the United States, and Americans got richer and richer. During the five years between November 1982 and November 1987 more wealth and services were produced than in any like period in history.

There were 60 straight months of uninterrupted economic growth, the longest string of steady peacetime growth in national production since we first began to keep such statistics in 1854.[1]

Close to fifteen million new jobs were created. It was the greatest five-year employment growth in U.S. history. At the end of 1982 the number of Americans working was 100,697,000. Five years later 115,494,000 were working.[2]

The production of wealth in the United States was stupendous. Reagan's run from the end of 1982 to the end of 1987 produced just a hair under $20 trillion dollars of goods and services, measured in actual dollars, unadjusted for inflation or changes in the quality of goods and services. The sum is so large that the value of the treasure is perhaps beyond comprehension. A million dollars is a lot of money. There are a thousand millions in every billion, and a thousand billions in every trillion, so basically a trillion is a million squared. Twenty of them is a lot.[3]

By the end of 1987 the United States was producing about seven and one-half times more every year than it produced the last year John F. Kennedy was president. By then we were producing 65 percent a year more than when Jimmy Carter left office in January 1981.[4] The U.S. economy is now an economic colossus of such size and scope that we have no effective way to describe its power and reach.

The numbers are stunning.

Yet one thing should be made clear. The Reagan economic expansion of the 1980s was not a perfect expansion; we shall never have one. In particular, the federal deficits we ran were too high, too many federal regulations lay unreformed, the trade deficit is worrisome, and there are dozens of details of the economy that urgently need attention, as any economist will tell you.

In fact, the Reagan economic expansion may not even have been the best economic expansion in history. Every economic expansion must be judged by many criteria: by the number of jobs created, the wealth produced, the steadiness of the production, the distribution of the benefits, the effect on tax rates, on inflation, on interest rates, on government regulation, and the impact on personal liberty. But if we use the word great in the literal sense of being large in size then, by the primary criteria we have used in the past to judge the size of an economic expansion—jobs created, wealth produced, constancy of increasing production—then the five-year economic run that produces 14.8 million new jobs, $20 trillion of new wealth, and does so steadily over a period of 60 months is, by that definition, the greatest economic expansion in history.

The results of the Reagan expansion were felt everywhere. Although personal income tax rates fell dramatically (the highest marginal tax rate fell from 70 percent to 28 percent, the largest percentage reduction in tax rates in U.S. history) federal tax revenue soared. As more people went to work and kept more of what they made, the amount they produced leapt upward. The total receipts of the federal government were $618 billion in 1982. Five years later, in 1987, those receipts totaled $1,016 billion, an increase of $398 billion.[5] That's almost a billion dollars a year extra to spend for every single congressman.

The first to feel the economic transfusion was the military. Fulfilling his presidential campaign pledge of defense first, President Reagan invested heavily in military manpower and defense weapons. In 1980, the year before he became president, the United States spent $134 billion on national defense. In 1987, the seventh year of Reagan's presidency, the United States spent $282 billion. That was an additional $148 billion, making the annual total more than twice as much as we were spending for national security before Reagan took office.

During the first seven years that Reagan was president of the United States he spent over $1.5 trillion on national defense, a staggering amount by anyone's standards, but an impossible one if it was not for the spectacular performance of the economy. The economy pays the bills.

There were other major reorderings of public spending priorities under Reagan. The best way to cut through the fog of explanation that involves some of the most exquisite political combat in the world is to simply look at the dollar outlay numbers for different years and compare them. How much did the federal government spend for certain public services before Reagan became president? How much is being spent for them after Reagan has worked his will, to the extent he could, for seven full years?

It is commonly believed that federal spending on social welfare programs was slashed during the presidency of Ronald Reagan. It is not true. Spending on social welfare programs increased surely and steadily, perhaps more than Reagan would have liked, but nonetheless it did increase. And this fact dramatizes a little-appreciated fact in American political life. The real power of the purse, the power to spend or not to spend, lies with Congress.

A president may be able to influence spending up in some areas and down in others, but ultimately he must get congressional approval for every nickel. On the other hand, he can somewhat restrain the spending impulses of Congress by the judicious use of the veto power. But the veto power can be used only sparingly. Often its effect is muted by the huge catch-all spending bills sent to the president for signature, which force him to veto the good programs along with the bad if he wishes to veto at all. In the final analysis, Congress can always, with a two-thirds vote, cheerfully override any presidential veto.

So while President Reagan cannot and should not be given full credit for all the spending that did take place, he also should not be blamed for cutting federal spending that was not cut.

The biggest percentage change in spending priorities came in the agricultural sector. As they have proved in country after country around the world, farmers are the champion lobbyists of all time, getting a large share of the public purse. In 1980 the federal government paid U.S. farmers and ranchers $8.8 billion. After seven years of having a president who prides himself on being a rancher, the United States was doling out over $31 billion a year—a 252 percent increase, far higher than the rate of increase of military spending.

But high as the percentage increase in public spending was for agriculture, the really big money went into social welfare programs. Reaganomics turned the economy into a money-making machine that allowed him to preside over the largest increases in social welfare spending of any country in history. In 1980 the United States spent just under $174 billion a year for the large social welfare programs—social security, medicare, and health—and by 1987, annual spending on these programs had increased by $145 billion a year to a total of over $319 billion a year, an 84 percent increase.

The Reagan administration gets a lot of credit for increasing national defense spending but, somehow, what happened in the huge area of spending for social security, medicare and health seems to have been neglected, benignly. In 1980 we spent $40 billion a year more on these programs than on national defense. After seven years of Reagan, after the largest military spending streak of any country in history, the United States is still spending $37 billion a year more on social security, medicare and health programs than it is on national defense.

The program receiving the next biggest spending increase under Reagan was welfare. Spending for the poor was just over $86 billion a year in 1980. By 1987 President Reagan had largely done on a national level what he did as governor of California—tried hard to get people off the welfare rolls who could take care of themselves, and then supported substantial increases in welfare spending. In 1987 federal spending for the poor was up by over $38 billion a year to a total of almost $125 billion a year—a 44 percent increase under Reagan.

Not everything went up. Federal spending on natural resources and the environment was maintained at the same dollar level it was during President Carter's last year in office—almost $14 billion a year. And federal spending on some programs went down. Cutting back programs he thought were ineffective or wasteful, President Reagan reduced spending in a few program areas—education, training, employment and social services, community and regional development, commerce and housing credit, and energy. Spending for all these programs totaled almost $63 billion in 1980. By 1987 Reagan trimmed them back some 22 percent, to just over $49 billion a year.

But on the whole, President Reagan set spending records right and left. Holding to his many pledges over the years to strengthen social security, the health care system, and welfare, and to build up our national defenses, he directed massive increases in social welfare and welfare spending and for national defense. That's where most of the money went.

There were other things that happened during this unprecedented economic expansion. Thrashing the conventional wisdom of economics, inflation plummeted as the economy rolled on. From high double digits in 1980, inflation dropped to low single digits and stayed there. Interest rates dropped. And the stock market boomed, setting new historical highs nearly every week, it seemed, in the optimistic summer of 1987.

But past expansions don't guarantee future ones. The almost unbelievable economic surge of the earlier 1980s may or may not continue in the late 1980s and early 1990s. The stock market may rise or it may fall. Nobody ever really knows.

Most of what we accomplished in this decade was possible because of economic growth, the main fuel for the spending engine, but we also had a little help from others. From 1980 through the end of 1987, President Reagan borrowed $1 for every $5 he spent, so that the national debt increased by $1.2 trillion dollars. The United States was one of the best credit risks in the world, people pressed money on us, and we obliged, borrowing easily, quickly, and almost guiltlessly. But credit carries with it danger and risk. Borrowing the trillion plus dollars may have been the smartest thing we ever did, but we will soon have to cut back our lust for borrowing.

There are still many problems. The federal deficit is too large. Our international trade deficit is too high. The huge debt overhanging the third world is a financial threat. The irresponsible call for protectionism is growing, although the historic October 1987 trade agreement between the United States and Canada, calling for virtually free trade by the year 2000, is a stunning step in the right direction.

Whether we can maintain the economic miracle that continues to unfold in front of us will perhaps depend largely on three things: (1) whether we can hang onto the economic policy reforms we have won so far, keeping tax rates low, government regulations sparse, and continuing to move in the direction of freer trade; (2) whether we can control the growth of federal spending, likely only with the passage of a balanced-budget amendment to the Constitution; and (3) whether we can move steadily in the direction of sounder money, toward a greater role for gold.

On Friday, May 22, 1987, at 10 o'clock in the morning I received a telephone call in my office at the Hoover Institution. My assistant told me it was the White House operator calling. Getting a telephone call from the White House puts your senses on full alert. Even though I knew that hundreds of people who work for the president place their calls through the White House operator, it didn't prevent me from thinking, "Maybe this time it is the president." It wasn't. Instead it was a young White House assistant named Karen Fuller. She worked for Tom Griscom who worked for Howard Baker who was President Reagan's new chief of staff.

Baker, who took over a few months earlier, after President Reagan fired Donald Regan, was a political heavyweight in Washington. A world-class amateur photographer, Baker was a man of unquestioned integrity and uncommon political sense. While not as conservative as Ronald Reagan, his many years as majority leader of the Senate gave him a keen sense of the importance of sound fiscal policy. On basic economic policy matters he was as solidly conservative as Reagan.

Karen Fuller had an odd request. "Would it be possible," she asked, "to get a copy of the policy paper you wrote on the idea of an economic bill of rights?" Fuller was three long steps removed from President Reagan, but I knew how the White House worked and took her request seriously. Griscom and Baker earlier in the day flew with President Reagan to Florida where he spoke to honor the thirty-seven American sailors killed when an Iraqi missile struck the USS STARK, a Navy frigate on patrol in the Persian Gulf. On the way back to Washington, aboard Air Force One, Griscom placed an air-to-ground telephone call to Fuller. Griscom almost certainly would not have made such a call unless he was responding to something that had Howard Baker's approval, and Howard Baker would not be looking for something that would not be of interest to President Reagan. So I told Fuller, "Sure, I'll send you a copy today by Federal Express and you'll have it tomorrow morning."

There was silence for a few seconds and then she said, "But I need it today. They want it when Air Force One lands in Washington this afternoon." I felt a rush of empathy for her, remembering all the times when seemingly impossible demands were made on me by a presidential candidate or a president.

I was surprised at the urgent need for a copy of a three-year-old essay on national economic policy but, remembering what it was like to work in the White House, I didn't question her. Instead I promised to somehow deliver a copy to the White House within the next few hours. After several phone calls my assistant, Brenda McLean, located one in the library of the American Enterprise Institute in Washington and arranged to have it copied and delivered to Griscom's office in the White House before his plane landed.

What they were looking for was a twenty-two page essay entitled "An Economic Bill of Rights," which I wrote in 1984. The essay was a longer, fuller explanation of an idea I first proposed to Reagan back in August 1979. The initial nine-page draft of Reagan's economic program, written over six months before the first presidential primary in 1980, contained both short- and long-term economic policies. Most of the long-term prescriptions were summed up toward the end of that draft in a section called an "Economic Bill of Rights." It was to be a single amendment to the Constitution with five sections:

Section 1. Limit the amount the federal government can spend.
Section 2. Require the federal budget to be balanced.
Section 3. Prohibit the imposition of wage and price controls.
Section 4. Establish a line-item veto power for the president.
Section 5. Require a two-thirds vote of Congress on all major spending bills.

However, as the 1980 presidential campaign rolled on and we discussed the entire economic policy plan with some of the most astute economists and politicians in the country, it soon became clear that the economic trouble we were in early in 1980 was so serious, and the pessimism of the voters so deep, that we had to focus on what could be done in the short term, on what a new president could reasonably be expected to do upon taking office.

Constitutional amendments could be enormously powerful tools for making major, long-term changes in economic policy, but few people in 1980 were putting much stock in promises that would require a two-thirds vote of both the Senate and the House, to say nothing of then gaining approval by the legislatures of thirty-eight states before any amendment could take effect. First things first. If Reagan was going to win the presidential election he was going to have to propose a set of economic policies that were doable, now, as well as being sound.

So purely for political reasons, all the long-term elements of Reagan's original economic plan were temporarily put aside, and all attention was focused on the short-term elements—on tax-rate reduction, spending control, regulatory reform, a stable, predictable monetary policy, and economic policy constancy. It was these short-term elements of the original plan that eventually became known as Reaganomics.

But President Reagan never forgot those long-term elements, several of which he considered essential to achieving a permanent, stable economic prosperity. His favorites were constitutional amendments that would (1) require a balanced budget, and (2) give the president line-item veto authority.

Ever since this country was founded, Congress has jealously guarded its power to send the president large appropriations packages, often forcing him to accept spending proposals he does not favor in order to get the ones he does favor. The president should have the power to pick and choose, to veto any spending program that he opposes, no matter how small. Under current arrangements, the president must submit his budget proposals to the Congress, which can then add or delete as it wishes. What it deletes cannot be put back by the president, but deletions are rare these days. The Congress is much better at adding to the budget, and when the additions to line items in the budget are sent back to the president in several large appropriations packages, it is impossible for him to veto relatively small items without vetoing the entire appropriation.

With line-item veto authority, the president could veto specific additions to any part of his budget. The only way Congress could put these deletions back in would be by the normal two-thirds vote necessary to override any presidential veto.

Again and again during his presidency, Reagan pleaded the urgency and import of a balanced-budget amendment to the Constitution. In numerous campaign statements, in both acceptance speeches at the Republican national conventions in 1980 and 1984, in six of seven State of the Union messages, in two national radio addresses, in the Economic Report of the President, and in both his inaugural addresses, he clearly and repeatedly made the passage of a balanced-budget amendment to the Constitution of the United States one of his top policy priorities.

But all to no avail.

Perhaps no revolution ever finishes. Every major part of it is constantly evolving, changing. Reagan's economic policy is no exception. Crafting an economic policy that will ensure steady, reliable growth was only begun with the Reaganomics of the 1980s. Until and unless we can control the powerful spending machine of the federal government our economic prosperity will be forever threatened. The stock market crash of 1987 was one potent reminder of the fact that no economy is invincible and will and can stand only so much fiscal abuse.

Today it is widely believed that federal spending is out of control. That, like many other pieces of conventional wisdom, is wrong.

It is true that we are running unprecedented deficits, on the order of $150 to $200 billion a year, as far into the future as we can reasonably see. It is true that the combined federal spending for national defense, social welfare programs, and interest on the national debt far exceeds the taxing capacity of our country. And it is true that there is much anguished wringing of hands over the fact that apparently nothing can be done about it. It looks like the budget is out of control.

But it really isn't.

The amount of money the federal government spends and the amount of money it raises by taxing us, and the deficits it runs by spending more than it raises in taxes, are all the result of careful, studied decisions taken with full knowledge of the economic and political consequences.

Federal budget deficits don't just happen or grow like Topsy. They are made with loving care in Washington.

Quite a few people bemoan what they see happening in Washington and say to me, "If they only knew what their policies are going to do."

Let me assure you. They know. The people in Washington— congressmen, senators, the president, White House aides, cabinet heads, and high-ranking bureaucrats—all those who have the final responsibility for causing us to repeatedly borrow upwards of $200 billion a year, they all know. They are easily the best-informed people in the country on matters of national economic policy. The amount of accurate, detailed information available for their use is awesome. They admittedly don't know everything, or even all they would like to know, but they know far more than those who are not in policymaking positions.

Then why are we running a triple-digit billion dollar deficit when everyone knows that large, sustained deficits will lead to economic disaster? Why don't we adopt responsible fiscal and monetary policies and balance the budget?

Well, we don't because those with the real power to decide how much we will spend it on, have consciously and deliberately decided to unbalance the federal budget. Their reason is simple and clear. The political consequences of adopting policies that would bring federal spending into line with revenue and balance the budget are believed to be far more painful than piling up the deficits.

Under our current political arrangements the real culprit in federal spending is the Congress of the United States. The U.S. Constitution expressly gives only the Congress the power "to lay and collect taxes . . . to borrow money on the credit of the United States . . . and to coin money." And, most importantly, it says, "No money shall be drawn from the treasury, but in consequence of appropriations made by law," and only the Congress makes laws. The president may propose the initial spending plan, the federal budget, but it is the Congress that disposes, that shapes, and approves the final spending plans.

The major economic problem we face today, the unfinished

part of the economic revolution that Reagan began, is the control and limitation of federal spending.

Federal spending continues to be the one element of United States fiscal policy that endangers future prosperity. Everyone knows it is wrong, everyone knows it is bad, but it rolls on unabated. The reason is simple. For a politician, being able to spend $200 billion extra a year on popular programs such as national defense and social welfare, and to be able to do it without doing the unpopular thing of raising people's taxes, to instead pay for this current largesse with borrowed money, is so compellingly attractive politically, that the current institutions of our political system are unable to withstand the power of the special economic interest groups who benefit.

The only way we are going to deal with that problem is to devise new institutional means to control and limit the U.S. Congress. And there is only one effective means available to us to do that—the Constitution. The founding fathers of this country never dreamed that the United States would ever become the economic colossus it has grown to be, never envisaged the enormous political power of economic special interest groups. But they were wise enough to recognize that they could not foresee the future, and that is why they built a mechanism into the Constitution for changing it, a difficult, hard-to-use mechanism that ensures that only the most important, most prudent changes will ever be made.

Time and time again President Reagan, as have many presidents before him, sent budgets to the U.S. Congress to limit and control federal spending. Time and time again, the Congress has rebuffed those plans, and substituted levels of spending they, and they alone, considered appropriate. But how does one go about forcing our elected congressmen and senators to take responsible positions on fiscal policy? We can reason with them, plead with them, exhort them, and we will have the same effect that we have had in the past—a negligible effect. The structure of economic interest groups in this country has produced a fiscal stalemate. Our political institutions are unable to override the combined political power of Americans with special economic interests, even though taking the national point of view would benefit almost all of us. The current rules of the economic political game make it impossible.

It is similar to the old economic example of six people who go out to dinner and beforehand agree to split the bill evenly among themselves regardless of what any individual orders. Given these rules, each diner has a powerful incentive to order the most desirable, most expensive dish on the menu, even though the result will be a bill that will exceed what any one of them wishes to pay. The solution to the problem, of course, is to change the rules—to require each to pay only for what he or she orders.

The same thing is true on the national economic scene. We need to change the spending rules. A balanced-budget amendment to the Constitution would do that. It would force Congress to balance the budget, to make the painful political choices among spending priorities and taxes. They would no longer have the option to borrow money freely to satisfy their current political needs. They would have to do the right thing. And, after all, that is why we honor them by electing them to high public office, that is why we compensate them handsomely with large salaries and expense accounts and huge personal staffs.

Politicians do not act in fiscally irresponsible ways because they are bad people. They act that way because the rules of the economic game are such that to act responsibly and vote for fiscal responsibility is, in effect, a vote for political suicide.

The debate on fiscal responsibility has been raging in the United States since the 1970s. It is still not settled. It is an unfinished part of the revolution, the unfinished business of the economy. Over the years I have become reluctantly convinced that if we really want a reliable economic policy, one that we can count on in the years ahead, we are going to have to hammer it into the Constitution of the United States. Like certain civil liberties, some economic powers are too important to entrust to elected officials and must be retained by the people themselves.[6]

And that is why I was so excited when the call came from the White House in May 1987. Three weeks later, on July 3, 1987, I understood the urgency behind the request for a copy of my old essay. The day before the Fourth of July holiday, standing on the steps of the Jefferson Memorial, President Reagan formally proposed adding an economic bill of rights to our Constitution. His proposal was broader and more sweeping than what I had proposed in my essay, but it did contain the most crucial elements: amendments to the Constitution that would (1) require a balanced budget, and (2) give the president line-item veto power. It took over six years but finally President Reagan went to the nation with a new policy program aimed at changing the basic institutional structure of government with regard to the making of economic policy.

Beyond its importance to our country, the concept is also an interesting example of an idea in transition, an idea that may or not become national policy. Born in the crucible of the 1980 presidential campaign, drawing upon the past thinking of many intellectuals who struggled with the problem of federal spending, it is still being vigorously debated. It has not yet passed into law, but it also has not faded away. The question of how to control federal spending and eliminate the federal deficit promises to be a major issue in the upcoming 1988 presidential campaign. Already at least two candidates, Senator Paul Simon on the Democratic side and Senator Robert Dole on the Republican side, have made it part of their campaigns.

It is not yet politically feasible. But then, when something *is* politically feasible, it almost immediately becomes national policy. The art of politics, and much of the fun and fascination of it, is to persuade enough people of the merits of a cause so that is does become politically feasible. If nothing else, it will be interesting to watch the future policy path of the balanced budget amendment unfold.

President Reagan has now laid down the agenda for that future policy debate. In his July 3, 1987, speech to the nation, he summed up his case by saying, "The centerpiece of the Economic Bill of Rights, the policy initiative we launch today, is a long overdue constitutional amendment to require the Federal Government to do what every family in America must do, and that is to live within its means and balance its budget.

"Be assured, I will again ask Congress to submit a balanced budget amendment to the States. And if the Congress will not act, I will have no choice but to take my case directly to the States."[7]

Thomas Jefferson would have approved. In a letter written to a friend, John Taylor, on November 26, 1798, Jefferson lamented what he believed to be the most serious flaw in our Constitution, adopted eleven years earlier. Wistfully he wrote, "I wish it were possible to obtain a single amendment to our Constitution. I would be willing to depend on that alone for the reduction of the administration of our government of the genuine principles of its Constitution: I mean an additional article, taking from the federal government the power of borrowing."[8]

If we do what Jefferson wanted in 1798 and what Reagan asked for in 1987, we will leave to our children a precious legacy—an economic prosperity enabling us to pay for the national defense necessary to keep us free, allow us to care decently for those who are not able to care for themselves, and provide new jobs and steadily increasing incomes to all who can work.

Five

Reagan in the White House

Reagan's management style is unique, making it possible for him to achieve legendary changes in economic policy and nuclear weapons strategy, magically and seemingly without effort. But it is a style with dangerous flaws that were masked until the Iran-Contra affair exposed them and nearly destroyed his presidency. It is a high-risk style; not deliberately so, but one that is his by instinct. When it works, it is spectacular. When it fails, it is also spectacular.

Chapter Sixteen

GETTING READY

In early November 1968, a few days after Richard Nixon was elected president, the deputy campaign manager, Peter Flanigan, eagerly opened about seven or eight big cardboard boxes, each stuffed with lists and résumés of people suggested for appointment to high government office. They were very important files. Some of these people would become the heart and soul of the new administration, the Republican troops who would take over the U.S. government and implement the policies that Nixon had campaigned and won on.

But when Flanigan and a few others from the campaign began reading through the neatly typed lists of suggested names and examined some of the accompanying résumés, the joy of winning and the anticipated pleasure of staffing the government with people who shared the political values we all worked so hard for over the years turned quickly to shocked despair. We could hardly believe what we were seeing. Most of the people on the lists were already in their jobs, or were Democrats or Independents. Many of them would have been excellent appointments if Hubert Humphrey, Nixon's liberal Democratic opponent, had won.

The staffing work was a disaster. The day after the boxes were opened there were hurried, secretive consultations among the top officials of the campaign and with Nixon. Then all the personnel recommendations, painstakingly and expensively accumulated during the campaign, were thrown out. Temporarily, the boxes were stashed in a bathtub in one of the rooms in the hotel we were using for transition headquarters; later they just disappeared. A week after the election, with just ten weeks before the inauguration of the new administration, the staff started over, from nothing, to find thousands of qualified people and match them up with the proper jobs.

The roots of the personnel disaster reached far back to the beginning of the campaign. Nixon rejected numerous recommendations, including a memo from me, to start preliminary planning on the long and difficult task of identifying several thousand highly qualified, willing men and women to fill the key policy-making positions if he should win the election. Nixon's reasoning was simple. His energies and efforts were focused totally on gaining the nomination. He was very skeptical of anything that would divert the resources of the campaign from that primary goal, whether it was staff or money or his time.

In fact, none of the top campaign staff had thought very much about what to do if he won the nomination, let alone the presidency. That was driven home to me when, a few days after he won the nomination, I attended a high-level campaign strategy meeting at our temporary headquarters in Newport Beach, California. For over a year I directed the research and policy development efforts of the campaign. I was anxiously awaiting to hear what our campaign strategy was going to be for the general election campaign so I could focus our efforts to support that strategy. I don't remember the exact words that John Mitchell, who was campaign manager, used to open the meeting but the thrust of them was "Well, we've got the nomination. Now let's figure out what to do to win the election."

At the time I was shocked, but in retrospect the lack of planning may not have been so unwise. Many people who run for the presidency forget that first you must get the party's nomination. Nixon did not forget. And the contest was so close you could argue that if he diverted a substantial part of the campaign resources to planning how to take over the government he might never have had a chance to use those plans. As it turned out, he won the presidency by one of the slimmest margins of the twentieth century.

But finally, in spite of Nixon's reluctance to plan ahead, he did listen to two of his close friends in the early summer of 1968. One of them was Donald Kendall, the president of PepsiCo, Inc. He strongly urged that Nixon put a friend of his, Dr. Glenn Olds, in charge of staff planning if he won. The other friend, Leonard Garment, a partner in Nixon's law firm, supported the idea and arranged to have Olds fly out to Wyoming to meet personally with Nixon. Nixon promptly approved him, probably because he didn't think it was that important and he didn't want to say no to his friends. It was one of the worst pieces of advice that Nixon ever received, and one of the worst he ever accepted.

Olds was an academician, then dean for international studies and world affairs at the State University of New York. He was not a conservative, had no political experience, had no record of ever supporting Nixon and, as far as we knew, was not even a registered Republican. (In 1986, over eighteen years later, Dr. Olds ran for the U.S. Senate from Alaska as a Democrat. He lost the race, 55 percent to 45 percent.) Given these factors it looked like a terrible choice and two of us—Richard V. Allen, who was in charge of foreign and defense policy development for Nixon, and I—objected strenuously about Olds to Bob Haldeman, Nixon's new chief of staff for the campaign. Haldeman listened politely, indicated sympathy for what we told him, and did nothing. Olds hired a few staffers, spent close to a hundred thousand dollars, and worked very hard for many months, proving once again that it often takes as much work to do something poorly as to do it well.

A few days after the opening and discarding of the personnel boxes I got a telephone call from Peter Flanigan. Most of the policy research and speechwriting staff was conscripted for personnel duty. None of us had any experience in personnel work, but within a few days we were settled comfortably in plush suites at the Pierre Hotel in New York City, Nixon headquarters for the transition and one of the most expensive hotels in the world.

Nixon recovered from the Olds fiasco quickly and tried to repair the damage. Now under crushing time pressures, he ordered the staffing of the government divided into three parts. By then Dr. Olds and his small staff had disappeared and would have nothing to do with the personnel operation for the remainder of the transition.

The first part included the selection of the cabinet and high-ranking members of the White House staff. These selections Nixon made himself, soliciting the advice of a handful of top campaign aides, including Bob Haldeman, John Mitchell, John Ehrlichmann, and Bryce Harlow. The cabinet appointments were all level I, the highest in the government.

The second part of the emergency personnel operation included all the subcabinet positions in the federal government, from deputies and undersecretaries down to assistant secretaries and other jobs with equivalent rank. They included all level II to V appointments. There were hundreds of them; we never did find out exactly how many. Early every morning throughout November and December 1968, we gathered in an ornate room at the Pierre Hotel overlooking Central Park. There were ten of us on the personnel selection committee, chaired by Peter Flanigan. Our job was to find people for all those subcabinet jobs.

The third part of Nixon's hurriedly put together personnel operation consisted of all appointed jobs below the subcabinet level. Harry Flemming, a young, inexperienced campaign aide, was put in charge of this level and dispatched to Washington, D.C. to run it from there. His operation was widely publicized and soon thousands of letters and phone calls from all over the country came in from people who wanted jobs.

Creating a massive personnel operation from nothing in a few weeks was an impossible administrative task. As one indication of how bad it got, I remember visiting Flemming's headquarters and noticing dozens of large cardboard boxes scattered all over the floors. On each box someone had written a date with a heavy black marking pen. When I asked what was in the boxes the reply was, "That's our filing system. All the letters that came in on, say, November 24, went into this box." When I asked how they would go about finding a person's application I got no answer.

There were over two thousand positions to be filled. And there simply were not enough hours remaining before Nixon's inauguration to analyze the positions, identify candidates for those positions, interview the candidates, make selections, offer the jobs and then, as occurred in many cases, be turned down and have to start all over again.

Toward the end of December we realized it was hopeless. Without an immense amount of prior planning and staff work it was going to be impossible to retain control of appointments. So it was decided that the remainder of the personnel selections would be delegated to the cabinet and subcabinet who were already selected. Nixon had no choice, but he did realize that a blunder was made. Immediately after agreeing to give his cabinet the authority to make appointments he remarked to an aide, "I just made a big mistake." [1]

The consequences of the Nixon personnel disaster were serious and long-lasting. The U.S. Government is so large and so complex that it takes thousands of dedicated, competent, loyal people to turn campaign promises into national policy. The Nixon administration never recovered from the personnel blunder. The departments were staffed primarily with people with an agenda different from that of the White House, and once Nixon missed that initial opportunity to put his own people in key positions it was too late.

We argued over what to do rather than about how to do it. The departments and agencies were full of people who basically disagreed with many of Nixon's policies. They were nice people, competent people, but we wasted a great deal of time arguing with them, cajoling them, persuading them. I recall going to policy meetings with a dozen or more people where I would be the *only* person in the room supporting President Nixon's policy position. All the time the clock was running, and once the initial appointees became embedded in their positions, it was all but impossible to dislodge them.

Nixon lost his opportunity to govern before he started.

The people around Reagan in 1980 were determined not to repeat Nixon's mistake. As far back as 1976, when Reagan made his first serious try for the presidency, I discussed this problem with Ed Meese and recounted to him what happened to Nixon. Meese had already thought about planning and, after hearing about the Nixon transition fiasco, was even more convinced that it was foolhardy not to do some extensive, prior work. By the time the 1980 campaign was under way, Reagan and all of his top campaign aides were committed to diverting some campaign resources to planning effective takeover of the government, with special attention paid to staffing.

Those planning efforts paid tremendous dividends after Reagan won the election in November 1980. Because then came the hard part. Throughout the campaign Reagan laid out a comprehensive program that seemed to make sense on paper. The difficult process of translating ideas into policy and law now lay ahead.

The Democrats had control of the House of Representatives and could, anytime they wished, block Reagan's program. Expectations were not high. The ranking Democrat, Tip O'Neill of Massachusetts, was almost chortling as he welcomed Reagan to the "big leagues." The conventional wisdom is that today's presidents are relatively powerless. Reagan had no great reputation as an administrator and the Democrats, smarting from their defeat, were anxiously looking forward to teaching him a lesson or two in the ways of Washington.

The transition period between presidencies is a very special and important part of the election process. Originally, presidents took office on March 4, but in 1937 the date was changed to January 20, lopping six weeks off the transition period.

Most people pay little attention to the transition. For the general voting public the election is over and they can get on with devoting full-time attention to their personal lives. The president for the next four years has been determined, and in a few weeks the old will be gone and the new will be in.

For a departing president who is leaving office undefeated it is usually a time of melancholy, an absence of frantic planning for the future, a time when pleasant and painful reminiscences are brought to mind as the files are packed. For a defeated president it is a time of anguish, of trying to come to grips with the fact, now brutally known to the world, that your countrymen have rejected you.

For a newly elected president the transition is a time of delicious chaos. The victor and his campaign staff and supporters can scarcely believe they have really won, and will rub their eyes in wonderment the morning after election day. Then the eleven-week span that lies ahead of them will be seen for what it is—a brief flash of time that is far, far too short for them to do what must be done before assuming the awesome responsibility of governing the most powerful, largest, most complex, most important institution on earth. Even if you work twelve to fourteen hours a day, including Saturdays and Sundays, less perhaps a day for Christmas, you only have approximately 1,000 working hours to prepare.

If you just concentrated on making major appointments, of which

there are over 2,000, you could spend only an average of 30 minutes on each appointment. And there is much more to do besides
making high-level appointments. The president-elect has to prepare a policy strategy. He has to accept many hours of briefings on
highly classified defense and intelligence information that was denied to him earlier. He and his family have to make arrangements
for moving (in Reagan's case, a coast-to-coast move). Most American families would take the better part of eleven weeks just to
move and get settled in a new home. And while the president-elect
is trying to do all this, the press is calling, congressmen and senators and governors are calling, dozens of world leaders are calling,
and they all want to talk to him now. The demands on the time of
a president-elect and his staff are bizarre and unreal.

One major task of the Reagan transition effort was the briefing
of incoming cabinet officers. As so often happens when a new administration takes power, the cabinet members are usually chosen
from outside the immediate campaign staff because these positions
require people with extensive experience, people who by seniority
and stature are less likely to be involved in the hurly-burly, revolutionary world of a presidential campaign.

On the other hand, it is the candidate and his campaign aides
who fashion the policy agenda. The problem every winning campaign faces is how to ensure that those with more distinguished
public reputations who will be chosen for the cabinet posts do not
betray the policies the campaign was fought on. In Reagan's situation, it was easily the most thorough and comprehensive effort undertaken in the history of American transitions. The president-elect
placed Ed Meese in charge of all transition activities, and Meese
came up with an approach that proved very successful.

Meese's plan for briefing new cabinet officers was a major reason why presidential scholars concluded that "the Reagan transition was the most carefully planned and effective in American
political history."[2] Rather than have one general orientation briefing, providing the new secretary-designate with a few suggestions
for personnel, and then leaving him or her to determine policy and
hire people for the key policy-making positions, Meese established
three separate briefing procedures.

Nobody ever said so, but basically it was an indoctrination course
for cabinet members, especially those who were not closely connected with the campaign or fully familiar with Ronald Reagan's

positions on major policy issues. There were two primary things we wanted to indoctrinate the new cabinet on: ideas and people.

Ideas are the key to creating policy, but people are the key to implementing that policy. The preparations on Reagan's issues and policy positions had been going on for many years, and were especially intense during the past five years. Dozens of advisory task forces of policy experts were hard at work for months, Reagan took hundreds of specific policy positions during the campaign, and hundreds of specific policy positions were spelled out in the Republican party platform.

Equally detailed and comprehensive efforts were made to identify highly qualified people for the thousands of government jobs that would open up if Reagan won. In the late spring of 1980, Ed Meese contacted an old friend, E. Pendleton James, a nationally known expert in executive recruiting, and asked him to draw up a plan for "filling the top positions in the government in preparation for a Reagan victory."[3] Unlike past efforts for the Nixon administration in 1968 and the Carter administration in 1976, the efforts of Pen James were professional and successful. James and his small dedicated staff worked long hours to write concise, detailed job descriptions for all the major positions in the federal government. They established clear priorities setting forth which jobs should be filled first after the election, and then long, long lists of qualified candidates, backed up with detailed résumés, for positions in every major policy-making area.

Reagan's planning precautions paid off handsomely. Once elected, he had a complete, integrated policy program, and with Pen James' lists—unlike the Glenn Olds file boxes in 1968—we had an invaluable source of high-level appointees.

On the one hand we had a fully developed, comprehensive policy program for the new administration and hundreds of names of qualified people, smart and tough, who were loyal to the Reagan political agenda. On the other hand we had a dozen or so newly selected cabinet officers, overwhelmed with the prospect of getting ready to take over their departments in a few short weeks, with little detailed knowledge of Reagan's policies and very few really good ideas of people to fill the key positions in their agencies.

Then the Meese briefings in the transition began.

The first briefing group was headed by William Timmons, an old political pro, with long experience in the campaigns and administrations of Nixon and Ford. Separate teams were established for each major government department and agency. Most of the people on the teams, besides being smart and tough-minded, had a lot of government experience. They knew how Washington worked. They fanned out across the city to compile reports covering just about anything a new cabinet officer might want to know about the government responsibility he or she was about to assume—where the office was located, how many people worked there, what government programs were involved, what congressmen and senators had special responsibilities for those programs, a detailed list of major decisions to make within a few weeks (in some cases days) after taking office in January, and any pending legal problems. The Timmons' reports were the sort of detailed dossier that might be put together on a large company being considered for purchase.

The second briefing group was directed by Pen James. A tall, intense Californian who ran a Los Angeles executive recruiting firm, James was an experienced hand at this, having worked for several years in Nixon's White House personnel office. He also worked easily with Reagan. Later, he would himself be appointed to the White House staff, in charge of all personnel selection for the early years of the Reagan administration.

The selection of political appointments was governed by three basic assumptions. First, the appointments were absolutely critical to the success of the administration. Second, the number and quality of appointments could only be achieved if we had a careful, thorough personnel organization. And third, control of appointments had to be centralized and controlled tightly by President Reagan and a few others on the White House staff.

The James group did not select subcabinet staff without consulting cabinet officers, but it was made clear to the incoming cabinet that they could not freely choose the people who would work for them. All key subcabinet appointments were cleared by Reagan and/or his top personal aides. They were treated as presidential appointments even when they were not. It was also made clear that, with very few exceptions, all incumbent political appointments should be fired. As Ed Meese put it, "We made sure that we cleaned out all the appointees of the past administration. We felt an empty office was better than to have a holdover."[4]

A special effort was made for the appointees to economic policy-making positions. Their selection was placed at the top of the list. In addition, we approached the selection of these people in a different manner. We did not begin by reading the job description and then looking for someone with relevant experience. Although that was a matter of some importance we began instead by asking different, what we thought were more relevant, questions: How will economic policy be made in a Reagan administration? Who will make it? Who are the critical people in the day-to-day economic policy-making process? Who will have the most to say about economic policy?

After thinking about this and reflecting on my experiences with economic policy-making during the Nixon administration, and what I had learned about how it worked for Presidents Ford and Carter, I concluded that economic policy was made ultimately, not by any one person, but rather by an ad hoc team, a team that, while it might vary somewhat from administration to administration, was remarkably constant in its basic composition.

It was very important that this team work well together, with the same objective. Any dissension, especially dissension about what *should* be done in economic policy, would, at the very least, delay our development of a realistic legislative program. And any significant delay of even a month or two would be almost certainly fatal to that policy. All the members of Reagan's economic policy-making team had to agree completely with the main elements of the comprehensive economic program he had set forth during the campaign. And they must be dedicated totally to implementing that program as soon as possible. We could argue over how it should be done, but not over whether it should be done.

The positions we identified as critical to the economic policy-making team included:

Secretary of the Treasury. The Treasury Department would be the lead agency on any tax changes, a vital part of Reagan's economic program. The secretary of the treasury was the highest ranking economic policy decision-maker in the cabinet and, by tradition, was usually the president's chief public spokesman on *all* matters of economic policy.

Undersecretary of the Treasury for economic policy, Assistant Secretary of the Treasury for economic policy, and Assistant Secretary of the Treasury for tax policy. The secretary of the treasury was going to be a very busy person, and would have to rely heavily on the policy advice of his chief lieutenants for tax policy.

Chairman of the Council of Economic Advisers. By law this person was the chief economic adviser to the president. It would be unthinkable to have someone in this critical post who was not fully in accord with the president's economic program. The last thing we needed was a brilliant academic theorist who had no appreciation for the reality of Washington and the stakes involved. We needed someone with economic wisdom who could exert his influence on the other members of the economic team.

Director of the Office of Management and Budget (OMB). OMB would be the lead agency on spending control, another vital part of Reagan's economic program. We needed someone who was not only in full agreement with the economic strategy that Reagan already spelled out, but also someone with a mastery of budgetary details, someone who would be tough enough and smart enough to apply the theory to particulars, or as in this case, to thousands of particulars.

The Deputy Director of OMB and the five Associate Directors of OMB. The director of OMB was going to be even busier than the secretary of the treasury. The 600 professional budget analysts on the staff of OMB, all career employees, were the best in the United States government, but they would need constant and direct policy guidance from Reagan administration appointees.

The White House Staff. President Reagan had always worked very closely with his personal staff, delegating heavily. It was therefore very important that his senior staff members understand and support his economic policy.

The White House senior staff was selected first. This wasn't much of a problem because the people who ran Reagan's campaign, and were running the transition, surprised no one by selecting themselves for the top White House jobs. Edwin Meese, who was in charge of the entire transition operation, became counsellor to the president with general responsibility for all government programs, including national defense and economic policy. James Baker was named chief of the White House staff, and Michael Deaver became his deputy. Meese and Deaver had been with Reagan since his early days as governor of California in the late 1960s. Baker was a relative newcomer, but quickly became an integral part of Reagan's personal staff, adding valuable political and government experience.

They became the president's three top aides, acting as a general management troika for him. They didn't have the title but they functioned as deputy presidents. They were involved with everything of importance, including economic policy.

My appointment followed theirs. As the president's assistant for policy development, I reported directly to Ed Meese and had specific responsibility for all domestic and economic policy. Neither Meese, nor Baker, nor Deaver had any formal economic training so, by default, I became the White House economist.

In retrospect, the transition personnel operation was superb, easily the best in the history of the United States. It wasn't perfect, mistakes were made, but perfection is not a fair criterion. According to one scholar, Professor Calvin Mackenzie, the Reagan administration "undertook transition personnel selection with more forethought, with a larger commitment of resources, and with more systematic attention to detail than any administration in the postwar period, perhaps more than any administration ever. Its personnel selection efforts were related to its policy and programmatic objectives in a way that had no precedent in the recent history of presidential transitions."[5]

James organized the personnel effort into five departments, referred to as issue clusters, reflecting our conviction that policy was the determining factor in selecting someone for a job, not the specific position to be filled. The five areas were human services, legal and administrative agencies, resources and development, national security, and economic affairs. Each one was headed by an associate director who reported to James.

The head of the economic affairs issue cluster was Annelise Anderson. During the campaign she traveled with George Bush as his policy adviser, was one of the few trained economists in the campaign, and also had prior personnel experience during a presidential transition (Nixon in 1968). We worked closely together, as we often did in past campaigns, on finding the right people for the most important economic policy-making positions. Those she suggested to the incoming treasury secretary, Donald T. Regan, included Beryl W. Sprinkel, who became the undersecretary for monetary policy and later chairman of the Council of Economic Advisers, Norman Ture, Paul Craig Roberts, and Steve Entin.

The last of the three briefing groups Ed Meese set up was something new to transition politics, something that had never been done in a systematic, organized way. It was called the Office of Policy Coordination, headed by my campaign deputy, Darrell Trent. On paper Trent was responsible for coordinating the issue reports of forty-eight policy task forces we established earlier in the campaign, and the efforts of the thirty people who reported to him, into a systematic program to forge the policy directions of the new administration. What was not written down was the real purpose of the Trent group—to educate the incoming cabinet and other key members of the administration on exactly what Ronald Reagan's policies were.

Over the years, Reagan and his people developed these ideas into a comprehensive, consistent, integrated policy that had been hardened, tempered, and confirmed during the presidential campaigns of 1976 and 1980. Now we wanted to make very, very sure that anyone who accepted a cabinet post would have no doubts about what was expected. We did not assume that everyone knew Reagan's policies. The elaborate briefing procedure on policy was to ensure that no one could ever say later, "I didn't know."

The overall transition management was essentially in the hands of the same people who later joined the White House staff. Baker and Deaver worked closely with Meese. The three administrative heads of the transition—Timmons, in charge of reports on the executive branch, James, in charge of personnel, and Trent, in charge of policy coordination—all reported to Meese. This was unusually thorough and comprehensive for a transition, but there was another unique arrangement that made it even more innovative. At Meese's suggestion, three of us were appointed senior policy advisers: Caspar Weinberger for budget matters, Richard Allen for foreign and defense policy matters, and myself for all domestic and economic policy matters.

Our responsibilities were sweeping, but not confining. On the organization chart we reported to Ed Meese. But our charter cut across all traditional organizational lines. Our mandate was policy. It was unprecedented and unconventional, but it seemed to work. We had the authority and responsibility to involve ourselves in anything related to our issue areas—whether it was a question of who should get a particular government job, or what policy position we should take on any issue, or questions of government organization or press relations or congressional relations.

By election day the overall economic policy plan was set firmly in principle; during the transition our focus switched from ideas and strategy to implementation and programs. This is not unusual. A transition is really the beginning of a new administration, not the end of a presidential campaign.

In effect, what we did during the transition was build an economic policy chute to channel actions in directions consistent with Reagan's philosophy. Just as in architecture form follows function, in the 1980 transition organization followed purpose.

There were many critical tasks to address during the transition, but in the limited field of economic policy we proceeded in the following manner: First, it was made clear to everyone that our policy was established. Whether or not we should cut tax rates or control spending or reform regulation was not a matter for future debate. Second, major attention was directed towards finding the key players of the team. The minimum qualifications included competence, experience, and absolute, complete loyalty to Reagan's economic policies. Third, once the key people were selected, we concentrated on briefing them fully. The political experts briefed them on all the operating details of the departments and agencies they were about to take over. The personnel experts provided them with several, and sometimes many more, suggestions of highly qualified people for every key policy position, and then the policy experts from the campaign staff gave them a complete briefing on all the positions Reagan took over the years.

If anyone was going to try to obstruct or change Reagan's program they were not going to be able to claim ignorance. Every key player in the decision-making process was carefully chosen and fully indoctrinated. It worked. There were a lot of arguments and discussions about how the policy should be implemented, but none about whether or not it should be done. By the time Reagan was sworn in on that cold January day, a powerful, smart, tough and very, very loyal team of economic policy decision-makers was in place and ready to run.

The stunning success of Reagan's economic policy and many of his other successes during the early years of his administration were largely due to the efforts of the transition team. They assembled a large, talented group of people, and briefed them thoroughly on what Reagan wanted done and how to do it. When Reagan took the field to begin his brilliant political quarterbacking, his team was ready.

Unfortunately, the kind of systematic and thorough staffing that took place during the transition was not sustained. Slowly, gradually, one by one, people less talented and less completely committed to Reagan's policy agenda began to fill the ranks of the administration. The results were disastrous. One consequence, for example, was the Iran-Contra fiasco, something that almost certainly never would have happened if Jim Baker, Ed Meese, Michael Deaver, and Dick Allen had remained close by the president, advising him in the White House.

Chapter Seventeen

THE WHITE HOUSE

The day the transition ended and the first term of the Reagan administration began was a day of dramatic change. In the morning we reported for work in the plushly carpeted offices of the White House instead of a run-down commercial office building in downtown Washington. The telephone service vastly improved. The coffee was hot and tasty, and we ate in the splendid White House mess, instead of having to rush out to a variety of fast-food restaurants and lunch counters.

Beginning at 12:01 A.M. on January 21, 1981, everything we did took on sobering dimensions. It was all for real now. We were no longer promising what we would try to do, as we did during the campaign. We no longer planned what we were going to do, as we did during the transition. Now we had to do it. From now on, whatever we did would be judged by the unyielding criteria of history—was it right, did it work?

As I walked into the west wing of the White House that first morning, I recalled something that happened a little over eleven years before in the same two-story white building I was now entering. I had received some advice I would never forget.

It happened on Tuesday, April 21, 1970. By then John Ehrlichman was Nixon's domestic policy adviser and every morning, at
7:30 sharp, he chaired a meeting of the senior domestic policy staff
in the Roosevelt Room, a few steps away from the Oval Office. I
had just sat down at the table and was nursing a cup of coffee, still
sleepy and marveling at how Ehrlichman could be so bright-eyed
and enthusiastic about government policy at this time in the morning, when the door at the far end of the room opened and President Nixon walked in. He had never done that before and, as far
as I know, never did again.

He looked tired, but it was obvious that he was high-strung
and alert. He talked to us for about fifteen minutes about some
minor domestic policy issues and abruptly left at 7:45 A.M. Less
than thirty minutes later he summoned the entire domestic policy
staff to the Oval Office.

President Nixon stood behind his desk, and we assembled in a
rough semicircle, standing in front of him. There were sixteen of
us there that morning, including John Ehrlichman, Peter Flanigan,
Kenneth Cole, Harry Dent, and John Whitaker. It was clear he
wanted to talk, and by God he wanted an audience. We were it.

We found out later he had been up all night, unable to sleep
after flying back from the Nixon western White House in California
and arriving in Washington at 2:30 A.M. He acted as if he had consumed six cups of strong black coffee. He was turned on, talking
fast, and making quick nervous gestures with his hands. He talked
to us about presidential leadership and what should be important
to us in our White House jobs. He kept driving at one basic point.

"Remember," Nixon said, "what happens around here on a
day-to-day basis is not really worth anything. What goes on in the
Congress is not that important. The important thing is the big picture. Here you have a chance to do things that normally take twenty-
five years to do. It is important to have a perspective of history, to
take the long view.

"The mark of a real leader is to keep aloof from all the details,
to keep your eye on the main things. You will only be remembered
for the big things you do here, and even some of the really big
things we will do here will be just a line in the history books.

"So it is important to be engaged in a major battle. The only
thing you will have to look back on is whether you accomplished
something major."

I thought about that advice often over the years, and everything I saw or did since then reaffirmed its validity. The urgent, daily details that are so necessary at the moment are all forgotten, some within days. Very, very few matters of public policy are ever important enough to etch themselves in the records of history. And almost no one ever gets to do anything of memorable magnitude all alone. Perhaps the best one can ever strive for is to be an important part of the battle which does make a major change, your actions being necessary for it to happen, but not alone sufficient to make it happen.

There were only a few major things I had been involved in. I had written a book recommending the abolition of the urban renewal program, helped Richard Nixon get elected in 1968, helped abolish the draft and establish an all-volunteer force, and then worked to defeat the guaranteed income in the early 1970s. Everything else had faded in the rush of new events.

So, when I walked through the door of the Reagan White House for the first time in 1981, I vowed to work on at least one important major policy issue, to do something to further it every day, regardless of what other urgent pressures came up. And the policy change I wanted more than anything else was a new, comprehensive economic policy that would halt the slide toward a semi-socialist state and move us toward a freer, more capitalistic society.

The only other issue of comparable importance to economic policy was national security policy. The United States desperately needed to rebuild its defense forces, but, except for my long-held interests in a protective missile force and staving off attempts to bring back the military draft, I realized that my talents and skills lay elsewhere, and so did my opportunities.

There are myths about working in the west wing of the White House. Many people have an image of noisy bedlam, of tense meetings of anxious aides who wrestle with torturous decisions, of people bowed under the crushing responsibilities of their jobs, images of a handful of aides strolling in and out of the Oval Office for brief, weighty chats with the president. Perhaps the most persistent myth of all is the myth of White House pressure, of how difficult the work is.

Actually, working in the White House is, in many ways, very easy. It is quiet, almost peaceful. Once you pass through its doors and hit the deep carpeted halls there is an air of unhurried calm. People talk softly and walk with a leisured pace. Nobody shouts or runs about. There is an unspoken policy of politeness. Even when the debate turns to controversial issues on which there may be passionate disagreements, tempers rarely flare.

It is a safe and secure place to work. It is probably the only office building in the United States which has heavily armed Secret Service agents, pleasantly dressed in their business suits, some with small Uzi submachine guns hidden in a zippered cloth pouch, casually standing outside the president's door. When you drive up to the gate at the south end of West Executive Avenue the White House guards always smile and, after making sure you are who you are supposed to be, cheerily wave you through. Unless you arrive with a guest. Then they will usually demand to see your White House security pass. A trifle embarrassing, but not a bad idea—for all they know, any White House aide driving up with someone they don't know could be a hostage. When you finally enter the building, there are more White House police, seated at a reception desk the top of which is covered with color mug shots of every White House staff member for easy reference and identification. One result of this extraordinary security is that you don't have to see anyone you don't want to see. Nobody pops in.

It has the best telephone service in the world. The White House telephone operators are legendary. They are friendly and work with startling effectiveness. Anytime you wish to speak to anyone, anywhere in the world, all you have to do is pick up the white telephone receiver, push one of the twenty or so lighted plastic buttons and tell the pleasant voice that answers who you would like to speak to. I never asked how they manage to find people so quickly in the most obscure places, but I suspect they are not shy about using the phrase, "This is the White House calling." Most people on the electronic pursuit path to their quarry are not apt to raise the question of who in the White House is calling.

The White House has the best research facilities in the world. You have access to a tremendous amount of information. If you know where to look and whom to ask there is a level of available expertise, facts, and studies that far exceeds that of even the most sophisticated research institutions. When you add to that the fact that you also have access to an extraordinary range of highly classified information, harvested by our multibillion dollar intelligence agencies, it is hard to deny that high-level policymakers in the federal government are fully informed.

Finally, the job was not stressful—at least not in the Reagan White House. The legendary pressure was nonexistent. This was largely due to Reagan and the long years he had spent in preparation. Personally, he was delightful to work for—he rarely had a bad mood, always had a warm greeting, listened attentively, soaked up new information and ideas quickly and easily, and, every now and then, said thank you.

The job could be stressful under certain conditions. If you ever get in over your head and don't know what the right thing to do is, or you do know but don't know how to go about making it happen, that can be real stress.

But with Reagan the making of national policy was relatively easy because he knew what he wanted to do and we knew what he wanted done. For five years before he was elected president he staked out clear positions on hundreds of policy issues, and on major issues he spelled out his proposals in some detail. That alone took away 90 percent of the sweat and anxiety that can afflict a White House aide. Most of the remaining 10 percent of the stress was eliminated by the unusual degree of collegiality and cooperation—at least during the early years—of the members of his administration. It wasn't perfect harmony, but the level of personal backbiting and petty obstructionism was remarkably low for a White House staff.

The only thing that could be called stressful was the sheer quantity of things one had to do. There were dozens of meetings scheduled every day, and you couldn't go to all of them. The number of people who wanted to see you was astonishing. The requests for speeches and appearances and dinners and cocktail parties always exceeded the number of days and nights available. And the phone calls poured in. Forty or fifty telephone calls a day was not unusual. Just answering phone calls could keep you occupied full time, and even then you would not come close to answering them all. Then there were the reporters—with their endless questions and requests for interviews.

Most of us were so busy, so tightly scheduled, that we had to carry a program of the day's events with us so we could keep critical appointments. Every night my assistant, an extremely bright, hardworking young woman named Barbara Honneger, would sift through and analyze the upcoming events and then prepare a neatly typed 3 × 5 inch white card listing all the major appointments I had for the following day, indicating the time, the place, and the purpose. I would slide this card into a clear plastic holder and slip it into my pocket. At times I felt that my life on the White House staff was ruled by that small, plastic-encased, appointment card. Others shared that feeling. If one paid close attention toward the end of any meeting in the White House, one could see a number of people in the room furtively pull something out of a pocket and then quickly glance down at it before refocusing their attention on the matter under discussion. They were just finding out where their appointment card had them scheduled to be next.

I have often been asked why I left the Reagan administration in 1982, generally in a curious, wondering tone of voice that expresses disbelief that anyone would voluntarily walk away from any job in the White House. But many have, for many reasons. My reasons were simple.

First, I never did enjoy government work. I always found it fascinating, important, and self-fulfilling, but I never thought it was either exciting or fun. While I never regretted a day I have spent in public service, I guess I regard it more as a duty, or an obligation, rather than as a real occupation or calling. To me it was very much like serving a tour of duty in the military—important, worthwhile, but not what I want to do for a living.

The day I left I went to the Oval Office to say good-bye to President Reagan. We talked briefly and I told him that "my job was the best possible job in the government that I knew of, but— it was still a government job."

"I know," he acknowledged with a small smile that implied that he may have had a similar feeling about his own job.

There were other reasons. I was convinced that 80 to 90 percent of all policy changes are made during the first year of a new administration. From then on, as the nature of the White House changes, you spend more and more time coping with Congress and preparing for the next election. Much of what I could do was done.

And finally, since 1975 I had been away from the academic world for a total of almost four years. It is obvious what people give up when they leave a business or professional career for public service—the financial gains, the promotions. What academicians give up is less obvious—the ideas not thought of, the books not written.

I had been away long enough.

Chapter Eighteen

POLICY CHOKEPOINTS

One morning in 1982 Michael Deaver, the deputy chief of staff, opened the door that led from his office into the Oval Office and walked in on President Reagan unannounced. Deaver was very troubled. The war in Lebanon was escalating. In June 1982 the Israelis moved across the border to attack the PLO. Soon their tanks and ships and planes were shelling and bombing the PLO strongholds in Beirut. Many people were being killed and wounded, and the casualties upset Deaver.

"Mr. President, I have to leave."

The president was startled.

"What do you mean?"[1]

"I can't be a part of this anymore," replied Deaver, "the bombings, the killing of children. It's wrong. And you're the one person on the face of the earth right now who can stop it. All you have to do is tell Begin you want it stopped."[2]

Reagan stared at Deaver with a look, as Deaver later described it, of "My God, what have we done?" and then asked his secretary to get Menachem Begin, the prime minister of Israel, on the phone.

George Shultz then joined Deaver and the president, and endorsed the idea of Reagan intervening with Israel. When the call to Israel came through, Reagan told Begin bluntly that the shelling and bombing of Beirut had to stop. Reagan's last words were, "It has gone too far. You must stop it." [3]

In twenty minutes Begin called back and said it was done. The shelling and bombing was stopped. Reagan was somewhat incredulous and said, "I didn't know I had that kind of power." [4]

That story is an unusual, extreme example of how decisions are made in the White House. But it illustrates two elements that are crucial to all important decisions made in the White House—the elements of access and information. The president makes all, every single one, of the big decisions, mostly by positive action, though sometimes by studied neglect. And he is mightily influenced by the facts that come primarily from the mouths and pens of the people he sees and talks to every day. Of course, his decisions are affected by his beliefs and philosophy, by what he reads and has read, but the personal daily discussions, briefings, and advice are the main driving force behind his actions.

And that is how someone like Michael Deaver, a White House staffer with no portfolio at all in foreign policy, could be pivotal in changing the course of American foreign policy at a critical time. He had information and he had access, and felt strongly enough to give advice that no one else was giving. There were other factors involved also. Mike Deaver did not happen to walk into the Oval Office that day by accident. He worked for Ronald Reagan for almost twenty years. The swirl of scandal that engulfed Deaver after he left the White House, which he largely brought upon himself, has obscured much of what he did while he was there and how he did it. Charged with violating the law that prohibits former employees from contact with the White House for one year while in the pursuit of private profit, he was investigated by an independent counsel named by the Justice Department, and eventually indicted and convicted. His lobbying business was ruined.

Deaver was quiet and intense, a small, slender, balding man who wore horn-rimmed eyeglasses. He revered Reagan and obviously drew intense pleasure from working for him. His pubic reputation was that of a public relations man, the fellow who was only interested in appearances, knew nothing of the substance of policy, and didn't care that he knew nothing. The reputation was false, although it grew as the years rolled by and he became widely known as some sort of supervalet. In truth, he was deeply involved—as were all of Reagan's other senior White House aides—in policy-making. And for a simple reason. Anyone who can talk to the president or write something that he reads and who has emotions and values will inevitably affect the making of national policy, for better or worse.

Deaver was the modern-day equivalent of a courtier to the king. Perhaps more than anyone on Reagan's staff he knew what the president valued, what he wanted, how he felt. And for many years he geared his life toward serving Reagan.

He also grew increasingly bitter that few people—even those in the press and in government—recognized this and that even fewer were grateful. Once, during the closing days of the 1980 presidential campaign, he turned to me in exasperation and said, "You know. I am Ronald Reagan. Where do you think he got most of those ideas over the years? Every morning after I get up I make believe I am him and ask what should he do and where should he go." Much of Deaver's advice, while not bearing directly on policy, affected policy. Most of it was good advice and Reagan came to value it more and more highly over the years.

There were two other factors, unique to Deaver, that inclined the president to listen to him. Guilt and gratitude.

In late 1979, after an especially vicious round of internal campaign politics, John Sears, together with Jim Lake (press secretary) and Charlie Black (head of political operations), ganged up on Deaver. On November 22nd—Thanksgiving Day—Nancy Reagan called Michael and asked him to stop by their house in Los Angeles. When the unsuspecting Michael arrived Nancy asked him to wait for a few minutes in their bedroom.

After cooling his heels for twenty minutes, he lost his patience and walked into the living room, where the Reagans sat with Sears, Lake, and Black. Michael's three colleagues had been plying the Reagans with tales of supposed financial misconduct. Almost the first words out of Reagan's mouth were, "Mike, the fellows . . . tell me I have to pay thirty thousand dollars a month to lease my space in your office building."[5] That was a whopper. Reagan's monthly office rental bill was $400. There were a lot of other expenses, travel for example, that were reimbursed and the total varied from month to month, averaging between five and ten thousand dollars.[6]

Deaver was stunned, in his own words, "angry and frustrated and bitter."[7] The man for whom he had worked for twelve years was taking seriously the charges of three relative strangers. Something in Deaver snapped and, in a few seconds, he walked away from everything those last twelve years of his life represented. Looking at Reagan, Deaver said evenly:

"You need to put somebody in charge, and if these gentlemen have convinced you that I am ripping you off, after all these years, then I'm out. I'm leaving."[8]

"No, this is not what I want," said Reagan, following Deaver out of the living room.

"I'm sorry, sir, but it's what I want," replied Deaver as he left the house.[9]

Reagan returned to the living room, having second thoughts about what he had allowed to happen, looked at the pleased faces of Sears, Lake, and Black and said bitterly, "Well, you sons of bitches, the best guy we had just left."[10]

Letting Deaver walk was one of the biggest mistakes Ronald Reagan ever made and he was furious with himself for doing it. A few months later in early 1980, the tide of the internal staff battle turned and Deaver returned, but it was never the same. Reagan never stopped feeling guilty for betraying him, and Deaver stopped looking out for Reagan's interests first and instead began looking out for his own.

What made the 1979 resignation even more painful to both Reagan and Deaver was an incident that occurred three years earlier in the summer of 1976. Michael Deaver had saved Ronald Reagan's life.

We had just finished two days of hard campaigning through the state of Ohio—Columbus, Akron, Lakewood, Cleveland, Dayton, and Cincinnati. We finished in Cincinnati on Sunday, June 6, 1976, and late in the afternoon were flying happily home to Los Angeles just a little over 2,000 miles away. We were in the air for about 15 minutes. The national press was in the rear of the plane, separated from Reagan by a heavy cloth curtain hung across the aisle.

Reagan was sitting in the first row of seats, next to the window, on the right-hand side. Nancy was sitting next to him on the aisle. As usual he was working, his stuffed briefcase open on his knees, steadily writing on his treasured 4×6-inch white file cards. I was sitting in the second row, directly behind Nancy, working through papers in my own briefcase. Michael Deaver was sitting in the second row, right across the aisle from me, behind two Secret Service men who sat across the aisle from the Reagans.

Suddenly Reagan stood up with his hand at his throat. He looked bewildered and his face was flushed. He was trying to talk but he couldn't. He lurched out into the aisle with a pleading look on his face. As I stood up, Nancy reached for him and the Secret Service men rushed into the aisle and asked him what was wrong. He couldn't answer, just kept clutching his throat with his left hand as his face got redder and his eyes widened.

My first thought was the unthinkable; Reagan was having a heart attack. Even if he didn't die from it, just the news of his having one would be enough to force someone his age out of the presidential race. And the entire national press corps was about twenty feet away behind the cloth curtain. One of the staff, a young campaign aide named Kurt Wurzberger, said it, "He's having a heart attack. I'll get the oxygen tank." We all stood there, frozen, helpless.

Then Michael Deaver realized what was really happening. Quickly pushing the rest of us out of the way, he came up behind Reagan and wrapped his small, slender arms around Reagan's powerful torso. He slipped his hands just below Reagan's rib cage, clenched his right fist and then grabbed his right wrist with his other hand and yanked with all his might—the famed Heimlich maneuver. Reagan seemed to know what Mike was trying to do. He didn't resist, but just bent slightly forward. Mike waited and then pulled hard again.

The second time Deaver's fists slammed into Reagan's stomach a shower of partially chewed peanuts sprayed out of Reagan's mouth into the aisle. Reagan gasped, noisily sucking in air as he slowly straightened up, the color of his face rapidly changing back to normal. He smiled weakly at us and said "thanks" to Mike.

Later I found out that about a year or so earlier he and Mike had by coincidence discussed what to do in a situation like this. Mike noticed the small bowl full of peanuts sitting on the armrest next to Reagan and figured out he was choking to death on a wad of peanuts.

It was quite a scene. Everyone was standing in the aisle surrounding Reagan, one of them with an oxygen tank and mask, ready to administer it if asked. Chewed peanuts covered the floor and Reagan was slowly shaking his head, rubbing his throat, getting his breath back. By then the press corps had noticed that something was wrong. There was too much activity in the front section, too many funny noises. We put the oxygen tank away quickly. If he took a few whiffs now and the press saw it they would be suspicious and we would never catch up with the rumors about his health. Reagan quickly sensed the potential for dangerous misinterpretation. Within thirty seconds of getting his wind back, he straightened his clothes and headed toward the back of the plane.

By then some reporters were peering around the pulled-aside curtain and figured out he choked on something. One of them asked what he choked on and Reagan replied, "A damn peanut." I added that it was probably one of Jimmy Carter's peanuts, then everyone laughed and relaxed as Reagan mingled with the press, telling them he had gotten a Jimmy Carter peanut stuck in his throat, nothing serious, probably just a plot by the Carter people. A few of the press didn't completely believe him because he still looked quite flustered, a lot more flustered than one would be on one peanut. Later, a few curious members of the press asked whether or not he was given oxygen (they had seen the tank in Wurtzberger's hands). We could truthfully say no. They seemed somewhat disappointed.

So, on June 6, 1976, presidential candidate Reagan came within moments of choking to death on a handful of peanuts. We almost gave oxygen to a man who was choking to death and if we had he probably would have died. The headlines would have read, "Reagan Chokes to Death on Peanuts." But the quick thinking and forceful action of Michael Deaver saved his life. The next day there were no headlines, only one small story on page 6 of the *Los Angeles Times* entitled, "Reagan Chokes on Snack, Calls it 'Carter Peanut.' "

Sometimes history turns on such small incidents as these. The Michael Deaver I came to know in 1976 when he saved Reagan's life and the Deaver I knew before Reagan forsook him that fall day in 1979 was a shy, friendly man who seemed secure and content. The Deaver that I became reacquainted with when I rejoined the campaign myself in 1980 was a man who was nervous and distant. An intelligent man, possessed of great cunning, he was now in some ways like a wounded animal, distrustful of everyone save his family. He seemed to draw into himself. Soon the stories began to circulate of how, by capricious and mean-minded actions, he was hurting other people. Slowly, one by one, some of his oldest and closest friends began to drop away.

By 1985, after he resigned from the White House staff and was well on his way to becoming a multimillionaire, he was one of the most disliked people in Washington. During this time, unknown to any of us, Michael was also slowly slipping into the desperate world of the secret alcoholic.[11] When the charges of influence peddling were leveled against him, the lone voice that spoke in his defense was President Reagan's. It was too late. Old scores were settled as both Republicans and Democrats rushed to help the media ruin first Deaver's business and then his reputation.

Deaver's personal relationship to Reagan was unusual and extreme, but it illustrates how, to a lesser or greater degree, every senior White House staff member interacts with the president from some historical base, from experiences and memories that strongly affect how much attention the president pays to that person's advice and counsel, and sometimes even whether or not the counsel ever gets to the president.

Now it is simply not possible for every member of the White House staff to stroll in and talk to the president whenever the urge strikes him. There is too little time and too many senior staff. All White House staff systems develop very strict rules to ration the president's time. It is the most precious resource in the White House.

Presidents also have little time for reading and the capacity of the federal government to write far exceeds anyone's capacity to read. This was especially true for Reagan who preferred the give and take of personal meetings to trudging through thick memos. This preference gave special importance to the meetings he attended. So, when you added it all up, there were three basic ways to participate in the policy process of the Reagan administration. The first was to talk to him personally and directly with no one to contradict or interrupt. This was the most effective, but opportunities were limited—during the early years only Ed Meese, Jim Baker, and Mike Deaver (and Nancy Reagan) had that option, and later Donald Regan shrank that circle even further. The second was to write and send memoranda. That was not very effective, given the way Reagan liked to work. That left the third way—

meetings. Cabinet meetings, cabinet council meetings, meetings with outside advisory boards, and ad hoc staff meetings.

In the White House all major decisions were made by Reagan. But before he could decide the choices had to be laid before him, along with the nature of the problem, the alternative courses of action, and the costs and benefits of each of those alternatives. All major policy ideas had to pass through a gauntlet of committee meetings, ranging from formal meetings of the full cabinet or the cabinet councils to smaller, more informal gatherings.

It was always much easier to block or derail an idea than to advance one. Anything less than unanimous support in these meetings could stop the making of a new policy in its tracks. Dissent always delayed things and was sometimes fatal. A strong, eloquent objection by even one senior member of a high-level policy group could be serious. And objections by two or more senior players would almost surely kill a new idea.

That is why every time a group of the president's senior policy advisers meets to discuss an issue, to comment on it, and especially to pass their comments and advice and recommendations on to the president, that meeting constitutes what we might call a policy chokepoint.

Among the things that worry any great naval power are navigation chokepoints, those narrow straits and channels through which their mighty warships must sail before they can break to the open seas. A warship is most vulnerable when sailing quietly through one of these chokepoints and a good part of naval war strategy must be devoted to assuring free and easy passage through them.

The economic policy that President Reagan wanted had to sail through many chokepoints in the White House before it became the law of the land. It needed the fast, full approval of a number of committees, groups, and counsels. It had to be fast because of the short length of the honeymoon period with Congress and the press. And it had to be virtually unanimous, because anything short of unanimity would seriously delay the process.

We knew what economic policy we wanted. We had chosen only people who supported that policy to be members of the economic team, and they were fully briefed on what the president wanted. The only task remaining was to transform those general principles into specific government policies, especially in the areas of spending control (OMB), tax rate reduction (treasury), and regulatory change (vice president). During the first year the main job was to control and monitor the policies we had, not to try to develop new, exotic policies. In Reagan's campaign we had been developing policy plans for over five years. Now was the time to close in on the more important ones and implement these policies.

Chapter Nineteen

CABINET GOVERNMENT

The cabinet meeting that President Reagan held on the afternoon of September 24, 1981, was one of the most important meetings of his first year in office. That evening he was making a nationally televised speech, appealing for continued support for his new economic program and specifically calling for an additional $80 billion in federal budget cuts. He felt those budget cuts were essential for the success of his economic recovery program, but he also knew it was risky politically, and he needed the complete, enthusiastic support of his entire cabinet.

It was the purpose of that cabinet meeting to brief them on the speech he was giving that night and to make sure they would all hold firm in their support for the substantial cuts they had all taken in their budgets. The meeting began at 3 p.m. Alexander Haig and William Casey could not attend so their deputies, William Clark and Bobby Ray Inman, sat in for them. This meant that when the meeting started Reagan was flanked on his right (the seat traditionally reserved for the secretary of state) by William Clark, his old friend and former chief of staff while he was governor of California, and on his left (the seat traditionally reserved for the secretary of defense) by Caspar Weinberger, his old friend and former state director of finance in California. Murray Weidenbaum and I were sitting directly behind him, and we commented on how relaxed and confident he seemed.

The president got to the matter at hand quickly.

"All I can say is," he began, "we have to go all out in standing behind this. We have to work our tails off. In my speech tonight I am saying that none of you are pleading for a break on these proposed cuts. We have to win this budget battle just as much as we had to win the other one.

"The time is now. I don't know when there will be another one."

The president's comments were received in silence. None of the cabinet members liked the box they were in. Cutting federal spending was a painful, messy business. But they knew they had no choice (unless they chose to resign), so they all pretended cheerfulness, masking their tension with tight, forced smiles.

Then the secretary of labor, Ray Donovan, who was sitting across and to the right of the president, cleared his throat and, in a deep, gravelly voice that never quite seemed to match his slender body, said, "Mr. President. For the sake of the pride of the people in my department I want to announce that the Department of Labor has cut its fungible funds 56½ percent since we have been here."

After Secretary of Labor Donovan sat back with a pleased, self-satisfied look on his face an anonymous soft, clear voice at the far end of the cabinet table said, "Well, you're halfway home."

Laughter swept the room and a few minutes later the president left for the Oval Office saying, "I'll go back and take pen in hand now (to veto spending bills). I've been doing this for three days."

The whole cabinet applauded.

After the president left, Ed Meese looked over the shell-shocked faces of the cabinet and quipped that there was a reason why the president left early, "He can't stand to see grown men cry."

It was a classic, powerful use of a cabinet meeting, to inform, persuade, and rally support.

Unfortunately, there are very few situations like this where a cabinet meeting is appropriate. Very few national policies fully and equally engage the attention of all cabinet members. Budget cuts across-the-board do, but most issues don't. A significant number of national policy issues fall within the jurisdiction of one department.

A cabinet meeting dealing with an obscure but important point of agricultural policy would be, at best, an excruciating bore for most members of the cabinet. At another extreme, a cabinet meeting dealing with the latest covert operation of the CIA would be unwise.

There are a small number of issues that can be usefully discussed at a full cabinet meeting. And there are also a small number of issues—farm policy, for example—that can be handled solely within the confines of a single department. But most issues cut across two, three, and sometimes four or five department lines. International trade policy, for example, involves the Department of Commerce, the Treasury Department, the Department of Agriculture, the State Department, and the Office of the Trade Representative. The organization of the federal government is not designed to cope with policy issues that are polyjurisdictional.

This leads to the critical policy organization question a newly elected president faces. How is he going to manage the development and implementation of national policies when many of those policies cut smartly across the traditional organization lines of the federal government? Multiplying the difficulty of the problem is the fact that potential policy conflicts between and among departments and agencies pop up frequently. You can reorganize the federal government every four years or so, but it won't make that much difference because as soon as you have finished reorganizing it things will begin to change.

President Reagan solved his policy organization problem by accepting an idea that Ed Meese came up with. He established a system of cabinet councils.

A cabinet council was really a smaller, tailor-made version of the cabinet. Each cabinet council was designed to deal with certain specific issues of national policy. When a cabinet council met it had the same force and authority in dealing with those issues as the entire cabinet did. The members of the cabinet councils were selected primarily on the basis that the departments they headed were deeply involved in the specific issues that would be discussed at the cabinet council meetings.

The cabinet councils were the basic policy chokepoints. Almost all of the policy work during the first few years of the Reagan administration was funneled through them. Some issues were discussed in full cabinet meetings, some were developed and handled by individual departments working with the White House staff, but the vast bulk of policy work flowed through the cabinet councils because only the cabinet councils could deal effectively with national issues that cut across two or more departments, and that included most of the issues.

President Reagan was the chairman of every cabinet council. But unlike the cabinet, which never met without the president, the cabinet councils could meet and take action without the president being there. Every cabinet council had, in addition to the chairman, a designated member who acted as chairman pro tempore.

The pro tempore chairman was a great advantage. The most limiting factor in White House decision-making is the president's time. The cabinet councils could meet frequently, allowing key members of the cabinet to fully discuss issues and to then distill their findings for the president's use. And often the president himself chaired the meeting, especially when informed by his staff that an important or interesting topic was to be discussed. During the first year the president chaired roughly one-fifth of all the meetings of his cabinet councils.

One of the unnoticed yet very important aspects of those meetings was where they took place. All meetings of the cabinet councils were held in the west wing of the White House—either in the Roosevelt Room or in the Cabinet Room, both just a few feet from the president's office. This made it easy for the president to attend when he was so inclined. And it did something else.

By the first week in December 1981 there had been 112 cabinet council meetings held in the White House. This meant that on 112 separate occasions a half-dozen or so cabinet members got into their cars and journeyed to the White House. They usually arrived ten or fifteen minutes early and stayed for a while after the meeting. Most of that extra time before and after the meeting was spent in discussion with other cabinet members and senior members of Reagan's White House staff.

Sometimes after a meeting a member or two of the cabinet would join a White House aide in his office for further discussions. These short impromptu discussions among and between the president's policy advisers were probably as important to the advancement and development of his policy as the meetings themselves. Valuable pieces of information were exchanged, disagreements worked out privately, and Reagan's advisers got to know each other personally, intimately. It created, for a while, an unusual degree of harmony between two normally antagonistic groups, the White House staff and the cabinet.

It was important for symbolic reasons also. All major policy discussions took place at the White House. Just the act of having to leave their fiefdoms, get into a car, and be driven to the White House was a powerful reminder to every member of the cabinet that it was the president's business they were about, not theirs or their department's constituents. Anyone who has actually walked into the west wing of the White House to conduct business will recall the aura the building throws off and the impact it has. It simply is easier to elevate the national interest above special interests in that building. It does not always happen, but it is easier.

Initially there were five cabinet councils. One on economic affairs, one on natural resources and the environment, one on commerce and trade, one on human resources, and one on food and agriculture. Later, a sixth one on legal policy was added. They were all pretty much organized the same way.

The cabinet members who were also chairmen pro tempore of the councils had a greater degree of influence on policy development than the other members of the cabinet. They participated in deciding when the meetings were held, how often, and most importantly, what was going to be on the agenda. In effect the chairmen of the cabinet councils were supercabinet members.

The cabinet council system was a fairly elegant solution to the problem of how to effectively use cabinet members in the development of national policy. The concept that Meese came up with provided a way for Reagan's cabinet to participate directly in the debate and discussion that helped shape his domestic policy.

The next critical step was to figure out how to staff the cabinet council meetings, how to conduct the detailed studies and analyses that the cabinet members would need to make intelligent and informed recommendations to the president, and how to handle the logistical work necessary to keep the system running smoothly— setting dates and times of meetings, notifying everyone in a timely fashion, setting the agenda for the meetings, and taking minutes and keeping records.

The administrative support for the cabinet councils came out of the Office of Cabinet Administration in Ed Meese's office. This office was headed by Craig Fuller, a young executive who formerly worked for Michael Deaver and Peter Hannaford in their public relations firm in Los Angeles. He had little interest in policy, but was extremely effective in setting up a computerized operation that tracked all the issues that soon began flooding through the cabinet councils. Most of the time we actually knew what was going on and where, and who was doing it, something almost unheard of in the higher reaches of the federal government bureaucracy.

The Office of Policy Development, which I headed, was responsible for developing and reviewing domestic and economic policy. On paper we were supposed to develop new ideas, suggest them to the cabinet councils or the cabinet, or to the president, and review and comment on all domestic issues as they came up. In reality, at least during the first year, I saw the purpose of my office as quite different.

We didn't need to develop any new policy ideas for Ronald Reagan. He had been examining public policy issues for most of his adult life. He had a long, long list of specific policy changes that he thought were very important and that he wanted to make right now.

Economic policy was at the top, way at the top, of his domestic policy priority list. The last thing in the world we needed was to go on some new policy wild goose chase. If we diverted our time and energy elsewhere that would only lessen our chances of achieving the policy changes Reagan had already determined he wanted.

What we needed was a policy implementation unit in the White House, a group of people who would try to keep the policy effort focused on those things that Reagan wanted done, and in the order he wanted to do them. We needed to control, channel, and monitor a whole truckload of policies we already developed, not to innovate and probe into sensitive, politically difficult issues. We also needed to make sure that Reagan's issues stayed at the top of the policy agenda, and we needed some way to make sure we could choke off less important and less relevant ideas that could only use up valuable time and keep us from accomplishing the big policy goals that we already had on our hands.

To help accomplish this I suggested to Meese that we establish a special staffing organization for the cabinet councils. Its primary purpose—unstated at the time—was to keep track of all major policy developments throughout the vastness of the federal government and to keep our resources tightly focused on those policies and those issues that President Reagan wanted. It was also to be flexible enough to suggest tactical ways of achieving those policy goals and to come up with new ideas that would make the policies even better.

Each cabinet council was provided with a formal support staff called a secretariat whose purpose was to provide the staffing on all policy issues to come before each council. An executive secretary was in charge of each secretariat. Every cabinet member appointed one person to the secretariat. This insured that the cabinet member was sure to be informed of all policy staff work taking place and that the secretariat had a reliable, fast way to get in touch with every cabinet member. Moreover, it helped the cabinet members to trust and feel comfortable with the staff work provided to them.

The executive secretaries in charge of all the secretariats of the cabinet councils were all chosen from my staff. They were White House staff members and carried the title of either senior policy adviser or special assistant to the president for policy development. In addition, I also named one or two other White House staff members to serve as members of each cabinet council secretariat. The executive secretaries were a critical part of the policy process. While they all worked directly for me, they also worked closely with the chairmen of the cabinet councils and the members to develop the agenda and background papers for the meetings.

The executive secretaries were a superb control and monitoring instrument. They were in constant touch with the cabinet members and their staff who were represented on their council, they met regularly with me in my office to discuss the current and future work of the councils, and they reported all administrative matters to the Office of Cabinet Administration in Meese's office, which, in turn, kept us all informed. The result was a knowledgeable White House staff with tight control of the domestic policy agenda. We had a clear picture of what policy issues were developing, how urgent they were, and when they were coming before the cabinet councils for discussion. I knew, Ed Meese knew, and so did Jim Baker, the chief of staff, and Michael Deaver, the deputy chief of staff. It did not operate perfectly. Every now and then an issue would slip through the policy net. But the cabinet council system did have a remarkably high batting average.

The senior White House staff—Meese, Baker, Deaver, and

myself—could also initiate policy studies and place issues on the cabinet councils' agenda and, perhaps even more importantly, could remove issues from that agenda, park issues temporarily by sending them back for further review and discussion, and assign them to the council that would most effectively handle them. It was a management system that placed enough power and flexibility in the hands of Reagan's senior aides so that they could shape and direct the course of discussion and recommendations to fit his priorities. This was done rigorously. Issues that the president had at the top of his list went to the top of our list and every effort was directed toward them.

Much of the policy analysis work of the cabinet councils was done through working groups, a concept I developed and suggested to Meese. Working groups were ad hoc teams established by the cabinet councils. They concentrated on specific issues. Their members were chosen by the executive secretaries after consultation with the chairman pro tempore of the cabinet councils and with me. Unlike the secretariat, which was a group representing the cabinet members of each council, the working group staff could be drawn from any department or agency, and even from the private sector if appropriate. The criterion for membership was expertise in the policy area under consideration. During that first year dozens of working groups were established to do policy analysis work for the cabinet councils. The policies they studied and made recommendations on ranged from natural gas deregulation to telecommunications to federal credit policy to civil rights to migrant workers.

The working groups proved to be a flexible management tool. They allowed us to concentrate the efforts of the best and brightest experts available without worrying about the territorial jealousies of departments and agencies. They also allowed us to postpone presidential action on controversial issues so we could focus on more critical policies. If interest groups complained about inaction on the part of President Reagan we could always point to the ongoing studies of the working groups. Almost without exception those special interest groups trusted Reagan enough to accept delay as long as the studies of the working groups were active and moving ahead. They saved us a great deal of political trouble, especially during the first year when we wanted to devote all our time and energy to economic policy. Finally, by *not* establishing a working group, we were able to submerge certain issues until we were ready to deal with them.

To ensure that the White House was fully involved in the deliberations of the working groups I assigned at least one member of my staff to serve on each working group. By judicious selection this enabled us to make sure President Reagan's views were represented faithfully throughout even the early phases of the analyses, and we were also ensured of being quickly informed if the direction of the analyses began to veer from Reagan's policies.

And then, just to make sure, the president appointed three people—Vice President George Bush, Ed Meese, the counsellor to the president, and James Baker, the Chief of Staff,—as ex officio members of every council. As a practical matter Bush, Meese, and Baker rarely attended the meetings of the cabinet councils unless the discussions reached a fairly critical stage. They largely left it to me to represent the president's views during the discussions.

I often reminded the cabinet councils of the president's campaign promises and his personal views on specific policy issues, and soon became known as the conscience of the administration to some, and as an irritating nag to others. After being reminded several times of Reagan's campaign commitments and being shown the actual statements, David Stockman referred to the written record of Reagan's earlier policy positions as the "scrolls."

During the first year I took part in more cabinet council meetings than anyone else and in October 1981 became the fourth ex officio member of all the cabinet councils.

The cabinet council meeting was the main policy chokepoint, a place where new ideas could be introduced, good ideas encouraged, and bad ideas sunk. The secretariats and the policy working groups served as effective sub-chokepoints, channeling the flow into cabinet councils. In effect, it was like a series of canals or channels with gates and traps. As long as the policy flow accorded with President Reagan's views we just watched and let it roll, intervening only when the process threatened to get off the tracks we laid down.

The operations of the cabinet councils were largely unnoticed by the media, and of those who cared about them at all, few ever understood their true purpose and function. In fact, most members of the White House staff did not seem to understand them, especially those who did not attend the meetings.

Some of the people who worked for me resented the process.

They had just joined the White House staff of a conservative president whom they revered. They wanted to develop new policy, to be creative.

Subsequently, they were upset when I insisted we focus our available time and energy on policies that Reagan already had decided on. They never seemed to understand or appreciate how easy it would be to fragment our policy efforts, and to end up trying to do everything at once, as President Carter had done, accomplishing nothing. Even to this day some of them have never forgiven me for not letting them craft their own policy proposals and vie for a small place in history. I do regret this, but I would have regretted it far, far more if we had not ruthlessly focused our policy efforts on the main game in town, on Reagan's comprehensive economic program.

The preeminent cabinet council was the Cabinet Council on Economic Affairs. Its work dominated the whole council process. During the first year of his administration, economic policy *was* domestic policy. This fact alone ensured that the Cabinet Council on Economic Affairs would be the main player. Of the one hundred and twelve cabinet council meetings during the first year, fifty-seven (just over half) were meetings of the Cabinet Council on Economic Affairs.

Another factor that contributed to its dominant role were the people who played key roles in its operation. The working chairman was Donald Regan, the secretary of the treasury. It took him a while to grasp fully what Reagan wanted done in economic policy, but once he had it he used all of the finely honed skills of a top Wall Street financial executive to implement that policy. Regan could be abrasive and gruff, but he was smart, tough, and thoroughly committed to Reagan's economic policies. I liked him and liked working with him.

Regan bore a startling resemblance to the late George Raft, the famous white-haired movie actor who played so many tough guy roles in the gangster movies of the 1930s and '40s. At times he even acted like the old actor. His long silver hair, the chiseled nose, and a naturally proud demeanor all combined to create an image that would have been just as much at home being a gangster boss in the movies as it was heading up the Cabinet Council on Economic Affairs. Regan used the cabinet council effectively and skillfully, with enthusiasm and force.

He was greatly aided by the person we agreed should serve as the executive secretary of his council, Roger Porter. Porter was bright, and a master of the paper flow. Fairly young, in his mid-thirties, his boyish face and curly hair made him look even younger, belying a vast experience in national policymaking. He had a unique background, having served as executive secretary of President Ford's Economic Policy Board in the White House from 1974 to 1977. Like Regan, he quickly adapted himself to every nuance of Reagan's economic policies and was indispensable in shepherding them through the cabinet council and helping shape them into our nation's new economic policy.

To further strengthen the staff support for this critical cabinet council I assigned two, instead of one, members of my staff to serve on the secretariat, including one of my most trusted assistants, Kevin Hopkins. Hopkins was a young economist, who pursued his Ph.D. in economics at UCLA but stopped just short of completing it to volunteer to work for the Reagan campaign in 1979. Since then he was closely and intimately involved with every single phase of the complicated development of Reagan's economic program.

The Cabinet Council on Economic Affairs discussed and made recommendations on the policy tactics of spending control, tax policy, monetary policy, and international economic questions. Besides the treasury, the other departments and agencies on the council were state (George Shultz), commerce (Malcolm Baldridge), labor (Raymond Donovan), transportation (Drew Lewis), the Office of Management and Budget (David Stockman), the Council of Economic Advisers (Murray Weidenbaum), the trade representative (William Brock), and the ex officio members, Bush, Meese, Baker, and myself.

While the Cabinet Council on Economic Affairs was the major instrument for implementing Reagan's policies, there were a number of other chokepoints in the White House. One was the cabinet, where economic policies of broad sweep were discussed. Most of the economic deliberations of the full cabinet were essentially briefings by the president and other senior advisers. But it was still a potentially powerful chokepoint. Any questions about the direction or validity of Reagan's program could be raised directly with him by any member of the cabinet. But the cabinet had been chosen well, and no one opposed the basic thrust of the president's policies.

The cabinet councils proved to be surprisingly effective for President Reagan during the early years of his administration. They allowed him to govern with a fully engaged, active cabinet. As two professors noted in a 1986 article in the *Presidential Studies Quarterly*, "Reagan's use of the Cabinet council process has been a most imaginative endeavor, a process which extended the transition and promoted implementation of the Reagan program."[1]

One Friday in August 1981 I invited Stuart Eizenstat to lunch at the White House. Eizenstat had been President Carter's domestic policy adviser from 1976 to 1980, and he was very helpful and gracious to Reagan's staff during the difficult transition period. Although we were far apart on the political spectrum—or at least as far apart as a left-wing Democrat and a right-wing Republican can get—he was honest, highly intelligent, and had good policy judgment. Over lunch we began swapping stories and I was soon telling him about the operational details of the cabinet councils. I probably told him more than he wanted to know, but he was the first person, aside from my immediate associates on the White House staff, who was not only interested in the system we devised, but was also quick to grasp and understand every nuance. Eizenstat later wrote to me that the cabinet council concept is "one of the more intriguing organizational efforts at cabinet-White House cooperation that we have seen in years."[2]

Chapter Twenty

SENIOR STAFF

The cabinet councils were not the only White House forums in which domestic policy was shaped. Another important economic policy chokepoint was the troika. Named after a Russian vehicle drawn by three horses abreast, the troika is the nickname normally used for the three people who are the president's top economic advisers—the secretary of the treasury, the chairman of the Council of Economic Advisers, and the director of the Office of Management and Budget. In the Reagan White House the troika had four members, the three I just mentioned—Donald Regan, Murray Weidenbaum, and David Stockman—and myself. I tried in vain to get people to call it a quadriad, even joking that someone might say that calling a group of four a troika showed that President Reagan's economic advisers could not count. But tradition dies hard in Washington, so we continued with the troika plus one.

The group met every Tuesday morning at 7:30 A.M. for breakfast in the elegant dining room maintained in the Treasury Building for the private use of the secretary of the treasury. Arriving at a small entrance on the side of the building nearest the White House, we were met by a security guard who would summon a tiny, slow elevator reserved for the exclusive use of the secretary of the treasury. We ate at a small table for four. Regan always sat opposite Stockman, and I always sat across from Weidenbaum. The seating was never planned, it just seemed to happen that way. The breakfasts were always excellent, prepared by Regan's chef and, unlike the breakfasts we ate in the White House mess, we didn't have to pay for them.

The meetings usually lasted 40 or 45 minutes, during which we exchanged information, argued, and then gave ourselves assignments. Anything relevant to the development of the economic program could be put on the table. The meetings were friendly and high-spirited. There was often disagreement on tactics, but never on the goals of the program.

There was even some friendly teasing. Donald Regan was old enough to be David Stockman's father and sometimes treated him as if that were the case—much to David's annoyance. By the end of the first year a certain amount of friction had built up between Regan and Stockman. On November 10, 1981, Regan decided to make a real overture to Stockman. It was Stockman's thirty-fifth birthday. Regan ordered up a foot-wide birthday cake with white, sugary frosting. Instead of candles the top of the cake was decorated with thirty-five little red plastic hatchets, symbolizing David's heroic efforts to control federal spending. Stockman was pleased and slightly embarrassed. And we ate it, even though it probably was the first time any of us ever had birthday cake for breakfast.

The warm glow of camaraderie we felt at Stockman's birthday party that morning soon dimmed, and then vanished. Later the same day the *Atlantic Monthly* magazine appeared on the newsstands carrying an article based on lengthy, detailed interviews Stockman gave to an editor of the *Washington Post*. Stockman had regularly and systematically (in eighteen or nineteen Saturday morning breakfast meetings at the Hay Adams hotel near the White House) leaked much of what was discussed in our breakfast meetings and at other meetings on economic policy. But he added something else in his early morning musings with the *Washington Post:* the charge that the essence of Reagan's economic program was a Trojan horse designed to benefit the rich. The charge was false, but the quote was accurate. Stockman had said it.

We all felt betrayed, especially President Reagan, and the breakfast meetings were never the same again.

Initially Stockman protested his innocence. Two days after the Judas-like piece appeared in the *Atlantic Monthly*, Stockman attended a meeting of the Republican congressional leaders with President Reagan in the Cabinet Room at the White House and tried to explain what he had done. Nervously he presented his case to his hard-eyed elders, saying, "It's hard to talk with your foot in your mouth. I'm truly flabbergasted. The article in the *Atlantic Monthly* is totally at variance with what I really think. I truly regret I have been shafted by someone in the journalism profession. But I truly believe in our economic program. I have been working on it twenty hours a day, and we should all continue to work for it."

No one said a word.

Finally, President Reagan cleared his throat and announced plans to move ahead with the MX missile and the B-1 bomber, and soon the Republican leaders were busily engaged discussing everything from national defense to abortion, bussing, and prayer in the schools.

Stockman sat quietly, his quick eyes darting around the room, trying to assess their assessment of him. It was too late. They did not believe him, and he would never regain their confidence.

David Stockman was profoundly pessimistic by nature. If he were ever to write a history of American baseball, he would probably describe Ted Williams of the Boston Red Sox, one of the greatest players of all time, this way: Even at the height of his career, Williams managed to get base hits only 40 percent of the time and struck out repeatedly.

On a number of occasions during 1981, when we were working day and night on Reagan's economic program, David would literally throw his hands into the air, exclaiming "it won't work." After a few words of reassurance he would calm down and return to work at his usual frenetic pace. But he was a driven man, haunted by the idea that only perfection was success. He couldn't seem to stand the idea that the Reagan administration was not going to get all the budget cuts he wanted. As budget director he was well aware that history would one day judge him on his performance, and he seemed afraid that he would be judged not on what he accomplished in terms of Herculean budget cuts, but rather on the size of the budget deficit that remained.

Soon after Stockman became budget director he proposed budget cuts far in excess of what any of us thought possible. Later, when we got about half of those budget cuts, we were all delighted that so much was achieved. But not David. He had been depressed. By the standard of the unrealistic goal he set for himself, he was a failure.

As the years went by and the federal budget deficits continued and grew, Stockman's disappointment congealed into bitter resentment—resentment that eventually found expression in his 1986 book, *The Triumph of Politics,* a self-righteous work with the tone of a screeching bluejay.

It is a curious book. Quickly and brilliantly written, it is full of rich and detailed anecdotes and facts, all accurate. But it also contains a few untrue statements at critical points, and it is marked by gaping holes in the telling of how Reagan fashioned his economic program. It deceived most by the crucial parts of the story left out, parts that in Stockman's version of history never happened. The result was a masterpiece of distortion, a book that damaged the reputation of Stockman far more than the targets of his ire.

The depths of his personal pessimism are starkly etched in the concluding words of the book. "Economic governance of the world's greatest democracy has been shown to be a deadly serious business. There is no room in its equation for scribblers, dreamers, ideologues, and passionate young men bent upon remaking the world according to their own prescriptions." [1]

How sad that someone who had been a scribbler, a dreamer, and a passionate, young ideologue who accomplished a great deal could ultimately find no sense of personal satisfaction in what he had done.

Before Stockman's perfidy was exposed, the weekly economic policy breakfast meeting in the Treasury Department's dining room was an effective, powerful policy chokepoint. During the first year of the Reagan administration little happened in terms of economic policy that the troika plus one did not know and approve of. Every major aspect of economic policy—taxes, spending, deficits, deregulation, economic forecasts, monetary policy—was discussed here before it went to the president.

At the conclusion of our breakfast meetings Stockman usually jumped into a waiting government car and was chauffeured back to his OMB office in the Old Executive Office Building a couple of blocks away, while Weidenbaum and I hurriedly walked over to the morning senior staff meeting in the White House. We were always twenty or twenty-five minutes late on Tuesday mornings, but everyone knew why and no one complained. If anything came up at the breakfast meeting that we thought should be shared with the senior staff, either Weidenbaum or I would make a brief report.

The senior staff meeting that began every morning at 8 A.M. was another economic policy chokepoint. People rarely discussed economic policy per se at those meetings, but they did bring up administrative, political, and media problems that often did bear directly on the making of economic policy.

After the senior staff meeting was over, Weidenbaum left and walked back to his offices in the Old Executive Office Building next door. And I went down the hall to Ed Meese's office for our morning policy meeting, the one that covered the entire policy waterfront—from missile defense and the military draft to farm and economic policy.

The morning policy meeting resulted from a suggestion I made to Ed Meese a few weeks after the president took office. Meese is a prodigious worker, and beneath that jolly exterior lay formidable brainpower that raced and crackled with energy. While other senior aides were tackling ten projects in a day and finishing nine, Meese would be involved in fifty and finishing forty of them. Meese loved national policy issues, all of them. The trouble was the ten or so he did not finish. Those projects you did not want to be involved with.

From the president's point of view, Meese was a wonder in the White House. Look at all he accomplished. However, from the point of view of the few who were not able to get Meese's attention because he was hopelessly overcommitted, Meese was a disaster. His briefcase earned the nickname of the black hole because it was reputed that anything that disappeared inside it never came out. I worked with Meese for years and appreciated his tremendous abilities, but I also knew that his natural working state was to be overcommitted. The trick to working effectively with Ed Meese was to make sure you got to spend time with him, personally. After discussing it with Richard Allen, now the national security adviser, who also reported to the president through Meese, I suggested to Meese that he set aside at least thirty minutes every morning, in his office, to sit down with the White House staff responsible for domestic and economic policy, foreign and defense policy, and budget policy.

He immediately agreed. Every morning after the senior staff

meeting a small group of us gathered around the small conference table in Meese's corner office on the first floor of the west wing. We had to sit at the table. Meese's desk was piled so high and covered so completely with reports, letters, documents, and notebooks that you literally could not see what the top of the desk was made of. But the view from his office windows was superb, over the front lawn of the White House, on out across Pennsylvania Avenue into Lafayette Park. Besides Meese and his immediate personal staff, those in attendance were Richard Allen, Edwin Harper, the deputy director of OMB, and George Keyworth, the science adviser to the president.

The morning policy meeting became another chokepoint in the making of economic policy. As a matter of fact, it was a critical chokepoint for the making of all policy during the early years of the Reagan administration. Everything from monetary policy to the strategic defense initiative to welfare reform and budget policy was discussed at Meese's morning meetings. Usually all the daily morning meetings in the White House ended by 9:30 A.M. and we could begin to do other things.

One other very important economic policy chokepoint was the late afternoon meeting of the Legislative Strategy Group (LSG). This group was chaired by James Baker and met regularly, usually beginning somewhere between 4:30 and 5:30 P.M. This group plotted the administration's legislative strategy, that is, how to get Congress to vote for the policies that President Reagan wanted. Although the focus of this group was completely on the implementation, not the development, of policy, its recommendations for compromises with Congress could have a significant effect on that policy.

There were several key members of this group. There was Max Friedersdorf, who was in charge of all congressional relations for President Reagan. Quiet and distinguished, Friedersdorf had a reputation for honesty and integrity and was highly regarded by senators and congressmen of both parties. He was indispensable to Reagan's extraordinary success with Congress in the first year. And there was Richard Darman, James Baker's right-hand man, who functioned as the secretary of the group and fashioned much of its legislative strategy.

Darman was an odd case. A man of unquestionably high intelligence with the rare capacity to come up with new, innovative, effective ways to solve problems, he was easily the most disliked man in the White House. Even his boss, Baker, didn't seem to care for him very much. It certainly wasn't because he didn't work hard enough. Many a night I left my White House office at 9 or 10 P.M. feeling somewhat virtuous that I was the last one to leave. But I never had that satisfaction for long. It seemed that no matter how late I left, there was always one lighted office in the basement of the west wing that I could see as I walked away from the White House and looked back—Dick Darman's.

There was some suspicion that he wasn't a loyal backer of Reagan's policies because of his former government service as a close aide to a prominent left-wing Republican, Elliot Richardson. But after watching Darman closely in meeting after meeting, for well over a year, I concluded that he never once advanced any policy position that was not fully consistent with President Reagan's. In fact, he was a more consistent supporter of Reagan's policies than were some of the senior aides who had been with Reagan for many years.

Then why did people resent him so? He had a quick, brilliant mind and could be arrogantly abrupt with people mentally slower than himself. He was a serious man who sometimes appeared cold and aloof, not the typical gregarious Washington politician. He had little time for being overly friendly, instead concentrating his time and energy on studying and calculating and plotting what the next political move should be. But his somewhat abrasive personality could not account for the depth of antagonism felt toward him. He was just one of many difficult personalities that populated the White House staff and the cabinet.

In retrospect the answer seems to be that he was the only senior White House staff member working for Reagan who did not help elect him. Darman alone stood by and did not lift a finger to help Reagan during the five long years he ran for president. And then, after he was elected, Darman was chosen by James Baker, for whom he worked earlier in the Department of Commerce, for a powerful position on the White House staff, bypassing dozens of others who worked long and hard for Reagan. Forgotten was the fact that Darman was extremely capable, forgotten was the fact that he contributed measurably to Reagan's success as president, remembered only was the fact that this fellow Darman had somehow acquired a political birthright that was not his.

The Legislative Strategy Group was responsible for devising and implementing President Reagan's legislative strategy for a wide range of issues. Economic policy was one of its most important concerns, but not by any means the only one. I was not a regular member of the group, but I did attend, by invitation, all the meetings that dealt with economic policy or other major domestic policy issues. Donald Regan, Murray Weidenbaum, and David Stockman were also invited to attend all sessions that dealt with how to get President Reagan's economic program adopted by a hostile, Democratically-controlled Congress. It helped that the Senate was in the hands of Republicans, but the House of Representatives was not.

In effect there were always two economic programs, the ideal one that Reagan and his advisers wanted and the one that could secure the approval of the House of Representatives. Jim Baker was in charge of the Congressional negotiations and had the unenviable job of negotiating with congressional leaders to get an economic program acceptable both to them and President Reagan. Many times, the result of the group's deliberations was to say to the president, "Look, we know you want 100 percent of what you asked for. But now you have a choice. You can either take 80 percent of what you want or nothing."

President Reagan always took the 80 percent.

In fact, he almost always got more than he would have been willing to settle for, because in the beginning he instinctively asked for far more than he could reasonably expect to get. Time and again he would ask for 200 percent, and then, after weeks or months of brutal, unyielding negotiation, he would suddenly settle for 80 percent of what he was asking for and walk away from the table with 160 percent. Less than what he asked for, more than what he would have ultimately settled for. Everyone seemed to be happy. He was satisfied and delighted with the result and Congress seemed well pleased with the victory they scored by beating him down in the negotiations.

One of the curious side effects of Reagan's negotiating style, particularly on economic policy that first year, was the bad reputation that Jim Baker got with conservative activists in the Republican party. Every time President Reagan settled with Congress for less than he originally demanded, some conservatives would start screaming that Jim Baker sold him out. After all, they reasoned,

Baker was George Bush's campaign manager in 1980, and even though he later joined the Reagan campaign and was instrumental in getting Reagan elected, he once had opposed him. He had to be a closet liberal. And how else could you explain how a man of such unyielding principle as Ronald Reagan agreed to these humiliating compromises with a Democratically-controlled Congress?

They never understood that Reagan was far more crafty than they, and that Baker loyally and doggedly pursued the President's agenda. It was Reagan, and Reagan alone, who decided that four-fifths of a loaf, especially a loaf that was perhaps too large to eat to begin with, was better than no loaf.

While the Legislative Strategy Group did not develop new economic policies, it sometimes did propose changes that significantly affected the final outcome of those policies. That is why it was a critical economic policy chokepoint. For example, the centerpiece of Reagan's program was a massive tax cut for individuals, a 10 percent across-the-board cut in income tax rates each year for three years. It was always referred to as a 30 percent tax cut, although the total reduction was only 27.1 percent because the base that the 10 percent annual chop was applied to was lowered by the previous year's cut. Unfortunately, Congress would not accept the idea of a 10 percent tax cut every year for three years, or ten-ten-ten as we called it.

Through Max Friedersdorf and Jim Baker the Democratic leaders told the White House they preferred a one-year tax cut, delayed as long as possible. That would have gutted Reagan's tax plan because the early tax cuts were the most important to early economic recovery. The American economy was a mess then. Postponing a tax cut for possibly a year or more would have been disastrous.

After hours of deliberations the Legislative Strategy Group came up with a counteroffer of five-ten-ten. I argued for a counteroffer of ten-ten-zero, a 10 percent cut right now, 10 percent next year, and leave the third year open. My reasoning was that even though we gave up a sure third year cut, we would get the maximum impact of the tax cut early and, if it was as successful as I thought it would be, we could use the economic record to go back to Congress after two years and ask for, and probably get, the last 10 percent.

Nobody but Jim Baker (who supported it for a couple of hours) liked this option, primarily because it looked as though the president was taking a real political licking, getting only a two-year tax cut program instead of the three-year one he called for all these years. So finally, by consensus, we recommended to the president that he agree to a tax cut plan of five-ten-ten. Congress accepted his counterproposal and that became the heart of his tax policy.

Another important economic policy chokepoint during Reagan's first year in office was something called the Budget Working Group. It had only eight members—David Stockman, who was the chairman, Ed Meese, James Baker, Murray Weidenbaum, Donald Regan, Tim McNamar, the deputy secretary of the treasury, William Brock, the trade representative, and myself. After a few meetings, Stockman, Weidenbaum, and I were the only regular attendees. In practice, the Budget Working Group functioned as a high-level budget appeals court, a supercabinet review group that directly reviewed disputed budget cuts with individual cabinet officers.

The control of federal spending was one of the most important parts of Reagan's economic program. The president was not calling for reductions in federal spending, or even for just holding the line. All he wanted to do was to stop it from growing so fast. Repeatedly, during the campaign, in the transition, and then at White House meetings, Reagan would look around him and say, "Federal spending is going up like this," (raising his arm straight from the shoulder at a 45-degree angle). "We have to bring it down to here," (lowering his arm to about a 30-degree angle).

That was the essence of Reagan's spending control policy. Just keep the rate of government growth at a reasonable level and economic growth, powered by judicious tax rate cuts, would gradually do the rest.

The legendary reputation Reagan acquired for cutting the budget stemmed almost exclusively from reducing large planned increases to moderate planned increases. To be sure, there were some absolute cuts in spending and a few programs were even eliminated entirely, but these were minor compared to the main action—cutting back the amount of increases demanded by the departments and agencies.

It almost looked easy when Reagan would raise his arm, talk about federal spending increases being irresponsible, and then lower his arm to what appeared to be a much more reasonable level. The Bible says, "It is easier for a camel to go through the eye of a needle, than for a rich man to enter the kingdom of God." Until Ronald Reagan became president and David Stockman became the director of OMB, there was more of a chance of pushing a camel through the eye of a needle than there was of cutting *any* federal spending program. It just wasn't done.

It had been that way in the United States for a long, long time. I remember one incident that drove it home to me in 1971 when I was serving as special assistant to President Nixon. In early 1971 two of us, Edwin Harper and myself, were asked by the president—as a special project—to review the budget that was prepared by Budget Director George Shultz and the cabinet, to see if we could find any programs that could be cut. President Nixon was looking for some federal program that was so bad or wasteful or extravagant that nobody could object if he eliminated it. We weren't looking necessarily for big budget items. We were looking for a symbol, a program that could be cut to establish the principle that federal programs were not blessed with eternal life.

We found one. It was the Board of Tea Experts. The federal government paid them to test imported tea. Part of the Department of Health and Human Services, it was founded by the Import Tea Act of 1897, some ninety years ago. The board is made up of seven expert tea judges who meet annually in Brooklyn, New York, to set the tea standards for the coming year. The tasting table is a work of art, in effect a large lazy Susan brimming with saucers and cups full of freshly brewed tea.

The board members sat at their slowly spinning table and tasted and reflected upon cup after cup of tea, day after day, and either granted or withheld their seal of approval. All the tea was privately packaged and the approval of the federal government was highly prized. The federal government was doing for the private tea industry what *Good Housekeeping* magazine has done for so many years for its advertisers—giving its seal of approval. There was one difference, however; the taxpayers were paying for something the tea industry should have been paying for.

Harper and I were outraged and delighted. We finally found a federal program that was so bad that no one would object to its demise. So we wrote a one-page memorandum to President Nixon recommending that it be abolished. Nixon enthusiastically agreed. We turned to that part of the budget and, with one hard stroke of the pencil, wiped it out.

Or so we thought. After a few days of self-congratulation, Harper and I were notified that the president did not have the authority to have this item deleted from the federal budget. The Board of Tea Experts had been established by a law passed by Congress, and it was going to take another law to kill it. Undaunted, we spent one full day drafting a small law that would do just that, and then we waited.

In a few weeks it became clear that eliminating the tea tasters was not going to be easy. First, the tea industry screamed. They begged us not to take away their tasters. They even offered to pay for the tasting as long as the federal seal of approval was put on their tea. We refused. We said it was the principle of the thing. The tea tasters had to go. So the tea lobbyists went to work on the congressmen who were members of the subcommittee that would handle the presumptuous legislation to abolish federal tea tasting. The days flashed by as Harper and I got diverted to many other more pressing, more important issues. Finally, we got the word. The subcommittee decided, most regretfully, that because the amount of the money was so small they really could not bother with a special law.

The tea tasters were still alive and well in the federal bureaucracy. That was just one of the small reasons why I was not too optimistic about our chances of cutting any substantial amounts of federal spending when Reagan took office in 1981. David Stockman changed all that. He joined the administration with the enthusiasm of a new puppy, eager and urgent, bounding and leaping through the federal budget with wild-eyed passion. He had the zeal of a newly born-again Christian, the craft and cunning of an Iranian mullah, the body of a thirty-four year old, and the drive to work fourteen-hour days, including Saturdays and some Sundays. He is the only person I ever met who actually read all of the federal budget and that, by itself, was no small advantage to start with.

During the 1980 campaign Reagan proposed federal spending reductions of $13 billion in 1981 and $18 billion in 1982—reductions from what spending was projected to be if no policy changes were made. We thought these were large amounts, and so did everyone else at the time. We also thought it was reasonable and could be done. We did not have the staff, time, and money to analyze specific government programs during the campaign. No presidential candidate has ever done it. Instead, I judged that it would not be unreasonable to recommend cutting all proposed government spending by 2 percent the first year (anyone with a personal budget or anyone who ran a business would readily understand that any budget could take a 2 percent cut easily), and then by another 2 percent the second year.

Reagan and all the campaign advisers quickly agreed that cuts of this magnitude in proposed federal spending could be done and should be done. So I took the budget total for 1981 ($633 billion) and multiplied by 2 percent, and the budget total for 1982 ($710 billion) and multiplied by 4 percent. The proposed spending cuts of $13 billion in 1981 and $28 billion in 1982 were very rough estimates but they established that Reagan was serious about reducing federal spending and he was thinking big, in terms of tens of billions of dollars, not hundreds of thousands of dollars.

Until we all met David Stockman after the election, and he told us what he thought could be cut from the federal budget, we thought these multibillion dollar spending cuts were pretty daring. Stockman, with the brashness of youth and the arrogance of someone who once admitted to an aide that his highest political dream was to be "Emperor of the Americas,"[2] made us all look like pikers. Within weeks he devised a plan to cut almost $50 billion from federal spending during fiscal year 1982. He was predicting budget cuts of over $100 billion by 1986. It was the most dazzling, daring attack ever launched against the forces of the federal budget.

It wasn't all Stockman's fault. Reagan and his senior staff encouraged and egged him on. We all knew that our efforts to control federal spending would be a vital part of the economic program, second in importance only to tax rate reduction. To accomplish that we decided to embrace and co-opt the Office of Management and Budget.

Based on my experience with and observation of earlier presidents, it seemed that all newly elected presidents began by relying heavily on their cabinet appointments to implement their policies. Nixon did it, Ford did it, and so did Carter. But it did not take long, usually a matter of months, for the cabinet officers to be seduced by the professional bureaucrats and the natural constituencies of their departments. Frustrated by the cabinet, the president and his staff would then turn to the professional staff of OMB, a group of about six hundred experts widely regarded as the best, most powerful policy staff in Washington. By then it was too late.

The OMB professionals, once eager to serve the new administration but studiously ignored, were cool toward late, halfhearted efforts to use their talents. Doubly frustrated, the White House would then turn inward and begin to expand its staff, attempting futilely to perform the staff work that was really the responsibility of the hundreds of experts in OMB and the thousands of experts in the departments and agencies. If the president managed to get himself reelected, as Nixon did, they would begin to realize there are not people or money enough in the White House staff structure to do the basic policy analysis work necessary to run the federal government effectively. And once again they would try, usually by the appointment of trusted lieutenants, to get control of OMB and the departments.

Of course, while this is going on, the years are slipping by, and little of the president's policy agenda is moving from something the president wants to do to the category of national law. We hoped not to repeat this history lesson from the past. The cabinet council structure was designed to draw the cabinet as close as possible to the White House on policy development. But how could we fully utilize the enormous talents of the six hundred OMB professionals? We did something that was almost revolutionary. We decided to let OMB know that we liked them, wanted them, needed them, and trusted them.

To emphasize the importance of OMB, Stockman was made an official member of Reagan's cabinet. I then suggested that Edwin Harper, who was going to be named deputy director of OMB, also be given the title of assistant to the president and made a full member of the senior White House staff. That was agreed to and Harper, in effect, became the day-to-day liaison with the White House, reporting directly to Ed Meese as well as to David Stockman. As a senior member of the White House staff, Harper attended all the daily senior staff meetings and served as an invaluable bridge to OMB, keeping them informed about the president's needs and keeping the White House staff informed about OMB's activities.

Stockman turned out to be a superb leader for OMB. He was the first director the professional staff of OMB saw who was not only as smart as they were, but in terms of budget detail, even knew a few things they didn't. He excited and intrigued them. Stockman also took over command of OMB with a very strong, talented personal team. Contrary to the impression given by most press reports, the leadership of OMB was not a one-man show. He brought three of his closest aides from his congressional days with him—Frederick N. Khedouri, Donald W. Moran, and David Gerson. All young, smart, and politically sophisticated, they had worked for Stockman for years. At times the four of them seemed to act as one superperson, with four brains and four voices, all in tune with one another.

To this core group, Stockman added four others: Larry Kudlow, a young economic forecaster from Wall Street who adapted readily and effectively to the corridors of power in the Executive Office of the President; Annelise Anderson, who worked for Reagan in two presidential campaigns, served as George Bush's policy adviser in 1980, and knew Reagan's policies backward and forward; William Schneider, one of the country's top national security experts with long experience on congressional staffs; and James Miller, one of the country's top regulatory experts.

These seven people were critical for the successes that Stockman did achieve. It was probably the most talented team to ever head the budget office. They provided a level of leadership and policy guidance that was unrivaled in OMB's history.

And critical to the success of this executive budget team headed by Stockman were the six hundred professionals, the budget experts. Their output during that first year was extraordinary. The studies of specific programs—concise and clear, accurate and insightful—poured out of their offices in such quantity that it was difficult to read them all. Every day, it seemed, one or two thick, blue, vinyl-clad notebooks would arrive in my office from OMB. Each one was packed with studies and analyses of specific government programs, all giving the key budget figures you had to know to ask intelligent questions. It was an astonishing outpouring of high quality, professional work. It was almost as if they were waiting for someone to say we like you, we want you, we need you, and we trust you. In effect, that first year we acted as if the OMB professionals were part of the White House staff and treated them that way. It worked dramatically well.

The Budget Working Group was Stockman's idea. Normally, the director of OMB gave all his proposed budget cuts directly to the individual cabinet officers involved. Any spending cuts the cabinet member found unacceptable he could appeal directly to the president. Under normal conditions that procedure worked well. There weren't that many cuts to begin with, and the number of appeals from the cabinet was bound to be limited. But the planned spending cuts were not normal. They were so massive and unprecedented that there was likely to be a flood of appeals from the cabinet, so many appeals that demands on the president's time could become unreasonable, and then the spending control efforts might be scuttled. So Stockman proposed an idea to Meese to set up a committee to "review all the remaining budget cuts with the affected cabinet members *before* they went to the president and the full cabinet."[3]

In practice this meant that any cabinet officer who wanted to fight a proposed cut in his budget had to appeal it to the board first, in person. The Budget Working Group was a hanging jury. The board members were all fully aware of the importance of overall spending control for the success of President Reagan's economic program. And no matter how eloquent or how plaintive the cabinet member's plea was to save the federal spending that OMB was lopping off his department, the board members shook their heads and firmly said no.

The Budget Working Group was effective. Billions of dollars of federal budget cuts which were appealed to the board and denied were not appealed to the president. The board played an important role in choking off the normal, instinctive moves of the federal bureaucracy to get every nickel they can from the taxpayers. It helped Stockman do his job of implementing a critical part of Reagan's economic program.

One of the most important components of economic policy is monetary policy. In the United States monetary policy is handled in a curious way. It is set by the Federal Reserve Board, independently of the other branches of the federal government. Any president has a strong interest in the monetary policy established by the Federal Reserve Board because it can have a major effect on the success of his overall economic policy. But how the president expresses that interest is a delicate and sensitive question.

Many people assume that the president makes monetary policy. He does not. The Federal Reserve Board does and it, as I once heard someone say, reports first to Congress and then to God. The president and his advisers can attempt to persuade or cajole the board, but one must be very careful about this. Even a hint of a compromise of the board's integrity would probably cause a back-lash, creating just the opposite kind of policy from what the president wanted. The major power a president has is the power of appointment. Every two years he gets to appoint one of the seven members of the Federal Reserve Board for a 14-year term, and every four years he gets to appoint one of those seven as the chairman.

At the beginning of Reagan's first term Paul Volcker, then the chairman of the federal reserve system, was acutely concerned about even the appearance of compromising his independence. So much so that he flatly refused to come to the White House for his first meeting with President Reagan and even turned down Reagan's offer to go to the Federal Reserve Board building and meet with all the members (this had never been done, and still hasn't).

Finally, we worked out a compromise that pleased everyone. Volcker agreed to have lunch with President Reagan on neutral territory, the treasury building. It was to be the first of a series of regular meetings between Reagan and Volcker.

The first meeting was somewhat bizarre. Instead of being driven the quarter mile or so to the treasury building, President Reagan decided to walk. Despite the concerns of the Secret Service he sallied forth from the front door of the White House, surrounded on all sides by senior aides and Secret Service men, with a sur-prised and delighted press corps trailing along behind him. It looked like a small circus parade as it turned right on Pennsylvania Ave-nue, marched east to 15th Street, and then turned right down to the treasury building and walked up the steps. It had been a long, long time since any president had been brave (or brash) enough to walk the streets of Washington, D.C. It was fun, everyone thor-oughly enjoyed it, especially Reagan, but it was also dangerous. And it never happened again.

It was a small group for lunch. In addition to Reagan and Volcker, those attending were Edwin Meese, James Baker, Donald Regan, Murray Weidenbaum, David Stockman, and myself. Paul Volcker sat to the immediate right of President Reagan. We were just barely seated when the president turned to Volcker and said, "I was won-dering if you could help me with a question that's often put to me. I've had several letters from people who raise the question of why we need any Federal Reserve at all. They seem to feel that it is the Fed that causes much of our monetary problems and that we would be better off if we abolished it. Why do we need the federal reserve?"

The president was serious.

I was sitting across the table from Volcker and the view was priceless. His face muscles went slack and his lower jaw literally sagged a half-inch or so as his mouth fell open. For several seconds he just looked at Reagan, stunned and speechless. It is a good thing Volcker had not had time to light one of his long cigars, because he might have swallowed it.

My God, he must have thought, here I am the head of the largest, most powerful banking system in the world and the very first thing this guy—who is going to be president of the United States for at least the next four years—says to me is to justify my existence!

To Volcker's credit he recovered quickly and smoothly, and replied, "Well, Mr. President, there have been concerns expressed along those lines, but I think you can make a very strong case that the Federal Reserve has operated well and has been very important to the stability of our economy."

And then he proceeded to give a brief lecture on the virtues of the Fed. The rest of the lunch was uneventful. Some general remarks about the economy were made, but mostly specific, factual questions were directed at Volcker.

And that was pretty much how the subsequent meetings between Reagan and Volcker went. President Reagan believed that a sound, stable, and predictable monetary policy was essential to restoring the economic health of the country. So did Volcker. Volcker was very concerned about the independence of the Federal Reserve and Reagan respected that concern. Others in the administration and in Congress often became impatient with Volcker and his fellow governors and urged Reagan to pressure the Fed, publicly and privately, to follow a different course. That would have been foolish and wrong, almost certainly having the opposite effect from what was intended.

The reason the monetary policy meetings between President Reagan and Volcker were an important economic policy chokepoint was not because of the good they accomplished, but rather because of the bad they avoided. After the first meeting at the treasury all the remaining meetings took place in the Oval Office at the White House. Volcker always came alone. Usually two or three of Reagan's economic advisers sat in on the meeting. I attended them all, accompanied by Meese or Baker or Stockman or Regan, and sometimes by all of them.

We rarely said anything. All the talking was between Volcker and Reagan, with Volcker doing most of the talking, presenting tables and charts, and explaining what the Fed was doing and why. Reagan never asked him to either ease or tighten the money supply. I think Volcker very much appreciated the lack of direct pressure. Given that Volcker was a Democrat appointed by President Carter, a surprising amount of goodwill seemed to develop between them. Basically we figured that Volcker was an extraordinarily capable individual who, if we treated him decently, would probably conduct himself in a professional, nonpartisan manner.

Proffering carrots and withholding the stick worked nicely, although it almost became derailed on July 21, 1981, when I received an angry, short letter from Chairman Volcker.

All it said was,

> Marty:
> I didn't know you distrusted my
> security that much!
>   Paul

Earlier, Volcker asked me for a few modest favors. He wanted a signed photo of President Reagan (which I arranged for) and a White House pass so he would not have to suffer the mild indignity of having to show his driver's license every time he came over to visit the president (this I thought I had arranged for). On July 15, 1981, Volcker was sent a snooty memorandum by John F. W. Rogers, one of Jim Baker's staff who was in charge of the physical administration of the White House. Rogers, a young man of little experience, informed the chairman of the Federal Reserve that, "We will be unable to honor your request" for a White House pass, and then sniffingly explained that "a decision has been made to reduce the number of White House passes in an effort to increase security and decrease extraordinary costs incurred with clearances," and then added righteously in parentheses "(one security clearance alone costs $3,000)."

It was just one example of the dozens of small, stupid things that happened now and then that could, if not taken care of, cause real damage. A staff functionary had just insulted a key person vital to the success of President Reagan's economic program, and indirectly everything the president wanted to accomplish, by implying he might be a security risk and then telling him it wasn't worth spending $3,000 to find out if he was or wasn't.

I immediately spoke to Meese and Baker, and John F. W. Rogers soon issued Chairman Volcker a shiny, new White House pass, and Volcker continued to follow a sound, relatively stable, fairly predictable monetary policy which was crucial to Reagan's economic program.

Chapter Twenty-One

SPECIAL PRESIDENTIAL ADVISERS

There were many economic policy chokepoints. One small but important one was the speechwriting unit. For many years now it has been impossible for any president to personally write or even dictate all the speeches, statements, and letters that need his signature or voice. There isn't enough time, even if he didn't do anything but that. He has to rely heavily on the talents of skilled writers who prepare manuscript drafts for him to review and approve, or edit and change, or, at times reject.

Presidential speechwriters are a rare breed. There is no formal course of study, no training available, no books to read. A good speechwriter has to make believe he or she is the president, know his policies and all of their nuances completely, be able to imitate his writing and speaking style, and then with verve and eloquence, write the words that will become an important part of history. There is even a special club for former full-time speechwriters to U.S. presidents, called the Judson Welliver Society. Judson Welliver was the first White House speechwriter; he wrote for President Calvin Coolidge.[1]

Most of the work I did for presidential candidates or presidents was in the policy area, but I occasionally attempted to write a speech draft. The soundest advice I ever received on the craft of presidential speechwriting came from Bryce Harlow when we were flying around the country during Nixon's 1968 campaign. We were assigned seats next to each other on the airplane. After reviewing the speech I had been working on for days, Harlow turned to me and said, "Remember—whenever you write for a president you can be forgiven for not being eloquent or brilliant, but you will never be forgiven for being wrong."

That did not exactly calm my rising anxiety about the speech, but it made an important point. The words of a president, and even the presidential nominee, are magnified enormously once he or she speaks or writes. It is almost as if you took a normal voice and hooked it up to a world-wide amplifier that multiplied the sound by 100,000 times. The slightest fault or distortion can be blown up into jagged, glaring errors.

Reagan's speechwriters were probably the most talented group assembled since the days of Kennedy and Nixon. The number one speechwriter during the beginning of Reagan's first term was Kenneth Khachigian. I knew Ken since 1968 when he came to work for me as a policy researcher in the New York City headquarters of Nixon's presidential campaign. Then in his early twenties and in his second year at Columbia University Law School, Khachigian literally walked in off the streets and volunteered to work.

Khachigian was one of the first of many young conservatives who would leave such a lasting mark on America. He had a quiet, easygoing personality, cared deeply about issues, worked long hours, and wrote beautifully. Before long he was a full-time staff member of the campaign. His pay was $100 a week. After the campaign, he finished law school and then joined the White House staff in 1971, where he rose to become one of President Nixon's top speechwriters, only leaving in 1974 when Nixon was forced to resign. In 1980 he responded to my urging, joined Reagan's presidential campaign, and was soon flying around the country at Reagan's side. His presence on the campaign plane and in the White House received very little press attention. He was just the voice of the president.

Khachigian was backed up by four other speechwriters: Dana Rohrabacher, a former reporter who was an ardent libertarian and worked in both the 1976 and 1980 campaigns; Bentley Elliott, one of the most talented and ideologically consistent writers in the country; Anthony Dolan, another conservative veteran of the 1980 campaign; and Mari Maseng, one of the first female presidential speechwriters. They were policy clones of Reagan on almost all issues. They knew what he wanted written without asking.

The potential power of a speechwriter to do good or bad is enormous. In the Reagan White House it was monitored by an extensive review system. The rough drafts of every major statement or speech were systematically sent to a dozen or so senior advisers for criticism and review. For example, days before the president made his first economic speech to the nation on February 5, 1981, Khachigian sent copies of the draft speech to Vice President Bush, Donald Regan, Ed Meese, Jim Baker, Michael Deaver, Murray Weidenbaum, David Stockman, Max Friedersdorf, David Gergen, Lyn Nofziger, me, and a few others. We, in turn, often photocopied the speech for our key staff members to review. The net result was a very fine review sieve that usually strained out any factual errors or deviation from policy.

The review group never had a formal name. Perhaps we should have called it the editorial board. In any event, the review process proved to be an effective way to fine tune and proofread the final versions of presidential statements on national policy as they were developed.

All spending and tax policy is based on an analysis of projected federal spending and tax receipts over a five-year period. How much we decide to spend on defense or welfare and what we do about tax rates is greatly influenced by those estimates of future budget numbers. All government policymakers use the budget forecasts, but perhaps not more than fifteen or twenty people in all of Washington have a clear understanding and appreciation of the crystal ball that produces the numbers.

Because of this the Economic Forecasting Group was another important economic policy chokepoint. Usually made up of the president's senior economic policy advisers, this group put together the government's annual economic forecast. The small group of people who churn out the official economic forecasts constitute the most sensitive economic policy chokepoint we have. Their estimates of how much money the federal government will spend under current policy and how much tax revenue will be coming in over future years often has a powerful and decisive effect on policy-making. The importance of the economic forecasts is widely accepted, but it is barely known how sensitive those forecasts are to the personal, very human judgments of the individuals who make them. It is truly an art, not a science.

Yet most policymakers treat the forecasts with the same degree of respect for accuracy they accord the daily published stock market results. Once the numbers are published they become the unquestioned base for most of the policy work that is done. And they are the product of some of the most sophisticated, most complex computer models ever devised by man. The only problem is that the complex forecasting equations must be given some raw numbers to start with, and this is where the personal judgment of the forecasters enters—with a vengeance.

All of the models that forecast federal revenues and spending are based on estimates of what inflation and the real rate of economic growth, interest rates, and unemployment will be each year for the next five years. They are particularly sensitive to the inflation and economic growth numbers. In effect, once you tell the computer model what inflation and the rate of economic growth will be every year for the next five years, it tells you what the federal government will spend every year and how much it will receive in taxes.

I remember the first time I sat around a table with Weidenbaum, Regan, and Stockman discussing the economic forecast numbers we were going to present to President Reagan. There was a sharp disagreement about the base data—the five-year projections of the annual growth rate of inflation and the annual rate of economic growth—to be fed into the computers. I had never spent much time thinking about what inflation or the rate of economic growth was going to be every year for the next five years, but as I did and listened to the conversation, it quickly became obvious that nobody else at the table had either, and that no computer model was telling them. They were making intuitive guesses, drawing on earlier discussions with their professional staffs. The treasury specialized in estimating revenue, OMB specialized in estimating expected changes in spending, and the CEA had the overall responsibility for the economic forecast itself.

But after all the computer models were built and all the experts were consulted, there were still two big facts that were unknown.

In order to make the computer model go you had to tell it what inflation and the economic growth rate were going to be for the next five years. If you didn't, it couldn't calculate what federal revenues and expenditures would be. And this we had to know. The Congressional Budget Act of 1974 *requires* the president to make a five-year budget forecast whether he wants to or not, and that means he must (or rather his advisers must) predict what the rate of inflation and the rate of economic growth is going to be each year for the next five years.

Now, of course this is very difficult. Nobody knows or has any way of finding out what those numbers will be. You can only make an informed guess. But the law is the law. So we sat around the table and tried to cloak our guesses in some kind of respectability.

It was not an idle exercise. A one-point change up or down in either the predicted inflation rate or the predicted economic growth rate could shoot the projected budget deficit up or down by tens of billions of dollars. For each of these critical estimates there was a range of what might be called professional judgment. Every month a private newsletter is published called the *Blue Chip Economic Indicators*. It lists forty-two forecasts of the most highly respected private economic groups in the United States including, for example, the forecasts of the Morgan Guaranty Bank, Chase Econometric Association, Prudential Life, and American Express. Of course, they don't know what is going to happen either, but they do provide a range of forecast judgments that, if you stay within its boundaries, at least will protect you from the charge of being unprofessional. Moreover, professional forecasters, those who are paid money to do this, rarely venture beyond one year in predicting the future, and they revise their forecasts early and often. As an economic forecaster once joked to me, "To err is human, to be paid for it is divine."

Making economic forecasts is tricky business. The forecast must be credible with the financial community. It must be internally consistent and within the same ballpark range the private forecasters are predicting. You must carefully weigh the impact of the forecast on future spending and revenues. If you are too optimistic you may start some programs now that you will not be able to pay for when the bills come due. If you are too pessimistic you may postpone important spending or tax policies. The group that makes that final economic forecast recommendation to the president wields a power that is little appreciated and understood. It is the invisible economic policy chokepoint.

One of the most difficult parts of Reagan's economic program to deal with was government regulation. The reform of federal regulations—changing, cutting back, eliminating and blocking new ones—was the fourth major leg of the comprehensive economic plan, in the same category of importance as tax policy, spending control, and monetary policy. Donald Regan and the Treasury Department, by tradition, were responsible for developing the detailed tax plan. David Stockman and the OMB were responsible for detailed spending cuts. Monetary policy was in the hands of Volcker and his fellow governors. But who was going to handle regulatory reform?

The federal web of regulation was extremely wide and deep, and very sticky. Thousands upon thousands of rules and penalties for not following them have poured from the agencies and departments for years. They crisscross every jurisdictional line that exists. Attempting to prune this web of regulation would be as close as any of us were apt to get to cleaning out the legendary Augean stables, and there was no Heracles on Reagan's new White House staff.

No department or agency could hope to cope with the regulations of their brothers. The other business of the cabinet would have stopped if we introduced complex regulation policy debates into that forum. The only agency that had a fairly good overview of the problem was OMB, but even they did not have the bureaucratic clout necessary to be effective. We did have one world-class expert on government regulation, Murray Weidenbaum, a noted scholar who had conducted extensive research and written widely on the subject. Unfortunately, the tiny analytical staff he commanded as chairman of the Council of Economic Advisers was unequal to the task before us. The CEA staff was geared toward providing economic advice to the president; they were not an operational arm of the government.

So, on the third day after President Reagan was sworn in, he announced at a Saturday morning cabinet meeting that he had asked the new vice president, George Bush, to chair the Presidential Task Force on Regulatory Relief. It was a deft move. Putting the vice president in charge of regulatory reform emphasized to everyone, especially his new cabinet members, how important it was to Reagan. It was a gesture of trust to Bush, giving him responsibility for carrying out a vital part of one of Reagan's most important policies. And it gave the vice president something to do that was not just ceremonial.

In addition to Bush, the president appointed seven others to serve on the task force: Donald Regan, William French Smith, Malcolm Baldridge, Raymond Donovan, David Stockman, Murray Weidenbaum, and myself. OMB was designated to provide basic staff support and the first executive director of the task force was James Miller, who had just been appointed director of OMB's Office of Information and Regulatory Affairs. C. Boyden Gray, the counsel to the vice president, and Richard S. Williamson from the White House staff, rounded out the executive staff of the task force.

Much of the task force work was done by the staff. The regulations were usually so fiendishly complicated that there simply was not time for task force members to review the details of the proposed changes. By and large we relied on what the staff told us. During the first few months the staff tore into their work with zest and determination. Only three months after we began, the task force had taken action on 181 federal regulations in 13 departments and agencies. The estimated savings were as much as $18 billion the first year, with annual savings thereafter of $6 billion.

But as important as the surgery was that the task force performed on existing federal government regulations, it was far less important than the effect the task force had in choking off a blizzard of new, even more onerous regulations. As Bush's task force began its long overdue pruning work the bureaucracy and special interest groups began to fight the reforms fiercely. Their intense preoccupation with keeping what they had seemed to take up so much of their time that they didn't have any time left over to dream up many new regulations. Beyond that, the very existence of a cabinet-level task force, personally appointed by the president, was enough to intimidate the proposal of any new major regulations.

Any significant proposal for regulation by any part of the Reagan administration would have eventually come up for review in Bush's task force. None ever came up because none were ever proposed. Any major new regulation threatening the success of Reagan's economic program would have had to attempt sailing through the very narrow strait of the task force on regulatory reform—and surely would have been sunk.

Unfortunately, the deregulation effort proved very difficult to maintain. Carving up old regulations on the books for years is not the most exciting or rewarding kind of government service. It is difficult to measure the precise results of what you do, and few appreciate them with the same kind of enthusiasm you get when you change taxes or spending. Bush, while fully and conscientiously committed, never seemed to develop any passion for his mission. Most of the work was left to the staff, and after a while the active effort to reform existing regulations seemed to peter out. But it still remained a potent policy chokepoint. Few new regulations attempted to sail through.

The last economic policy chokepoint in the White House was really not in the White House. It was a group of private citizens who regularly met directly with the president and advised him on economic policy. It was called the President's Economic Policy Advisory Board (or PEPAB for short).

The idea for an economic policy advisory board of private citizens first occurred to me after a discussion I had with Richard V. Allen during the 1980 campaign. Allen was thinking about reestablishing a board that President Carter abolished shortly after taking office in 1976. It was the President's Foreign Intelligence Advisory Board (PFIAB), a distinguished group of private citizens who oversaw the entire range of U.S. intelligence operations and made recommendations for policy changes directly to the president. Originally instituted by President Eisenhower in 1956, it was formally established by President Kennedy in 1961, and had enjoyed an excellent reputation over the years. Why President Carter wiped it out is still a mystery. Allen thought Carter's action was a mistake and told me he planned to recommend its resurrection to Reagan if he was elected.

I agreed, and urged him to do it. Then I began thinking about the problems that lay ahead of us in economic policy. We would need all the help we could get. Why not an independent, high-level advisory group of private citizens with expertise and experience in the making of economic policy. At least a dozen or so of the best economists in the country who worked closely with Reagan during the campaign were, for one reason or another, not going to join the administration. Why not keep them together in the form of a presidential advisory board?

The more I thought about the idea the more I liked it.

To begin with, it would be good for outside experts to advise the president from time to time on national economic policy. I knew from my earlier Nixon administration experience that it would not be long before the senior economic advisers became increasingly dependent upon their professional staffs and increasingly isolated from voices of independent criticism. It would be good for the president to hear directly from private economists who were independently analyzing and judging his policies. And if his senior economic advisers knew he would regularly meet with outside experts who were not bashful about telling the president things he would not like hearing, as well as things his staff and cabinet might not want to tell him, then they might be considerably more careful about the policies they recommended to him. It is a fundamental rule of White House internal politics for a president not to limit his sources of advice and counsel to those who work for him.

Second, these well-known economists who advised Reagan during the campaign were highly individualistic. If they had no formal connection with the new administration, before long they would be lobbing criticial bombshells at various parts of the economic program. The national press corps would egg them on, playing off one against the other as they sought comments for the daily news stories. But maybe if they continued as a team, at the highest level, to personally advise the president on economic policymaking, then maybe they would continue to focus on the main elements of that policy on which they agreed. We had to bring them inside the Reagan tent.

Third, I was going to need all the help I could get in the internal policy debates that lay ahead. The domestic policy shop in the White House was not set up to get heavily involved in economic policy. Most of the positions of the domestic policy staff had to be allocated to people who could cover a wide range of general domestic policies. On the other hand, the chairman of the CEA would be supported by dozens of experts, the director of OMB by hundreds, and the secretary of the treasury by thousands. If I was lucky, I might have one or two people on my staff that I could depend on for first-rate economic analysis.

Moreover, while I was confident that Murray Weidenbaum would be a staunch and consistent defender of the economic plan Reagan laid out in the campaign, I wasn't so sure about Stockman and Regan. I knew Weidenbaum since the days when he and I served on President Nixon's White House staff and I followed his scholarly work closely over the years. Murray was the sort of person who reminds everyone of a friendly, easygoing uncle, but I knew that he would stubbornly pursue the policies he believed in and fight for them. And from the campaign I knew he believed in Reagan's economic policies.

Much of what I knew about David Stockman was good. I had met him several times, and once spent a couple of days with him in 1978 flying around the country on a Republican party sponsored campaign for lower tax rates. He was smart and energetic and a fervent advocate of the supply-side tax cut that was part of Reagan's economic program. He had valuable congressional experience and was a master of budget detail. On the other hand, Stockman had no degree or training in economics. He was self-taught, and Adam Smith was the last good, self-taught economist I knew of.

During the 1980 presidential campaign Stockman came to Reagan's side very late. The man he really wanted to be president was John Connally, and Connally's economic policies had a streak of fascism in them. Anyone who could love John Connally, the godfather of wage and price controls under President Nixon, couldn't be all good. And Stockman was very ambitious. Such a man could not be trusted.

I would have been even more nervous if I had known then what I know now. Thirteen years earlier, as a student at Michigan State University, Stockman embraced Marxism,[2] attended meetings of the radical Students for a Democratic Society,[3] and served on the steering committee of the Greater Lansing Community Organization, "a multi-issue left-wing group."[4] Of course, he had since disavowed the political views he held as a young man, and he was a registered Republican.

I knew even less about Donald Regan. By reputation he was a very smart, tough Wall Street financier who had made millions. He never served in government and Reagan scarcely knew him. He came to us via the single-minded effort of William J. Casey, chairman of the 1980 campaign. William E. Simon was Reagan's first choice for secretary of the treasury, but when that fell through Casey put forth the name of his old friend from New York City and sold the president on him. Regan was not an economist either, but the thing that most disturbed me was the whispered word from one of my colleagues that Donald Regan donated a substantial amount of money to President Carter's campaign in 1980 as well as to Reagan's. Anybody who could contemplate supporting the economic policies of both Carter and Reagan earned a skeptical eye for at least a while.

That is why I really wanted some checks on the economic policy deliberations that were about to start. I could think of nothing better than a group of economists, all more distinguished professionally than any of Reagan's inside senior economic advisers, all in agreement with one another and with Reagan on key economic issues, all either good friends of Reagan or highly respected by him, and all well known to me, some of them close friends and colleagues for fifteen or more years.

I thought of PEPAB as a secret intellectual weapon, one that could be called upon if Reagan's economic program started to veer off the track. And, too, it was a nice and appropriate way to honor and reward these distinguished economists for their help in electing Reagan.

Most everybody liked the idea of an outside economic advisory group when I proposed it—Meese, Baker, Deaver, and the president—except for the other senior economic advisers, who were downright frosty. I expected they would be concerned about the potential encroachment of their policy turf, but I didn't expect they would get as upset as they did. Even Weidenbaum wasn't pleased and he told me so, but grumpily he agreed to go along when I explained the advantages it would have for President Reagan. At first Stockman and Regan said nothing, just smiled thinly. Then I began to hear rumors about how they really felt. They felt threatened.

Someone leaked their concerns to Evans and Novak, a highly respected and influential team of political reporters. By the time the story was printed in their January 21, 1981, *Evans-Novak Report,* my modest proposal had turned into an end run around Regan and Stockman.

"What worries all of them [Weidenbaum, Regan, and Stockman] is Martin Anderson, RR's domestic policy advisor. He has dropped incredibly (and uncharacteristically) indiscreet hints that Stockman, Regan and Weidenbaum are just not qualified to make economic policy and perhaps there should be an outside board of senior economists (called 'graybeards' by their detractors), such as Greenspan, ex-Fed Chairman Arthur Burns, ex-Treasury Sec. George

Shultz and ex-CEA Chairman Herbert Stein. Who would they report to? Presumably Martin Anderson. Thus, this is regarded as an end run by the new Treasury team, which wants no part of it."

Oh well. I missed this piece when it ran and only discovered it many years later while going through some old files. But the suspicions were soon picked up and amplified in other stories in the *New York Times*, *National Review*, the *Baltimore Sun*, *Business Week*, and the *Conservative Digest*. I missed those stories also and soon, unbeknownst to me, I acquired a false reputation as being in the anti-supply-side camp, being strongly allied with Arthur F. Burns and Alan Greenspan, who also acquired the false reputation of being opposed to Reagan's economic program.[5] It was understandable why many of my old colleagues seemed somewhat cool to me during the early months of the administration in 1981.

These suspicions were enhanced by the natural resentment people working on the inside of an administration have toward any outsiders, which is how the President's Economic Policy Advisory Board was viewed. As soon as people begin to work for a president they seem to sprout an instinctive urge to have the president all to themselves and begin to resent deeply any contacts by outsiders, especially competent people the president likes and respects. Most people who work for a president become quite jealous of him. I saw it happen to President Nixon's people and I was seeing it happen again.

There is a consensus among a few former White House aides and advisers I talked to that a clear effort was made by someone to sow dissension among the loosely knit group of supply-siders who favored tax cuts as the primary part of Reagan's new comprehensive economic program. Wedges of suspicion were driven between the White House and Treasury, between the Council of Economic Advisers and Treasury, and between the White House and the Council of Economic Advisers. It is highly doubtful that we will ever know who did it and for what reason. The press treats confidential leaks to them with more sacred care than a Catholic priest treats the confidential confession of sin. Reporters will go to extreme lengths to protect the identity of their sources, including going to jail, even when they have been lied to. And that is why someone can betray or misrepresent the views of colleagues with virtual impunity.

Donald Regan's natural suspicions of an outside group of economic advisers were heightened by these stories and confirmed by warnings about me given to him by Paul Craig Roberts, the assistant secretary of the treasury, who assumed that what he read must be true.[6] After a while Roberts discounted the stories, but not before the Treasury Department made some unusual attempts to weaken PEPAB's influence with the president. When they were unable to block the advisory group, a different approach was tried.

First, Donald Regan suggested that the proposed PEPAB report directly to him as secretary of the treasury, rather than to President Reagan. That suggestion was rejected.

Then the Treasury tried to take over administrative control of the advisory board. I had sent a draft of the president's executive order establishing PEPAB to a number of senior aides for review and comment. When the copy I sent to the Treasury came back, it was carefully rewritten and retyped. In the original draft the president's domestic policy adviser was designated the board's secretary, with the implied power to call meetings and set the board's agenda. All of PEPAB's expenses were to be paid by the White House and their budget would be part of the budget of the domestic policy staff.

The suggested revision that came back from the Treasury proposed that PEPAB's budget be paid (and controlled) by the Treasury Department, and that their staff would handle the basic administrative functions of the board. I almost missed it. But my practice had always been to do the tedious proofreading of important documents myself, and I discovered the suggested changes in time to delete them.

On February 10, 1981, President Reagan established the first economic policy advisory board in the history of the United States. It reported directly to him. I was its secretary and the White House controlled its budget.

The twelve charter members were an elite group, unmatched in their collective reputation. The first chairman of PEPAB was George Shultz, former secretary of the treasury, former secretary of labor, and former director of OMB. Shultz was an effective chairman. He worked hard at it; there were dozens of telephone calls between him and the White House as we set meeting dates and shaped the agenda. Though Shultz wasn't being completely altruistic. His constant and regular contact with President Reagan and his top aides gave him an opportunity to show off his talents and he deftly parlayed his opportunities into becoming the sixtieth secretary of state.

The other members, with one exception, had advised Reagan throughout the presidential campaign and the transition: Arthur F. Burns, Milton Friedman, Alan Greenspan, Arthur Laffer, James T. Lynn, Paul McCracken, William Simon, Thomas Sowell, Herbert Stein, Charles E. Walker, and Walter Wriston. They were truly the board of directors for the development of Reaganomics.

The one exceptional member was Herbert Stein. His jowled face, pierced by dark, sad eyes, looked perpetually mournful. He was a pessimistic, cynical man, a heavy personality that was lightened from time to time by his flashing, wry wit. His stature as an economist came largely from public service, stemming from his membership on the Council of Economic Advisers under President Nixon from 1969 to 1974, the last three years as chairman. Stein's tenure with Nixon was marked by rising inflation, increasing unemployment, the imposition of wage and price controls, and the United States' unilateral abandonment of the gold standard.

Stein had nothing to do with the development of Reaganomics during the campaign or the transition. He made no effort to support Reagan during the campaign, and I made no effort to solicit him. I remembered his private counsel to President Nixon all too well. Herbert Stein is a good economist with considerable talent, but his economic analyses, regardless of the issue, seem to always have one conclusion: raise taxes. Stein rarely saw a tax he didn't like. But while I was putting together the proposed membership list of PEPAB I noticed that we had virtually every former holder of key economic policy posts in past Republican administrations— with one obvious exception. So in order to have a clean sweep I recommended Stein. He never disappointed us, recommending tax increases (in vain) at almost every meeting of the board.

During the critical first year, PEPAB met six times with President Reagan, every time strongly reinforcing his long-held views on economic policy. Reagan loved meeting with them. Many of the members were old friends and his eyes would twinkle and his face would beam when he joined them in the Roosevelt Room or the Cabinet Room. What they did for him more than anything else was to reassure him that the course he was following was right. It was they who pressed him to resist any tax increases, it was they who strongly urged more and more cuts in federal spending, it was they who pushed for more deregulation. And most importantly, it was they who praised him, to his face, for his consistent, determined effort to restore the economic health of the United States.

Regan, Weidenbaum, Stockman, and other senior White House staff aides attended every meeting and always came away with the courage of their convictions on Reaganomics strengthened and reaffirmed. The counsel of these economic gurus was taken with great respect. The combined force of their individual positions, when taken together, was irresistible. It would have been very difficult for the Reagan administration to long pursue any important economic policy if it was strenuously opposed by the board. Their presence was especially important toward the end of that first year when many of Reagan's senior advisers, including Stockman and Baker and Regan, were buckling under the pressures of the increasing budget deficit and began pressing the president to change his adamant opposition to tax increases. PEPAB was summoned as quickly as possible and they personally reassured the president that he, and not his advisers who wanted to boost taxes, was right. Milton Friedman and William Simon, two of Reagan's favorites, were very eloquent and persuasive on this point.

As the board continued on, the membership changed slightly—Walter Wriston replaced George Shultz as chairman when Shultz became secretary of state, Tom Sowell resigned for health reasons, Rita Ricardo Campbell, a senior fellow of the Hoover Institution was added, and I joined the board in 1982 after leaving the White House staff—and it continued to meet regularly, but less frequently. The resentment of the traditional economic advisers to the president—the fiefdoms of Treasury, CEA, and OMB—lingered on. They never got used to the idea that a group of outsiders, with no responsibility for the day-to-day conduct of national economic policy, could waltz in, sit down with the president, and second-guess what they were doing. It seemed to annoy them greatly. Perhaps that is why none of them ever thanked me for setting it up.

There was one bizarre footnote to the history of PEPAB. The board was ambushed in October 1985, in a manner that was to foreshadow the string of misjudgments leading to Reagan's most damaging crisis, the sale of arms to Iran and the secret provision of money to the freedom fighters of Nicaragua.

On the morning of October 22, 1985, Milton Friedman called me at the Hoover Institution from his oceanside retreat in Sea Ranch, California. He had just been called by the White House and asked to attend a meeting with President Reagan to discuss international trade policy, and asked me if I knew what it was all about. Was I going? Was it a PEPAB meeting?

I was puzzled. I had not been invited and there was no scheduled PEPAB meeting. But if a group of outside economists was coming in to discuss trade policy with President Reagan they were supposed to be members of PEPAB. I told Milton I would try to find out what was going on and immediately placed a telephone call to Jack Svahn in the White House. Svahn now held my old job and, as the executive order setting up PEPAB in 1981 specified, he was its secretary. He would know.

Surprisingly, he was unaware of the meeting but said he would check into it. The next day he called back. "Sure enough," he said, "there is an outside group of twelve economists coming in to talk to the president about trade policy and protectionism. Some of them are members of PEPAB, such as Milton Friedman and Alan Greenspan, but others are not; Walter Heller, for instance."

Walter Heller? *The* Walter Heller, the prominent left-wing Democrat, the economist who was a passionate foe and critic of Reagan's economic policies? What the hell was going on? As these thoughts were flashing through my mind, Svahn began to explain it to me.

"You see," he said, "the executive order that established PEPAB expired on October 1st and Don Regan has refused to renew it. So in effect, you're all fired." And then he laughed and joked that "we all want you to know how much the president has appreciated your service."

We had all been fired, in effect, for three weeks without even the courtesy of a notice. No letter, no thanks. And it was all done in the dead of night. Even the chairman, Walter Wriston, did not realize he had been unemployed for three weeks. Svahn, domestic policy adviser to the president and the man in the White House with responsibility for PEPAB, had not known. Not even Beryl Sprinkel, the new chairman of the Council of Economic Advisers and a trusted confidant of Regan's, was consulted.

Apparently Donald Regan was attempting to settle an old score. He was a proud, headstrong man who did not like to be frustrated—in anything. For five years he must have brooded about those private economic advisers poaching on his policy turf. Even though he admitted that they were useful, that they provided a fresh point of view, he now seemed to feel they were no longer needed or necessary. As chief of staff, with unprecedented power delegated to him by President Reagan, Regan evidently decided to tidy up the policy advisory structure.

There was one hint that something was brewing. On September 30, 1985, *U.S. News & World Report* noted that on economic policy "Divergent views will be largely screened from Reagan. Economists will continue to be viewed with disdain. The group of outside economists that used to meet with Reagan four times a year has seen him only once this year."[7]

The whole thing was outrageous.

Twelve of President Reagan's top economic advisers, some who had loyally supported him for over a decade, were rudely dismissed without a word. And nobody outside of a small group in the inner, upper reaches of the White House knew it. Probably not even President Reagan. It was an ominous sign.

It was a small incident but it revealed something about Donald Regan's character—such a strong degree of assurance and self-confidence in his own judgment—that he unhesitatingly followed his impulse, apparently unaware of the potential cost to President Reagan. It was a hint of a character flaw that would be deepened and widened by the decisions forced upon him in the months that followed, a flaw that perhaps helped plunge President Reagan into the abyss of the Iran-Contra affair within a year.

After my conversation with Jack Svahn I decided to cast a little light on Regan's pocket veto of PEPAB. One by one I telephoned every member of PEPAB, beginning with the chairman, Walter Wriston, and broke the news to them that they were fired. I found them in New York, in California, in Germany, in Washington, D.C., in Missouri, and Michigan. All of them were shocked. Most of them had never been fired from anything in their lives. Some were coldly furious.

Then I waited. The calls were made on Wednesday and Thursday. The weekend came and not a word. No mention in the press, no calls from the White House. Finally, early Monday morning I got a phone call from Jack Svahn.

"Hi," he said "a funny thing happened to PEPAB on the way

to expiration. Friday I was told that eliminating PEPAB was a mistake. We'll be having our next meeting as soon as the president gets back from the summit with Gorbachev. And the meeting scheduled with those other economists on October 30th has been canceled."

Tuesday morning I got another call from Beryl Sprinkel, chairman of the Council of Economic Advisers. I was told he went up in smoke when he heard about the attempted ambush of PEPAB. He was upset and grim when he emphatically told me that he looked into the matter and was convinced that "PEPAB should not be killed. It would be a disaster to stop. If I hear anything to the contrary I sure as hell will let you know."

As a footnote to a footnote, the President's Economic Policy Advisory Board was reestablished by Executive Order for a new two-year term, and later renewed for another two-year term, lasting until September 30, 1989.

Chapter Twenty-Two

THE MARK OF THE BEAST

A few major policy decisions managed to escape channeling through the cabinet councils. The Reagan administration was about five weeks old before the councils were established on February 26, 1981. One issue that escaped the council net was immigration policy. It didn't fit neatly into any of the five cabinet councils we established and it clearly cut across many department lines with most of the action located in the Justice Department. The new attorney general, William French Smith, had enough clout with the new president to insist that he head up a special ad hoc policy group to deal with immigration policy. So, in early March 1981, less than two weeks after the basic cabinet council structure was put in place, President Reagan established the Task Force on Immigration and Refugee Policy. It was chaired by the attorney general and included the cabinet members from the Departments of State, Defense, Education, Labor, Health and Human Services, Transportation, and the Treasury. It also included the director of the Federal Emergency Management Agency.

The Task Force on Immigration and Refugee Policy operated very differently than the cabinet councils, much more along the lines of traditional interagency groups. Most of the meetings were held in the Justice Department. Few members of the cabinet attended the deliberations of the task force after the early meetings, and increasingly they sent their deputies or their deputy's deputies. The influence of the entrenched professional bureaucracy was enhanced and soon the draft recommendations for the task force lost any flavor of Reagan ideology. By the time the task forces final recommendations were presented to President Reagan in a full cabinet meeting on the afternoon of July 16, 1981, they included provisions for employer sanctions, which made it a crime for an employer in the United States to hire anyone who came across the border looking for work without entry papers, and a national identification card, similar to the internal passports used by the Soviet Union. Because the policy was developed in the more traditional way, few of the cabinet focused closely on the complex issues involved.

It was a controversial issue, marked by passionate disagreement among the White House senior staff, the cabinet, and Congress. It was an especially hot issue in western and southwestern states. Attorney General Smith made his initial proposals in a cabinet meeting two weeks earlier, but the discussion got bogged down and, at Ed Meese's suggestion, Smith agreed to systematically go over the issues and make a final presentation at this meeting.

As the immigration policy discussion started, the president interrupted and said, "Good Lord. We're back to immigration already."

We all settled back in our seats and the briefing and presentation continued. When it was finished I was appalled.

The attorney general had just finished proposing to the members of Reagan's cabinet sitting around the old wooden table in the Cabinet Room that every person in the United States be required to have a counterfeit-proof identification card issued by the federal government. The call for a national identification card was not the major thrust of the complex immigration reform proposal but it was there—in fine print—as an integral part of the whole package.

Such a card is an indispensable tool of a totalitarian state, for before a government can really begin to control your life it must know who you are and where you are, and it must be able to demand proof of your existence whenever it encounters you—applying for work, moving to another address, walking down the street. Without a national identification system, it is very difficult for a small number of people to control a large society. With one, it is much easier.

Few people see or believe in the sinister side of a national identification card. It is always put forward for the best of reasons. How could a common thing like an identification card be abused in the United States, the freest country in the world? Don't we already have social security cards and driver's licenses and birth certificates? Why not just have one and make it foolproof, and list everyone's number on a giant, central computer system in Washington, D.C. Law enforcement officials dream about it. The State Department would like the card to be large enough so it could double for a passport. Hotels could ask for it when you checked in. Banks could demand it before you could cash a check. Welfare recipients would have to produce their passbook before they got their monthly check. The uses are endless, and so are the potential abuses, which are limited only by the ingenuity of government officials.

The proposal for a national identification card was smuggled in wearing the clothing of a new immigration policy. The critical part of the new policy was concerned with how to deal with people who came into the United States illegally. For the most part this meant Mexican citizens who endured hardship and risk to secretly enter the United States in search of work. Usually they worked hard for relatively low wages, sent most of the money back to families in Mexico, were careful to stay out of trouble, and rarely went on welfare. Some economists thought this was even good for the U.S. economy. But others raised a hue and cry about illegal aliens, and the political establishment was casting about trying to figure out what to do.

The attorney general's presentation on immigration was straightforward. The reasoning went like this. Illegal aliens are flooding across our borders. We are powerless to stop them. We aren't willing to spend enough money for agents to guard every foot of the border. We aren't willing to throw up barbed wire fences, or build a Berlin-like wall and mount machine guns on top of it, or patrol the borders with dogs. No, we can't stop them. So the only solution is to change the situation so they decide not to come, to make them *not* want to come to the United States. Why do they come? For jobs. Then let's make it impossible for them to work. We can't destroy all the jobs in the United States but we can make it illegal for American employers to hire illegal aliens. If an American hires a Mexican we'll put the American in jail and ship the Mexican home. That ought to do it. But then the question was raised as to how an employer could tell an illegal alien from a genuine American citizen. The answer was simple. Ask him for identification to prove that he was an American and if he wasn't, don't hire him. That seemed reasonable, but there was one remaining problem. We don't have a national identification system.

So that is how, one day in 1981, the attorney general came to present his border control plan—for reasons he thought were good—to the president and his cabinet. Attorney General Smith was a patrician lawyer from Los Angeles who was smart and able, and he had done his homework very well with other members of the cabinet. Smith was Reagan's former personal lawyer and held his trust and confidence. He was seated, in accordance with long tradition, almost directly across the table from President Reagan, speaking directly to him.

I was seated a couple of feet behind the attorney general, in one of the soft leather seats along the back wall that were reserved for senior White House staff, again in accordance with long tradition. I could see the back of Smith's head, nodding slowly up and down, as his agile brain directed the flow of a flawless, brilliant presentation. It was working. As he moved on from point to point, the members of the cabinet were becoming persuaded. The national identification system was described simply as upgrading the social security cards to make them counterfeit proof. Not a single objection. It all went down smoothly. A few minutes later Smith was through. He stopped and I knew he was smiling. The president looked up and around the room to see if anyone had any comments. I knew there weren't going to be any. The subject was complex. Nobody else in the cabinet had spent much time on it. And Smith's presentation was very, very good.

So I raised my hand.

I knew I was breaking an unwritten rule, the rule that says senior staff members may sit in on cabinet meetings but they are not to speak unless spoken to. But in the second or two I had to think about it I reasoned that I did not want to be part of the administration that foisted a national identity card on Americans, especially when most of the cabinet seemed to be quite unaware of what they were doing. The worst that could happen to me was to be fired, and if I were fired I would have to go back to sunny California, which didn't seem like a bad prospect at the time.

After a few seconds went by there were no comments coming from the cabinet and the president noticed me. I guess it was pretty obvious, my hand was raised directly over the back of the attorney general's head. He simply said, "Yes, Marty."

And I began to speak. One reason I loved Reagan was his casual neglect of unnecessary protocol and formality. He liked to do things that worked. I assume he figured I had something worthwhile to say or I wouldn't have raised my hand. Anyway, the room grew quiet and a lot of eyes, some topped by slightly raised eyebrows, focused on me. I knew this wasn't the time for a longwinded, theoretical critique of national identity cards, so I decided to try humor, leavened with a little shock.

"Mr. President," I said, "one of my concerns about the national identity card is that the Office of Management and Budget has estimated that it could cost several billions of dollars to produce a counterfeit-proof social security card for everyone." That statement didn't seem to make much of an impact. By that time a billion dollars or two didn't bother anyone in the cabinet.

"I would like to suggest another way that I think is a lot better. It's a lot cheaper. It can't be counterfeited. It's very lightweight, and impossible to lose. It's even waterproof.

"All we have to do is tattoo an identification number on the inside of everybody's arm."

There were several gasps around the table. A couple of the cabinet members looked as if they had been slapped. No one said anything for a long time.

The first person to speak was James Watt, the secretary of the interior. Watt was a seasoned bureaucrat who left a clear and lasting legacy on the natural resources of this country. He loved the environment, but was not an elitist. He wanted to preserve the environment not from people, but for people to use, and he was fearless in the pursuit of what he believed was right. He was also fearless in speaking out in other areas.

His thick eyeglasses sparkled as his booming voice rolled across the table, "Why, it sounds to me that you are talking about the mark of the Beast. That's terrible."

Most of the people seated around the cabinet table looked puzzled. Except for the president, few of them knew that the mark of the Beast was a biblical reference to Revelation 13: 16–18. But now they were alert. Watt was an astute politician, especially knowledgeable about the political thicket populated by right-wing Republicans. You could see the questioning looks come over their faces, each one crinkling and moving in his or her own special way. Nobody seemed to know quite what to say. First the image of Nazi concentration camps and now the mark of the Beast. What next?

The attorney general started to shift back and forth in his chair, getting ready to quell the incipient mutiny. But President Reagan cut him off. The president spread his hands forward across the polished surface of the table, leaned back and looked directly at the attorney general. Smiling broadly he joked,

"Maybe we should just brand all the babies."

For about ten seconds everybody laughed and smiled, and that was the end of the national identification card for 1981.

The most important question is how Reagan's cabinet got in that position in the first place. How they came so close to approving a new national policy that obviously neither they nor the president wanted.

The answer lies in the fact that immigration policy was not checked by a system of cabinet councils. Immigration policy's special ad hoc task force, a normal way of doing business in many past administrations, allowed the issue to go awry. The establishment of the cabinet council structure prevented that kind of problem from happening again in the domestic policy area, especially in economic policy. Curiously, what was done to implement policy on the domestic side was not done on the foreign policy side. This, as we shall see, led to some disastrous consequences in Reagan's second term.

Chapter Twenty-Three

THE "GOVERNOR"

Ronald Reagan is an unusual man.

His personality is opposite that of his closest political soulmate, Richard M. Nixon. During the 1968 presidential campaign, Nixon was usually referred to by his staff as the boss when he was not around. Even after he became president, many still called him the boss. Ronald Reagan was never called the boss by anyone. Until Reagan became president, he was invariably referred to as the governor by those working for him. Only after he became president did people begin calling him the president.

The distinction between boss and governor is not a frivolous one. The two words sum up the dramatically different styles the two men used to manage and administer. Nixon used a no-nonsense, authoritarian style, barking out commands right and left. He is intrinsically a shy man, loathing public appearances, tolerating meetings with small numbers of people, and longing for the total seclusion of a locked door. He rarely felt comfortable with people, save for a few intimate friends. Nixon's instinct is to plan and plot, the kind of man who thinks seven or eight moves ahead in a chess game. Nixon governed—and bossed.

Reagan was just the opposite. Totally at ease socially with everyone—from the factory worker who shook his hand to famous celebrities to the stewardesses on the campaign airplane to visiting heads of state. He received them all with equanimity. He liked people, liked all of them, a lot. He liked to meet them, talk to them, hear their problems. He rarely planned and never plotted. And he does not bark commands.

Reagan is a strikingly handsome man, enough so to have become a movie idol in the 1940s. His deep, distinctive voice with its mellow timbre opened the door to his unusual career path—from radio announcer to actor, from speaker on the U.S. lecture circuit to one of the most masterful political campaigners of the twentieth century.

He is highly intelligent, with a photographic memory. He has a gift for absorbing great amounts of diverse information, and is capable of combining various parts of that information into new, coherent packages, and then conveying his thoughts and ideas clearly and concisely in a way that is understandable to almost anyone.

Even his health is unusual. Reagan is a doctor's dream. Every time he returned to the presidential campaign trail after his periodic visits to the doctor for a routine medical check he proudly told us what the doctor said.

"The doctor was amazed," Reagan would report with an air of bemused satisfaction, "he said I have the body of a man ten years younger."

It isn't all due to nature. Reagan has some very unusual health habits, or rather a collection of mundane health habits which, when taken together, form an unusual whole. For example, when traveling around the country campaigning he almost always went to bed early. When the day's work was done, and it was eight or nine o'clock in the evening, he did not sit around and chat with the staff. He just smiled, said goodnight, and left for his room.

He exercised regularly. Every night, not just now and then, but every night, he did twenty to thirty minutes of carefully designed exercises. Sometimes during the campaign trips he even brought along a specially designed wheel with an axle that he grabbed with both hands and turned himself into a human wheelbarrow. He was very enthusiastic about the virtues of that exercise wheel.

He gets a good, solid eight hours of sleep every night, eats a full meal for breakfast, and by eight or nine o'clock in the morning, is ready to put in another twelve-hour day.

The pressures of the White House have not deterred Reagan from his healthy life-style. In the fall of 1986 he told a skeptical reporter, "I have a little exercise routine I do at the end of the day. I go home from here [the Oval Office] and exercise, then take my shower. And contrary to what a lot of people think must go on in the White House, a great many evenings, most of them as a matter of fact, you'll find Nancy and me in pajamas and a robe having dinner, and then early to bed."[1]

When he is working he works steadily all day long. He does not take naps, contrary to the widely believed rumor that he takes them regularly. Never once during all the hundreds of days of campaigning with him did I ever see him curl up and take a nap in the middle of the day.

He does not smoke. No cigarettes, no cigars, no pipes.

He does not drink. Once in a great while he might have a small, single glass of wine.

He does not take any pills. Not even aspirin as far as I observed.

He doesn't even drink coffee or tea. Except once in a very great while, when he somewhat guiltily gulps a half cup of coffee before an important speech. He rations himself carefully because even the caffeine in a half cup of coffee will make him acutely alert.

He also stays away from sugar. No candy bars, no cookies, or cake. He is partial to popping a jelly bean or two into his mouth every now and then, but the number he eats never came near justifying the notoriety those jelly beans received in the press.

When he does have a little tea or coffee he always uses a sugar substitute, saccharin. One of his proudest possessions on the campaign trail was a dispenser loaded with a dozen or so saccharin pills that looked just like a fountain pen, pocketclip and all. He would pull the saccharin pen from his inner coat pocket, hold it poised over the cup, push the cap top, and release a solitary saccharin tablet like a bombardier. He never went anywhere without that pen.

In sum, he took care of himself just as we are all supposed to do.

One of the most extraordinary things about Reagan's presidency was his management style, the techniques he used to guide and direct the huge bureaucracy to develop and carry out the policies he believed in. It was a style that carried him past the doubts of those who believed the presidency was no longer manageable, to the awed wonder of those who marveled at what he accomplished in economic policy during the early years, and then plunged him into the depths of dismay as he wallowed through the muck of the Iran-Contra affair.

Reagan's management style is unique, making it possible for him to achieve legendary changes in economic policy and nuclear weapons strategy, magically and seemingly without effort. But it is a style with dangerous flaws that were masked until the Iran-Contra affair exposed them and nearly destroyed his presidency. It is a high-risk style; not deliberately so, but one that is his by instinct. When it works, it is spectacular. When it fails, it is also spectacular.

The executive skill of any leader is largely a reflection of the person's personality, appearance, and intelligence. In any organization, no matter the size, the chief executive's style has a profound effect on how and how well that organization works. In the White House that effect is greatly intensified. Every aspect of his personality, appearance, manner, and thought processes is amplified enormously. The pulse of the federal government beats to his rhythms. The nature of a president's personality does not ultimately determine the course of policymaking, but it can have a powerful impact on that course—a strong, positive president can accelerate the flow of policy, a weak president can slow it

As Reagan prepared to take office in 1981, expectations were low. For the past twenty years the job of president has taken some of our most able men and crushed them. John Kennedy was assassinated before he could finish his first term. Lyndon Johnson was driven from the Oval Office by the debacle of the Vietnam War. Richard Nixon was forced to resign by the bungling of the Watergate affair. President Ford, appointed to the post, was defeated in his first election by a relatively unknown governor of a small southern state. President Carter just couldn't seem to cope with the awesome complexities of his job. The humiliating combination of fifty-two Americans held hostage by the fourth-rate military power of Iran, while the American economy careened wildly with double digit inflation and double digit interest rates, seemed to overwhelm Carter and snuffed out his bid for reelection.

The chilling conclusion was that the office of the presidency had become unmanageable. President Eisenhower was the last American president to complete two full terms in office. The power of a president to work his will, to change policy, to guide and lead the nation was thought to have been weakened irreparably. And that was the view of the office when held by strong and capable men. As Reagan prepared to come to Washington, expectations were even lower. He was still seen by many as an ex-movie actor with few management skills, a tremendous political campaigner who could speak with mesmerizing force, but who possessed none of the brilliant toughness needed to be president. As Richard Nathan, a highly respected political analyst from Princeton University, put it, "Most close observers of the Washington scene and system saw Reagan as a media success who would be overwhelmed by the immense substantive and managerial demands of the presidency."[2]

Reagan's official welcome to Washington, D.C., was cool and contemptuous. In December 1980, a few weeks before Reagan took office, Tip O'Neill, the very powerful Speaker of the House of Representatives and a key leader of the opposition, issued a stinging warning, "The governor of a state plays in the minor leagues. When you're president, you're in the big leagues. Things may not move as fast as you want them to."[3]

It was not an unreasonable warning. The office of the presidency had been chewing up its occupants, all of whom came to it with far greater reputations for managerial skill than Reagan, ever since the late 1960s.

But Reagan surprised and baffled all the experts, friend and foe alike. He entered Washington like a conquering general, quickly and deftly grabbed the levers of power, and soon had it doing his bidding. Within a year Tip O'Neill's contempt turned to relatively silent awe and there was no more talk about the big leagues.

Reagan succeeded in restoring the power of the presidency. He got things done, and he got them done fast. As *Fortune*, perhaps America's premier management magazine, noted in late 1986 two months before the Iran-Contra affair descended upon the country, "One extraordinarily important if little-noted element of the Reagan legacy is already established: He has proved once again that the presidency is manageable."[4]

His reputation for being an effective, powerful president was largely due to his accomplishments in economic policy. If he had failed in the first year to enact the major parts of his economic program, it is very likely he would soon have been mired deep in the same political quicksand that swallowed up his predecessors. The story of how he escaped that fate, of how he transformed an economic vision into a new, concrete, national economic policy is partly a story of innovative, bold management.

Before Reagan became president it appeared to almost everyone that he and his staff had little, if any, executive skill. The fascination seemed to be with superficial aspects of Reagan's personality: how he looked, how he smiled, what he said, why people liked him, and whether or not he dyed his hair.

He does not dye his hair, by the way. During one political campaign a couple of reporters even followed him to his barber shop, waited patiently and, just after he left, scooted in and grabbed a few handfuls of freshly cut hair off the floor. They sent the hair samples to a laboratory to be tested scientifically for the presence of dye. The tests were negative; they found no trace of dye. Up close, it is now possible to discern a few pure white hairs here and there on Reagan's head. Not many, but enough to authenticate all the other dark brown ones.

While so many focused their attention on his physical appearance and his personality, few seemed to even suspect that he had some very definite ideas about managing, and that he pursued those ideas relentlessly and skillfully. Very few acknowledged that he was responsible for the successful administration of the largest state in the country for eight years. They acknowledged that affairs of state in California ran quite smoothly. They acknowledged that he had in fact been governor. But they never seemed to connect the two. Nor did they give him much credit for selecting and choosing the people who filled the key positions in his administration while he was governor.

The most important part of his management philosophy was that he knew what he wanted to do, but he also had ideas on the means he would use to accomplish his ends. These were the main management techniques he used.

Establish Strategic Priorities. Everyone knows this is what should be done. But Reagan was different from most people. He actually set priorities: national security was number one, and economic policy was number two. Everything else belonged to a different order of importance and urgency and was subordinated to national defense and economic policy during the early years of his administration.

When he took office the economy was in shambles and our national defenses were dangerously weakened. As Reagan told us privately during the campaign, "If we don't do something about defense and the economy we won't be able to deal with the other problems, but if we can restore the strength of the military and get the economy healthy then everything else will become possible."

He crystallized these basic strategy priorities in 1980 and has not deviated from them since.

Change Tactical Priorities. While he stubbornly held to his major, long range goals, he was as agile and deceptive as a pro football halfback in making his way to those goals. He cajoled, he persuaded, he exhorted, and sometimes he threatened. He explored every possible means to achieve his ends. He would try one approach and if it did not work he would quickly give it up—with no apparent remorse or regrets—and move on to a new approach. For example, in the drive for his economic program he adjusted quickly to political opposition or changing economic forecasts.

Friedrich Nietzsche once said, "Many are stubborn in pursuit of the path they have chosen, few in pursuit of the goal." Reagan was stubborn in pursuit of the goal he chose and was willing to try, and try again, almost any path to get there.

Delegation of Authority. His delegation of authority was legendary. Reagan delegated easily, effortlessly. Once he delegated authority, he did not interfere as long as that person acted reasonably. He did not attempt to fine tune those working for him. And as long as they were working for him, striving for the same goals he was aiming for, he backed them up. He liked perfection, but did not expect it. Honest mistakes were accepted and forgotten.

Negotiation. President Regan loved to negotiate, a love that was carried over from his days as president of the Screen Actors Guild in Hollywood. All his adult life Reagan used a simple bargaining technique to achieve his goals. He has always been very straightforward about it, yet none of his opponents ever seemed to grasp what he was doing to them. He always asked for much more than he was either expecting to get or willing to accept. This was never acknowledged, perhaps even to himself.

The fact that he wanted what he demanded, and felt secure and right in those demands, simply added to his relative power in the negotiations. He would ask blithely for twice what his subconscious minimum demands were. After long and arduous negotiations, his opponent would finally make an offer that was actually far more than Reagan's minimum. Reagan would accept it quickly and quietly, never once boasting how he put one over on the other fellow, but self-content in the knowledge that, once again, he achieved a substantial victory. As he once put it, "I've never understood people who want me to hang in there for a hundred percent or nothing. Why not take seventy percent or eighty percent, and then come back another day for the other twenty or thirty percent?"[5]

If he didn't get what he wanted, he would withdraw and wait. Reagan always felt there would be another day; he had a calm, stubborn patience that served him as a powerful weapon.

Reagan's decision-making process has been the subject of much speculation over the years, most of it ill-informed, apparently shaped more by a desire to reinforce prejudices about the man than to gain insight. Some of his more left-wing enemies are convinced that he is rather stupid and stumbles into decisions, making many of them by default. Some of his right-wing critics seem convinced that he is manipulated by moderate and left-wing staffers into betraying his right-wing political principles. Others simply see him as rather detached from the decision-making process, someone who really doesn't understand much of what is going on, and doesn't care very deeply about what he does know. All these views are wrong, and very seriously and mistakenly underestimate Reagan as a manager of people.

On reflection we can see that this has to be true, for there is simply no way that anyone could successfully govern the United States, and earlier have successfully governed California for eight years, with that kind of happy-go-lucky, uninformed, ignorant, easily manipulated management style.

Then how does one account for his apparent success as a manager? In 1984 Meg Greenfield, editor of the editorial page of the *Washington Post*, wrote an essay for *Newsweek* in which she explored the question of "How Does Reagan Decide?" A liberal Democrat, she is one of the more astute political analysts in Washington, and she observed something that even many of Reagan's closest conservative supporters failed to understand—that he makes decisions like a labor negotiator for a workers' union.

Greenfield summed up part of his style this way, ". . . the long waiting out of the adversary, the immobility meanwhile, the refusal to give anything until the last moment, the willingness— nonetheless—finally to yield to superior pressure or force or partic- ular circumstance on almost everything, but only with something to show in return and only if the final deal can be interpreted as furthering the original Reagan objective."[6]

In addition to his little appreciated skills as a negotiator Reagan has a few other personal characteristics that are crucial to his lead- ership. The first is his outward behavior toward other people, es- pecially those who work for him. There are no reprimands, no yelling, no chewing out, and no complaining. Sometimes he might look a little disappointed when things go wrong, but generally he is disturbed only under great strain. He is almost too easy to work for. You rarely feel a sense of failure or humiliation, but you might very well feel guilty for not having achieved something.

On the other hand, Reagan was not overly thoughtful towards those who worked for him. He did not remember their birthdays with cards or small gifts. He rarely acknowledged what they had done for him. If he approved of their work he accepted it and used it, but never praised it. If he did not approve, he never uttered a word of criticism, he just did not use it. He seemed to have the attitude that we all should do our best: he should do his and we should do ours. And one does not get special thanks for doing what one should do.

Another trait that I believe accounts for a substantial part of his success is his facility for making decisions. He makes decisions promptly and decisively, and then goes on to something else. As Donald Regan observed, "The President has a unique talent: He is serene internally. When he has made a decision, he lives with it. He doesn't fret over it. And most of all, he doesn't change his mind."[7]

This does not mean that Reagan is some kind of superhuman who can not be riled or upset. In fact, one of the most unappre- ciated facets of Reagan's character is his towering temper which rarely flares but is memorable when it does. If Reagan is crossed, crossed badly, he exudes what can only be called a black Irish rage. His face darkens, his jaw muscles clench and bulge, and his lips get thin and tight.

In public he might show sporadic flashes of displeasure, but he never gets really angry. Some may conclude from this that he does not get angry. They would be wrong. We discovered during the campaigns that the surest sign he was furious was when he grabbed his eyeglasses by the right side of the frame, ripped them from his face, and then hurled them across the room into the far wall. It didn't happen often, but it did happen.

During one campaign stop in 1976 Reagan held a brief impromptu press conference in a narrow alley leading to the back entrance of the building where he was headed for a meeting. A few of the local reporters were unusually impertinent and pressed questions, which, while not difficult to answer, were asked in an insulting tone. Jim Lake, Reagan's press secretary stepped in after a few minutes, raised his hand and said his usual, "One more question." Reagan answered another one, and then turned, went through the door, and then, surrounded by aides and Secret Service agents, began to walk slowly into the interior of the building. One of the reporters outside yelled, "What's the matter? Are you afraid to answer the question?" Reagan stopped. You could sense, if not see, the hairs on the back of his head start to rise.

Abruptly he turned and headed back out the door to the alley. Unfortunately, I was standing directly in his path. When he reached me his eyes were blazing, focused on his tormentor outside. He felt rather than saw me, and, with one swift thrust of his arm shoved me aside, slamming me against the wall. Outside he angrily answered the reporter's question, and then turned and came back in.

One of the very few things that irritated him to anger was having one of his speechwriters rewrite his original drafts with too much zealousness. He appreciated constructive criticism, but when the criticism lapped over into changing the intent or thrust of what he was trying to say, he became angry.

I recall one day on the campaign plane when Peter Hannaford, one of his oldest and most valued speechwriters, handed him back a thick rewritten draft of a major speech. Reagan smiled, slipped on his reading glasses, and started reading. After two or three pages his brow developed deep furrows and his jaw started to tighten. Then, when he finished reading the next page, he grabbed it, raised it high into the air and slammed it down, hard, onto the small pile he just read. He continued to read, slamming each succeeding page down harder and harder, while Hannaford and I sat quietly a few feet away, wincing slightly as each page hit home.

We concluded he didn't like the rewrite.

But Reagan's flashes of anger are judicious. He never gets upset or angry over trivial matters. Even the most serious matters rarely disturb his tranquility. He is far more tolerant than perhaps anyone I have ever known, but there is a finite limit to his tolerance. When appropriate, he can become very, very angry. He is so damned good-natured so much of the time that it is very easy to conclude that anything goes. That would be a very bad mistake to make.

Let us all hope that the Soviets at least understand that.

Reagan has another distinctive trait that is almost totally hidden by his warm, friendly manner. He is very tough-minded. When people first meet him they can get the impression that this is an easy man to manipulate. They will say to themselves, "This guy is so good-natured he'll do anything I suggest." The impression is that of a soft, friendly pillow. What they fail to see is the two-inch rod of chrome steel within.

Reagan is one of the toughest men I have ever known, far tougher, for example, than his predecessors Carter, Ford, and Nixon. Once Reagan has determined what he thinks is right, and what is important to do, then he will pursue that goal relentlessly.

The personal feelings of others and their emotional distress, while something he is always sympathetic to, will never alter his course. What others would be cursed for, Reagan does in a friendly, evenhanded way that disarms criticism. Perhaps it is because he never acts with malice and he never takes pleasure from the discomfort of others. But if it is necessary he will cause that discomfort, freely and easily.

Reagan may be unique in that he is a warmly ruthless man.

Another important aspect of Reagan's personality is his inherent humility. He is not an arrogant or haughty man. He is aware of his limitations as a mortal, and that generally causes him to act with caution. I remember one incident that brought this home to me vividly and showed me that even great men sometimes have doubts about their ability to cope with the problems facing them.

It happened late one afternoon during the 1976 presidential campaign. I was sitting with Reagan in the back seat of a black Cadillac limousine on the way to a television studio where he was going to give an interview that would be seen by millions of Americans. He was unusually quiet and thoughtful. It was becoming clear that he had a reasonably good chance of winning the nomination of the Republican party. As the dream of being president began to turn into reality the awesomeness of the job came home to him.

We were discussing what policy points he should try to make during the television program when he stopped, shook his head slowly, and said, "I don't know if I can do this. I'm not sure I'm qualified to be president."

For a few seconds I was stunned. He was probably going to be the next president of the United States and now he was wondering whether or not he could do it?

And then I decided that he was just like every other candidate who ran for president before him, a person with enormous talent and ability, but also a person whose abilities, no matter how great, could never meet the demands of that impossible job. Reagan wasn't perfectly qualified; he was just better qualified than anyone else around and available at that time.

I turned toward him and said, "Sure you can. You ran the state of California for eight years, and that's like running the seventh largest country in the world. You're the only guy to run for president who actually majored in economics. And you know your policies are the right ones for the country."

"Well," he said with a little smile, "maybe."

Then the limousine stopped in front of the television station. He went inside and did another brilliant job of communicating his vision of what had to be done in this country. I never heard those doubts mentioned again.

Ronald Reagan also had one distinctive personality trait that was highly unusual, perhaps unique for someone who rose to the high level of managerial responsibility he attained.

He made no demands, and gave almost no instructions.

Essentially, he just responded to whatever was brought to his attention and said yes or no, or I'll think about it. At times he would just change the subject, maybe tell a funny story, and you would not find out what he thought about it, one way or the other. His style of managing was totally different from the model of the classic executive who exercised leadership by planning and scheming, and barking out orders to his subordinates.

It was something that all those who had worked closely and intimately with Ronald Reagan knew. Ed Meese knew. Mike Deaver

knew. And so did Dick Allen and Lyn Nofziger and Peter Hannaford and John Sears. Bill Casey learned it when he joined the campaign in early 1980 and Jim Baker later in 1980. But we rarely
talked about it among ourselves and never to outsiders.

We kept it a secret.

We just accepted Reagan as he was and adjusted ourselves to
his manner. If that was the way he wanted to do things, fine. At
the time it seemed like a small thing, an eccentricity that was dwarfed
by his multiple, stunning qualities.

So everyone overlooked and compensated for the fact that he
made decisions like an ancient king or a Turkish pasha, passively
letting his subjects serve him, selecting only those morsels of public policy that were especially tasty. Rarely did he ask searching
questions and demand to know why someone had or had not done
something. He just sat back in a supremely calm, relaxed manner
and waited until important things were brought to him. And then
he would act, quickly, decisively, and usually, very wisely.

He is not aloof. In fact, he is very approachable. He welcomes
people. He likes to have people come to him. But he is almost shy
about doing it the other way—that is, going to others.

This kind of behavior in a political candidate is unheard of.
From the viewpoint of a jealous, competitive staff it is potentially
chaotic. For any staff member could, if he or she took advantage
of Reagan's unusual hospitality, sit or talk to him whenever and for
as long as he or she wished. Somehow during the campaigns this
potential for disaster was recognized by all those around him and
there was a clear, unspoken and unwritten rule that no one would
ever abuse the privilege of access.

On Nixon's campaign plane in 1968, Nixon sat in a separate
compartment, splendidly alone, usually cut off from his staff and
guarded by his chief watchdog, Bob Haldeman. Because it was unusual and difficult to talk to Nixon personally, everyone wanted to
do so even when there wasn't a good reason for it. Access was
status. But on Reagan's campaign plane in 1976 and 1980 it was
just the opposite. He sat in the same compartment with the staff.
There were no staff acting as guards. Anyone who wanted to talk
to him simply walked over—Secret Service men, stewardesses, and
advisers. He always smiled, stopped whatever he was doing, and
talked to them. After a while, when it became clear that anyone
could talk to him whenever they wanted to, they stopped. Without

ever discussing it, everyone seemed to understand that if they each took advantage of this easy access it would soak up so much of Reagan's time that he wouldn't be able to do the things that we had all come out on the airplane to get done. So most of the time he sat and enjoyed the same splendid isolation Nixon did in 1968, except he did it without walls or guards.

This part of Reagan's personality is unusual. Perhaps the most public manifestation of it through the years has been his peculiar behavior at press conferences. At the end of the press conference it is understood that the questioning is over, that reporters will not ask any more questions, and that if they do the president will not answer them.

This rule is important because it prevents the president from being surprised and caught off guard. Presidents are rarely asked about trivial matters, and their answers can have great consequences. A hasty or careless answer to a sudden question can have disastrous consequences—it can roil foreign policy, upset the financial markets, and destroy careers. Reagan was fully aware of the dangers of quick answers to complicated questions.

But reporters soon discovered that if they shouted a question to Reagan, loudly enough for him to hear, he was incapable of not stopping, turning, and answering. For years his closest and most trusted advisers and friends have pleaded with him not to do this. He has always agreed with them that he should not do it. But he continues to do it repeatedly. He has never told his advisers and friends that he would not do it, he just agrees that he should not do it, and then goes on and does it anyway.

It seems to be an instinctive part of Reagan's personality to respond to anyone who addresses him. Whether it is a new policy proposal from a senior adviser or a letter from a total stranger or a question rudely shouted at him by a hostile reporter, he will answer. But he will not initiate those contacts. He would be perfectly happy and content if he did not know or hear of people's attempts to communicate with him. But when their spoken words reach his ears or he reads their written words, then he seems compelled to respond.

The consequence of this unusual trait is that Reagan is very dependent upon his personal advisers. Because he does not actively and constantly search out and demand things, he must rely on what is or is not brought to him. When his staff is very, very good, talented, wise and loyal, and almost selfless, it works brilliantly. But when his staff is ordinary—talented, smart but not wise, and loyal more to themselves then to Reagan policy or to the man himself—then mediocrity rules. And if any of his personal staff chooses to abuse his or her position and deliberately withholds key information or misleads him, Reagan is helpless—and disaster can strike. This is particularly true for matters where much of the information is secret and classified and there is no normal press coverage.

The people President Reagan surrounded himself with in his presidential campaigns and during the early years of his presidency were critical to his success. Even his political enemies noted and acknowledged this. Robert Strauss, perhaps the toughest and most savvy Democrat in the United States, praised Reagan's original White House staff, saying it was "simply spectacular. It's the best White House staff I've ever seen." [8] In fact, outstanding advisers were indispensable to Reagan—as was later proven so tragically by the Iran-Contra affair—given his unique management style.

And the degree to which he trusted and depended on his advisers is probably the key to understanding the Iran-Contra affair that crippled Reagan's presidency during his second term of office. Reagan's style was like a loaded pistol without a safety, a powerful and effective weapon, but dangerous if mishandled.

One other factor that undoubtedly contributed to Reagan's unique and complex personality was his many years as a movie star. Being a national celebrity is something that few of us will ever experience. The people who do achieve this rarified status are put under special pressure and go through changes that are difficult to understand without experiencing them.

One of the things they experience is approval and adulation from complete strangers. Strangers will accost them in public with the attitude of someone who has been their friend for years and talk to them as if they knew them. It can be disconcerting, and you have to train yourself to deal with it.

I first realized that Ronald Reagan was a different, special presidential candidate when I stepped into a hotel elevator with him during one of the early 1976 campaign trips. Two women were already in the elevator, both of them in their late forties or early fifties. They must have been teenagers when Reagan was acting in the movies.

When the ladies realized that the man standing next to them was Ronald Reagan they began to move and talk excitedly. Finally, one of them could not restrain herself and blurted out to Reagan, "Can I touch you!?"

Reagan smiled warmly back at her, held out his hand and said, "Hello. I'm Ronald Reagan."

She seized his hand quickly, trembling with delight. Her friend started to giggle. A few seconds later the elevator door opened and we were off campaigning again.

The incident was a potent reminder that there were millions of Americans across the country who had watched Reagan in his movie roles for years, and followed his career in Hollywood and later with the General Electric Theater.

Ronald Reagan's style was also marked by the fact that he had a trusted partner who was an important part of most of his decisions—Nancy Reagan. They are literally inseparable.

Nancy Reagan came from a broken home. Her father divorced her mother when she was only a year old, and her mother virtually abandoned her to pursue her own acting career on the stage in New York City. When she was seven years old, her mother married again, this time to a famous, wealthy neurosurgeon from Chicago. He turned out to be a superfather, and she was tough and smart enough to recover from the misfortunes of her early childhood and to take advantage of her new opportunities.

She did well in school and went on to Smith College in Massachusetts, one of the finest schools in the country. After she graduated from Smith she single-mindedly pursued an acting career. Combining beauty and brains with an impeccable academic background she soon became one of the most glamorous young women in the country, performing in major movies with top actors. When she met Ronald Reagan she was independent and highly successful, and so was he.

They are happily, openly in love with one another. On the plane, after the campaign day was over and we were heading home, she sometimes pulled up the seat divider between them and then curled up with her head in his lap and went to sleep. Sometimes when they were both in high spirits they even cuddled a little on the plane. They obviously adored each other and if they ever fought, they never did it when anyone else was around.

Nancy Reagan was an important and active participant in virtually all the important discussions that took place during the campaign. She was highly intelligent, with a sixth sense for asking insightful, penetrating questions. Above all, her judgments on public policy issues, political strategy, and personnel were superb. It was easily as good as the advice Reagan got from his top campaign aides.

She was also wise enough to sense that her role could be easily twisted by a less than understanding national media who would try to portray her as a domineering wife, meddling in areas that she didn't know anything about and should stay out of. The national news media in the United States is dominated by middle-aged males and they have some difficulty believing that a wife could also be a bona fide adviser. But Reagan recognized a good mind when he encountered one, and he consulted her constantly on just about everything. It was just done in a restrained, low-key manner. On the other hand he would never hesitate to overrule her counsel, although he seldom did so because she was usually right.

Someday the Reagans will have quite a story to tell. During the course of the Iran-Contra affair, President Reagan surrendered portions of his personal diary. The national press, obsessed with the Iran-Contra affair, reported the diary episode strictly from the viewpoint of whether or not it showed that Reagan was culpable. It didn't. What was little remarked on was the very existence of the diary itself.

Reagan's diary, long and detailed, written virtually every day in ink on lined, bound notebook pages, is probably, in the words of one person who has seen them, "the most extraordinary record ever made by a modern president. Everything is in the diary—Reagan's private thoughts, his descriptions of key events, his evaluations of people he met—everything."

Nobody ever had the slightest clue that President Reagan was keeping any personal records, not even Michael Deaver, his closest personal aide. In March 1985 Deaver had even become so alarmed that Reagan was not keeping any notes for history that he convened a special meeting of experts in the White House—including Samuel Vaughan, Doubleday editor, and Daniel Boorstin, Librarian of Congress—to discuss what might be done about it. The conclusion was to strongly recommend to the president that he begin to keep some kind of diary, even an oral one dictated into a tape recorder.

Little did we know that he secretly had kept a personal diary, a treasure trove of notes and facts. I am also told that Nancy Reagan has been keeping her own secret diary. A pair of secret diaries should make the Reagan memoirs quite memorable.

President Reagan's management philosophy was best summed up when, toward the end of his sixth year as president, a reporter said, "Your friend Roger Smith, chairman of General Motors, says that you've done a great job of focusing on the big picture without getting bogged down in detail. How do you decide which problems to address personally and which to leave to subordinates?"

President Reagan replied, "You surround yourself with the best people you can find, delegate authority, and don't interfere as long as the overall policy that you've decided upon is being carried out. In the Cabinet meetings—and some members of the Cabinet who have been members of other Cabinets told me there had never been such meetings—I use a system in which I want to hear what everybody wants to say honestly. I want the decisions made on what is right or wrong, what is good or bad for the people of this country. I encourage all the input I can get. . . . And when I've heard all that I need to make a decision, I don't take a vote. I make the decision. Then I expect every one of them, whether their views have carried the day or not, to go forward together in carrying out the policy."[9]

The only true test of a management style is whether it works or not. In the early years of his presidency it worked brilliantly. Supported by a large number of capable aides he rode easily in the saddle of the presidency, husbanded his energies, and focused them sharply on his chosen top policy priorities. In those early years his executive skills were largely responsible for the stunning successes he achieved in economic policy.

In the closing years of his presidency the high rolling, high risk methods that served him so well earlier now betrayed him. His unique management style had enormous power and efficacy when implemented properly, but it was a flawed style, with high risk and potential for disaster. Its Achilles' heel was exposed by the Iran-Contra affair.

Six

Reagan's Achilles' Heel

In the broad sweep of history the painful saga of the Iran-Contra affair will be at best a small footnote. But if it reminds us once again that our republic is vulnerable, that it does matter who is president, and who the president's men and women are, then it will not have been endured in vain.

Chapter Twenty-Four

KHOMEINI vs. REAGAN

Monday, November 24, 1986, was a typical day in northern California. When I drove onto the Stanford University campus that morning, the day was sparkling and sunny, and the air was cool and dry. The students and staff looked serene.

We were all blissfully unaware of the dark cloud of scandal that was about to pass over the Reagan administration, casting a black shadow on the Reagan revolution that had so utterly dominated public policy for the past six years. President Reagan was near the crest of his power. His economic program was, so far, spectacularly successful; he was moving forward with a massive new missile defense program; and, reelected by one of the largest margins in history, he was on his way to going down in the history books as one of America's most successful presidents.

Then came the Iran-Contra affair.

That November evening, the night before the full force of the Iran arms scandal hit the Reagan administration, I had dinner with Robert Gates, the deputy director of the Central Intelligence Agency. Gates had come to California to give a luncheon address at the Commonwealth Club of San Francisco on President Reagan's missile defense program. It was a major policy speech and Gates' remarks were broadcast nationally on radio. After his speech he drove to the Hoover Institutition, about one hour's drive south from San Francisco, to give a seminar at 4 p.m. That evening there was a small dinner in his honor at the Stanford University Faculty Club. In attendance were a half-dozen or so of my colleagues from the Hoover Institution, including Henry Rowen, the former chairman of the National Intelligence Council of the CIA, Dennis L. Bark, a member of the board of the U.S. Institute of Peace, and Angelo Codevilla, a former senior staff member of the Senate Intelligence Committee.

About halfway through dinner the door to the small private dining room opened and a quiet, almost unnoticeable man, one of Gates' traveling companions, came in, walked up to him, bent down, and whispered something. Gates was sitting directly across the table from me. As the whispering sunk in, Gates lowered his head, frowning. When his aide finished, Gates excused himself, dropped his napkin on the table, and then hurriedly followed the other man out of the room.

About ten minutes later Gates rejoined our dinner party. He came back into the room looking stricken, his face drained of most of its color. But he sat down quietly and, after a few moments, recovered his composure and rejoined our conversation.

I was curious to know what he had just learned that seemed to affect him so strongly. But, of course, no one asked.

On the morning of the next day, Attorney General Edwin Meese held a White House press conference and it became clear what the whispered message at dinner must have been about. Meese announced to the world that somewhere between $10 million and $30 million of the profits from the sale of U.S. arms to Iran had been diverted to secret Swiss bank accounts for use by the Contra rebels in Nicaragua, in apparent defiance of a congressional ban on such aid. What was to become known as the Iran-Contra affair had begun, a sprawling scandal that effectively paralyzed the Reagan administration for almost a year.

From the beginning of the Reagan presidency, Iran played an unusual, important role. During the election campaign of 1980 the captivity of the fifty-two Americans held by the Iranian government was a politically explosive, sensitive issue. The humiliation suffered by President Carter because of the hostage crisis did not by itself cause his defeat, but it certainly contributed to Reagan's large margin of victory. To anyone who took part in that presidential campaign, the contempt and disdain on the unsmiling face of the Ayatollah of Iran will be forever branded in memory. Khomeini was the closest the United States has come to having a personal enemy since the days of Hitler in World War II. He epitomized the random evil that seemed to be appearing sporadically with greater and greater frequency around the world. Ronald Reagan despised him.

And then suddenly—after being held hostage for 444 days, after the course of an entire presidential campaign, the fifty-two Americans were released just a few hours before Ronald Reagan took the oath of office on January 20, 1981. The timing of the release was so exquisite that it confirmed a sense of triumph in Reagan and his supporters. At the same time, it reinforced President Carter's utter defeat.

The sudden, dramatic release of the American hostages just before Reagan became president ended the most humiliating episode in modern American history, perhaps the most humiliating episode in the entire life of the young republic. The national security of the United States was never endangered, and virtually all Americans carried on their lives throughout the entire affair as if nothing happened. But never before had any nation so openly and brazenly abused so many American citizens for so long, and gotten away with it, without paying a fearful price. Iran discovered a potential weakness in the power of America, the same weakness that exists in any powerful person when someone he or she holds dear is taken hostage—the American weakness of valuing human life almost above all else.

When the Iranians realized just how reluctant we were to risk harm to the hostages, they gloated at their newfound power, as they mocked and taunted the United States on the evening network television news.

Americans were outraged and shocked. Shocked that innocent Americans were taken hostage and deprived of their liberty, outraged that we were powerless to do anything about it, and worried by the knowledge that any serious attempt to punish the guilty would mean sure death for the hostages.

That sense of just fury would mark American politics for years to come.

The day in early 1981 when the hostages were released was

one of profound relief for most Americans. That morning all things seemed possible and the powers of the evil Ayatollahs of this world seemed weak and distant, even though the weather was in direct contrast to our bright spirits. It was a cold, damp day in Washington, D.C., and the sky was dull, with a heavy overcast.

At President Reagan's inauguration I sat with other senior members of the White House staff in the small group of coveted seats on the platform just behind and to the right of the president. We could look out over the heads of the assembled crowd facing us and, looking west from the Capitol toward the White House, take in the magnificent view which for the first time the president would be able to see while being inaugurated. Ever since Andrew Jackson's inaugural in 1829 the ceremony had been held on the east side of the Capitol with its cramped view and limited audience capacity. The new view toward the west seemed to be just one more symbol of Reagan's new beginning.

The view was spacious and inspiring—the Washington Monument and the Lincoln Memorial—and, if you turned around and looked back, the thick, pale white marble walls of the Capitol building itself were very reassuring. Perhaps it was the combination of so many good things that contributed to a feeling that all things were now possible.

Everything was perfect.

It got even better. President-elect Reagan stood and took the oath of office, administered by the chief justice of the United States, Warren Burger. Then came his inaugural address. Reagan walked to the podium and, as he raised his head to look out at the crowd assembled in front of him and speak, a strange and wonderful thing happened.

The dark cloudy sky over his head began to part slightly, within seconds there was a gaping hole in the gray overcast, and a brilliant, golden shaft of wintery sun burst through the clouds and bathed the inaugural stand and the watching crowd. As Reagan spoke a slight breeze ruffled his hair and the warm golden light beamed down upon him. Later, a few minutes after he finished speaking, as if on cue from some master lighter backstage, the hole in the clouds shrank, the sky darkened, and Washington grew gray and cold once again.

It was a fortuitous coincidence of timing and weather, but for those who did not know that, it sure could have looked like a sign from Heaven. At the very least it was a bright, golden symbol of the passing of the old and the coming of the new, one more proof that even when it came to weather Reagan was lucky.

Six years later the warm sun went down on the Reagan administration. Once again Americans were being held captive in squalid prison cells somewhere in the Middle East. And once again Iranian government officials had humiliated and outfoxed the government of the United States.

The essentials of the Iran-Contra affair were simple and straightforward. The United States agreed to sell military weapons to Iran, primarily modern antitank missiles to counter the large tank force of Iraq. The sales were done secretly, in blatant contradiction of not only our own announced policy never to sell any arms to nations like Iran who were involved in international terrorism, but also in contradiction of our policy of asking other countries not to sell arms to them either.

It was hypocrisy and severely undermined the credibility of the United States in the conduct of its foreign diplomacy. But more than that it displayed a moral insensitivity that was breathtaking. Selling U.S. military weapons to Iran? It wasn't as bad as if the United States sold weapons to Germany and Japan right after World War II—but it was close.

What made the whole weapons deal with Iran even more distasteful and shameful was the fact that we did it largely under the pressure of their threats, not out of any grand design or cold-blooded calculation of geopolitical advantage to the United States. Iran was once again responsible for Americans being held hostage in the Middle East. And we had agreed cravenly to pay their hostage demands, namely by selling them weapons.

After knuckling under to Iran and adopting the moral cloak of an international arms dealer—in an amateur attempt at secrecy—we capped the whole sorry episode by misleading our own Congress and attempting to get around a law passed by Congress and signed by President Reagan. The law expressly forbids our intelligence agencies from providing military aid to guerrillas intent on overthrowing the new communist dictatorship in Nicaragua. Through trickery and deceit a small band of people in the White House and the CIA managed to take some of the profits made on the sale of U.S. arms to Iran and use them to purchase weapons for the freedom fighters in Nicaragua.

Some of those involved thought it was a neat idea—cutting secret deals with international arms dealers who had the moral values of Mafia thugs; paying ransom for American hostages in order to bask in the momentary adulation of the U.S. public as the victims straggled home one by one; tilting the chance of victory in the Iran-Iraq war towards Iran and prolonging a bloody war in the hope both sides would lose; and, finally in a delicious irony, using the Ayatollah's blood money to pay for the Contras' attempts to win back their freedom from the communist rulers in Nicaragua.

The United States paid dearly for those brief moments of sly, self-satisfaction. When the secret arms sales, the ransom payments, and the diversion of money broke into the open in November 1986, the United States was plunged into a political scandal that dominated the news for the next year and effectively paralyzed the government.

The Reagan political revolution was stopped in its tracks by the Iran-Contra affair for almost a year. Developments in economic policy, nuclear weapons defenses, and arms control slowed measurably and in some cases stood still. The top officials of the executive branch, key congressmen and senators, and the leading political commentators and analysts in the national media were all obsessed with the unfolding drama and preoccupied with its details.

The greatest cost of the scandal was time. The year consumed in dealing with it could have been spent formulating and driving home the policies that might have assured the continuation of many of Reagan's policies well into the twenty-first century.

During this period of time President Reagan was deeply affected. For the first time in his life, his personal credibility was challenged, and soon the majority of the American people were convinced he lied to them. His honor and integrity were on the line and the public's doubts seemed to seriously depress him. Day in, day out, the Iran-Contra affair was a constant, drumming distraction, preventing President Reagan and his top aides from concentrating on affairs of state. As one anonymous senior aide commented in the summer of 1987, "In the long run maybe Iran will be a footnote, who knows. But it's immobilized the President. It's forced him to go on the defensive—so much that everything he does turns back on Iran."[1]

The scandal was substantial and serious, but it was old-fashioned U.S. politics that made it the spectacle it became. In the late fall of 1986 the presidential prospects for the Democratic party were as cold and damp as the oncoming winter in Washington.

Ronald Reagan had rewritten the national policy agenda during the presidential campaigns of 1976 and 1980 and now much of that agenda was turned into law. His administration was driving to finish that agenda before the end of his second term, to institutionalize the defense and economic policy changes he wrought in the years before. All this put the Democrats in serious political trouble. If Reagan succeeded, if his policies really worked, well, it might be good for the country but it would be politically disastrous for the Democrats. They couldn't say this publicly, but it was increasingly clear that Reagan somehow had maneuvered them into a position where what was good for the country was bad for them politically and vice versa. The Democrats desperately searched for viable alternatives to Reagan's economic policies and his nuclear missile defense policies. They found none. The best they could muster was defiant, shrill opposition to programs the American public supported. They found themselves on the eve of the 1988 election with no big issues and no distinguished, well-known candidates willing to carry their banner—just the prospect of losing the presidency once again, and perhaps slipping into political limbo for the rest of the twentieth century.

Then, the Reagan administration virtually handed the Democrats the political club of the Iran-Contra affair. The Democrats seized on it gleefully; it is hard to fault them. The Republicans should not have been surprised that, when they handed a desperate political enemy a fine weapon, it would be used.

Unlike Watergate, which grew from a burglary, the Iran-Contra affair grew from bad policy judgments—policy judgments that scorned the wisdom of history and agreed to pay ransom and sell weapons to our enemies, policy judgments that put ends above means, that broke one of the fundamental rocks our republic is built on—that no man is above the law. The mystery of the Iran-Contra affair is the mystery of how such bad policy judgments came to be made, how for a brief moment of time, bad ideas triumphed over good ideas.

Chapter Twenty-Five

REAGAN'S FOREIGN POLICY DIRECTORATE

Less than two months after he took office, President Reagan was scheduled to attend a summit meeting with Pierre Trudeau, the Canadian prime minister, in Ottawa, Canada. So, in addition to the awesome task of setting a new administration in motion, we had the burden of preparing for a major foreign trip on March 10, 1981. Because it was his first foreign trip President Reagan's performance would be closely watched and analyzed.

As the complex preparations for Reagan's foray to Canada got under way, I discovered, to my surprise, that I was expected to be part of the presidential party traveling with him. A substantial part of the agenda of the talks between Reagan and Trudeau were bilateral issues (the State Department's term to describe United States domestic issues that are of significance to our northern neighbor) and as Reagan's domestic policy adviser, I and other members of my staff were to assist with those issues. As was his custom, Reagan involved other senior members of his staff with the preparations for his first foreign trip. Edwin Meese, Michael Deaver, and James Baker, although none of them were foreign policy experts, were right in the middle of everything. We were there because Reagan wanted us there.

This infuriated Alexander Haig, the newly appointed secretary of state, who saw himself literally as the vicar of foreign policy. He was convinced there was only one person necessary to the president when it came to foreign policy, and that was Haig himself. He was somewhat contemptuous of the views of anyone who was not a certified, blue-ribbon, foreign policy expert. He was baffled by Reagan's insistence on including these foreign policy amateurs in the inner circle of the summit planning. The thing that seemed to annoy Haig most was Reagan's habit of involving trusted advisers in policy discussions on issues in which they were not expert. Haig was incredulous that President Reagan might consult anyone else on any element of foreign policy, no matter how small. Word of his unhappiness and disbelief soon seeped back to the White House staff, which serenely ignored Haig's concerns.

One morning, at one of the final White House briefings for President Reagan before his departure for Canada, I made the mistake of showing up in the Cabinet Room about ten minutes early. I figured no one would be there and planned to read some material my staff prepared for the meeting which I hadn't had time to read. I never got to it. When I walked in Secretary of State Haig was already there, standing behind the cabinet table, bent over, reading. As soon as he saw me he straightened up, drew himself together like a small Charles de Gaulle, and bellowed, "What the hell are you doing in *my* meeting, Anderson?"

I should have known then that Ronald Reagan was going to have more than his share of troubles in foreign policy. This was not the kind of collegial staff member that Reagan was used to working with. Although I was not a good friend of Haig's I had known him for a long time. When I was a special assistant to President Nixon in 1969, Haig was one of Henry Kissinger's key deputies on the National Security Council staff. I had worked fairly closely with him on a couple of matters involving international trade and the military draft, and he once gave me some sound advice on how to handle a Soviet KGB agent who wanted to be my "friend," and was besieging me with telephone calls and invitations.

Some of my colleagues were a mite suspicious of Alexander Haig because he formerly had worked for Joseph Califano, one of the most effective and committed liberal Democrats in the country, while they were both in the Defense Department during Robert McNamara's tenure as secretary of defense. Haig was a career military man and his political views were largely unknown. But I found him very competent and easy to work with, that is, if you could get past his occasional, initial gruffness.

So I smiled across the cabinet table at him and answered his question, "Mr. Secretary," I said, "anytime I get the chance to brighten your day I take it."

He looked at me for a few seconds, smiled briefly, and with a quick shake of his head acknowledged that I was going to stay. But he didn't really like it. He liked it even less when Meese and Deaver and Baker joined the gathering a few minutes later.

Haig quickly became the most celebrated symbol of Ronald Reagan's early and continuing difficulties with foreign policy. Proud and headstrong, the former general and White House chief of staff for Richard Nixon was an unusual choice for Reagan. Other strong candidates for secretary of state included Caspar Weinberger, William Casey, and George Shultz, all of whom played major roles in Reagan's election, and none of whom had Haig's prickly personality. But Haig did have far more extensive foreign policy credentials than any of his rivals. Many of Reagan's old friends in his kitchen cabinet from California, including Alfred Bloomingdale, Joseph Coors, Justin Dart, and Jaquelin Hume, were vastly impressed with Haig's hard-line reputation and no-nonsense style, and prevailed on Reagan to select the more famous relative stranger rather than one of his less famous, longtime political suporters. The recommendation was not unanimous. At one point in the deliberations, Glenn Campbell, who predicted Haig's appointment would be a disaster, warned his colleagues, "Gentlemen, anti-communist bluster is no substitute for a well-thought-out foreign policy."

It was a fateful choice. It placed a stranger, far removed in style and temperament from President Reagan, at the heart of his foreign policy, a policy not yet fully formed. Haig never did understand Reagan very well or work effectively with him. The year plus that he served as secretary of state, from January 1981 to June 1982, was marked by severe policy disputes and strained personal relationships. There was something about Haig—he seemed to ruffle the feelings of almost everyone, and almost everybody seemed to ruffle his feelings. Reagan's foreign policy never did recover from that shaky start.

As any modern president must, Reagan relied heavily on the advice of experts when he made decisions. This was particularly true of foreign policy, because his knowledge and experience there were substantially less than in the broad range of issues that made up the domestic policy agenda. When an issue involved foreign policy, or a related defense or intelligence issue, he made decisions more tentatively, and listened to the experts.

Compared to the vivid, sharp blueprint of the economic policy he worked on for years, the Reagan foreign policy blueprint was blurred and pale. Reagan did hold strong convictions on the conduct of foreign policy, on the question of nuclear arms reduction, and the necessity of rebulding our defense and intelligence capabilities. And he clearly understood that the first and foremost responsibility of the president is to maintain our national security. But when it came to implementing those general policies and achieving the broad goals of his foreign policy in particular, Reagan was much more dependent upon his advisers. This is not unusual for American presidents. It has been true for every one of our presidents since World War II, with the exception of Eisenhower and, to a lesser degree, Nixon. For this reason, the selection of a president's foreign policy advisers is more sensitive and important than the selection of his domestic policy advisers.

To help him make those foreign policy decisions, President Reagan did not create a foreign policy vicar to be his sole deputy as Alexander Haig urged him to do. He also did not rely exclusively on the institutional framework that grew up over the years— the National Security Council. The National Security Council was established by Congress in 1947. It is chaired by the president. Its statutory members, in addition to the president, are the vice president, the secretary of state, and the secretary of defense. The chairman of the Joint Chiefs of Staff is the military adviser to the council and the director of the Central Intelligence Agency is the intelligence adviser. As envisaged by Congress, the purpose of the NSC is "to advise the President with respect to the integration of domestic, foreign, and military policies relating to national security." [1]

Instead, Reagan did what he so often did before, and what so many successful leaders and executives do throughout the world: he fashioned his group of advisers to fit his needs and their talents. Basically, he established a foreign policy directorate, a small group of people—eight men and one woman—to whom he turned for counsel and advice on all important issues during the early days of his administration. The group had no formal name. He did not often meet with them seated formally around a table. But he did consult with each of them, steadily and regularly.

President Reagan used his foreign policy directorate the same way he used his other ad hoc advisory groups. He believed in one person, one vote, but some people's votes were always more equal than others. In weighing what his advisers told him, Reagan was strongly affected by the length of his relationship with that person and the degree of confidence he placed in that person's judgment. An old, trusted confidant of the president was rarely overruled by the wisdom of new advisers, no matter how impressive their credentials or their reasoning.

Reagan also believed strongly in letting everyone have a say. No matter how much he leaned on the advice of his key specialists, he also liked to cross-check that advice against the views of other advisers whose judgments he valued. Beginning with his days as governor of California, he rarely relied on the counsel of a single person. Instead, he encouraged all those at a meeting to comment on the issue from their own point of view. It was a valuable technique that often brought a fresh perspective, a new and better way of solving a problem, but it was not without costs. It took time, and it sometimes annoyed and irritated those who resented having their areas of expertise invaded by nonexperts. That feeling of resentment was especially true of people who had not been associated with Reagan for a long time and did not appreciate or understand how he liked to work. And while he believed in letting everyone have his say, he did not give equal time to all his advisers. How much he did listen to them and how much attention he paid to what they said was heavily affected by the nature of the issue under consideration. All other things being equal, after everyone spoke, he tended to rely very heavily on the advice of the person who had the main responsibility for the implementation of the policy being discussed.

Four of the original directorate of nine were traditional choices— Alexander Haig, secretary of state; Caspar Weinberger, secretary of defense; William Casey, director of the CIA; and Richard V. Allen, assistant to the president for national security affairs.

Alexander Haig played the lead role in foreign policy. Given his distinguished military background and long service on the staff of the National Security Council, as the head of NATO, and his experience as chief of staff for President Nixon during the dark days of 1974, Haig made effective use of the natural power base of the secretary of state. He was not a conceptual, strategic thinker, but his instincts were sound and supportive of Reagan's general policy. His relative weakness as a member of the directorate was that he was the new boy in town, competing for the president's attention with others who were long associated with him, some for upward of fifteen years. Haig played the lead role, but it was not a commanding lead.

Caspar Weinberger filled the traditional role of being a civilian in control of the Defense Department. He had served as a captain in the Army infantry during World War II but for the last thirty-five years concentrated on civilian concerns. Weinberger was a superb lawyer with a distinguished record of public service. As director of the Office of Management and Budget under President Nixon, he acquired a legendary reputation as "Cap the Knife" for his efforts to cut federal spending. Later, as secretary of health, education and welfare under President Ford, he spearheaded the development of a radical welfare program that, if it had been accepted, would have dwarfed any of the plans of left-wing Democrats. Whenever he took a job, he clearly set out to be the best anyone had ever been at it. And that was the kind of single-focus intensity he brought to bear on national defense. He paid little attention to general questions of foreign policy (except arms control) or the details of intelligence, and instead focused on restoring the military might and power of the United States. He succeeded brilliantly in his single-minded drive, but in accomplishing that Herculean task he forsook a more general advisory role on foreign affairs.

The third traditional member of the foreign policy team was William J. Casey. Casey was a very unusual, special man with unique ties to President Reagan. During the early years of the administration he husbanded those talents and resources, and focused his energies on rebuilding the nation's intelligence capabilities, which in his and Reagan's view were decimated during the four years

Jimmy Carter was president. Our eyes on the world were not blind, but our vision was badly impaired, rife with dangerous blind spots.

Perhaps the most important player in the formulation and shaping of Reagan's early foreign policy was Richard V. Allen. Allen joined up with Reagan in 1976 and fought and bled with him in the primary campaign that he eventually lost to President Ford. But from then until Reagan took office in 1981 Allen was Reagan's guide in the wilderness of foreign policy. It was Allen who hammered out the main conceptual outlines of Reagan's foreign policy in the 1976 and 1980 campaigns, it was Allen who helped draft the foreign policy planks of the Republican platform in 1976 and 1980, who personally introduced Reagan to scores of well known foreign policy experts, who organized Reagan's foreign policy task forces, who drafted his major foreign policy campaign speeches, who played a major role in staffing the key foreign policy jobs in the new administration, and who deliberately followed a low profile path as Reagan's national security adviser, trying, with some success, to coordinate and reconcile the warring dukes of his foreign policy kingdom—Haig, Weinberger, and Casey.

Above all, Allen was the only foreign policy adviser who was a geopolitical strategist. Not a military man, he came out of the classic mold that has given the United States its most effective national security advisers. Allen was an established scholar, knew the national political scene, and had extensive experience in foreign policy making, having served on President Nixon's staff as principal deputy to Henry Kissinger.

The fifth member of the group was Jeane Kirkpatrick, a Democrat in name, if not in substance. As ambassador to the United Nations she ably represented the United States. A noted scholar, she was not shy about using her quick mind and strong debating style to speak out forcefully in support of United States policies. Her sense of policy and her intellectual skills made her a significant voice among the members of the foreign policy directorate during Reagan's first term.

The other four members of Reagan's first foreign policy directorate were George Bush, Edwin Meese, James Baker, and Michael K. Deaver.

Vice President Bush had the most foreign policy experience of these last four members—one year as head of the CIA, and one year as ambassador to the United Nations. Bush had a special relationship with Reagan. Even though he had been Reagan's closest rival for the Republican presidential nomination in 1980, Reagan scrupulously avoided saying anything bad about Bush, and Bush, in return, was only mildly critical of Reagan and his policies. After Reagan soundly beat Bush in the primaries and selected him as his running mate, he pledged that Bush, unlike other vice presidents, would play an important role in his administration. Reagan followed through on that pledge, drawing Bush deep into the inner sanctums, virtually letting him sit by his side as he conducted his presidency.

The last three members of the foreign policy directorate—Meese, Baker, and Deaver—had no foreign policy experience whatsoever. They had no significant military experience, no diplomatic experience, and no intelligence experience. What they had instead was political brilliance, a sense of strategy, common sense and, above all, a long record of loyal service to Reagan. This was especially true for Meese and Deaver, who were with Reagan from his earliest days as governor of California. Baker was a relative newcomer, but after serving as George Bush's campaign manager he served Reagan skillfully during the presidential campaign of 1980 and contributed materially to Reagan's success. Baker won his spurs with Reagan only recently, but his strong talent as an administrator and his keen, if somewhat cautious, political judgment soon had him operating on a level close to that of Meese and Deaver.

During the first year or so, Haig and Allen dominated foreign policymaking. Weinberger and Casey were almost totally preoccupied with the huge tasks of restoring our defense and intelligence capabilities. Bush, Meese, Baker, and Deaver had a multitude of other responsibilities and thus did not initiate much in the way of foreign policy, but they served as a powerful and effective check. In spite of the difficulties with Alexander Haig, which led to his resignation in 1982, and the unfounded political charges that forced Allen's own resignation a few months before Haig's, the first year of Reagan's foreign policy was fairly successful.

Not one of its least accomplishments was the fact that nothing went seriously wrong, a policy success that is often very difficult to achieve, but rarely noted or appreciated.

A crisis—a sudden, critical state of affairs—is the most difficult test of any group of national policy advisers. Reagan's foreign policy directorate got its first test barely two months after he took office. By then Haig demonstrated that his deteriorating relations with the president and his colleagues was due to more than a touchy and testy personality.

Haig hungered for power and openly grasped for it. The job of secretary of state has such innate power in its mandate that it usually more than slakes the thirst for power of those who hold it. But not Alexander Haig. He constantly and persistently drove for more and more power at every opportunity, striving for the day when he would direct foreign policy singlehandedly.

The most celebrated instance of Haig lunging for power and recognition happened the day President Reagan was shot by would-be assassin, John W. Hinckley, Jr. It was Monday, March 30, 1981, only sixty-nine days after Reagan became president. In the early afternoon one of my assistants, Barbara Honegger, rushed into my office and told me in a tone of disbelief that President Reagan had been shot. A few minutes later I left my office and walked to the Situation Room, two floors down.

Many of the president's senior aides and members of his cabinet were starting to assemble. There was no formal call; they just seemed to come, one by one, and file quietly into the small room, standing and sitting around the conference table that filled most of the room. The reports from the hospital were sketchy, but it was very clear that while Reagan was still alive, the wound was serious and he might die.

People spoke in controlled, hushed voices. Everyone was calm, but tense and apprehensive as we waited for more reports on the president's condition.

Four members of the foreign policy directorate were in the Situation Room—Allen, Casey, Haig, and Weinberger. Ed Meese, Jim Baker, and Michael Deaver were at the hospital with the president and were joined by Nancy Reagan. Vice President Bush was hurriedly flying back to Washington on Air Force II from Texas and was due to arrive in a couple of hours. The press secretary, James Brady, was shot in the head and Lyn Nofziger, Reagan's press secretary when he was governor of California, was pressed back into service as the spokesman at the hospital.

In the Situation Room Richard Allen chaired the meeting that steadily increased in size as the hours passed. By 3:30 p.m. most of the cabinet was there. Weinberger and Casey sat at the end of the table directly across from Allen. Haig sat by himself at the other end across from Allen. Donald Regan, then secretary of the treasury, sat on Allen's right. I was on Allen's left, sitting between him and Haig. There were about twelve people in the room.

The discussion went on about various matters, including the condition of President Reagan (no one knew for hours what his true condition was), whether or not the vice president should take over as provided for by the twenty-fifth Amendment to the Constitution (the consensus was no), and whether or not Weinberger changed the alert status of our defense forces in preparation for a possible attack from Soviet Union (again, no).

Things went smoothly. The only problem we had was communications. In the Situation Room there was one telephone, custom-built and hidden neatly under the far end of the conference table. To our chagrin it chose that afternoon to stop working, making it necessary for us to shuttle back and forth to the room next door to make and receive calls until another phone was hooked up.

It was somewhat embarrassing, but not serious.

A little after 4 p.m. someone asked, "Where's Al?" Haig was gone. His seat was empty and, as I looked around, I couldn't see him anywhere in the room. Odd. I hadn't noticed him leave. Just behind where he was sitting was a small color television set mounted flush in the wall about six feet off the floor. It was on and serving as the main source—sometimes the sole source—of news during those depressing hours. My eyes focused on the television screen.

Suddenly Alexander Haig appeared on that screen, nervously clutching the podium in the White House press room, his eyes bright with excitement, badly out of breath. Someone said, "My God, there he is, it's Al." And then all eyes in the Situation Room watched the television set in stunned fascination as the secretary of state tried to reassure the nation and the rest of the world that everything was OK.

After a few preliminary remarks Haig stated bluntly, "As of now, I am in control here, in the White House."

Those remarks set off an explosion of concern. He may have meant well, but for millions of anxious Americans watching for news of whether President Reagan was alive or dead, Haig's words sounded ominously like a veiled grasp for power. His nervous appearance and the shaky tremor in his voice added to his unsettling choice of words.

The reaction of the people in the White House who were talk-

ing to Haig just minutes before was even more incredulous than
that of the millions of Americans watching him in their homes and
offices. The public was not sure whether or not Haig was in control. We knew he was not.

Haig later justified his actions by pointing out that just before
he rushed on stage he and Dick Allen discussed the remarks that
Larry Speakes, the official White House spokesman, was making
about the assassination attempt. According to Haig, both men were
concerned that Speakes was not knowledgeable about what was
happening and should not be talking. Allen and Haig rushed to the
press room to get Speakes off the air."[2] But then, to Allen's astonishment, Haig took the podium.

We all knew what Haig was doing. Had he announced that he
wanted to address the nation from the press room, he would have
been overruled. Had he ordered anyone in the room to do anything, he would have been politely ignored. He wasn't in control
of anything.

The man who was in control, Ronald Reagan, was temporarily
indisposed. His three top deputies were with him, and his vice
president, who would take control if the president did become in-
capacitated, would be back in an hour or so. The president's national security adviser, his commander of the armed forces, and the
head of the CIA were sitting with us.

Haig's quaint notion that he was in control was a fantasy existing only in his mind. But he probably knew that, too, perhaps even
better than anyone in the room. What he saw, and seized, was an
opportunity to talk to millions and millions of people and to give
them the impression that he was in charge. It was literally a once
in a lifetime opportunity to show his stuff to the country. Haig had
toyed with the idea of running for president before he became secretary of state, and the idea may not have completely left his head
that day when Reagan was shot. We will never know precisely what
went on in his mind that afternoon. He acted on his own, precipi-
tously, without consulting or informing his cabinet colleagues.

As the years went by, the size and composition of Reagan's
foreign policy directorate changed. By early 1985, at the beginning
of Reagan's second term in office, the diverse directorate of nine
metamorphosed into a tightly focused directorate of six, obsessed
with secrecy. Only three of those six were members of the original
nine.

Alexander Haig was replaced by George Shultz, the man many of Reagan's advisers thought should have been secretary of state in the first place. Shultz was one of the most highly respected men in America, having served with great distinction in a series of cabinet posts in the Nixon and Ford administrations, in academia, and in the business world. A large man who once played varsity football for Princeton University, he had an extraordinary reputation for judgment and integrity, a reputation enhanced by a strong, expressionless face that any professional poker player would kill for. In spite of his appearance as a banker's banker, he was not timid or stodgy. He had risen to the rank of captain in the Marine Corps, with all that that entails, and there was an intriguing, undenied story circulated in 1987 to the effect that, while a student at Princeton University, he had a tiger tattooed on his buttocks.[3]

Shultz did not have any direct foreign policy experience but his international business background and the international economic policy he was involved with as secretary of the treasury gave him a strong, running start. And soon he was well on his way to becoming one of our most effective secretaries of state. By the beginning of Reagan's second term Shultz had clearly risen to the status of first among equals in Reagan's foreign policy directorate. His role became increasingly important toward the end of Reagan's second term. More than any other person it was George Shultz who, with skill and patience, engineered the nuclear arms reduction treaty with the Soviet Union that President Reagan had stalked for so many years.

Weinberger and Casey stayed on and grew stronger with each passing year. Both immensely successful in restoring the strength of their departments, they began to exercise more and more influence in areas of foreign policy outside their own areas of concern. By early 1985 they joined Shultz in an exalted status. Like three old bulls, each one controlled a primary area of American foreign policy—the State Department, the Defense Department, and the intelligence community. In their own pastures they were unchallenged, and every now and then they wandered off into each other's territory.

The fourth member of the group was Vice President Bush. Except for Casey and Weinberger, and the president himself, Bush was the only member of the directorate who was there from the beginning. He went to all the important meetings, met regularly with the president for private weekly lunches, and was intimately tied to the entire foreign policy community. He was everywhere, but he left few visible tracks, sometimes not even fingerprints.

The fifth member of the group was Donald Regan. When he took over as chief of the White House staff in January, 1985, he effectively replaced three of Reagan's most powerful aides.

James Baker simultaneously swapped positions with Regan, becoming the new secretary of the treasury. It was a good move for both of them. Cabinet members always lust after the power of a senior White House aide. White House aides always envy the status and prestige of the cabinet. In one deft move, Baker and Regan both got what they had long coveted, and President Reagan retained the services of both.

Baker kept his formal appointment as an ad hoc member of the National Security Council, but his influence on foreign policy swiftly diminished. Busily involved in economic policy and international monetary affairs, he was blissfully ignorant of any of the secret dealings that led to the Iran-Contra affair. As an example of how rapidly his status changed when he moved his office from the west wing just a few hundred yards down the street to the Treasury Department, he was not even informed, let alone consulted, even as a matter of courtesy as a member of the National Security Council, on the major foreign policy moves that were taking place in the Iran-Contra affair. Within a few months after Donald Regan came to the White House both Edwin Meese and Michael Deaver left. Meese became the new attorney general. From then on, instead of being deeply involved in all major foreign policy moves as counsellor to the president, he was usually only consulted when a specific legal question came up. Michael Deaver returned to private life, dropping out of the formal foreign policy-making process totally.

Donald Regan was a talented man who gained valuable political and administrative experience during his four years as secretary of the treasury. But he did not have the political sensitivity and eye for political danger of any of the three men he replaced. His style was straightforward, abrupt, and sometimes impetuous. When in doubt, he charged. In many worlds he was extraordinarily effective, but in his new job he was handicapped by a lack of political finesse that was compounded by his lack of expertise in foreign policy. When President Reagan replaced Meese, Baker, and Deaver with Donald Regan he gained a hard-charging executive and lost his three best full-time political advisers. Meese and Baker, of course, did remain as members of the cabinet, but it was not the same as being in the same small building, on the same floor with the president, constantly, day after day.

The sixth and final member of the foreign policy directorate in late 1985 was Admiral John Poindexter. Poindexter was the epitome of a superb naval officer. He was loyal, efficient, and had a very strong sense of duty to his country. He also had a Ph.D. in nuclear physics, smoked a pipe, and went about his duties in a quiet, unassuming way. He was the perfect staff man.

Poindexter was also Reagan's fourth national security adviser in less than five years. While the key execution arms of foreign policy—the State Department, the Defense Department, and the intelligence community—were headed by men with strong, aggressive personalities with years of leadership experience, the post of national security adviser was constantly restocked with men of less and less renown. The critical job of coordinating all foreign policy was chewing people up and spitting them out regularly and systematically.

Richard Allen served as national security adviser one year and was replaced by William P. Clark. Clark served Reagan loyally and well, but fled to the Department of Interior after a year and a half. He seemed much happier as secretary of interior than as the national security adviser.

Reagan's third national security adviser was Robert C. (Bud) McFarlane. McFarlane's career began as an officer in the Marine Corps, where he eventually rose to the rank of lieutenant colonel. In 1971 he joined President Nixon's White House staff as a military aide in the legislative liaison section, and soon he was promoted to military assistant to Henry Kissinger who was then the national security adviser to Nixon. McFarlane served Kissinger for approximately four years, leaving after Jimmy Carter beat President Ford in the 1976 election. By the end of the 1980s McFarlane was a member of the professional staff of the Senate Committee on Armed Services, one of the sea of gray-suited aides that keeps the machinery of Washington running. After the election of President Reagan, McFarlane's career took off. He was appointed counselor of the Department of State, a coveted subcabinet position. When President Reagan summoned Bill Clark from the State Department in 1982 to come to the White House, McFarlane came along as Clark's deputy. When Clark resigned in 1983, Lieutenant Colonel McFarlane succeeded him.

McFarlane was a notch below Allen and Clark. He didn't have the intellectual strength of Allen, nor the luxury of virtually unlimited trust that Clark developed with President Reagan over a period of almost twenty years. McFarlane was an able, intelligent man who, through a series of fortuitous circumstances, got promoted to a very difficult job. He did not have the reputation, the intellect, or the strong personality that were minimal requirements for anyone trying to coordinate the likes of George Shultz, Caspar Weinberger, and Bill Casey—to say nothing of satisfying the new chief of staff, Donald Regan. McFarlane may have been a lion in the foreign policy field, but this jungle was filled with old rogue elephants. In a little over a year he was gone, a crushed and bitter man.

McFarlane's replacement was of even less renown than McFarlane. John Poindexter began his career with President Reagan in a low level position on the National Security Council staff, a military assistant to Richard Allen. He was a good naval officer, and a competent, conscientious staff man. But when McFarlane suddenly resigned just before Christmas in 1985, Poindexter was abruptly elevated to a position that he probably never even dreamed of attaining. Most Americans fully appreciate the importance of being the national security adviser to the president, but to a man trained in the military, it is close to becoming the right hand man to God. Poindexter took his work very, very seriously but, to an even greater degree than McFarlane, he wasn't up to the job.

So, there it was. By the time Reagan's second term of office was well under way, there was a dramatic change in the size and composition of the group of people he relied on most for advice in foreign policy matters. The original group of nine shrank to six. Gone were the seasoned political advisers (Meese, Baker, and Deaver). Gone were the intellectuals, the strategic thinkers (Allen and Kirkpatrick). Gone were the loyal, old trusted friends (Meese, Clark, and Deaver). Now there were only six—Casey, Shultz, Weinberger, Regan, Bush, and Poindexter. These were the advisers the president huddled with in early 1986 to discuss the advisability of selling U.S. arms to the Iranians to effect the release of Americans held hostage by small bands of Middle East terrorists.

George Shultz and Caspar Weinberger were very strongly opposed to the idea right from the start. When Weinberger first came across the notion of selling arms to Iran in a memorandum that crossed his desk, he whipped out his pen and scrawled in the margin "this is almost too absurd to comment on."[4] Mysteriously, President Reagan went against the advice of both his secretary of state and his secretary of defense, the two people who in the eyes of most of the world, were his preeminent foreign policy advisers.

Why would Reagan, a president who relied to an unusual degree on his key policy advisers, and especially on his foreign policy advisers, ignore the urgent pleas of his two most important foreign policy aides?

The answer was Bill Casey.

Chapter Twenty-Six

REAGAN'S MASTER SPY

Bill Casey was known as a shrewd businessman, a smart, tough lawyer, a rough-and-tumble financier who, every now and then would dabble in national politics. Perhaps his best known role, before he became the head of all of America's secret intelligence services, was chairing Ronald Reagan's successful run for the presidency in 1980. Walter S. Mossberg, a senior *Wall Street Journal* reporter, described him in 1987 as a "political crony of the president."[1] Most people thought of Bill Casey as a Wall Street financial type, a New Yorker who talked fast in a mumbling, soft voice—a master of slightly questionable financial dealings that made him millions of dollars, often skirting right up to the edge of the law, but never over it. The legend was widespread. And it was wrong.

The portrait that the media and others have drawn of Casey over the years is far off the mark. Much of what they know and say of him may be true, but it misses the essence of the man, which was much more sharply and truly defined by things to which very few people seemed to pay any attention.

Casey was a tall man of medium build, who walked and moved

quickly and deftly, in spite of a slight stoop and a gangling awkwardness that seemed to have his hands and arms going off in random directions. In person he was warm and friendly, his lively, brilliant mind masked by the disarming face of a kindly old man. The balding head, the shock of white hair, the metal-rimmed glasses, and the swinging jowls beneath his chin all added to that impression. But when he spoke that image melted, replaced by a hard, focused competence. He seemed the kind of man who got things done, and done right, the first time. People are most often of two basic types—those who always have an excellent reason why they are not able to do something, and those who always get their tasks done, somehow. Casey was clearly in the latter group.

The first small indication I got of Casey's abilities occurred late in the Nixon campaign in mid-October 1968, as we headed into the final stretch. He worked as an intermittent volunteer at campaign headquarters in New York City, and I was flying around the country with Nixon on the campaign plane. As the campaign drew to a close, the press became increasingly critical of Nixon, charging him with failing to provide any specific details of the national policies he was advocating and promising to implement if he were elected. The charges infuriated Nixon. One day on the campaign plane he summoned four or five of us to his seat. As we stood and crouched beside him in the cramped aisle, he launched into an attack on the press. Referring to recent articles charging him with presenting only fuzzy generalities he became angry and indignant. "That's not true," he said emphatically, "I have been very specific. I've taken specific positions on at least seventy or eighty different issues. They are absolutely wrong."

Then he looked up at us.

"Isn't that right?" he asked.

None of us had thought to add up the number of specific policy position he took during the campaign, but we all grunted or nodded yes.

"All right then," Nixon continued, "I want to publish a complete collection of all my policy positions. And I want a copy of the book given to every single reporter on this airplane."

I was in charge of policy research, so unfortunately that task was mine. The problem, to put it mildly, was that we only had about three weeks left in the campaign. Most of the policy research staff had been working night and day for over a year, and they were close to exhaustion. Publishing a book, even for a major book publisher with a fresh, experienced staff, usually takes many months.

Nixon couldn't mean a real book. So I asked, "Do you want this typed up . . ." and before I could finish the sentence, Nixon interrupted and said, "No, I want the whole thing set in type. I want it published. It should be a book."

One thing about working for Richard Nixon: There was never any question about what he wanted done. You might have questions about whether or not it should be done, or even whether it could be done, but never about what he had in mind.

I knew there was no point in telling him that what he wanted was impossible. In the few weeks remaining in the campaign there wasn't time to comb through all our policy files, identify all the specific issues, sort and arrange them, edit them, and then publish them as a book. But Nixon didn't know about all that. Standing there we must have appeared somewhat bewildered as he looked up and added, "I'd like to have this in a week." Unfortunately, he was looking at me.

Later that same day I telephoned campaign research headquarters in New York City and told them I had a little job for them. In our New York office Richard Allen was in charge of foreign policy research, and Alan Greenspan was in charge of domestic and economic policy research. They were already working 14 to 16 hours a day, seven days a week, and received the book request with disbelief. I assured them Nixon was serious.

Allen and his people started working on it immediately. Greenspan was then in Key Biscayne at a planning meeting with other members of our research staff. He couldn't return to New York so he delegated the domestic policy editing task to Annelise Anderson, who flew back to New York the next morning. A former editor at Beacon Press in Boston for two years, she was one of the few people in the campaign with any publishing experience.

When she walked into campaign headquarters Bill Casey was already happily at work on the book project. The unsolved problem was the physical production of the book. Even working literally day and night it still would take several days to just edit and assemble the policy material. That would leave only three or four days to set the type, print the pages, and bind the book, a process that can easily take six months or more under normal conditions in the publishing world. How were we going to get it done in three or four days?

The answer was Bill Casey. As he did so many times in his life, Casey accepted the impossible task and then devised a step-by-step, precise plan to make it happen. He owned a publishing company that specialized in financial and accounting books. Casey made all the production arrangements. His publishing firm began to hum, working around the clock, twenty-four hours a day. Every two hours, day and night, a courier arrived from the publishing company to pick up new copy for typesetting and dropped off the latest completed page proofs.

One week later, on October 17, 1968, the book was done, on schedule, error free, handsomely bound and printed. It was a paperback book with a khaki green cover and a bold white lettered title, NIXON ON THE ISSUES. One hundred and ninety-four pages long, the book contained a collection of specific policy positions that Nixon took on 227 different issues, making his point overwhelmingly. The book was a minor publishing miracle.

Within hours after finished copies of the book began rolling off the printing press our campaign plane touched down at a New York airport. As the plane rolled to a stop, one of the young staff members of the campaign, Mary Froning, stepped out of a car waiting for us near the runway and walked toward the plane holding a large cardboard box. I walked down the steps of the airplane, thanked her, and lugged the heavy box back into the plane. Inside the box were about forty copies of the book.

One copy, wrapped in paper, sat on top. Bound in thick brown leather to be presented to Nixon, this copy of the book had a different title. Emblazoned on the front in 24-carat gold leaf were five words: "NIXON SOCKS IT TO 'EM."

When I handed the leather-bound copy to Nixon he was as delighted as a five-year-old child with a new toy on Christmas morning. He loved the special title on his copy. He quickly opened the book and started riffling through the pages, noting with satisfaction that his estimate of the number of specific policy positions he had taken was low.

"OK," he said, "Now let's give this to the press. Let's hand them out."

So I went back to my seat, picked up the box of books, and started down the aisle of the airplane, lightly dropping one copy into the lap of every reporter traveling with us. The reporters were obviously surprised. It was probably the first book ever published by a presidential campaign in the history of the United States. For the remainder of the campaign there were no more stories in the press about Nixon ducking the specifics of policy issues. Nixon's book gambit worked.

Doing the impossible was not unusual for Bill Casey. But perhaps the most impossible thing he did was masterminding the penetration of Nazi Germany by American secret agents during World War II.

In the fall of 1944 the Allied armies in Europe were preparing to invade Nazi Germany, but unlike the other parts of Europe they had recently taken, they knew little about what was really going on inside the Third Reich. There was a desperate lack of hard, accurate intelligence, a lack that was going to cost the Allies dearly in dead and wounded when they invaded Germany. The critical task of getting that intelligence fell on the shoulders of William J. Donovan, known reverently as "Wild Bill" Donovan. Donovan was in charge of the Office of Strategic Services (OSS), the United States spy machine.

Finding out the Nazi's secrets looked impossible. The Allies had few agents inside Hitler's Germany. When we turned to the British for help, they, the most highly regarded intelligence service in the West, essentially shrugged and said it couldn't be done. The British preferred to rely on the German agents they recruited to their side and on the carefully guarded secret that they had broken the German code and were reading the Nazis' most sensitive radio communications.

But the United States wanted the kind of intelligence that could only come from human sources, on the ground inside Germany. So "Wild Bill" Donovan gave the young man he had just named the chief of all our secret intelligence operations in Europe the daunting task of infiltrating Hitler's Third Reich. The young man was thirty-two years old and his name was William J. Casey.

Casey's story is told in a fascinating book by Joseph E. Persico entitled *Piercing the Reich*."[2] The story remained hidden for almost thirty-five years until Persico discovered some newly declassified material on the exploits of the Office of Strategic Services (OSS) during World War II. The tale Persico spins of Casey's deeds in the last year of the war would make remarkable fiction if not true, but the tale is true, a great story of brilliant spying and personal heroism.

In the fall of 1944 Casey moved to London and set up his headquarters at 72 Grosvenor Street.[3] Within months his intelligence operation was able to "recruit 200 crack agents to penetrate the heart of the Nazi fortress—forge documents authentic enough to defy the closest scrutiny—manufacture convincing identities to deceive the cunning Gestapo—devise a complex yet infallible network of communications—arrange monitoring, fact gathering, and on-the-spot analysis."[4]

It was an extraordinary feat. Starting from virtually nothing, Casey was able to put together a sophisticated spy network that reached deep into Nazi Germany, up under Hitler's nose. It was a dangerous, dirty business. Some American spies were killed. But information the Allied armies so desperately needed was obtained and undoubtedly saved countless American lives during the invasion of Germany later in 1945.

Casey's spectacular spying went completely unsung for thirty-five years. He never mentioned a word of what he did. Very few knew or appreciated the fact that Casey was America's master spy in World War II.

Whether others knew or not, Casey himself was profoundly affected by his World War II experiences and took from them some lifelong lessons. During the last year of the war a controversy arose about whether our intelligence services should recruit members of the Communist party to secure information. Donovan set the tone for the OSS, declaring, "I'd put Stalin on the OSS payroll if I thought it would help defeat Hitler."[5] And Bill Casey, who later became known as an ardent anti-communist, issued a directive to his secret intelligence staff in London on February 22, 1945, to recruit potential American spies from "the Free Germany Committee or other Communist groups, anybody who fought in the Spanish civil war."[6]

He also developed an enormous respect, almost awe, for the brave young men and women who willingly risked their lives to spy for the United States. Casey described his attitude toward his secret agents this way: "They got any damn thing they wanted. These guys were the kings. We were all working for them, to get them off in the right frame of mind, to get them functioning in the right place, the right way."[7] When the war was over Casey never seemed to forget the power of a single-minded pursuit of a desirable goal, and the importance of complete loyalty to the people who work for you.

While Casey made a lot of money in business and was a master spy during World War II, these avenues, either one of which would have been more than enough for most people, didn't seem to command his main interest. As he grew older he became more and more fascinated with politics. After flopping dismally as a candidate when he ran for Congress in 1966, he turned to presidential campaign politics—in other people's campaigns. As reward for his service in Nixon's presidential campaigns he was appointed chairman of the Securities and Exchange Commission in 1971 and served until 1973, overseeing the regulation and conduct of the financial markets in the United States. Utilizing his spying background he served on the President's Foreign Intelligence Advisory Board in 1976 during President Ford's administration. He also served as undersecretary of state for economic affairs while Henry Kissinger was secretary of state. Having made enough money to live comfortably doing whatever he wanted to do, he seemed to gravitate more and more toward national and international politics as the years went by.

In 1979 he joined the Executive Advisory Committee (a fancy name for Reagan's expanding kitchen cabinet) of Reagan's budding presidential campaign. By January 1980 the campaign was close to bankruptcy and the internal political warfare among the staff factions—one headed by John Sears and the other headed by Ed Meese—virtually paralyzed campaign operations. While the staff sulked and plotted and the campaign slid deeper in debt, Bill Casey, in mid-January 1980, got himself appointed by the Executive Advisory Committee "to conduct a management audit of the national campaign operations." [8]

Casey interviewed all the key people in the Los Angeles campaign headquarters and carefully examined the files and financial records. After a few weeks he probably knew more about the campaign than anyone, so he was exquisitely positioned when Reagan was forced to fire the campaign manager, John Sears, on February 26, 1980. Casey worked himself into the position of natural heir to running Reagan's campaign—perhaps by accident, perhaps not.

The firing of his campaign manager, the man who masterminded the effort which now had Reagan rounding the corner far ahead of any other candidate, perfectly positioned to romp to victory, was stark evidence of the disastrous state of campaign affairs. The mainstay of the campaign, John Sears, became the main problem. Near-bankruptcy and chaotic management are the norm rather than the exception in presidential campaigns. That could be dealt with. What could not be handled was the apparent change in Sears' personality. As Reagan began to emerge as a strong candidate in the fall of 1979, Sears' ego seemed to swell with Reagan's rising polls and he developed a touch of what one might call megalomania. The somewhat shy, brilliant man with a self-mocking sense of humor, whom I had known and worked with off and on for over ten years, suddenly turned into a secretive stranger who bristled at the slightest opposition to any of his ideas. The man who never lied to me started telling me things that were not true.

The first to leave the campaign late in 1979 was Lyn Nofziger, one of Reagan's oldest and staunchest supporters. Nofziger just couldn't get along with Sears any longer. I was the next to go. Sears took affront at my opposition to some of his politically inspired policy proposals. I had no objection to a good political move, but I felt strongly that endorsing a bad policy, one that violated Reagan's general policy principles, for a short-term political gain would only hurt Reagan in the long run—which in terms of presidential politics could be a few months or less. Sears and I clashed more and more on policy, and it was clear that he thought my disagreement was somewhat presumptuous. Then the problem seemed to go away, and all was quiet for awhile—until I discovered that Sears had secretly set up a parallel policy development operation some 2,500 miles away in the Washington, D.C., headquarters. Sears recruited a young man named Gary Jones, the administrative aide to William Baroody, Sr., the president of the American Enterprise Institute, to run the Washington policy shop.

I was outraged. Not so much by the addition of Jones and his researchers in Washington, because we could use all the help we could get, but rather by the underhanded way it was done. In all politics—campaigning as well as governing—trust is the coin of the realm. So much happens so fast that you don't have time to sit down with people and sign agreements. I couldn't work for a campaign manager I could not trust. I thought about going to Reagan with the problem but realized quickly that would not work. Reagan never involved himself with administrative details of the campaign and it was highly unlikely that he would ever intervene to the detailed extent of ordering Sears to shut down the shadow research operation on the other side of the country in an office he had never seen. I talked to Michael Deaver, but he was having his own problems with Sears, and I ended up doing more listening than talking. I couldn't figure out what to do. If this situation prevailed, I would continue to be known as the head of policy development, but with all the money flowing to the Washington policy shop, I would rapidly become just a figurehead, or worse, a fig leaf for the real policy operation.

Finally, after a few days an inspiration came and the more I thought about it the more it appealed to me. I decided to go on strike. To withdraw my services from the campaign. Just like a labor union. So late in the fall of 1979, just as Reagan's 1980 campaign was ready to take off, I quit. Sears was shocked and spent hours trying to talk me out of the decision. But the longer I talked to him the more convinced I became that I was doing the right thing. Reagan was a little surprised, but he rarely questioned the coming and going of his staff. So, as he did with Nofziger, he wished me a fond so long and hoped I would return soon. The next day I packed and drove my old 1973 Corvette four hundred miles back to Palo Alto in northern California.

A short time later Michael Deaver, Reagan's closest aide, also resigned and joined me and Nofziger in campaign exile.

For the next few months Sears worked steadily to gain complete control of the campaign. At times he seemed to think he was more important than the candidate, granting press interviews and projecting himself, not the candidate, as a national figure. There were whispered reports from the traveling staff that sometimes, perhaps on a bad day, he would not even deign to speak to Reagan. Sears's remaining target was Ed Meese, the one aide who seemed to stand between him and total control of the campaign. So Sears demanded in early 1980 that Reagan get rid of his old friend and former chief of staff. That was a mistake. Reagan, now fully aroused and furious, instead fired Sears and his friends—Charles Black and James Lake.

Ed Meese stayed, William Casey was hired to replace Sears, and within a few months Nofziger, Deaver, and I returned from our brief respite in exile and rejoined the campaign. When I reviewed the progress of policy development in the campaign since I

President Reagan's economic policy advisers in 1981.
[Photo © Dan Kramer, 1981]

Stockman tries to make a point about the politically sensitive social
security reform plan at a meeting of the Cabinet Council on Economic Affairs in the
Roosevelt Room on May 1, 1981. [White House photo, Karl Schumacher]

President Reagan discusses the defense budget with his advisers at a special meeting
in Los Angeles on August 18, 1981. Clockwise from Reagan: Caspar Weinberger,
Frank Carlucci, Lawrence Korb, General David Jones, Martin Anderson, Donald
Regan, Richard V. Allen, Bobby Inman, James Baker, Edwin Meese, Alexander
Haig. Behind Reagan and taking notes is Robert McFarlane.
[White House photo, Karl Schumacher]

At a reception given by
the Hoover Institution in
Washington in 1981.
Left to right:
Annelise Anderson;
Martin Anderson;
W. Glenn Campbell,
director; Caspar
Weinberger;
Rita Ricardo Campbell.
[Hoover Institution
photo]

President Reagan makes a point on
the defense budget to his national
security adviser, Richard V. Allen.
Allen was instrumental in sharply
increasing spending for national
defense. [White House photo,
Karl Schumacher]

Staff meeting of
the Office of Policy
Development in
the White House on
February 23, 1982.
[White House photo,
Jack Kightlinger]

Washington Post article on November 29, 1981.

Very special treatment for Federal Reserve Chairman Paul Volcker. President Reagan receives him informally in the living quarters of the White House on February 15, 1982. [White House photo, Bill Fitz-Patrick]

President Reagan, Arthur F. Burns, and William Simon. [White House photo, Jack Kightlinger]

A special meeting of some members of the President's Economic Policy Advisory Board (PEPAB) and Reagan administration officials in my White House office on November 4, 1981. Clockwise from left: Murray Weidenbaum, Donald Regan, David Stockman, Paul McCracken, Alan Greenspan, Martin Anderson, George Shultz, Walter Wriston. [White House photo, Jack Kightlinger]

Breakfast meeting of the Troika-Plus-One economic policy planning group on November 10, 1981, the same day the infamous article on Stockman broke in the *Atlantic Monthly*. The birthday cake, with small red plastic hatchets stuck in the frosting, was Donald Regan's surprise to celebrate Stockman's birthday. [Photo courtesy Donald Regan]

The President's Foreign Intelligence Advisory Board in 1982, before the purge.
Clockwise from left: Paul Seabury, John Foster, Thomas Moorer,
Edward Bennett Williams, Ross Perot, Robert Six, Clare Boothe Luce, Leo Cherne,
Anne Armstrong, Seymour Weiss, William Baker, David Abshire, Martin Anderson,
W. Glenn Campbell, Leon Jaworski. [White House photo, Bill Fitz-Patrick]

Chance meeting with
the President on West
Executive Avenue on a
windy day in April 1983.
[White House photo,
Karl Schumacher]

Meeting of Reagan administration officials in the Situation Room of the White House on March 30, 1981, just after President Reagan was shot and moments before Alexander Haig (standing right of center) told a puzzled national television audience that he was "in control here, in the White House." Seated at table clockwise from Haig are William Casey, William French Smith, Donald Regan, Richard V. Allen, and Martin Anderson. Standing from left: Max Friedersdorf, Drew Lewis, Daniel Murphy, and Richard Williamson. [White House photo, Karl Schumacher]

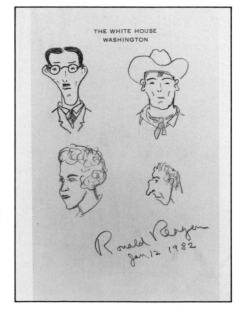

President Reagan sometimes sketches small portraits during long meetings. This group was drawn during the Cabinet meeting on January 12, 1982. The sketch at the upper right is a self-portrait. No comment on who the others may be.

President Reagan meets with his key foreign policy advisers
during an emergency meeting in the Situation Room
during the TWA hijacking episode in July 1985. Left to right:
Caspar Weinberger, George Bush, President Reagan, George
Shultz, William Casey, and Donald Regan.
[White House photo, Terry Arthur]

Floor plan of the third floor of the Old Executive Office Building,
next door to the White House, during the making of the Iran-Contra
affair in 1985–1986. Bill Casey's office was in the northwest corner
and Oliver North's on the middle corridor.

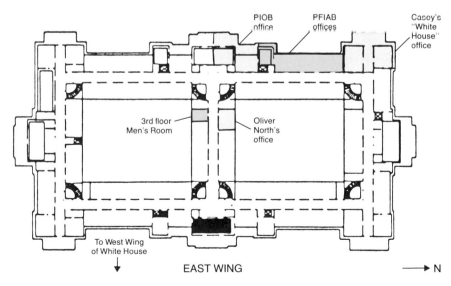

December 8, 1987. Ronald Reagan and Mikhail
Gorbachev after exchanging the pens that signed
the INF treaty. [White House photo, Bill Fitz-Patrick]

The real Reagan. [White House photo, Bill Fitz-Patrick]

left I felt both regret and a sense of vindication. There were no new ideas. But it could have been worse. At least there were no new bad ideas.

It was a sad chapter in presidential campaign history. And it was a personal tragedy for one individual. John Sears never became a part of the Reagan presidency, never once stepped foot inside the Reagan White House. Yet without John Sears it is doubtful if Reagan would ever have become president, and no one can ever take away from Sears the distinct and rare mark he left on political history. But it is also true that if Reagan had not fired Sears in February 1980, the very afternoon of his impressive victory in the New Hampshire primary, it is doubtful that he would have been elected president of the United States.

Unlike the famous legend of the Mighty Casey, who came to bat in a baseball game with the bases loaded and struck out, William Casey took over the 1980 campaign with all the management bases empty and hit a homerun. Strong leadership was needed and Casey provided it in spades. He took charge of campaign management, slashing costs and restructuring operations. Soon the entire campaign was back on track. Reagan fully recovered from his earlier loss in the Iowa primary and went on to win a thumping victory at the Republican convention, and later the election itself.

Casey, who barely knew Reagan a year earlier, was now the chairman of the whole damn thing, the head man of an operation that punctured the power of left-liberal politics in the United States and installed a deeply committed conservative Republican as president. It was a feat that rivaled his World War II exploits in penetrating Nazi Germany.

When the 1980 presidential campaign was over Bill Casey was in an enviable position. As chairman of the winning effort he had a claim to the spoils of victory. Any appointment was his for the asking. And Casey knew what he wanted, the most prestigious political appointment in the United States government—secretary of state. It would cap off an extraordinary, illustrious career that began in the black corridors of World War II espionage, ran through Wall Street, and then the highest levels of the federal bureaucracy, first at the SEC and then at the State Department. He probably would have preferred being a senator or even president, but one brief, abortive experience with elective office seems to have convinced him that that was not his destiny. But secretary of state—

now that was a splendid office. His background and experience, his demonstrated ability to manage, and his brilliant, crafty mind easily qualified him for the job. And his service to Reagan, being instrumental in getting Reagan elected, gave him a political birthright.

Regrettably, Secretary of State Casey was not to be. Although he let it be known that he wanted the job, it was denied him. The only criticism I heard about Casey was that he was too inarticulate to be secretary of state. He did mumble at times, but that seemed hardly a sufficient reason. Exactly why he was denied the job is still unclear, but the influence of Reagan's old friends in his kitchen cabinet increased sharply for a time after the election, and they seemed to be far more impressed with the swaggering, ramrod-straight Alexander Haig than they were with the soft-spoken, fast-talking, stooped William Casey. In effect Casey was told he could have any job in the new administration he wanted—*except* secretary of state.

So Casey took the job as head of the Central Intelligence Agency—a job that almost everyone else would think a tremendous honor—as a consolation prize.

God, he must have been bitter. He, who had led Reagan's campaign, who helped elect him president, who made it possible for Reagan to have incredible power, now had to endure the humiliation of watching the one position he coveted go to Alexander Haig. It was not that Haig was a bad choice. He had a strong military background, and a lot of White House experience in national security affairs, but—and this was the point that hurt—he hadn't lifted a finger to help Reagan secure the nomination of the Republican party. There wasn't going to be another chance for Casey either. This was it. He was 67 years old. It was not likely he would ever again be even this close. It was maddening and galling.

Most people seemed to view Casey's appointment to the CIA as a juicy political plum, a job Casey wasn't even remotely qualified for, a job he must have been delighted to get, a chance for a New York businessman to play at being a spy. Instead, it was a bitter, vengeful old man who grudgingly accepted the job as the best he could get at the time, a man who was very familiar with the intelligence world he was headed for.

But before he picked up his old cloak and dagger, he demanded two things. First and most important, he asked the president for full cabinet rank. The request could not be denied. Given his past campaign service and the keen disappointment at not getting the State Department appointment, it seemed like a small favor. It was not. Agreeing to Casey's demand for cabinet rank automatically gave him a seat at the cabinet table, including the right to participate in debating whatever issue might be discussed. And that gave him—as director of the CIA—a direct voice in national policymaking. Until then in this country we had been careful to separate intelligence from policy, primarily on the grounds that once the intelligence gatherers became involved in policymaking the temptation to slant and bias their intelligence could become irresistible. With Casey's appointment to Reagan's cabinet the wall between intelligence and policy came tumbling down.

The second thing Casey demanded and got was an office in the White House complex. That office may have contributed more to his growing influence and power over the years than his seat at the cabinet table. As in most large organizations, the location of one's office in the city of Washington is very important. The most prized locations in Washington are in the west wing of the White House, but as there is room for only a dozen or so senior aides and their very small staffs, the competition is focused on the much larger building, the Old Executive Office Building (fondly called the OEOB), located just a few feet across a short, private street from the west wing.

The OEOB is a marvelous, magnificent building containing hundreds of offices. It comfortably houses about 1,800 people, and during World War I it was stuffed with 4,500 people. The largest solid granite building in the world, it is a brilliant embodiment of French Renaissance architecture. Six massive floors tall, it is 474 feet long and 266 feet wide. Today its interior is honeycombed with the offices of the most important sections of the Executive Office of the President. A major part of that honeycomb contains the offices of the president's National Security Council and certain related intelligence activities. Contrary to the popular impression given by the U.S. press, the staff of the National Security Council is *not* located in the basement of the White House. Most of them are across the street, way up on the third floor of the OEOB, happily ensconced in those spacious, ornate old offices with eighteen-foot high ceilings. Only the Situation Room, the national security adviser, and a small handful of his personal staff are located in the west wing, and they are on the ground floor, with windows and everything—not in some dark, dank basement.

The place that Casey chose to nest was a handsome suite of offices in the northwest corner of the third floor. From his corner office (room 345½) he did not have one of the prized views of the White House or the Washington Monument, but he did have some very interesting neighbors.

The door to Casey's office was one of 1,314 huge, two-inch thick doors in the building, made of thick pine and veneered on both sides with richly grained, quarter-inch thick mahogany. The heavy brass doorknob was custom cast on the premises over one hundred years ago. Out that mahogany door and about sixty-five feet to the right was the entrance (room 340) to the President's Foreign Intelligence Advisory Board (PFIAB), responsible for overseeing the operations of the entire intelligence community.

About 140 feet farther on down the corridor in room 330½, were the offices of the President's Intelligence Oversight Board (PIOB), a much smaller group with the more focused and unenviable task of informing "the President of intelligence activities that any member of the Board believes are in violation of the constitution or laws of the United States, Executive orders, or Presidential directives."[9] Then, as you turn left, there is another long corridor that runs through the middle of the building to the other side. The first door on the right is the men's room (391M) for the third floor. Across the hall from the men's room is the suite of offices (room 392) once occupied by Oliver North, the Marine lieutenant colonel who figured so prominently in the Iran-Contra affair, and Fawn Hall, his very smart, loyal, strikingly beautiful secretary.

The rest of the corridors on this floor were lined with the offices of the National Security Council staff, but none held offices of such sensitivity and importance as the corridor that led to Casey's corner. If any place in the White House complex deserved the name of Spook Alley this was surely it.

As a practical matter, having his own office and secretary up there on the third floor of the OEOB meant that Casey could easily and secretly confer with just about anyone on the National Security Council staff. All he had to do was pick up the phone and ask them to take a stroll down the marble tiles of that cavernous corridor. No one would notice, let alone keep track. Casey could also use his office for meetings he wished to conceal from his own bureaucracy over at the sprawling headquarters of the CIA in Langley, Virginia. The phone calls he made and received at the OEOB were truly private, not tape recorded and carefully logged as they were in his CIA headquarters. And finally, the office did wonders for his prestige. Every time he left CIA headquarters at Langley and headed for his OEOB pied-à-terre, the professional intelligence staff had no way of knowing whether he was conferring privately with the president or just taking a nap on the couch in his office there. It was an ideal setup.

Any head of the Central Intelligence Agency with Casey's brains and drive was bound to play an important role in any administration. Armed with his seat at the cabinet table and his office in the White House complex, he played an increasingly formidable role in the Reagan administration. In the beginning he concentrated on rebuilding and strengthening the intelligence community, especially the CIA.

William Casey did a superb job of building up the intelligence capabilities of the United States, using his special relationship with the president to secure massive increases in funding, a critical first step in any rebuilding effort. But he went far beyond getting money for intelligence activities, increasing both the quantity and scope of the intelligence product and sharply increasing the morale of his agents and staff. When he left, the CIA wasn't perfect, but each year he spent with the agency left it better than it was the year before.

During those early years Casey's most important influence on public policy was probably the impact he had on the defense budget, and thus on our whole economic policy. Some press accounts seemed to implicitly assume that the defense budget was largely shaped by decisions made on general tax and deficit policy, and by domestic spending, with the amount spent on defense being essentially a residual—what was left after the other elements of fiscal policy were determined. Some accounts assumed that defense spending was somehow determined at the same time as other program spending levels were set. It didn't happen that way; it was just the other way around.

President Reagan's first priority, as he stated repeatedly over the years, was national defense. He really believed in the old idea that the first duty of a U.S. president was to secure the republic, to ensure that the nation was safe from conquest by a foreign power.

On numerous occasions I remember Reagan saying, "The defense budget cannot be determined by other programs, what we spend on defense is what we must spend to maintain our national security, and how much we spend depends largely on what the Soviet Union does."

And that's the way it was. The national security advisers— Weinberger, Allen, Haig, and Casey—would tell President Reagan how much money they needed to counter the Soviet threat and generally they would get every dollar they asked for. Reagan would listen patiently as David Stockman, the young budget director, argued the case for restraining defense spending in order to reduce the budget deficit and then Reagan, after listening to his argument, would overrule him.

The defense budget drove fiscal policy, not the other way around. First, the level of the defense budget was set and then, and then only, were the other key elements of taxes, domestic spending, and the size of the deficit considered.

While the defense budget was driving fiscal policy, estimates of the extent and seriousness of the Soviet threat drove the defense budget. When Secretary of Defense Caspar Weinberger asked for multibillion dollar increases in defense spending he acted from his deep concern about the growing Soviet military threat to the United States. The same was true when Secretary of State Haig asked for increases in his budget. The serious and increasing concerns that Weinberger, Haig, Allen, and President Reagan all had about the Soviet military machine were largely based on the intelligence estimates provided to them by the intelligence community through William J. Casey. Those intelligence estimates played a critical role in affecting the administration's overall policy thrust. There was a straight and direct linkage. The increasingly revitalized CIA and other elements of the intelligence community provided Casey with the intelligence he needed to brief everyone else. Casey's intelligence estimates drove the defense budget, the defense budget drove fiscal policy, and fiscal policy had an enormous impact on what could and couldn't be done in the other areas of national policy.

But Casey was really a frustrated policymaker. The head of U.S. intelligence services has traditionally been viewed as somewhat of a high-class servant. The intelligence reports are referred to as the product, and the people to whom those intelligence reports go are called clients. The assumption has always been that the clients of intelligence are to be served by the producers of intelligence, that intelligence is to be produced in the most ruthlessly objective way possible, to enable the policymakers to get the kind of thorough, accurate, balanced information they would need to make informed judgments and decisions. Providing accurate, objective intelligence is a difficult, demanding, honorable task, but it wasn't enough for Bill Casey. He wanted to enter the higher status ranks of the policymakers.

And he did. As the years passed by Casey became an increasingly important member of Reagan's foreign policy directorate. His influence increased far beyond his responsibilities for providing sound, accurate, timely intelligence. His counsel was increasingly proffered, and accepted, in matters which had significant impact on foreign and defense policy. In the area of covert activity he soon achieved almost complete dominance.

As head of the Central Intelligence Agency, Casey did not delegate the conduct of these limited secret wartime activities to the intelligence professionals. He seemed fascinated by covert activity and soon became deeply and personally involved in its execution. By the time Reagan's second term began, Casey was clearly in command of all covert activity. Normally the level of covert activity is determined by the nature of our foreign and defense policies, but under Casey it soon seemed that some of our covert activities were beginning to have an increasingly significant impact on our overall foreign policy.

Casey's rise to power as a policymaker, and his increasing influence on foreign and defense policy, was not always smooth. At times he came in for strong, even fierce criticism. Three incidents along the way stand out, all of them involving serious charges concerning Casey's judgment, honesty, and integrity.

All high-level government officials are required to report, in great detail, their financial assets and any business dealings that might involve them in a conflict of interest. In addition to reporting, many also place all their assets in a blind trust, turning over to disinterested professionals control of their financial assets. But Casey chose not to do this. Instantly suspicions were aroused, and his reports were scrutinized extra carefully when they were submitted in 1981. Casey's financial reports caused an uproar. Carelessly prepared and incomplete, they drew heavy criticism from the Senate Select Committee on Intelligence, which found that he had "omitted at least nine investments valued at more than a quarter of a million dollars, personal debts and contingent liabilities of nearly $500,000," and a number of other relevant facts.[10]

All this was from a Senate committee controlled by Casey's own political party, not the Democrats. It was an embarrassment to the Reagan administration, but Casey stubbornly held to his position and the issue faded quickly.

The second incident was the Hugel appointment. Max Hugel was one of Casey's campaign deputies, a New Hampshire businessman who Casey selected in 1981 to head all covert activities for the CIA. Although Hugel was an able, intelligent man, he knew nothing about espionage and secret wars. The political payoff is a common and noble tradition in Washington, but there are basic standards of competence and experience that must be met. The intelligence community was incensed at Hugel's appointment, taking it as a personal affront to their professionalism.

Barry Goldwater, the grand old man of the Republican party and the chairman of the Senate Select Committee on Intelligence, was so outraged that he publicly called for Casey's firing. Eventually Hugel was forced to resign, but President Reagan continued his loyal support of Casey and he stayed on, and soon that controversy also died away.

The third incident that Casey became embroiled in before the Iran-Contra affair exploded was something the press often referred to as the "Carter papers" scandal. It happened in the summer of 1983. Looking back on it, it was somewhat of a forerunner of the Iran-Contra affair. It even had its own Congressional investigating committee.

In July 1983, a book was published alleging that during the 1980 presidential campaign "a Reagan mole in the Carter camp had filched papers containing the main points the President planned to make when he met Reagan for the debate."[11] In other words, the Reagan presidential campaign was accused of placing a spy in the White House and stealing the secret briefing papers that President Carter used to prepare himself for the one critical national debate he had with Reagan during the 1980 campaign. As expected, a great outcry took place, and soon people were going back, reviewing the three-year-old campaign records, and trying to sort out what exactly did happen.

When the debate between Reagan and Carter was agreed to

there was great consternation at our national headquarters and great glee among the "Capsule Command," as Theodore White called them, on Reagan's campaign plane. That decision to debate set off a flurry of activity back at national headquarters. The normal way Reagan prepared for a debate was to sit down for an hour or two with a half-dozen or so of his aides and engage in a mock debate. The aides would take the role of the press and throw the hardest, meanest questions they could think of at Reagan. He would parry and answer them as best he could, often commenting later that the questions he actually got during the debate were a lot easier than the ones during practice.

But this time, back at national headquarters, James Baker was placed in charge of debate preparations. Baker had a much more organized way of doing things and probably was somewhat appalled at the seemingly casual way we approached debates in the past. It really wasn't as casual as it seemed, because we worked very hard on asking the kinds of questions and raising the types of issues most likely to be raised during the debate. But Baker did not want to leave anything to chance, and he set about developing what was certainly the most elaborate and detailed preparation in the history of the U.S. presidential debates. As we did for the debate with third party candidate John Anderson, a mock debate studio was set up in a large, empty garage on a spacious estate in a heavily wooded suburb of Washington, D.C.

The estate we rented was Wexford, then owned by Elizabeth Taylor and Senator John Warner. By coincidence the house was once President John F. Kennedy's. He only used it briefly, just before he was assassinated in 1963. As we walked through the corridors from room to room, meeting and conferring on the upcoming debate, the hauntingly beautiful photos of President Kennedy and his wife Jacqueline and his small children were a sad reminder of the price that some paid for public service.

The old garage, outside to the rear, next to the horse riding trail, was furnished with bright studio lights, television cameras and recorders, rough plank tables for the aides who would take the part of the reporters, and small, blinking red, amber, and green lights that would control the timing of the questions and answers during the debate. The studio and its furnishings were crude and make-shift, but everything was done to exact scale, thus recreating to a large degree the feel and ambience that would greet Reagan on the stage in Cleveland. David Stockman took the role of President Carter. The panel of reporters was played by a number of aides and advisers, including Dick Allen, Alan Greenspan, and myself.

As part of the preparations for the debate, James Baker asked two of his aides, David R. Gergen and Frank Hodsoll, to put together a special policy briefing book for Reagan. Gergen and Hodsoll were part of the old Bush campaign staff. After Reagan beat Bush in the 1980 presidential primaries and then selected him as his vice presidential running mate, the Reagan campaign became the Reagan-Bush campaign. It is an old tradition in American politics. Two candidates, archenemies in the fight for the party's nomination, will join together in an effort to defeat the greater enemy, the nominee of the opposing political party.

One of the most difficult parts about merging two rival campaigns into one is assimilating the losing campaign staff. Understandably disappointed in losing, they generally have no deep and abiding love for the candidate who does win, or else they probably would have worked for that candidate in the first place. But somehow, they have to be made part of the new campaign team. The new Reagan-Bush campaign solved that problem in 1980 by assigning all the old Bush aides to our national headquarters.

Back at headquarters the former Bush aides were trying to carve themselves a new niche and were actively looking for ways to make themselves useful to Reagan's closing drive for the presidency. Gergen and Hodsoll were talented, dedicated people and when Baker gave them the debate briefing book assignment they attacked the project with skill and great determination.

Traveling on the plane, preoccupied with the task of keeping on top of the fast moving issues in the campaign, I was only vaguely aware of the intense debate preparation effort back at headquarters in Virginia. I began to focus on it when I received a call from one of my top aides, Kevin Hopkins, in the same headquarters where most of the policy research and development team was based. Hopkins was upset. "Gergen and Hodsoll are cutting us out of the debate book," he complained. "They won't show us any of the papers they are producing. And they're real secretive. They even lock the doors of their offices when they leave for the night."

I told Hopkins to ignore them and concentrate on the major issues they were working on. I assumed that Gergen and Hodsoll were being secretive and keeping the drafts of the briefing book all to themselves to ensure, in the old bureaucratic game of internal politics, that they got all the credit for preparing it. What Gergen and Hodsoll and Baker did not know was that Ronald Reagan did not like briefing books, especially thick, heavy black ones. Over the years, traveling with him on the road, I noticed that he would read and absorb large quantities of written material given to him in the form of loose papers, or articles, or separate reports. But if someone organized a looseleaf notebook of briefing material on a range of issues it was rarely used. Reagan would accept the large notebook cheerfully and then, without even glancing through it, lay it down on the seat beside him or on the floor.

As it turned out, Gergen and Hodsoll had very good reasons to be highly secretive. They were in possession of hundreds of pages of policy briefing material prepared for President Carter, material they were busy using to guide them in the preparation of their policy briefing book for Reagan. The knowledge of the Carter papers was very closely held within a small cell of aides on the Reagan-Bush campaign staff, all of them former Bush campaign aides or others who recently joined the Reagan campaign.

On the campaign plane we were blissfully unaware of the secret gambit our new campaign colleagues were conducting. We didn't even know about it when they proudly presented us with their completed policy briefing book. The book was a thorough, professional job, reflecting both the able skills of Gergen and Hodsoll and a little bit of help they had from their friends, the Carter papers.

Unfortunately, or fortunately, depending on your point of view, the Gergen-Hodsoll briefing book was barely touched by Reagan. As usual, he relied instead on the give-and-take of practice sessions with his senior aides, none of whom used the new briefing book to work out the dozen or so questions for Reagan in the mock debate.

When the secret of the stolen Carter papers came out in 1983 it set off a firestorm of criticism and a series of seemingly endless investigations. The big question was: who obtained the Carter papers and how did they do it?

After the air of the investigation cleared and a 2,413-page-long, mind-numbing report was produced, it all came down to this. James Baker gave the Carter papers to the debate briefing team headed by Gergen and Hodsoll. They, in turn, used the papers and gave many of them to David Stockman to use in preparing for the debates. But where did Baker get those interesting presidential papers?

On June 23, 1983, Baker, then Reagan's White House chief of staff, said "it is my best recollection" that he got the papers from William Casey. Casey, now head of the CIA, immediately denied the charge, saying he had "no recollection" of the papers.[12] Casey later elaborated further, saying it would have been "totally unchar-acteristic and quite incredible" for him to have obtained those Carter papers. "It could have destroyed the campaign," said Mr. Casey. "After being involved in seven Presidential campaigns, I know that's dynamite. I wouldn't tolerate it. I wouldn't touch it with a ten-foot pole."[13] Baker insisted that he told the truth and "was not about to face a perjury rap" to protect Bill Casey.[14]

There the whole matter ended. The White House chief of staff called the head of the CIA a liar, and the head of the CIA called the White House chief of staff a liar. Neither one would back down, and all the investigations and all the FBI agents couldn't find out for sure who was telling the truth. All we know for sure is that one was and one wasn't. If one had to bet on who was telling the truth, most people I know who were familiar with the two men would bet on Baker.

Bill Casey was a man with at least two sides. One of those sides was brilliant, energetic, wise, and thoughtful. It was the side of Bill Casey that powered him to many successes in life. The other side was crafty and cunning, a side that sometimes winked at the law and trafficked near unethical behavior, a side that wasn't al-ways scrupulous about telling the truth when it interfered with achieving a desirable goal. This was the side that kept getting Bill Casey in trouble of one sort or another throughout much of his spectacular career.

Chapter Twenty-Seven

CASEY'S CAPER

When the issue of selling arms to Iran and paying ransom for American hostages moved onto the agenda of Reagan's foreign policy directorate in 1985, the major player was Bill Casey. This was the ultimate in covert activity. In order to get the hostages back, the United States was flirting with the idea of breaking our vows never to pay ransom or to sell military weapons to Iran. Wow. Perhaps the only thing more politically explosive would be to consider buying and selling drugs, such as cocaine and heroin, in order to secure the release of the hostages.

Right from the beginning, Casey seemed to like the idea of selling arms to Iran and soon he became the dominant force in the meetings and consultations held on the subject. The most critical meeting took place on January 7, 1986. It was held in the residential part of the White House to ensure secrecy, even from the prying eyes of the White House staff. As they did earlier, Secretary of State George Shultz and Secretary of Defense Caspar Weinberger argued vehemently against the plan. They pointed out it was in flat violation of our long-held policy to prevent the sale of arms to Iran from any country. To violate that policy secretly would destroy our credibility with our allies throughout the world. They would think we were liars. Shultz and Weinberger argued that paying ransom was self-defeating, that it would only encourage Iran and their terrorist friends to seize even more American hostages in the future. Even if done secretly it was a bad policy, and if it should ever become known it would make the United States look foolish and irresponsible.

But the passage of five years had greatly strengthened the normal compartmentalization that occurs in the federal government. Shultz and his State Department were in charge of foreign policy, and while selling arms to Iran obviously touched on foreign policy, it was a covert activity and thus outside of Shultz's policy territory. Similarly, Weinberger and his Defense Department were in charge of our military forces, but it was not in their policy territory to decide whether or not secret, covert activities might secure the release of the American hostages. Covert activity was the territorial imperative of William Casey, and he argued forcefully for going ahead with the plan.

Casey seemed to put the safety and return of the currently held hostages—especially the high-ranking CIA agent, William Buckley—above all other considerations, appealing deeply to Reagan's emotional anguish over their seizure. Buckley was our station chief in Lebanon. He knew many of the CIA's most important and sensitive secrets. But he was kidnapped on March 16, 1984, and was being brutally tortured in an effort to extract that information from him. We knew this because Buckley's torturers had thoughtfully sent the CIA a videotape, with sound, of the actual torture Buckley was undergoing. Casey arranged for that sickening videotape to be shown to President Reagan. Casey, who developed an enormous respect for the courage his secret agents showed in the face of danger during World War II, wanted Buckley out at all costs.

Further arguments were made about a strategic opening to Iran, stressing the fact that the Ayatollah was over eighty years old, and how important it was to establish contacts with so-called moderates who might soon inherit his power. Intelligence, given to President Reagan by John Poindexter, talked of "Iran's deteriorating position in the war with Iraq."[1] And the argument evidently was made that supplying arms to Iran would maintain the military balance in the Iran-Iraq war.[2]

The arguments had a high degree of plausibility about them,

although some of the plausibility rested on premises that were not true. There were no powerful moderates in Iran likely to inherit the Ayatollah's mantle, and the internal intelligence estimates of the CIA showed that Iran was winning, not losing the war with Iraq as Reagan had been informed.

Casey's emotional arguments about Buckley, false intelligence about the Iran-Iraq war, combined with the normal reluctance of a president to overrule key advisers on their own policy turf, eventually led President Reagan to approve the ill-fated plan. Reagan's decision was undoubtedly encouraged by the response of the remaining three members of the foreign policy directorate.

John Poindexter, just appointed Reagan's fourth national security adviser a few weeks earlier, enthusiastically supported Casey and the arms for Iran proposal. It would have been unusual and courageous for him not to support it. Poindexter was brand new to Reagan's inner circle, and there he sat surrounded by five of the most senior, most powerful members of the Reagan administration. Covert activity was Casey's policy turf and Poindexter knew that if he opposed it, Casey would exact revenge. In early 1986 Poindexter's situation was new and shaky enough that opposition was somewhat foolhardy, at least from the viewpoint of internal politics. Moreover, Poindexter seemed to genuinely approve of selling arms to Iran.

Donald Regan was a different case. Initially opposed, he gradually came around to Casey's point of view and no longer raised any objections. Regan was certainly aware that he had no background in intelligence matters or covert activity. And beyond that he almost certainly remembered who made it possible for him to be where he was. It was his old friend Bill Casey who singlehandedly made him secretary of the treasury five years earlier and who was a staunch and consistent friend throughout his entire government service. One would need very good, very sound reasons to be so ungrateful to such an old friend.

The last and perhaps critical vote was that of George Bush. As a past director of the CIA, he was the only person in the room with the credentials to challenge Casey on his own turf. He was knowledgeable about covert activity, had headed the crisis management group for President Reagan, and was spearheading the anti-terrorist efforts of the administration.

George Bush is an enigma in American politics. Tall, taller than

Ronald Reagan, with the physical energy of someone twenty years his junior, by early 1988 he had the reputation of being something of a wimp, standing for nothing, timid and small. But how could that be? He is a thoroughly decent man, with sound political values and a sharp mind. As a young man he was a genuine World War II hero, a fighter plane pilot. He was a successful businessman and then held and served with distinction in a number of important government posts. He was the man who came closest to defeating Ronald Reagan in 1980. He was vice president for seven years, serving Reagan loyally and capably. And yet, after all that, even a friendly columnist, George Will, referred to him contemptuously as a "lap dog." What is wrong?

Perhaps part of the answer is that Bush was born a blue blood with a silver spoon in his mouth, and that he was taught early in life to downplay his achievements, not boast of what he did. Bush seems to have taken the lessons of his youth seriously, and what might be gracious in a young man from a wealthy family can lead to disaster on the national political scene. In American politics, accomplishing something worthwhile is difficult. Getting proper credit for what you accomplish is often more difficult. Bush seems to have hidden too many of his lights under the proverbial bushel basket.

For example, toward the close of that critical meeting on the sales of U.S. weapons to Iran, there is no record of what the vice president said when eyes turned to him. All indications are that he neither objected nor approved. When President Reagan was asked sometime later if Bush raised any objections to the arms sales plan when it was being discussed, he replied simply, "No."

In the final analysis, the vote of the foreign policy directorate early in 1986 was four to two. The administration's lead man on covert activities, William Casey, was strongly in favor of the arms sales to Iran. The national security adviser, John Poindexter, supported him. Both the chief of staff, Donald Regan, and the vice president, George Bush, endorsed the plan by not opposing it. In policy meetings of this type, to raise no objections is to implicitly endorse the policy under discussion. Only Shultz and Weinberger opposed it in the end. President Reagan made the final decision, siding with the other four against his secretary of state and secretary of defense.

Looking back, it is clear that President Reagan made a serious policy mistake, even though it may have been an understandable one. From that fateful decision flowed the whole series of disastrous events that came to be known as the Iran-Contra affair.

Once the decision to sell arms to Iran was made, it was only a matter of time before members of the White House staff became involved with international arms dealers. Then began the sorry slide into corruption and deceit, the furtive activities of men trying to do too much, in way over their heads. Soon they were tempted and seduced into using some of the millions of dollars in profits generated by the arms sales to benefit the Contras fighting for their freedom in Nicaragua. By then they were enmeshed so tightly in the web they were spinning it seemed natural to keep their new activities secret from not only the secretary of defense, the secretary of state, and the Congress, but even from the president himself. The whole Iran-Contra affair is a fascinating, intricate tale of deceit, bravery, courage, and corruption, and, finally, the betrayal of the president by some of his closest and most trusted aides.

In looking back at the fateful decision reached on that cold day, January 7, 1986, one thing still puzzles me. Once the decision was made to sell arms to Iran I can understand how all the other events followed. Once four of President Reagan's closest advisers, led by his old trusted friend Bill Casey, endorsed the plan, I can understand why the president approved it. But what I cannot understand is why Bill Casey pushed the idea of selling arms to Iran in the first place.

Casey was smart and politically sensitive. He would have been the first to see the gaping holes in the logic of the basic scheme. He would have been the first to sense that it was political dynamite, with risks far out of proportion to the likely gain. He would have been the first to speak up, confidently and surely, to tell President Reagan that the whole thing was a dumb, cockeyed scheme.

But he didn't. Instead Casey led the fight for the Iran arms sales scheme. Why? Perhaps it was the other side of Casey triumphing in later life, the side that was a little crafty, the side that was willing to bend the rules, the side that liked risk. But that explanation is not satisfying. There was more here than just being a little crafty and devious, of taking some risk for risk's sake. This was a massive break with established policy, a blunt refutation of our long-held policies not to sell arms to Iran, or any other terrorist nation for that matter, and never to pay ransom. No, there had to be something else at work here.

Let's examine one possibility.

On Monday, December 15, 1986, just three weeks after the Iran-Contra affair broke open, and the day before Bill Casey was due to testify before Congress for the third time concerning his role in the rapidly expanding scandal, Casey was stricken, twice, with convulsive seizures. He was taken immediately to Georgetown University Hospital in Washington, D. C. The press did not report any details of the seizures that struck the aging CIA director, but any convulsion of this sort is serious. A convulsion is a "pathological body condition, characterized by abnormal, violent, and involuntary spasmodic contractions and relaxations of the voluntary muscles, taking the form of a fit."[3] Just the thought of the director of the CIA thrashing about on the floor is unsettling.

Three days later the worst fears were confirmed. Casey had a brain tumor and the indications were that it was cancerous. He went into surgery at 7:40 A.M. on Thursday morning. The doctors operated for five hours and twenty minutes, opening his skull with a small circular electrical saw and then removing as much of the cancerous tissue as they could. The size of the tumor was never made public, but tumors such as this are often as large as a lemon or even a small orange. After a week of further tests it was confirmed that Casey did, indeed, have a malignant cancer in his brain. In medical terms it was a "B-cell lymphoma of the large cell type."[4]

B-cell lymphoma is an unusual form of brain cancer, occurring in less than one percent of all brain cancers.[5] It was a remarkable coincidence. Just days before Casey was about to be cornered by the congressional hounds, he was struck down by one of the rarest and most deadly cancers known to man. Of the nine kinds of cancer that can afflict the brain, lymphoma has the highest death rate. The occurrence of the rare lymphoma cancer is thought to be the result of some damage to the body's immune system, the intricate network of natural cells that attack and kill dangerous bacteria and viruses that invade our bodies.

Casey never recovered from the operation on his brain, and his condition grew steadily worse. He died on May 7, 1987, after being moved to the Community Hospital in Glen Cove, New York, near his home. He was seventy-four years old. When Casey died many of the answers to the Iran-Contra affair mysteries died with him.

A search of the medical literature on lymphoma brain cancer

turns up two interesting sets of findings. Lymphoma brain cancer is a difficult disease and the medical profession is still searching for an effective way to diagnose and treat it. Of the hundreds of cases studied worldwide during one recent three-year period, there were two isolated cases cited of people treated with the injection of drugs—dexamethasone, a steroid, in one case and cytarabine, another powerful anti-cancer drug, in the other—in which the cancer miraculously disappeared. But those were rare and unusual cases.

The normal treatment is either surgery or radiotherapy (X-ray treatment), both widely used over the years. A careful review of the results of these two normal treatment methods, however, shows a dramatic difference in the results. According to one 1986 study of eighty-three well-documented cases, the patients who received radiotherapy treatment lived on for an average of thirty months. Those who had surgery lived only for an average of slightly over three months.[6] Part of this discrepancy in survival rates may be due to the fact that the most seriously ill patients are the ones most likely to be operated on.

The second finding is more disturbing. Though the evidence is scant, it seems clear that the onset of a brain tumor can cause drastic changes in a person's judgment and personality. As the cancer begins to grow, from a speck so small you could not see it, to the size of a pea, to in some cases the size of an orange, it kills brain tissue and exerts steady, increasing pressure on the brain itself, pushing it ever tighter against the inner walls of the skull.

Some of the symptoms of a cancerous tumor growing in the inner left side of the brain, as Casey's was, include "mental changes . . . convulsions," and in some cases, "severe dementia," the medical term for madness or insanity.[7] A growing brain tumor can also cause paranoia, an irrational suspiciousness and distrust of others.[8] Because brain tumors are so rarely detected early, the symptoms can go on for months, in some cases for up to two years, as one brain surgeon told me, before there is a medical explanation for the increasingly odd and bizarre behavior of the victim.

According to Dr. William R. Shapiro, professor of neurosurgery at the Memorial Sloan-Kettering Cancer Center in New York, the type of brain tumor Casey had is "particularly insidious because it grows like a network within brain tissue rather than in a ball or lump. . . . As a result, the tumor can induce gradual, subtle changes in personality or mental functioning that may go unnoticed by associates or may be attributed to stress until there is a dramatic symptom, such as a seizure."[9]

Another noted expert, Dr. Nicholas Zervas, chief of neurosurgery at Massachusetts General Hospital, said that when a brain tumor is discovered, "You can usually find a six-month interval before, when the family begins to question things," adding that "changes in personality or functioning are more common when the patient is elderly. . . . besides damaging nerve tissue, tumors sometimes provoke electrical disturbances within the brain, causing seizures too mild to be noticed but that interfere with thought processes."[10]

Is it possible that Bill Casey's mind, his sense of judgment, his ability to discriminate, to reason, to think clearly was becoming increasingly impaired as the Iran-Contra affair unfolded? The answer is clearly yes, it is possible. If the symptoms began subtly, perhaps as much as two years before the tumor was detected, his brain would have started to feel the effects in early 1985. By the summer and fall of 1985, when the foundations for the general scheme of selling arms to Iran, paying ransom, and secretly diverting money to the Contras were laid in place, it is possible that Casey's brain was feeling the ravages of cancer, suffering memory loss, making bad decisions.

The testimony of some of his closest friends and associates tends to support the idea that Casey was being betrayed by a secret enemy within his own body.

William Safire, a *New York Times* columnist, a close friend of Casey for over twenty years, and a sensitive and astute observer of people, was one of the first to notice a change in Casey's mental state. Commenting about the time period in late 1985, Safire wrote, "It was about this time that Casey's personality changed radically. He found he had prostate cancer (and so informed the President, who had cancer worries of his own); time was short. He grew testy with friends, easily infuriated at criticism and hypersensitive to leaks: after I took a pop at him in print, he hollered at me over the phone and later blew up at me at a large party."[11]

In another event in late 1985 one of Casey's deputies refused to brief President Reagan's Intelligence Oversight Board on the full extent of the CIA's current covert activities, as required by the president's own executive order. Somewhat astonished, the chairman of the board, W. Glenn Campbell, also a very old friend of

Casey's, protested directly to him. When Casey balked at giving Campbell the secret information, Campbell exploded and said, "Who decides this?" (implying that Casey had no right to withhold the information).

Casey thundered back, "I do."

Chairman Campbell retorted, "You don't have the authority." [12]

On that particular covert action, Casey gave in under great pressure, but he never did tell the President's Intelligence Oversight Board anything about the Iran-Contra affair—in direct defiance of President Reagan's executive order.

There were also small things, not notable at the time, that were out of character. In November 1986, just after the Iran arms dealings became public, Casey wrote a "blunt, private letter to President Reagan urging him to replace Secretary of State Shultz with former U.N. Ambassador Jeane Kirkpatrick to assure loyalty to the president and his policies." [13] More wrongheaded, less astute advice has rarely been given. It is unthinkable that a fully functioning Bill Casey could have ever made such an ill-timed political recommendation.

No one will ever know for sure, but there is evidence to suggest that Bill Casey was not thinking straight for a long period of time, a period that very closely coincides with the development of the Iran-Contra affair. A cancerous brain tumor grew slowly and insidiously for months, perhaps years, inside Casey's brain, damaging and sabotaging that exquisite instrument that had done so much for his country. No one will ever know precisely to what extent subtle changes in the physical functioning of his brain were responsible for the bizarre and confusing series of events that occurred.

There is a good chance that by the time the Iran-Contra affair was under way, the wise old bull of the intelligence community was transformed by an invisible assassin into the equivalent of a crazed, rogue elephant, driven wild by an unseen tormentor, rampaging and destroying whatever lay in his path. And the Reagan administration's foreign policy blueprint was in that path.

Chapter Twenty-Eight

THE PURGE

In hindsight we should have seen the Iran-Contra affair coming. There were plenty of clues that something was seriously wrong in the national security community of the Reagan administration. But at the time the clues did not add up in any logical, connected way. In fact, some of the events were simply baffling, with seemingly no rhyme or reason behind them. One of them stands out sharply in my memory.

In October 1985, the same month that saw the attempted purge of PEPAB, the president's economic policy advisory board, there was another telling purge—the purge of PFIAB.

PFIAB is the acronym for the President's Foreign Intelligence Advisory Board. PFIAB, as it was usually called, is a very difficult organization to write about. PFIAB's main business concerns the entire range of the most secret operations of the U.S. government, and every member of the board has potential access to the most tightly held, most closely guarded military, diplomatic, and intelligence secrets in the country. The material they handle routinely is so secret that even the degrees of classification and compartmentalization are themselves classified.

I was a member of the President's Foreign Intelligence Advisory Board for almost four years. When President Reagan appointed me to it on March 2, 1982, I signed the same secrecy agreements that every other member of the board did, pledging never to reveal or discuss any of the secrets shared with us during the performance of our duties. However, the existence of the board is not secret, nor is its purpose and membership, which is clearly spelled out in public documents. But the specifics of the operations of PFIAB are secret and, with that handicap in mind, I will try to explain as best I can what happened.

One afternoon during the first week of November 1985 I was going through my mail at the Hoover Institution when I uncovered a small, pale green envelope about seven inches long and four inches high. The only return address in the upper left-hand corner was one line "THE WHITE HOUSE," in dark blue engraving. I knew immediately who the letter was from.

Almost all letters sent from the White House are written on pure white stationery. All of the correspondence of the hundreds of White House aides is white, as is most of the president's correspondence. The pale, pale green stationery is the president's private stock, and is reserved for his personal use only.

Intrigued, I lay down the rest of the mail and, with a slight ceremony, carefully slit open the envelope with a very sharp knife. When I started to read the letter I noticed that the greeting had been personalized. The "Dr. Anderson" part of "Dear Dr. Anderson" was scratched out by pen and in its place was a handwritten "Marty," the name the president always addressed me by in person.

I eagerly began to read the letter.

And discovered I had just been fired.

It was a nice enough letter. Reagan thanked me for my "contributions to the work of the President's Foreign Intelligence Advisory Board" and pointed out that during my "membership on the Board, the PFIAB made important contributions to improving our intelligence capabilities."

Then came the slow pitch, "As you know, my senior policy advisers and I have made various changes in the area of national security to better equip our country to meet future challenges. It has become clear that the PFIAB has grown to a size which makes it difficult to focus intimately and actively on some of the new critical intelligence problems we will have to address. I intend, therefore, to reconstitute and streamline the Board."

And then the fast ball, high and inside, "Your service to our nation has been greatly appreciated, and I know that in the years ahead you will be able to look back with pride on your accomplishments."

"With kindest personal regards, sincerely," and it was signed "Ron," the way he usually signs personal letters to his friends.

It was the first time in my life I was ever summarily fired. It was a shock. Of course, it was only a part-time job, requiring flying to Washington, D.C., every two months for a couple of days, plus spending one or two days a month in related tasks. The board members did not get paid for the three or four days a month it cost them in terms of travel, study, and attending meetings, so I wasn't upset about the financial loss. In fact, PFIAB members had to pay a $400 a year special assessment for the sandwiches and soft drinks that were brought into our nonstop meetings, so actually I was going to be ahead a little financially.

What did hurt was the public embarrassment of being fired by the president for no apparent reason. During my four years of service on the board I received numerous compliments and commendations on both the quality and quantity of my contributions. The president and the White House staff and the chairman and vice chairman of the board always seemed enthusiastically satisfied with what we were doing. And then suddenly, without any real explanation—after ten years of intensely loyal service to Reagan—he fired me.

The President's Foreign Intelligence Advisory Board was established by President Eisenhower in 1956, and was first known as the Board of Consultants on Foreign Intelligence Activities. The board was continued by every president since then, except President Carter, who abolished it in 1977. President Reagan brought it back to life on October 20, 1981, with Executive Order No. 12331.[1]

As reestablished, the PFIAB was charged with assessing, "The quality, quantity, and adequacy of intelligence collection, of analysis and estimates, of counterintelligence, and other intelligence activities."

To assist PFIAB in carrying out its charter the board was given the authority to, "Continually review the performance of all agencies of Government that are engaged in the collection, evaluation, or production of intelligence or the execution of intelligence policy . . . [and] to assess the adequacy of management, personnel, and organization in the intelligence agencies."

PFIAB is potentially a very powerful organization. Its members have access to all the secret information the United States government possesses. They have access to the secrets of the Central Intelligence Agency, the Federal Bureau of Investigation, the National Security Agency, the Defense Intelligence Agency, and every other nook and cranny of the intelligence community. It is an extraordinary degree of access, exceeded perhaps only by that of the president himself, whose effective access is sharply limited by the time he has available to read and study intelligence reports.

The power that stems from the possession of that information is increased further by the direct access the board has to the president. Not only can PFIAB find out what is going on in highly secret, tightly compartmentalized parts of the government, but the members can also do something about it. They can tell the president. It is a unique capability, making PFIAB potentially one of the most powerful checks against the kind of irresponsible, wasteful, and sometimes dangerous activity that can grow and flourish in an environment which, by its very nature—secrecy—makes it impossible for the normal checks and balances to operate.

Since Eisenhower's time every member of PFIAB has taken "an oath not to reveal any classified information acquired through their service on the Board,"[2] and I have no intention of violating that oath. However, there have been a few public studies of PFIAB which can give us a general idea of the kind of work it undertakes and the importance of that work. The most comprehensive public work on PFIAB is a twenty-five page pamphlet published by the Hale Foundation in 1981. The Hale Foundation is a nonprofit organization dedicated "to enhancing the capability of U.S. intelligence to serve the fundamental objectives of the Constitution."[3] The pamphlet cites a major analysis of the operations of PFIAB from 1956 through 1974 by the Congressional Research Service of the Library of Congress. Noting that PFIAB's findings and recommendations are classified and that no specifics about its recommendations are available, the Hale pamphlet goes on to list some of the general subjects that the recommendations of PFIAB have dealt with over the years:

- Control and coordination of the intelligence community, particularly in the area of covert action.
- Improved strategic warning systems.
- Management of the National Security Agency.
- General development and improvement of U.S. intelligence capabilities.
- Improved methods of handling sensitive intelligence.
- More effective coordination and evaluation of covert action.
- Review of CIA paramilitary operations.
- Revisions of functions of the National Security Council group which approved or disapproved covert action and paramilitary operations to ensure political control and review of such activities.
- Investigations into satellite reconnaissance systems.
- Deficiencies in the collection and analysis of intelligence from Southeast Asia.[4]

As the Senate Select Committee to Study Intelligence Operations concluded in 1976, "PFIAB has served, in effect, as an intelligence 'Kitchen Cabinet.' The Board has been useful, in part because its advice and recommendations have been *for* the President." A final reason for the tremendous value of the board to our national security has been the objective quality of its work. The members of the board have, almost without exception, hopelessly favored the intelligence community, believing deeply in the importance of its mission. The PFIAB members love the intelligence community, but it is tough love. While PFIAB is a strong and powerful backer of our intelligence system it is also, as Professor Lyman Kirkpatrick, a former inspector general of the CIA, describes it, "one of the severest critics of the intelligence system."[5]

Getting fired from PFIAB was infuriating and very, very puzzling. It just didn't make any sense. Though the one consolation I had was that I was fired in some very good company. Ten other members of the board were fired at the same time. They were: General Robert Barrow, former commandant of the United States Marine Corps, one of the country's top military and intelligence experts whom President Reagan had named just three months earlier to his new Commission of Defense Management; Dr. Alan Greenspan, one of the world's most noted economists who, a year and a half later, was chosen by President Reagan to become chairman of the federal reserve system; Admiral Thomas H. Moorer, a former chief of U.S. Naval Operations and chairman of the Joint Chiefs of Staff, one of our most experienced and respected retired military officers; Peter O'Donnell, an intelligent, wealthy business-man from Texas, and one of Reagan's earliest and most consistent political supporters; Eugene Rostow, the former director of the Arms Control and Disarmament Agency and noted foreign affairs scholar; Senator Harrison Schmitt, a former astronaut and former senator from New Mexico, noted for his space technology expertise; Dr. Paul Seabury, professor of political science at the University of California (Berkeley) and noted authority on intelligence and foreign policy matters; Robert F. Six, the founder and chairman of Continental Airlines, who worked closely with the intelligence community for many years and was an old personal friend of President Reagan; Seymour Weiss, the former director of the Office of Strategic Intelligence and Research in the Department of State, one of the country's top intelligence experts; and Edward Bennett Williams, a former member of PFIAB in the 1970s, perhaps the country's leading criminal lawyer, and a noted intelligence expert.

We all got the same letter at the same time. There was no warning, no nice retirement dinner with speeches thanking us for our years of service, not even a small gold watch. Afterwards I talked to each member who was fired. They were not amused. Like myself, it was the first time most of them had ever been fired. One exception was Edward Bennett Williams, who took it somewhat more philosophically than the rest of us. A staunch Democrat, he was a member of PFIAB when President Carter disbanded the board in early 1977 just after taking office. Williams thought our firings were one of the "most graceless" things he had seen during his many years in Washington but then, looking at the bright side of it, noted that he was perhaps the only person in history who had been "fired from PFIAB by two different presidents."

Those who survived the purge and remained on the board made up an equally, if not more distinguished group: Anne Armstrong, the chairman, Leo Cherne, the vice chairman, Howard Baker, Jr., William O. Baker, W. Glenn Campbell, John Foster, Jr., Henry A. Kissinger, Clare Boothe Luce, William French Smith, and Albert Wheelon.

But what was curious and added even more mystery to the purge was the addition of four *new* members just two weeks later. The ostensible reason given in the president's letter was that the board had become too large to work effectively. But if that were the case, why were four new members added shortly thereafter? The new members were indisputably capable—Jeane J. Kirkpatrick, the former ambassador to the United Nations, Albert Wohlstetter, one of the country's best national security scholars, James Q. Wilson, a Harvard/UCLA political scientist who was the country's top expert on crime, and General Bernard A. Schriever, who was the commander of the U.S. Air Force Systems Command from 1961 to 1966. If the problem with the board was its size, why fire eleven and hire four—why not fire seven? Obviously something else motivated the purge.

There are hints that the size of the board had bothered the chairman for some time. During 1984 she and the vice chairman, Leo Cherne, both complained that they thought the board was too big, and expressed concern that the intelligence professionals might be reluctant to part with their really secret information to twenty-one board members plus a half-dozen or so staff. The counter arguments were: (a) there had never been a leak from the board, (b) the range of activities we were supposed to review and assess was so great that we needed twenty-one people, a relatively small number when subdivided into working subcommittees, and (c) the intelligence professionals had no authority to be reluctant—they reported to us, we did not report to them.

The chairman's first order of business at the November 1984 meeting was to tell us calmly and sweetly that she was asking us all to submit our resignations because "this was customary whenever a president was reelected to a second term." I was surprised to see my fellow board members agree one by one, nodding their heads yes as if that indeed was the normal way to proceed. Didn't they understand that as soon as they submitted their resignations, she could accept a select number and achieve her bureaucratic goal of a small, easily manageable group—ineffective perhaps, but one that would not cause anyone much trouble?

So I raised my hand, waited patiently to be recognized, and pointed out that what she just said was not true. I said "it was not customary to submit resignations. The only time I know of when that was done was in 1972. Nixon demanded the resignations of his entire cabinet and many other high-ranking government officials and it was one of the worst mistakes he ever made."

Chairman Armstrong was not pleased at my rebuke. "Perhaps

you would like to check it with the White House," she replied with a forced smile that I was sure did not reflect her true feelings.

"Sure," I said, "I'll be glad to."

During lunch I called John Herrington, the stiffly conservative head of White House personnel. Herrington was one of the key advance men during Reagan's campaign, performing the critical task of making the thousands of logistical arrangements that are necessary for the success of a modern-day presidential campaign. Herrington—whose job now was placing qualified people loyal to Reagan and his ideas in government jobs the president could fill by personal appointment—was appalled when I told him why I was calling.

"Hell," he said, "We aren't requesting anyone's resignation, especially PFIAB's. It's one of the few groups that is doing a terrific job for the president. That's the dumbest thing I ever heard of."

Later on that day, toward the end of the meeting, Chairman Armstrong called on me to see if I had anything to report from the White House. She was probably gambling that I either had not called or was unable to speak to anyone in authority who would contradict the story she made up. So I told the board that I spoke to the appropriate people in the White House and was told that "no resignations were being asked for and that, besides, they thought PFIAB was doing a great job."

I thought that would finish it, but Mrs. Armstrong persisted, demanding, "Is that all? Was there anything else?"

I should have resisted the temptation, but her glare of frustrated contempt was too great an invitation.

"Yes," I said. "They said it was the dumbest thing they had ever heard of."

Everyone laughed.

She was never very friendly to me after that.

Anne Legendre Armstrong was an unusual choice for chairman of PFIAB. She is a medium height, slender woman with an attractive face with high cheekbones. Born on December 27, 1927, she went to Vassar College in New York, was elected to Phi Beta Kappa, the honorary scholastic society, and graduated in 1949. Even though she is from New Orleans, she has the look of the East Coast horsey set. She was in her mid fifties when she took over the chairmanship of PFIAB. Before becoming chairman she had no prior knowledge of intelligence or military matters. The whole world of spies and intercepted electronic signals and satellites and nuclear missiles was new to her. She had no close political ties to Reagan, having worked for George Bush against Reagan until Bush lost. Then she joined the Reagan-Bush team as the cochairman of the campaign. She had no significant experience as an administrator, although she served with distinction as Ambassador to Great Britain during 1976–77.

Basically she was a very talented politician, married to a wealthy Texas rancher. She was never elected to public office, but she was very good at working for and with politicians, and acquiring increasingly important political appointments. When President Reagan won the presidency in 1980 she quickly claimed the prize she wanted—the chairmanship of the President's Foreign Intelligence Advisory Board. Richard Allen, Reagan's new national security adviser, was incredulous. "She's just not qualified," he argued, and fought the appointment. But George Bush, who had not asked for much from the new administration, was asking for her appointment. James Baker, Bush's former campaign manager and the new White House chief of staff, also backed her appointment. With Bush and Baker supporting her it was only a matter of time before she got the coveted position.

The one thing that seemed to elude Mrs. Armstrong more than anything else was the respect she so desperately appeared to want from the other board members and, most importantly, from the major players in the national security field—William Casey, Alexander Haig, George Shultz, Casper Weinberger, Richard Allen, William Clark, and Bud McFarlane. It was a losing fight. It seemed to me that Casey, Shultz, Weinberger, and Clark only tolerated and humored her. Casey, in particular, was in private quite contemptuous of her abilities, but cheerfully solicitous to her in public. Among most of the board members, she was regarded with a mixture of toleration and amusement, but with little of the respect that was accorded to members such as Clare Booth Luce, Henry Kissinger, Alan Greenspan, and Edward Bennett Williams. Even the overtly loyal vice chairman, Leo Cherne, would sometimes look up at the ceiling and roll his eyes when she made some of her most interesting suggestions. One of the strongest and best known members of the board—Ross Perot, the billionaire businessman dynamo—resigned from the board in exasperation, seeing it largely as a waste of his time under her leadership.

During 1985 the situation surrounding PFIAB became increasingly unhappy. Bill Casey's resentment of the board was growing. Every two months the director of Central Intelligence (or the DCI as he was called) reported to and was interrogated by the board.

When Casey entered the high ceilinged PFIAB conference room, lanky and moving fast, he always reminded me of an old mountain lion making his way down a steep bank to a favorite watering hole— seemingly casual but acutely alert. Casey hated his bimonthly meetings with PFIAB. His annoyance with the probing, critical questions was barely concealed. But he knew he had to do it, so he sat there, like an animal being baited, and endured the indignity of our questions.

Mrs. Armstrong was having an increasingly difficult time coping with the likes of Casey and Shultz, who could barely tolerate being overseen by her. They began to balk, not in person of course, but through their bureaucracies. The board began to encounter delays in getting information, officials called to testify before the board were not entirely forthcoming—if you didn't ask precisely the right question, you got the wrong answer, and the recommendations of the board were being implemented slowly, if at all.

The executive director of the board was Gary Schmitt, a young graduate of the University of Dallas in Texas, who worked briefly on the staff of the Senate Intelligence Committee for Senator Daniel P. Moynihan, the Democrat from New York. One night Schmitt complained to a friend that Mrs. Armstrong felt strongly that many of the board members were not "granting her proper respect and that the kind of questions they were asking were upsetting the intelligence community, making it impossible for her to work with the key people, especially Casey." Some of us would have to plead guilty about the respect, but as far as upsetting the intelligence community, well, that was simply part of what happened if the board did its job properly. Overseers are supposed to be respected, not liked.

The concerns of Armstrong, Cherne, and Casey went unslaked for a full year, until the mass firing on Halloween in 1985. That purge transformed the character of PFIAB, changing it overnight into what I would call a celebrity board. All members of presidential advisory boards are usually pretty busy people. The old board, with twenty-one members, had enough people to ensure that fourteen or fifteen showed up for the two days of meetings every two months, and included a number of people who devoted much more time. The new board, with fourteen members, had a much higher proportion of very distinguished, very busy people. It was difficult enough to get Henry Kissinger, Jeane Kirkpatrick, Howard Baker, and William French Smith even to come to a meeting, let alone get them to do a lot of study and preparation and independent investigation. Once people such as these were given facts and information, their superb judgment and high intelligence would produce terrific conclusions. But they were so busy generally that the board became, overnight, greatly weakened in terms of the raw, available manpower of its board members, and thus it was forced to rely more on the small staff of PFIAB and the material provided by the bureaucracy. This was a matter of degree, because the old board also relied heavily on the small PFIAB staff and the bureaucracy.

The old board had a substantial number of members who liked to instigate things. They asked a lot of questions, some of them embarrassing. They were persistent, they pressed their case. They were not intimidated by rank or past political service to President Reagan. At times they could be irreverent. And they were all fired. While the new board was one of extraordinary ability and distinction, there were very few boat rockers among its members, and those who were most capable of doing some vigorous boat rocking were usually those too busy to do so.

Finally, the members of the old board were appointed for unlimited terms, which meant that barring the unforeseen, unlikely event that they would be fired, they could proceed with their work without fear of being replaced. The new board was dramatically different. Every member was appointed for two years, adding a measure of insecurity and instability that the old board did not have.

In effect, the old PFIAB, the aggressive intelligence critic with its "tough love," was defanged and declawed. The old tiger became a purring lap cat.

Perhaps the most interesting question is why was it done? How was President Reagan persuaded to fire eleven people abruptly? At first we assumed it happened because Mrs. Armstrong wanted it to happen. But that could not be true. The purge of PFIAB could not take place without the active, strong support of at least several of President Reagan's key foreign policy advisers, members of his foreign policy directorate. And that is what happened.

Over the years I came to know quite a few people scattered

throughout the federal bureaucracy and Congress. For a long time after the purge, everyone who knew anything about it was too concerned and nervous to speak up. Most of the key players effecting the purge were sworn to deep secrecy. No one would talk, period. But, after a while, the nervousness and concerns faded—bit by bit—and people began to talk. From a number of different sources, most of them still nervous enough not to want their names used, it was possible to piece together a fairly accurate picture of what happened. The explanation is in part speculation, and there are surely things we will never know, but the basic story seems clear.

To put it mildly, Bill Casey did not like the old PFIAB. He indicated his displeasure to numerous friends and acquaintances. According to one reliable source, who in this instance asked to be anonymous, a longtime professional colleague of Casey admitted that "Casey had nothing but contempt for PFIAB." As his years as head of the CIA piled up, he seemed to become more and more arrogant, and increasingly resentful of *anyone* who dared to criticize or question him. This heightened sensitivity to criticism may very well have been the result of a growing brain tumor. Whatever the cause or reason, his displeasure with PFIAB was fairly widely known at the beginning of Reagan's second term of office in 1985. Casey was too wily an operator, even with a brain tumor, to openly attack PFIAB. Instead, he waited for an appropriate opportunity.

When Mrs. Armstrong began to complain about the board's size, it probably did not take Casey long to discern the virtue of her concern. Probably somewhat reluctantly he allowed her to convince him, to win him over to her point of view, giving her suggestions on whom to replace and whom to keep. With the skill of the folklore character Brer Rabbit begging the fox not to throw him in the briar patch, Casey graciously allowed Mrs. Armstrong to be his stalking-horse. He was aided in this endeavor by his old friend, Leo Cherne, the vice chairman of the board. Cherne lobbied McFarlane hard to have the size of the board drastically reduced.[6]

For a long time, no one paid any attention to Mrs. Armstrong's petulant complaints about the size of the board. But after she picked up Casey as an ally in her cause, people listened. McFarlane listened. If Bill Casey and Mrs. Armstrong wanted to change the board, then McFarlane was for it. Later McFarlane expressed regret over what happened, saying, "It wasn't my finest hour. I just punted. I caved in to Anne. I didn't fight it." What McFarlane did was understandable. The late fall of 1985 was an incredibly pressure-packed time for the national security adviser and he had more important things to do—including the upcoming summit meeting with Mikhail Gorbachev—than check out the validity of what Anne Armstrong and Leo Cherne were telling him.[7]

McFarlane assigned the task of working out the messy details to one of his aides, Kenneth de Graffenreid, and swore him to deep secrecy. De Graffenreid, beginning in the early fall of 1985, drafted the new executive order, the press releases, and the firing letters for Reagan's signature.

The decision was helped along with a small bit of disinformation, as they call it in the intelligence trade. The argument was made that the old PFIAB was so internally torn with dissension that it was impossible for it to function effectively. When the *New York Times* ran a story on the firings the following day, the reporter, Peter Kilborn, quoted a senior administation official as saying that the group had become an unwieldy "monstrosity. . . . strife-ridden and contentious," and that "there were so many people who normally disagreed so much it became useless."[8]

That was not true. Either the source lied to Kilborn or someone lied to the source, who believed he was telling the truth. In fact, the old board was an unusually harmonious group. Never have I seen so many people agree so totally and completely on such a wide range of important policy issues. There was dissension and strife and contentiousness, but it was not among the board members, it was between the board and the intelligence agencies whose work they vigorously reviewed. I later talked to Kilborn in an effort to find out who believed this. Like all good reporters he would not reveal his source, but he did indicate that it was a very high, very reliable source—and to me that meant someone right next to the president.

The day after I received the letter firing me from PFIAB, I boarded a plane and flew to Washington to attend a special luncheon on November 6, 1985, at the White House that President Reagan gave for the executive committee of the board of governors of the Ronald Reagan Presidential Foundation. The foundation was building the Reagan Presidential Library and the executive committee was beginning a major fund-raising drive. It was not an intimate luncheon. Perhaps as many as forty people attended. There was no opportunity to take up the little matter of my firing with the president. At least not without causing an awkward scene. And besides, it was done, the *New York Times* had made it official, and there was no putting Humpty-Dumpty back together again. All the others who were fired came to the same conclusion and never raised the issue with the president.

But after lunch I spotted Donald Regan standing off by himself. I recalled the story in the previous day's *New York Times* quoting a high-ranking government official using the words "monstrosity" and "strife-ridden." In my experience there was only one White House senior official who used such colorful, strong language with such a sense of certainty. It sounded just like Donald Regan.

I walked over to Regan and after exchanging greetings got right down to the PFIAB business. I said, "I realize it's a fait accompli now, but I think you should know it's not true there was a lot of dissension and strife among the PFIAB members. There was an extraordinary degree of harmony among the members. Sure the board was sometimes very critical of the State Department and the CIA, but . . ."

Before I could finish, Regan flared up in a defensive huff and exploded, interrupting me in an angry, defiant voice, "The board just wasn't working. There was so much fighting and disagreement among the members it just wasn't effective anymore."

That was interesting. Donald Regan never attended a PFIAB meeting, so he must have learned that from someone else. And he surely sounded like the senior official who was quoted in the *New York Times*, or else they were both briefed by the same person on the same argument.

"I don't know who told you that, Don," I replied, "but it's totally wrong. It's not true."

Regan's face was a lot redder now, and I could see that he was about to become really angry. He was not a man who liked being told he was wrong. But before either of us could say anything else, I noticed William French Smith approaching us. After Smith resigned as attorney general in early 1985, he joined PFIAB and had been a member now for almost a year. So I said, "Don, why don't you ask Bill. See if he thinks the board was 'strife-ridden.' "

Regan turned to Smith and briefly explained to him what we were discussing, pointing out how PFIAB was so torn with dissension that it could not function. Smith looked puzzled and his face furrowed.

"No," Smith said, "Marty's right. There was no dissension among the board members."

Now it was Regan's turn to look puzzled. As the redness drained from his face all he said was, "Oh."

So what did happen? How did the upper reaches of the White House come to believe that the PFIAB board was contentious and so large that it was unwieldy?

This way. One day, late in October 1985, the carefully drafted letters firing over half the board landed on President Reagan's desk, courtesy of Robert McFarlane, neatly bypassing Chief of Staff Regan. When President Reagan read the letters he was puzzled, so he picked up the telephone and called Regan. "Don, why are we firing all these people?" inquired the president.

Regan was caught by surprise. "I don't know, Mr. President, but I'll find out."[9]

Regan immediately summoned Anne Armstrong to his office. Mrs. Armstrong earnestly argued her case. "The board is much too large," she told Regan. "It has gotten contentious, and many of the members lack sufficient expertise." She explained that she was not off on some wild toot by herself, stating that her position was strongly backed by many of the key members of Reagan's foreign policy circle.

Casey was enthusiastically behind the purge, and once Mc-Farlane accepted the idea he quickly suggested an old friend, Albert Wohlstetter, to serve as one of the new members.[10] Secretary of State George Shultz and Vice President Bush apparently raised no objections to the firings. Shultz's neutrality was understandable, for PFIAB had pounded the State Department regularly with brutal effectiveness. Bush's neutrality was also understandable. He was not about to cross one of his most important political supporters from his political base, Texas.

On October 29, 1985, Vice President Bush named Anne Armstrong one of seven national cochairmen of his official political action committee, Fund for America's Future, the driving force behind his presidential candidacy for 1988.[11] By late 1987 Mrs. Armstrong was the official representative from Texas on the national steering committee of the 1988 Bush for President campaign. In the earlier days of PFIAB there was an unwritten rule that any member who wished to engage in partisan political activity would gracefully resign in order to preserve the board's reputation as being above politics. But that quaint tradition apparently had been quietly abandoned.

Donald Regan was skeptical about Armstrong's story. And he was nervous about summarily firing so many of the president's close friends and political supporters. Bob Six, Edward Bennett Williams, Alan Greenspan, Tom Moorer, Sy Weiss—what the hell was going on? So Regan double-checked. Just to make sure, he called Leo Cherne and asked him to come to his office.

Leo Cherne is a Democrat, born Leo Chernetsky on September 8, 1912, in New York City, an ardent left-winger of the 1930s who gradually shifted to the political right, especially on foreign policy issues. Cherne was one of Bill Casey's best friends. He had known Bill Casey for about forty years, giving Casey one of his first jobs when he hired him to work for his organization, the Research Institute of America. Cherne loves PFIAB. All the other members, even Chairman Armstrong, treat it as a part-time job. Cherne treats it as a full-time job.

He seems to spend more time in his PFIAB office than he does in his home, New York City. He is intensely interested in all the arcane mysteries of the secret world, and probes them deeply, endlessly. In his mid-seventies, he is a short man, with an ingratiating manner that borders on fawning. Most everyone likes him, and appreciates his hard work and the endless hours he selflessly devotes to the intelligence community. He seemed to be the ideal person for Regan to check with to see if Mrs. Armstrong was telling the truth.

In a brief meeting in Regan's west wing office, Cherne backed up Mrs. Armstrong's story completely, reassuring the chief of staff that everything she said was true.

But something was still unsettling Donald Regan. He had done two strong, personal checks, far beyond and above the call of duty of an impossibly busy White House chief of staff, but he still felt uneasy. This was not something he wanted responsibility for. If the president wanted to fire all these people, he was going to have to hear the story himself and make his own judgment. Regan was not about to put his body between President Reagan and the eleven to be fired.

So he arranged for Mrs. Armstrong to meet with the president personally to plead her case. She did, and evidently gave him the same misinformation that she gave to Donald Regan and Robert

McFarlane, the same misinformation that Leo Cherne corrobo-rated.

President Reagan approved the firings.

Donald Regan later joked, "You know the President, he could never say no to a woman.[12]

The brief two or three month period during the fall of 1985 was a critical time for the foreign and intelligence policies of the Reagan administration. Much was going on. For example, there were intense preparations for the upcoming summit meeting with Soviet General Secretary Gorbachev on arms control. The Soviet coding of their missile test data was raising serious questions whether our intelligence could provide adequate verification of a new treaty, if one should occur.[13] Plans for the development of a U.S. missile defense system were moving forward. A ruckus was being raised about the new Soviet embassy compound located on a 350-foot hill in Washington, D.C., giving it a clear line of sight to the White House and the Capitol.

While the criticism and pressure were building on the intelligence community, some striking changes were taking place in its power structure. Casey rose to virtually unchallenged supremacy and solidified his control over the entire domain of intelligence, including covert action. His old friend Donald Regan had long since replaced one of Casey's earlier nemeses, James Baker, as White House chief of staff. Casey now had a powerful friend in court. Vice President Bush was generally supportive of Casey and non-critical. McFarlane was simply no match for Casey and rarely opposed him. Oliver North, one of McFarlane's key deputies for covert action, became deeply attached to Casey and soon functioned as if he worked for Casey, not McFarlane. When McFarlane left the National Security Council in frustration and despair, he was replaced with someone even more worshipful of Casey—Admiral John Poindexter.

PFIAB was one of the last remaining thorns in Casey's side. George Shultz and Caspar Weinberger were unafraid to tangle with Casey, and the congressional committees were, as always, feisty and willing to question even someone as exalted as the head of our intelligence services. But, with the exception of PFIAB and the small three-man PIOB, the President's Intelligence Oversight Board, there was little else to restrain Casey's enthusiasms. When the twenty-one member strong PFIAB, that used to probe widely and deeply without caution, was transformed into a much smaller board, dominated by famous, very busy people, one of the last effective potential checks on Casey and the intelligence community was gone.

It is impossible to say for certain that if the old PFIAB was in place the Iran-Contra affair would not have happened. As later testimony before Congress would bear out, Casey and Poindexter and North would probably have had no more compunctions about misleading the board than they had about misleading anyone else. But a large, vigorous board would have made it more likely that the skullduggery would have been discovered much, much earlier. The offices of PFIAB were located on the same floor of the same building, directly between Bill Casey's office and Oliver North's office.

Perhaps Casey's fear of a large PFIAB was the fear that something would leak into it. For if it had, if any member of PFIAB had discovered that the United States was selling arms to Iran for a huge profit and then diverting that profit to the Contras in Nicaragua, they certainly would have brought it to the attention of the entire board. And the board would have been outraged and taken it to President Reagan at once. Much the same way that Edwin Meese, William Clark, Michael Deaver, or James Baker would have reacted if they had known. But no one did know.

After the purge of PFIAB in October 1985, the pesky restraints were largely gone, and the way was clear.

The Iran-Contra games could begin.

And they did.

Chapter Twenty-Nine

THE MIDDLE EAST CABAL

One of the strangest and most bizarre tales in the Iran-Contra affair was the one told by Suleiman (Sam) Bamieh in March 1987. Bamieh, a forty-eight-year-old businessman of Saudi Arabian birth, lives in San Mateo, California, a wealthy suburb of San Francisco. For many years he operated a trading company in the market jungles of the Middle East and was personally acquainted with some of the powerful people who rule those sandy kingdoms. Until those days in early March 1987 when he told his tale, Mr. Bamieh seems to have been a typical Middle Eastern businessman living and operating in the United States, keeping a low public profile, cultivating influential and powerful friends who could help his business.

And then suddenly he called newspaper reporters and deliberately injected himself into the burgeoning Iran-Contra scandal. This was odd behavior for a normally secretive international businessman who usually shunned publicity. But Bamieh said he had good reasons. He told the reporters he had received four threats on his life in recent weeks and concluded that only publicity would keep him alive. Evidently, he reasoned that if he told his story to the world, there would no longer be any reason to kill him in order to prevent him from telling that story.[1]

This is the tale Bamieh told in March 1987.

On Monday, May 20, 1985, many months before the United States began selling arms to Iran, Sam Bamieh was visiting King Fahd of Saudi Arabia. Saudi Arabia covers a huge territory, 865,000 square miles of sandy, desolate soil, largely worthless except for the tremendously valuable pools of oil that lurk deep beneath the sand dunes. While Saudi Arabia is rich in land and oil, it is decidedly short on people, having a population of less than ten million to guard its riches. It is a nervous nation, surrounded by populous states inhabited by old enemies with large, well-armed military forces. Syria and Iraq to the north, Israel and Egypt to the west, and Iran, with its fifty-five million people, just a few miles to the east across the Gulf of Oman. Saudi Arabia's King Fahd, one of the last reigning monarchs in the world, was especially worried about the threat that Iran posed to his country.

Iran and Iraq, bitter enemies themselves, had been at war for five years, locked in one of the most vicious, bloody conflicts of the twentieth century. From the beginning, Saudi Arabia supported Iraq and gave them billions of dollars to buy arms to kill Iranians. But now, to King Fahd's growing horror and surprise, Iran was slowly gaining the upper hand in the war. Iran might win, and, if she did, the consequences for Saudi Arabia could be grim. If Iran conquered Iraq, Saudi Arabia would suddenly be sharing a common border, hundreds of miles long, with a vindictive enemy. In Iran's eyes, Saudi Arabia was a despicable, weak, rich, cowardly country that used its unearned oil wealth to arm Iran's archenemy Iraq. Retribution would not be long in coming, at least not as long as the Ayatollah was still alive and there were millions of fanatical Iranians willing to do his bidding. Saudi Arabia's survival was at stake.

Bamieh's tale continued. That day in May 1985 he was visiting his friend King Fahd on private business. The meeting with the king took place in the Old Presidential Palace in the city of Jiddah on the eastern shore of the Red Sea. Bamieh says he was allowed to sit in while "Prince Bandar bin Sultan, the Saudi ambassador to Washington, briefed Fahd on a campaign to persuade the United States to serve Saudi interests by making a new diplomatic overture to Iran."[2]

Evidently, the Saudis had been concerned about the potential threat posed by Iran's revolutionary government. According to Bamieh, in an attempt to curry favor with Iran the Saudis reportedly offered Iranian officials $20 million to agree to secret talks. The Iranians initially rebuffed the Saudis, but there was something the Iranians did want very badly—U.S. arms and military spare parts. Before the Iranian revolution expelled the Americans from Iran in 1979, the United States was the primary supplier of weapons to the former Shah's military forces. Now many of those weapons, which Iran needed to fight the Iraqis, were useless because of a lack of spare parts. Perhaps, the Saudis may have reasoned, if we help the Iranians get those U.S. weapons and spare parts, they will spare us if they defeat Iraq.

Bamieh said that in his presence, Prince Bandar bin Sultan briefed King Fahd on the contents of a document he carried with him outlining such a plan. Part of the plan included an effort "to assist the National Security Council to convince the president to go for an opening to Iran to get the hostages out. . . . to persuade President Reagan to mount a U.S. diplomatic overture by selling arms and military spare parts to Iran."[3]

To implement the plan, Bamieh indicated that "the Saudis then turned to international wheeler-dealer Adnan Khashoggi, a Saudi citizen with close ties to the royal family."[4] Khashoggi was one of the world's richest men. Born in Mecca on July 25, 1935, he was the son of one of the personal physicians of the king of Saudi Arabia. Khashoggi briefly went to college in the United States—first, one term at California State University at Chico and then a second term as a transfer student at Stanford University. With one year of higher education finished, he left school and went into international business. By the early 1970s he was extraordinarily wealthy.

Khashoggi made hundreds of millions of dollars on arms sales operating in the murky, dangerous underworld of international arms dealers. He was smart, crafty, and ruthless. A friend of mine who once worked for Khashoggi for nearly two years confirmed that he would never refuse a request from the royal family of Saudi Arabia. The royal family was his base. When the king called, Khashoggi would drop whatever he was doing and take up the king's bidding.

The Saudis had already taken one major step to endear themselves to the United States administration. When Congress passed the Boland Amendment prohibiting military aid to the rebel Contras whom President Reagan was supporting in Nicaragua, the Saudis agreed to secretly aid the Contras—aid that may have amounted to as much as $25 million or $30 million. Beginning in June 1984, the Saudis quietly began sending $1 million a month, and later $2 million a month, to the Contras to buy weapons and supplies.[5] It was one of the best kept secrets in the United States government. Congress knew nothing about it. One U.S. official who did know was Robert McFarlane, who must have felt some degree of indebtedness to the generous King Fahd.

As Bamieh continued to spin out his tale, he said that the goal of the Saudis was "to enhance their influence with the Ayatollah, the Libyans, the Syrians, the PLO, and other anti-American factions in the region."[6] To most people, providing weapons to one's mortal enemies would seem crazy, or at best, somewhat foolhardy, but Bamieh insisted that the Saudis have historically "tried to maintain relations even with their enemies."[7] It is a way of thinking that is foreign to most peoples of the world, particularly Americans, and is perhaps why so little attention was paid to what was occurring.

What gives Bamieh's story a certain amount of credibility is what happened next. Adnan Khashoggi apparently went right to work on his assignment from the king. Just six weeks later, on July 1, 1985, Khashoggi delivered a fifty-page document to Robert McFarlane. According to Bamieh it was the same document that Ambassador Bandar discussed with King Fahd in his presence. The document was the joint product of Khashoggi and Manucher Ghorbanifar.[0]

Ghorbanifar is an Iranian arms dealer with curious connections to high-ranking officials in the Iranian government and to Iranian intelligence circles. A number of people who knew him either distrusted him or disliked him or both. Ghorbanifar and Khashoggi had met a number of times since January 1985 and the document Khashoggi gave to McFarlane contained "Ghorbanifar's views on Iranian politics."[9] The Ghorbanifar-Khashoggi document argued that the United States "could undermine the radical regime of Ayatollah Ruhollah Khomeini" by resuming contact with Iran[10] and proposed a plan of action for the United States to follow, including the sale of military weapons and spare parts to Iran.

The Saudis may have taken out some insurance on Khashoggi's efforts. Sam Bamieh also reported that at the May 20 meeting Ambassador Prince Bandar bin Sultan "recommended to King Fahd that (Michael) Deaver be recruited to gain National Security Council approval for an overture to Iran proposed by Saudi arms merchant Adnan Khashoggi," an idea suggested by Frederick G. Dutton, the Saudis' "principal political adviser in Washington."[11] Deaver had left his influential White House post just ten days earlier and was then in the process of setting up a private consulting firm in Washington, D.C.

A short time thereafter the Saudi Arabian government engaged the services of Michael K. Deaver and Associates, paying him $500,000 in 1986 in four quarterly installments of $125,000 each.[12] In early 1987, the Saudi's dropped their contract with Deaver, probably as a result of a criminal probe into his lobbying activities after he left government service. Dutton told the special prosecutor investigating Deaver's activities that "the former White House aide did no work for the Saudis" in return for the $500,000. And Randall J. Turk, Deaver's lawyer, when asked about Mr. Bamieh's allegations, said the Saudis "never approached him about anything like that."[13] Whether or not Deaver made any discreet inquiries or contacts on behalf of the Saudi Arabian government to try to persuade the U.S. government to change its mind about selling arms to Iran we will probably never know. But Deaver did get to keep the $500,000.

Besides Saudi Arabia there were two other nations deeply interested in arranging for the sale of U.S. arms and spare parts to Iran. The nation most interested, of course, was Iran. Although the leadership of post-1979 Iran called the United States an evil "Satan" and displayed unremitting hostility and bitterness in all their actions, they were quite practical when it came to the survival of their country. They had been attacked by Iraq and were now engaged in a fight for their lives, a fight that could hinge on whether or not they could buy U.S. arms and spare parts. They were desperate, ruthless men who saw no reason to stop at anything in their drive for survival and power. They believed deeply in Allah, the omnipotent God of Islam, surrendering themselves to God's will. And God's will in the 1980s seemed to clearly favor killing Iraqis and hating and despising Americans. But the Iranians found it difficult doing God's will without American weapons, and so set out deliberately to deal with the great American Satan, as Khomeini often referred to the United States, under terms one usually uses in dealing with the devil—you may do whatever is necessary to achieve what you need.

The third nation involved in the arms sale was Israel. This may seem strange because most observers see Iran as unremittingly hostile toward Israel. But Middle East politics is a strange business in strange lands. Israel is located on the northwestern tip of the Arabian Peninsula, tightly sandwiched between Syria and Egypt. The only reliable friend they have in the entire region is Saudi Arabia, and that is a friendship born more out of Saudi military weakness than of Saudi love and admiration for the Israelis.

Israel's situation was, and had been for many years, precarious and dangerous. Her actions in the Iran-Contra affair as it unfolded may seem strange, but they are much more understandable if we try to look at it from Israel's perspective. Think how Americans would react if they shared borders with a heavily armed Canada and Mexico and were subject to periodic military invasions and continual terrorist attacks from the north and the south. I suspect that what we would do in those circumstances would make anything the Israelis have done during the last twenty years look tame.

The United States embargo on the sale of weapons and spare parts to Iran was working remarkably well. By the summer of 1984, the Iranians seemed to be getting desperate, making repeated approaches to international arms merchants to get TOW missiles. They even tried the CIA. One of the top officials of the CIA testified to the president's investigating commission that by then the CIA was getting "30 to 40 requests per year from Iranians and Iranian exiles to provide us with very fancy intelligence, very important internal political insights, if we in return can arrange for the sale of a dozen Bell helicopter gunships or 1,000 TOW missiles or something else that is on the contraband list."[14]

The TOW antitank missile, known in the U.S. military as the BGM-71, is a small, deadly missile that can hit a tank up to two miles away, punching through the thick outside armor and turning the tank's interior into a fiery hell of ricocheting chunks of metal. A single TOW missile can slice and char the crew members of the tank beyond recognition. All tank crews fear it.

Throughout the world it is called a TOW missile, a curious name but a precise acronym for the words that describe how it works: tube-launched, optically-tracked, wire-guided. The missile launcher can be mounted on a truck or a jeep or—and this is what makes it so effective—it can be carried by a small group of men. The complete launcher weighs 172 pounds, but it can be broken down easily into five elements, none of which weighs more than fifty-three pounds. The missile is fired from a launching tube. It has two motors. The first motor quickly pops it out of the tube, and only then does the flight motor ignite. As anyone who has ever fired a hand-held missile will confirm, this is very important because it prevents the red-hot exhaust gases and propellant particles from burning and cutting up the face and hands of the person launching the missile. The gunner aims the missile with a high magnification optical sight, complete with the traditional cross hairs. While the missile is in flight it is connected to the launcher by two very strong, very thin wires. As the missile flies, the wires uncoil from two separate spools, and the gunner transmits any steering commands he has for the missile through those wires.

The TOW missile itself is only forty-six inches long and weighs just under forty pounds. There are two sets of four fins that jut out and girdle its six-inch diameter body, one set of flight fins at the tail of the projectile and one set right in the middle. The head of the missile is round and rather bulbous. In fact, it almost looks cute, like a giant toy. But it's no toy. It is a great equalizer on battlefields where tanks play a dominant role. A TOW missile launcher in the hands of a few infantrymen, on foot, has the power to destroy a multimillion dollar tank, in spite of the tank's armored walls and powerful guns.[15]

So, at the beginning of 1985 there were three countries in the Middle East with a real stake in changing the United States policy of not selling arms or spare parts to Iran. Iran wanted U.S. weapons and spare parts to press its war against Iraq. Israel and Saudi Arabia wanted to earn credit with Iran by helping to procure those weapons and parts, and Israel, in addition, had a longer-range goal of keeping the Iranians and Iraqis fighting.

At about this time the efforts of Iran, Israel, and Saudi Arabia received an unexpected ally in the person of Bill Casey. Many reasons could have persuaded Casey that his government's position of not selling arms to Iran was wrong. He may have agreed with the Israeli assessment that it would be in our best interests to prolong the war between Iran and Iraq, and that submitting to extortion was an acceptable way to deal with the clerical fascists of Iran. Casey was also deeply troubled by the imprisonment and torture of

William Buckley. In the best of health, Casey would have dealt with the devil if it meant he could rescue one of his men. For whatever combination of reasons, at the time of Buckley's kidnapping Casey decided to try to change U.S. policy on selling arms to Iran and paying ransom for American hostages.

Soon officials at the highest levels in the governments of Iran, Israel, Saudi Arabia, and the United States were embarked on a lobbying effort to reverse the United States policy that prohibited sales of U.S. arms and spare parts to Iran and urged other countries to do the same. Lobbying is defined as the "conduct of activities aimed at influencing public officials."[16] It is an old and honorable art, when practiced openly and domestically. But when practiced secretly, on an international scale, it can border on hostile, aggressive action.

A cabal is defined as a "number of persons secretly united to bring about an overturn or usurpation, especially in public affairs."[17] This particular cabal is reported to have begun "with a meeting between an Israeli official, two Israeli weapons dealers, and an Iranian arms merchant in late 1984."[18] The group met secretly and frequently throughout 1985 in various places in the world. From the testimony given to the President's Special Review Board and other sources, we know that from late 1984 through the end of 1985 there were at least thirteen meetings. Three took place in Germany, four in Israel, two in Washington, D.C., in the White House, and the rest were scattered around Europe—including Paris and London. The main powers always represented were Iran, Israel, and the United States.

The first meeting of the cabal with the United States present took place in January 1985. It met in Hamburg, West Germany, one of the world's largest seaports, a lusty, cosmopolitan city, cold and damp during the winter months—the temperature hovering about the freezing mark, a thick fog pouring in from the North Sea—with an average daily sunshine of only two hours. You don't see many tourists in Hamburg in January.

The countries represented at the meeting were: Iran—Manucher Ghorbanifar was an Iranian arms merchant with close ties to the highest levels of Ayatollah Khomeini's regime; Israel—Yaacov Nimrodi served for ten years as the Israeli defense attache in Tehran, Iran, in the days of the Shah. He is an Israeli arms merchant, and a close friend of the then prime minister of Israel, Shimon

Peres. Nimrodi also speaks Farsi, the language of Iran; Israel—
Adolph Schwimmer is a personal friend of and, since September
1984, a special adviser to Peres. He is also a wealthy arms merchant
and founded Israel Aircraft Industries;[19] Israel—Amiram Nir is a
high-ranking Israeli official, and an adviser to Peres, in charge of
Israel's counterterrorism programs; and the United States—Roy
Furmark is a businessman who lives in New York who was a close
friend and associate of William Casey for twenty years. Furmark
was a legal client of Casey's, knew him in business matters, and
had even attended the OSS reunion dinners that Casey liked so
much.[20]

A pattern of representation prevailed when the group met to
plot how to change U.S. policy. Usually five people attended—
one Iranian, three Israelis, and one American. At the core of the
cabal were three men—Ghorbanifar, Nimrodi, and Schwimmer. All
three were present at eleven of the thirteen meetings, while Nir
and Furmark were often replaced with other representatives from
Israel and the United States as the year wore on.

Most of those who attended that January 1985 meeting were
there for obvious reasons. Ghorbanifar represented the highest levels of the Iranian government who wanted U.S. arms. Nimrodi,
Schwimmer, and Nir represented the Israeli government who wanted
Iran to get U.S. arms. As Adnan Khashoggi later put it, "I did not
look at Nimrodi as a businessman. I looked at him as representing
the Israeli government in putting the package together."[21]

But how about Roy Furmark? Why was he there? And how did
he get invited? It would be rather unusual for a New York businessman, no matter how well connected internationally, to drop in
on a secret cabal plotting to change U.S. policy in a most sensitive
area. There seems to be only one plausible explanation—that Bill
Casey was not only aware of the meeting, but blessed it and sent
a personal, secret emissary. And if that is true, it means that Casey
was aware of the efforts to persuade the U.S. to sell military arms
to Iran almost a year before other high-ranking U.S. officials—Oliver
North and Robert McFarlane—became involved.

The key members of the group shared a common interest that
may have transcended their duties to the governments they represented. Many of them were international arms merchants, people
who made their living—and huge fortunes—by buying and selling
military weapons and spare parts for those weapons.

Thirteen Reported Meetings of the Middle East Cabal Held at Various Locations around the World during 1984–85 to Discuss the Sale of U.S. Weapons and Spare Parts to Iran[22]

1) Late 1984	*2) JAN 1985/***Hamburg**	*3) APRIL 1985/***Tel Aviv**
Ghorbanifer *(Iran)*	Ghorbanifar *(Iran)*	Ghorbanifar *(Iran)*
Nimrodi *(Israel)*	Nimrodi *(Israel)*	Nimrodi *(Israel)*
Schwimmer *(Israel)*	Schwimmer *(Israel)*	Ledeen *(U.S.)*
Kimche *(Israel)*	Nir *(Israel)*	
	Furmark *(U.S.)*	
*4) MAY 1985/***Hamburg**	*5) JUNE 1985/***Hamburg**	*6) JULY 1985/***Tel Aviv**
Ghorbanifar *(Iran)*	Ghorbanifar *(Iran)*	Ghorbanifar *(Iran)*
Khashoggi *(Saudi Ar)*	Nimrodi *(Israel)*	Nimrodi *(Israel)*
Furmark *(U.S.)*	Schwimmer *(Israel)*	Schwimmer *(Israel)*
	Kimche *(Israel)*	Kimche *(Israel)*
	Khashoggi *(Saudi Ar)*	Ledeen *(U.S.)*
*7) JULY 1985/***Tel Aviv**	*8) AUG 1985/***Israel**	*9) SEPT 1985/***Paris**
Ghorbanifar *(Iran)*	Ghorbanifar *(Iran)*	Ghorbanifar *(Iran)*
Nimrodi *(Israel)*	Nimrodi *(Israel)*	Nimrodi *(Israel)*
Schwimmer *(Israel)*	Schwimmer *(Israel)*	Schwimmer *(Israel)*
Nir *(Israel)*		Kimche *(Israel)*
Khashoggi *(Saudi Ar)*		Ledeen *(U.S.)*
Furmark *(U.S.)*		
*10) OCT 1985/***Europe**	*11) OCT 1985/***Wash. D.C.**	*12) NOV 1985/***Wash. D.C.**
Ghorbanifar *(Iran)*	Ghorbanifar *(Iran)*	Ghorbanifar *(Iran)*
Nimrodi *(Israel)*	Nimrodi *(Israel)*	Nimrodi *(Israel)*
Schwimmer *(Israel)*	Schwimmer *(Israel)*	Schwimmer *(Israel)*
Kimche *(Israel)*	Ledeen *(U.S.)*	Ledeen *(U.S.)*
Ledeen *(U.S.)*	North *(U.S.)*	

*13) DEC 1985/***London**

Ghorbanifar *(Iran)*	Kimche *(Israel)*
Nimrodi *(Israel)*	North *(U.S.)*
Schwimmer *(Israel)*	McFarlane *(U.S.)*
	Secord *(U.S.)*

If there are no arms sales there are no profits for arms merchants. Unless someone is selling to them and buying from them they cannot make money. Dealing privately in military weapons can be a quick way to make many millions of dollars, but like dealing in cocaine and heroin, it has certain risks and difficulties. Perhaps the most difficult part to becoming a successful international arms merchant is locating a reliable supply of high-quality weapons. Not just anyone can walk in off the street and buy weapons from the U.S. armory. If we could, perhaps even you and I could become millionaires quickly, for there seems to be no lack of demand for the powerful, accurate, high-quality weapons made in the United States. A successful arms merchant must keep one thing always foremost in his mind—he must have a reliable supplier of high-quality weapons. The demand will usually take care of itself.

As the deliberations of the cabal continued throughout the year they talked of many things—the need for a new relationship between Iran and the United States, the desirability of stopping terrorism, the necessity of obtaining the release of the American and other hostages, the need for peace in the Middle East, and the need to halt the Iran-Iraq war—but always, somehow, the answer to these urgent questions seemed to involve the sale of United States military weapons and spare parts to Iran.

By the time the cabal met again in late July, in one of Nimrodi's homes in Tel Aviv, Israel (apparently Nimrodi had many homes, including one in London where the cabal met later), the agenda was well advanced. The group included the original five plus Adnan Khashoggi. According to testimony Mr. Furmark gave to the Special Review Board (known as the Tower Commission because the chairman was Senator John Tower) established by President Reagan to investigate the Iran-Contra scandal, the participants at the July 1985 meeting in Tel Aviv discussed a program "to open up relations between the U.S. and Iran."[23] Furmark's recollection of some parts of the meeting are a trifle hazy, but it is clear that agreements were reached and the thrust of those agreements was to enable U.S. arms and spare parts, either from Israeli or U.S. stockpiles, to be sold to Iran. As Furmark put it, "The U.S. had agreed, the Israelis had agreed, the Iranians had agreed to do some business."[24]

Incredible. The U.S. had agreed? Who in the U.S.? Roy Furmark was the only American in the room. Did he agree, on his own, to commit to an Iranian and the Israelis representing the highest levels of their governments that the United States would condone the sales of U.S. weapons to Iran? Very unlikely.

Especially when just a few weeks earlier, back in Washington, Secretary of State Shultz and Secretary of Defense Weinberger had battled with Bill Casey over a similar plan. McFarlane had sent a draft memorandum spelling out a new policy that would allow the United States to sell arms to Iran. Casey strongly supported the idea, writing, "I strongly support the thrust of the draft."[25] Shultz and Weinberger objected very strongly. Shultz said it was contrary "to our interest." Weinberger was less polite, saying that "this is roughly like inviting Qadhafi over for a cozy lunch."[26] Shultz and Weinberger won the day, or so they thought. McFarlane reported to them that the idea was dead. That is, until Furmark's secret trip to Tel Aviv in July 1985.

The cabal ran into one hitch at the meeting and it soon became clear why Khashoggi was invited to attend. According to Furmark, "Nobody would trust each other. The Iranians would not pay for anything until they received and inspected the goods. . . . And of course the Israelis would not send anything until they were paid in advance. So now you had a stalemate. Khashoggi then said, 'Well, I will trust the Iranians, I'll trust the Israelis, I'll trust the Americans, I'll put the money up.' So the first transaction I understand was a million dollar transaction which he deposited into a numbered account which the Israelis told him to put the money in."[27]

So, in effect, King Fahd's man put up the money necessary to make the U.S. arms and spare parts begin to flow to Iran.

During the latter half of 1985 the group met frequently to sort out the problems that can arise in any secret, complex activity like this. Furmark apparently attended no more meetings after July, being replaced as the American representative by Michael Ledeen, a consultant to the National Security Council and close associate of Robert McFarlane. Ledeen was a typical young, impecunious scholar at the Center for Strategic Studies in Washington, D.C., before he became acquainted with Alexander Haig, who then invited him to join his personal staff when he became secretary of state. Ledeen reported directly to McFarlane, then counsellor to the State Department. Ledeen eventually left the State Department but his friendship and association with McFarlane continued after Mc-Farlane became President Reagan's third national security adviser. Toward the end of 1985, Ledeen's place at the cabal meetings was taken by Oliver North, one of McFarlane's key deputies on the National Security Council staff, and General Richard Secord, a retired military officer recommended by Bill Casey. Secord was an American arms merchant, in partnership with a fellow named Albert Hakim, an Iranian-American, an experienced international arms merchant.

But the Iranian and Israeli presence was constant and steady.

Ghorbanifar attended each and every one of the thirteen meetings, traveling at considerable cost—in terms of time, money, and personal effort—to the far corners of the globe. Nimrodi and Schwimmer rarely missed a meeting. Together, the three of them—Ghorbanifar, Nimrodi, and Schwimmer—must be considered the hard core of the cabal. But the key person, the prime mover, was Manucher Ghorbanifar. As Michael Ledeen testified later, "Ghorbanifar is really the driving force behind this whole thing. I mean, one can speculate about Americans and Israelis, but it is clear that the guy really—I mean, these ideas did not come either from the Government of the United States or the Government of Israel or arms merchants. These ideas came from Ghorbanifar. He was the person who introduced them. He was the one who put them forward, and he was the one who claimed to have the capacity to achieve them." [28]

That, in itself, is not surprising. A smart, clever Iranian pushing something that is in the vital interests of Iran. But what is surprising is that all those listening, all those who participated in the cabal, did not understand precisely what he was up to. Besides, Ghorbanifar was not a subtle man. Once when asked how he dealt with people who crossed him he replied menacingly, "People betray me, I betray them. People are honest with me, I give them everything; if not, I cut their throat." [29]

But he was a suspicious man, an Iranian citizen living in France, in his mid- to late-fifties, very wealthy. He was reported to have been an agent of SAVAK, the former Shah of Iran's secret police force. And he had strong, powerful connections to the revolutionary dictatorship of the Ayatollah Khomeini. [30]

In other words, in addition to being an international arms dealer, Ghorbanifar was almost certainly a secret agent of the new revolutionary regime in Iran. Yet that thought never seemed to dawn on any of the Americans. When Michael Ledeen described how "Mr. Ghorbanifar picked up the telephone, dialed the private number of the Iranian prime minister, and spoke to him as only a close confidant can," it was with a tone of reverence and awe. [31] Did it not occur to them that there might be a very good reason why Ghorbanifar had such easy access to high Iranian officials, that he could in fact be one of them, not just a simple businessman in happy pursuit of profit?

If Ghorbanifar was the spark plug of the operation, the Israelis were surely the engine and tires. In addition to Nimrodi and Schwimmer, either Amiram Nir, Israel's chief of counterterrorism, or David Kimche, a former Israeli intelligence officer who was then serving as director general of the Israeli Foreign Ministry[32] and was a close friend of Robert McFarlane, attended eight of the thirteen meetings. There were at least two, and usually three, Israelis at every meeting of the cabal, more than enough to dominate the flow of discussion and the likely conclusions.

Saudi Arabia was a relatively minor player in the whole affair. They had no real military power, only lots of oil money, and were evidently only brought into the picture when their cash was needed. Khashoggi claims to have lost $10 million dollars on the deal. Truth-telling is not his strong suit, but on this issue he may just be telling it straight.

The real lambs in the whole affair were the Americans. Reports of the cabal's meetings indicate that at times the American representatives were almost innocent bystanders, impressionable and gullible. Furmark seems to have just listened and absorbed and reported back everything that occurred. Ledeen, who attended six of the meetings, seemed to be particularly smitten with Ghorbanifar, the Iranian wolf. While McFarlane finally came to the conclusion that Ghorbanifar was "the most despicable creature he ever met," and General Richard Secord considered him "a vulgar con man,"[33] Michael Ledeen, who met with Ghorbanifar upwards of thirty times, was a real fan, describing him to the CIA as a "wonderful man. . . . almost too good to be true."[34]

With Furmark and Ledeen carrying the ball for the United States in the early meetings of the cabal against the Iranian-Israeli wolf pack of Ghorbanifar, Nimrodi, Schwimmer, Nir, and Kimche, it's lucky the United States didn't end up selling Iran an atomic bomb or two.

The meetings of the cabal were unusual meetings.

The men who attended were unusual men. Most of them were fairly old, in their fifties or sixties, wealthy almost beyond belief, worldly, sophisticated men with many powerful and wealthy friends like themselves. The chief occupation of the core group that attended the meetings was international arms merchant, a demanding profession with no textbooks, and few rules to guide the players.

My personal experience with powerful, wealthy men is that they rarely do anything idly or act on whim. They are driven, terribly hardworking people and, as they enter the twilight of their lives and realize they may only live for another ten or, if they are very lucky, perhaps twenty years, they become passionately jealous of their time. Time becomes the new coin of their realm, far more valuable than money and possessions. Time is the one thing their wealth and power cannot buy.

Yet these men of the cabal, at the peak of their careers, met regularly and systematically throughout the world. Counting travel and preparation, each trip took at least two days of their time, some perhaps more. The cost of the Concorde air travel tickets, and the luxurious hotels, and whatever other expenses they incurred scarcely would be noticed by them. But the time it cost them was noticed.

They always met in secret. The fact of their meetings and the purpose of those meetings was not announced to the world. And when they traveled to their rendezvous, they did not travel as care-free, independent businessmen with a yen to do good for others in the world. No, they traveled as de facto agents of national pow-ers—as the agents of Iran, Israel, Saudi Arabia, and the United States.

The record of their meetings that has so far come to light clearly indicates that they considered what they were about was a matter of great importance and urgency. Besides the plenary meetings we know about, there is evidence that many of them did a great deal of work preparing for the meetings, some even preparing memo-randa as long as fifty pages. We don't know how many telephone calls they made to each other, how many letters they exchanged, or how many other people they contacted in their quest.

What we do know is that this was no idle venture. They were embarked on deadly serious business. And they succeeded.

It was no contest. Soon some of the most powerful, wealthy, wily forces in the world—the mullahs of Iran, the Saudi royal fam-ily, the Israeli government backed by the Mossad, perhaps the best intelligence agency in the world, and a half-dozen smart, rich, and ruthless arms merchants—had massed together and pooled their talents and resources for an assault on the policy that proscribed the sales of U.S. military weapons and spare parts to Iran. Carefully gauging their target, they homed in on Reagan's White House, the point of maximum leverage for a change in national policy. More specifically, they focused on the key advisers to the president in this area of foreign policy—on the national security adviser, first

Robert McFarlane, and when he left in December 1985, John Poindexter, McFarlane's replacement, and on the key deputies of the national security adviser, the staff who gathered the information and wrote the memoranda on which decisions were based.

First Ledeen, and then North, and then McFarlane and Poindexter fell to the blandishments and false promises and dubious reasoning of the Middle East cabal. Iran, Saudi Arabia, and Israel working from the outside, combined with Bill Casey working from the inside, were a powerful and effective lobbying force. Shultz and Weinberger objected consistently, to the end. But Vice President Bush, and finally Donald Regan, raised no objections to the proposed change in policy and soon Oliver North was enthusiastically following Casey's instructions, most of the time with the blessings of McFarlane and then Poindexter.

Soon the U.S. arms and spare parts were flowing to Iran, first from Israeli stockpiles, and later direct from armories in the United States. Some American hostages were released, and some more were taken, so the number being held during the Iran-Contra fiasco stayed relatively constant. The arms merchants made millions of dollars. And the Reagan administration was shaken to its foundations.

One of the most sacred duties an adviser to the president has is to give the president accurate, timely, balanced information on which to base decisions. The aide must be especially wary not to allow himself or herself to be used by anyone. Many subtle and powerful pressures are brought to bear on White House aides. What some of them fail to understand is that when most people deal with a White House aide they don't see a person at all. What they see is a clear pane of glass, and, on the other side, the president, the man with the power to do what they want, whatever that happens to be at the time. People will go to great lengths to influence a presidential decision, and if that means that they have to bamboozle a White House aide then many of them will try to do just that. The rewards for successful bamboozling are great.

If any of Reagan's older, more politically sophisticated staff members—Richard Allen, James Baker, William Clark, Michael Deaver, Edwin Meese—had remained at the White House, the Iran-Contra affair almost certainly would have been nipped early in the bud. But by 1985 the old guard was gone, and the new guard just wasn't up to coping with the wolf pack from the Middle East.

Chapter Thirty

THE IRAN-CONTRA GAMES

By the beginning of 1986, the sixth year of Ronald Reagan's presidency, there was a dangerous witches' brew bubbling and boiling in the foreign policy cauldron. President Reagan and most of his key advisers were serenely unaware of the poisonous potion cooking deep in the bowels of the bureaucracy.

All these ingredients simmered through 1986, finally exploding into a major scandal in late November. The parts of the scandal that received the most media attention—the juicy financial intricacies of international arms deals, the possibility of personal corruption, and the endless speculation of what the president knew and when he knew it—were the predictable fallout of the powerful forces put into play years earlier. Once the U.S. arms spigot to Iran was opened, the rest of the events flowed naturally.

Two of the most powerful motivating forces known to man— survival and self-interest, the fear of being conquered by foreigners and the desire for great wealth—merged into a powerful battering ram of persuasion and deception aimed straight at the foreign policy door of the Reagan White House.

A few hard thumps and the door splintered open.

There were two major parts to the Iran-Contra affair. The Iran part was President Reagan's decision to break a long-standing U.S. policy not to sell military weapons to Iran, and especially not to do so in a way that clearly implied the paying of ransom for American hostages held by terrorist groups in the Middle East. This was a policy error that established the groundwork for the rest of the scandal.

The second part of the Iran-Contra affair, the Contra part, was a side effect of the arms sales to Iran, but it was potentially more serious, not in terms of policy but rather in terms of lawbreaking. The charge in general was that high-ranking members of the Reagan administration deliberately set out to circumvent, and may in fact have broken, the law which forbade military aid to the Contras of Nicaragua. The potentially most serious charge of all was that President Reagan knew of, and perhaps ordered, the diversion of money made on the sale of U.S. weapons to Iran to the freedom fighters of Nicaragua. Both President Reagan and many high-ranking members of his administration were under suspicion of breaking the law. That is very serious business.

Breaking the U.S. embargo on arms sales to Iran came in steps. The first step was to get the United States to condone the sale of U.S. arms that Israel purchased earlier and had in her armories. In July 1985, while President Reagan was in the hospital recovering from an operation, Robert McFarlane briefed him on the Israeli proposal. Reagan agreed to explore contacts with Iran but said no to arms sales. On August 6, 1985, President Reagan met with his foreign policy directorate in the White House residence. McFarlane again briefed the president on the Israeli proposal. All the United States was being asked to do was to replenish the arms Israel sold to Iran. In return, four American hostages would be released, and because it would be done secretly, the United States could deny knowledge of the entire transaction.[1]

According to later testimony by McFarlane, those who supported the plan included Vice President Bush, William Casey, and Donald Regan. Shultz and Weinberger continued to oppose the Israeli sale. President Reagan did not make a decision at this meeting.

Then on August 30, 1985, three weeks later, the weapons began to flow. Israel shipped 508 U.S. TOW antitank missiles to Iran. After the fact, President Reagan approved the sale and authorized the United States to sell TOW missiles to Israel to replenish their stockpile. It is not clear whether or not he also explicitly approved the sale before it happened. According to McFarlane, sometime in August after the August 6th meeting, President Reagan gave oral approval. Later, Reagan could not recall doing so, saying, "I cannot recall anything whatsoever about whether I approved an Israeli sale in advance or whether I approved replenishment of Israeli stocks around August of 1985. My answer, therefore, and the simple truth is, 'I don't remember—period.' " But he also added that he was surprised the Israelis shipped arms to Iran, and that this led him to doubt that he had ever given approval in the first place.[2]

In any event, a huge crack in the U.S. embargo on arms to Iran opened up. Other arms shipments to Iran from Israel followed, but the real prize sought was to get the United States to ship arms directly. On January 7, 1986, a crucial meeting was held in the Oval Office. New proposals had been put forth by Amiram Nir and Ghorbanifar to trade U.S. arms for American hostages. One plan called for the United States to sell 2,000 more TOW antitank missiles to Iran. Reagan's entire foreign policy directorate—Bush, Casey, Shultz, Weinberger, Regan, McFarlane, and Poindexter (who had just taken over from McFarlane)—was there. Attorney General Edwin Meese joined the group to give his legal opinion on the proposed action. Bill Casey and John Poindexter argued strongly for the plan. Shultz and Weinberger once again opposed the whole idea. But Vice President Bush and Donald Regan raised no objections, and Edwin Meese, on what he later called a "51–49 decision" also reluctantly went along.[3]

President Reagan was obviously torn. He wanted the American hostages back, he wanted to do everything he could to reestablish a sensible relationship with Iran in the hopes it would help put an end to the Iran-Iraq war, then in its sixth year, and he wanted to reduce the vicious terrorism that continued unabated. But he knew it was wrong to sell U.S. arms to Iran, effectively paying ransom for the hostages. When the meeting ended, President Reagan had not settled the issue one way or the other. He did not approve the sale of arms, but on the other hand he did not shut the initiative down either.

Ten days later he did make a final decision. On January 17, 1986, President Reagan personally signed a finding which for the first time authorized the sale and, in addition, directed that it be carried out in the utmost secrecy to the extent that not even the U.S. Congress was to be informed. A finding is a provision in U.S. law that, in effect, allows the president to exempt himself temporarily from laws passed by Congress. When Congress earlier passed laws severely restricting the power of the president to act in many areas of foreign policy, particularly on covert activities, it added a small proviso allowing the president some flexibility. He could, if he himself determined it to be in the interests of our national security, act without telling the Congress. All he had to do was put it in writing and later notify Congress of what he had done in a timely manner. There are times when a president must act quickly in the interest of national security, so the ability for him to make such findings allows him to act now and tell Congress later. The ability to make a finding also makes it possible for a president to effectively not inform Congress, simply by delaying indefinitely his timely notification.

This is, in fact, what happened. Whether it was done deliberately or inadvertently, the timely notification stretched on for weeks and then months, and when the scandal broke in late November 1986 Congress still had not been notified. Congress was not amused when they did find out and this small omission may have contributed to the zeal of their subsequent investigation as much as anything else. Consequently, that particular loophole was plugged in 1987. A president may still sign findings in national security emergencies but now has agreed to report to Congress within forty-eight hours.

After President Reagan signed the finding authorizing the sale, the arms shipments increased. On February 16, 1986, the United States shipped 1,000 TOW antitank missiles to Iran. In late May 1986, McFarlane even traveled to Iran with plane loads of weapons in a futile effort to try to trade them for more hostages. In September 1986 McFarlane made a second trip to Iran, bringing with him twenty-three tons of U.S. weapons.

In return an American hostage or two was released every now and then, usually after a major arms shipment. That was the good news. The bad news was that the clever terrorists usually picked up a new hostage or two to keep things even. After playing the ransom-hostage game with Iran and her terrorist friends, there were still nine American hostages held captive in the Middle East in the summer of 1987, three *more* hostages than when the first shipment of U.S. TOW antitank missiles was sent in August 1985.[4]

As soon as Iran realized how highly we valued getting those hostages back, they apparently kept a good supply of hostages to ensure we would do their bidding. After a time some American officials even feared stopping the flow of U.S. arms to Iran because it might endanger the lives of the hostages currently held. It was a classic demonstration of the futility and stupidity of dealing with kidnappers and terrorists. When we acceded to their demands we only earned their scorn, and rightfully so.

On the other hand Iran succeeded in buying a lot of U.S. weapons and spare parts needed to ply its war against Iraq. Saudi Arabia and Israel gained favor with Iran for helping make all this happen. And the international arms dealers were getting richer and richer. Where the whole Iran arms sales fiasco would have gone if it was not exposed in early November 1986 is unknown, but there was no end to the Iranians' appetite for our hostages and our weapons, and no shortage of international arms dealers willing and able to help.

The use of international arms dealers was absolutely necessary to make the scheme work but it was also the element that eventually brought the whole plan crashing down on the Reagan administration. The arms dealers were necessary because the countries involved did retain a certain residual amount of propriety. Iran wasn't about to buy directly from the United States government, and the United States wasn't about to sell directly to the Iranian government. Instead they agreed to sell and buy secretly from third, private parties. This method of operating through a middleman made it easier to keep the sales secret and allowed for some degree of deniability if the secret was found out.

But operating through private international arms dealers created a different kind of problem. Once the arms dealer had possession of the U.S. weapons he was free to set any price the market would bear. In the case of Iran, the need was desperate; they were willing to pay almost any price, and Iran was charged a terrific premium for the weapons she received. For example, Iran was charged $10,000 for TOW antitank missiles that the United States priced for sale at $3,500.[5] A $6,500 profit per missile is almost a 200 percent markup, high even for an international arms dealer. The price differential produced enormous profits. Those huge profits soon led to envy and other temptations.

The entire U.S.-Iran arms sales operation was engineered primarily by four arms dealers—one from Iran (Ghorbanifar), two from Israel (Nimrodi and Schwimmer), and one from Saudi Arabia (Khashoggi)—and in the beginning they had all the action. However, as events developed, the Americans decided to use their own arms dealers. The obvious reason was to get a greater degree of control of the enormous profits that were being made. The new arms dealers that the Americans began to shift the business to were General Richard Secord, a native-born American who had substantial experience in weapons dealing, and Albert Hakim, a naturalized American citizen born and raised in Iran who had many years of trading experience in the Middle East.

As the shift was made, the previous arms dealers from Saudi Arabia and Israel were understandably annoyed. They had gone to a great deal of trouble in terms of time and effort—and spent a lot of money—to get this operation going. Being cut out just when things were looking quite profitable did not please them at all. Some speculate that the secret arms sales were revealed as an act of revenge. We don't know if that is true or not, but there certainly was provocation.

The huge profits generated by the arms sales also drew the attention of some American officials who did not hope to profit personally from them, but who had a problem those arms sales profits could help. Almost halfway around the world from Iran, down in Latin America, the United States had a very troublesome foreign policy problem with Nicaragua. A communist regime forcibly took power and was rapidly developing strong and friendly ties to the Soviet Union. Worse, Nicaragua was arming itself with billions of dollars of Soviet weapons, and was rapidly becoming a source of all kinds of trouble very close to our shores and borders. We already had one Soviet semi-satellite—Cuba—armed to the teeth just 90 miles off the coast of Florida. President Reagan did not want to let another Soviet semi-satellite develop on his watch.

The one hopeful sign in Nicaragua was a group of rebels who went into the hills and launched a guerrilla war against the new communist dictatorship. The guerrillas were popularly known by those who liked them as the Freedom Fighters and by everyone else as the Contras, because they were against the current government. An intense debate developed in the United States over whether or not we should aid these guerrilla fighters in their fight for freedom against the communists. President Reagan was solidly on the rebels' side, proudly calling them Freedom Fighters and likening them to the revolutionary soldiers who won our freedom from England. Reagan and most of the Republicans in Congress wanted to send them economic and military aid.

Others weren't so sure. They weren't sure of the guerrillas, suspecting them of not being too fussy about human rights as they went about their struggle. They weren't sure that the new communist government of Nicaragua was all that bad. And they weren't sure that our help wouldn't eventually lead to American troops fighting down there. The debate went on and on, and by 1985 it was pretty much a draw. Some economic and military aid went grudgingly to the Contras, but not much. By 1985 all military aid was cut off and the prospects for more were small.

This did not please the president's men who were responsible for our Nicaraguan policy. They knew how strongly President Reagan felt about helping the Contras, but they had little power to do what he wanted. The legislation that cut off military aid to the Contras was sponsored by Congressman Boland and henceforth was known as the Boland Amendment.

There was no mention of private aid or help to the Contras, or for that matter the communist government of Nicaragua, but it was very clear that it was the will of Congress that no military resources be used to help the Contras in their battle for freedom. We will argue for years as to who was right in this debate, but one fact is beyond argument: President Reagan and the Republican party suffered an important foreign policy defeat when the Boland Amendment was passed. The policy of the Democrats prevailed as the official policy of the United States.

Some have argued that the Boland Amendment is unconstitutional, that it unfairly and unwisely restricts the power of the president to conduct foreign policy. That is part of an old and enduring argument in the United States about the relative powers of the president and Congress in the conduct of foreign affairs. The basic argument is that the president has special prerogatives in the making of foreign policy, that he should not be unduly restrained by Congress, if at all, and that the Constitution gives him these powers. Whenever there are arguments about what the Constitution of the United States means, it is often helpful to read it. Very few people actually do read it and it is too bad, for the founding fathers wrote with a grace and precision of language rarely found today.

The Constitution is particularly instructive in the area of foreign policy. Written in the summer of 1787, the writers could scarcely have imagined the world of nuclear superpowers and terrorist states that we live with today. Yet they are very clear on the prerogatives and powers of Congress in relationship to the chief executive, the president. When the founding fathers wrote the Constitution they had a healthy and wise distrust of *any* chief executive.

By the words of the Constitution, Congress, not the president, was given the power to:

- Regulate commerce with foreign nations.
- Define and punish piracies and felonies committed on the high seas, and offences against the law of nations.
- Declare war and make rules concerning captures on land and water.
- Raise and support armies.
- Provide and maintain a navy.
- Make rules for the government and regulation of the land and naval forces.
- Provide for calling forth the militia.
- Ratify all foreign treaties.
- Veto ambassadors to foreign countries.
- Appropriate money from the treasury.

They didn't leave the president out of it all together. The Constitution names him the commander-in-chief of the army and the navy, and gives him the "power, by and with the advice and consent of the Senate, to make treaties," provided two-thirds of the senators present concur. He also gets to nominate, "and by and with the advice and consent of the Senate," to appoint ambassadors to foreign countries.

And that's it.

Rather than giving the president special prerogatives in the foreign policy area, the Constitution does just the opposite. It hands the real reins of power—armies and money—to the Congress.

The president is preeminent in the field of foreign policy when it comes to talking. He speaks for the United States. But when it comes to fighting, Congress takes over. The enormous military power of the United States—the power of billions of dollars and sophisticated, powerful weapons and millions of combat-ready troops—has never been entrusted to the whims of any president, no matter how beloved or trusted.

The actions of Congress may be frustrating, maddening, and at times, even angering. But the alternative of a powerless Congress is worse. For it is only a powerful, cantankerous Congress that shields our constitutional republic from the power lunges of a chief executive and his unelected staff.

That isn't how President Reagan and his chief foreign policy advisers saw it when Congress, controlled by the Democratic party, effectively cut off aid to the Contras in late 1984. They were outraged, convinced the Democrats were badly mistaken, even morally wrong. How could you not support people fighting for their freedom? Stymied by congressional Democrats, they did not give up on the Contras, but explored other ways to help and soon money and supplies were pouring in from other foreign countries and from private donations in the United States. This activity was legal, but it was time-consuming and frustrating. Asking other countries for help was referred to in private as tin-cup diplomacy, and every effort was made to keep the contributions secret. The two countries that provided the most help secretly to the Contras were Saudi Arabia ($25 to $30 million) and Brunei ($10 million). Taiwan and South Africa provided a smaller amount of assistance.

Trying to keep the cause of the Contras alive was very frustrating for the people who worked closest to the president and knew how deeply he cared about them. Like all good presidential advisers they wanted to please their boss. Most of them understood when the president said he wanted them to "do anything they could" to help the Contras that he meant anything that was ethical and lawful. A few presidential advisers apparently got carried away with their desire to please the president, and crossed over the ethical and legal line that spelled political disaster.

Here's how it happened. With the CIA, the Defense Department, and the State Department prohibited from giving military aid to the Contras, the basic responsibility for doing what could be done fell to the National Security Council staff in the White House. First Robert McFarlane and then John Poindexter took on the seemingly impossible task of aiding a revolutionary army over 2,000 miles away in the jungles of Central America. They also had many other things to do, so the task was largely delegated to a young Marine lieutenant colonel, Oliver (Ollie) North.

North was an American success story. His parents were not wealthy or well-connected, but North—entirely by his own effort—eventually propelled himself up into the higher levels of the National Security Council staff in the White House. He was born in 1943 in Texas, but grew up in a small town in northern New York. He was not a noted scholar, but he was very determined. In 1963 he was admitted to the United States Naval Academy at Annapolis, Maryland. Though he was not a big man (only 5'9" and 147 pounds), he fought his way to the Naval Academy's middleweight boxing championship, demolishing more skilled fighters by simply bludgeoning them into submission.

North graduated from the Naval Academy in 1968, got married, went on his honeymoon, and then shipped out to fight in Vietnam. He was only there for eleven months, but came back with the Silver Star, a Bronze Star with a V for valor (the nation's third and fourth highest combat medals), and two Purple Hearts.[6]

When he returned from Vietnam, an American war hero still only in his late twenties, he plunged into a career as a Marine Corps officer. There his meteoric rise came to an end and he spent the next ten years or so moving slowly through the ranks, finally earning promotion to major and a post at the Naval War College in Newport, Rhode Island.

It was during this decade in the career belly of the Marine Corps, in December 1974 while he was on active duty in Okinawa, that Oliver North was admitted to the Bethesda Naval Medical Center and hospitalized for ten days. He was reportedly suffering from emotional distress. According to one report, never denied, North was "babbling incoherently and running around naked, waving a .45 caliber pistol."[7] We do not know the exact nature of his mental problems, only that they were serious enough to require hospitalization for ten days. The record of North's hospitalization for emotional distress was later secretly removed from his military files, reportedly by General Richard C. Schulze,[8] an extraordinary and probably illegal act on the part of the general. This was a critical factor in North's later advance on up through the ranks of the National Security Council staff. If his hospitalization had been known, he almost certainly never would have been promoted to the sensitive, highly demanding position he eventually held. In fact, former national security adviser Richard Allen said later that he would never have hired North in the first place had he known about his previous record of hospitalization for mental problems.[9]

In 1981 Oliver North was thirty-eight years old and moving on a very slow career path in the Marine Corps. The old hero days of Vietnam faded into memories and he was getting close to the point where many young officers have to decide whether they have a chance of making it to the top of their service. And then suddenly North managed to extricate himself from the dull posting in Rhode Island. Somehow he managed to catch "the attention of Navy Secretary John Lehman, who was impressed by a paper the young major wrote about the uses of the modern battleship. Lehman recommended North to National Security Adviser Richard Allen, who hired him for the NSC's Defense Policy Staff."[10]

It is a custom for the national security adviser to bring several young military officers into the White House staff as military aides. As Richard Allen said later, North's main job was "to handle easels and carry the charts."[11] He was quite surprised at North's later transformation into an important national security adviser to the president.

Allen underestimated Oliver North's ability to thrive in the world of White House aides. North obviously recognized he had a very rare opportunity, and he took every advantage of it. He worked incredibly long hours, took on difficult, dreary assignments that others avoided, and carefully followed orders. Soon he was indispensable. By 1985 the young major was promoted to lieutenant colonel, had his own office and secretary, and had survived three different national security advisers. He became a major player in many of the most sensitive and important activities of the National Security Council staff. He helped coordinate the United States plans for the 1983 invasion of Grenada, played a major role in freeing the hostages taken when TWA Flight 847 was hijacked in Beirut, Lebanon, and directed the capture of the terrorist hijackers of the Italian cruise ship, the *Achille Lauro*. He even helped select the targets when U.S. warplanes bombed Libya in retaliation for one of Khadaffi's more provocative acts of terrorism, the bombing of a German nightclub that killed American servicemen.[12]

In addition to all that and the countless other tasks that came across his desk, he also had the prime responsibility for directing the efforts of the United States to help the Contra forces in Nicaragua. It was a task that fell to North by default. North noted the president's keen interest in the Contras and soon was embarked on a wide range of activities to help them. He spoke to private fundraising groups, hoping to induce them to contribute money. He met with the Contra leaders, assuring them of the president's support and offering them moral support and whatever help he could within the limits of the law, and sometimes help that exceeded those limits. He put the Contras in touch with private U.S. citizens who gave them large sums of money. He requested and got highly classified CIA reports and maps of the battleground in Nicaragua and then secretly gave this intelligence to the Contras. Soon he was known in Latin America as the "Comandante." All this he did in addition to his other duties.

But North was only one man, and he was stretched very thin. Soon he was busily recruiting others to help oversee and operate his rapidly growing operation. Because of the restrictions of the Boland Amendment, it was necessary for him to conduct his activities through so-called private citizens, people who by the letter of the law were not government employees, but who would act and function and report to him as if they were his private employees. To make this elaborate charade work, he recruited two key lieutenants: General Richard Secord and Albert Hakim.

These two American arms dealers were soon happily at work, buying and selling weapons and using part of the proceeds to funnel weapons and other military aid to the Contras. Only a small pecentage of their profits were spent on the Contras, but even this small percentage accounted for millions of dollars in aid.

One of the most intriguing things that North did was to establish his own worldwide communications network—secret and totally secure. From virtually anywhere in the world—from Nicaragua or Honduras, from Europe or the Middle East, from any part of the United States—his colleagues and coconspirators could send messages to one another in unbreakable code. To accomplish this, North commandeered fifteen of America's most sophisticated, very secret communications devices from the National Security Agency. The machine was called a KL-43. North blithely distributed them to his partners in the covert activities, in spite of the fact that few of them possessed the necessary security clearances to use them.

The KL-43 is actually a small, commercially available personal computer made by the GRiD Systems Corporation that has been fitted with a special, super-secret encryption chip. Encased in solid black magnesium, it's a little over a foot square and only two inches thick, and has an unusual plasma screen, which folds out, displaying vivid, bright orange letters against a black background. It's an elegant piece of equipment that anyone with several thousand dollars can own—minus the encryption chip, of course.

In its full flower North's operation was spectacular. From his command post on the third floor of the Old Executive Office Building, he directed a worldwide network of operations—everything from his own private war in Nicaragua to secretly engineering the sale of U.S. weapons to Iran. Because of his close personal association with Bill Casey, who at times seemed to treat North, who was more than thirty years younger, as a son, he had access to virtually all the resources of the intelligence community. Through the business enterprises of Hakim and Secord he had airplanes, weapons, and even his own oceangoing ship. His status inside the White House was rising. He was not a senior adviser to President Reagan but, like several hundred other White House aides at his level, he did meet once or twice a month with the president directly. There were always a half-dozen or more people in the room when he met with Reagan, but he did get to meet with him face to face, one of the ultimate tests of status and power in any White House. By early 1986 he was flying high. Even his office location was better. Instead of being on an inner corridor across from the men's room, he was now operating out of a suite of offices with a grand view of the Washington Monument.

Then temptation seems to have struck, a temptation so delicious and desirable that he apparently could not resist it. It would lead to his ruin. The temptation was money, the lure of the ages.

It happened when two of North's many operations were joined together—the effort to sell U.S. arms to Iran and the effort to provide military help to the Contras. The arms sale provided substantial profits to the two American arms dealers reporting to North. The smarmy Hakim and the blustering Secord made a formidable pair. The enterprise, as they liked to call their collection of businesses, was thriving and producing millions of dollars in profits. While technically and legally the profits probably belonged to Hakim and Secord, the spirit of their understanding with North and his boss, John Poindexter, and Bill Casey, was such that North and Poindexter and Casey tended to treat some of those profits as *government* funds, not the private monies of Hakim and Secord.

On the other hand, the effort to provide military help to the Contras had fallen on very rough times. Congress had stopped the flow of government funds and North soon discovered that raising a few million dollars through private donations was a time-consuming, frustrating process. The Contras were desperately short of all kinds of supplies—guns, medicine, food, ammunition—and there was not enough money to replenish them.

So as 1985 ended and 1986 began, one of North's secret operations—selling U.S. arms to Iran—was generating a substantial surplus of cash, while another one—aiding the Contras—was desperately short of cash. It was just a matter of time before someone would come up with the idea of putting the two operations together. Why not use the money made by one operation to fund the expenses of the other? Why not? Why not take the profits from selling U.S. arms to Iran and spend it on weapons and other supplies for the Contras in Nicaragua?

It was such a simple idea, such a brilliant solution to the vexing problems caused by political opposition in Congress, that it is curious nobody thought of it sooner. But no one did. In fact, the idea never did occur to Oliver North, or John Poindexter, or Robert McFarlane, or even William Casey. No, the idea seems to have come from a smarter, more clever source—Amiram Nir, the senior adviser to the prime minister of Israel, the man in charge of Israel's quite effective counterterrorism program, and one of the more active members of the Middle East cabal.

On January 2, 1986—two months after PFIAB was purged, a few days after McFarlane left and Poindexter took his place, and two weeks before President Reagan signed the finding authorizing the sale of U.S. arms to Iran—Amiram Nir came to Washington, D.C., and met personally with John Poindexter and Oliver North in the White House. Poindexter had just assumed, over the holidays, a job with awesome, difficult responsibilities. The demands on his time that January 2 must have been very high, so it is not unreasonable to conclude that he considered Amiram Nir an important visitor. In any event, it turned out to be a fateful visit.

At the meeting with Poindexter and North, Nir reportedly proposed "a fresh start to the Iran initiative, minus Nimrodi and Schwimmer."[13] That was interesting. Others were trying to oust Ghorbanifar and Khashoggi, two of the original arms dealers, from the operation, and now Nir, one of Israel's highest officials, recommended dropping the two Israeli arms dealers. I can't think of anything more certain to cause trouble than to cut out of some potentially very profitable arms deals the very same four Middle Eastern arms dealers who made the whole thing possible in the first place. It could make them very, very mad. But that wasn't Nir's most explosive suggestion. Nir is reported to have suggested to North that the "Iranians could be overcharged for U.S. weapons and that the profits be funneled to the . . . Contras in Nicaragua." Israel strongly denied these allegations.[14] Later, North changed his recollection of who first gave him the idea of using the arms sales money to fund the Contras, maintaining in testimony in July 1987 that he got the idea from Manucher Ghorbanifar, "somewhere in Europe, probably," at a meeting in a bathroom.[15] Ghorbanifar is not a shy man who shrinks from taking credit, but this was apparently one credit too many and he quickly denounced North's statement as a lie.

"Imagine it!" the arms dealer protested. "I'm supposed to have taken a man who is chief of operations for the National Security Council and said, 'Come to the bathroom, screw me, overcharge for the weapons, finish me in Iran, and then send the money to your friends, the Contras.' Honest to God, this is the biggest joke I have ever heard in my life. I was never alone with him."[16]

Regardless of who suggested the idea, it was irresistible. We might be forced to sell U.S. weapons to Iran in order to get the American hostages back, but we would fix the Ayatollah. First we would charge him outrageously high prices, gouging him good. And then we would take the money we got from Iran—the Ayatollah Khomeini's money—and buy weapons and supplies for the Contras fighting the communist dictatorship in Nicaragua. What poetic justice! Getting the Ayatollah to provide the funds our own Congress denied us. That would show the Congress, too. In one deft stroke we could help the Contras, take advantage of the Ayatollah of Iran, and thumb our noses at Congress. Ollie North thought "it was a neat idea."[17] John Poindexter "thought it was a neat idea" also,[18] and later approved the plans that North and his colleagues—

notably Hakim and Secord—developed. Whether the idea came from the Israeli, Amiram Nir, or the Iranian, Manucher Ghorbanifar, the Americans, North and Poindexter, lunged at it like hungry trout leaping for newly hatched mayflies.

Soon the two operations were joined as one. Profits from the weapons sales flowed into the enterprise owned by Hakim and Secord, and some of those profits then found their way into the hands of the Contras in Nicaragua. Very few senior people in the United States government knew about the operation. In fact, there were probably only three. One was Oliver North, and the first person with whom he raised the idea was Bill Casey. According to North, the head of the CIA was ecstatic about the idea, referring to it as "the ultimate irony, the ultimate covert operation. . . ."[19]

North's boss, John Poindexter, was the other one to know. Right away he thought it "was a very good idea,"[20] and personally gave North approval to go ahead with it. As far as we know, nobody told President Reagan. Both North and Poindexter swear they did not tell Reagan. North never had a good opportunity and Poindexter thought the secret diversion of funds was so politically volatile that he took it upon himself not to tell the president.

"The buck stops here with me," Poindexter later testified, "I made the decision. I thought I had the authority to do it. I thought it was a good idea. I was convinced that the President would, in the end, think it was a good idea. But I did not want him to be associated with the decision."[21]

We will never know for sure whether Bill Casey told the president or not. Casey has that knowledge with him in his grave. President Reagan has consistently denied that anyone ever told him about the idea to divert secret funds to the Contras and, given the sworn testimony of North and Poindexter, the evidence is overwhelming that Reagan never was told.

And that is a chilling thought. That a senior White House aide felt free to make that crucial and sensitive a decision all by himself is astonishing. Poindexter knew the secret diversion of funds to the Contras was potential political dynamite. He admitted as much in his sworn testimony. Yet he plunged smugly ahead, jeopardizing the entire policy agenda of the Reagan administration. Poindexter took the risk, himself, that the sly secret scheme to fox the Ayatollah and con Congress might blow wide open and threaten the president's economic program, the Strategic Defense Initiative, his defense buildup, and the possibility of a sound nuclear arms reduction treaty with the Soviet Union.

Poindexter's gamble failed, but he wasn't the only loser. Although President Reagan and the Republican party were the big political losers, the entiré nation may have lost something too— the opportunity to push further ahead toward the two goals that, until then, had fueled Reagan's revolution: economic prosperity and a secure, well-defended nation.

The most sinister part of the Iran-Contra affair is something that did not happen—the creation of a superCIA. But it was not for lack of trying. We came very close to the establishment of a powerful secret organization that would have operated with complete independence, plunging into delicate, dangerous foreign policy matters free of any government restraint whatsoever.

Let private businessmen make lots of money selling U.S. arms to Iran. Then have them direct this money to the Contras in Nicaragua. Nobody knows. It doesn't cost the taxpayers any money. And Congress cannot interfere. An idea so neat and brilliant has much broader applicability. Why confine the fund-raising part to arms sales to Iran? Why not arms sales in general? Why confine the use of those funds to covert activity in Nicaragua? Why not Afghanistan or Angola or anywhere else in the world where people were fighting for their freedom?

Bill Casey was entranced by the idea. The money would be raised privately, secretly. Congress would not have to appropriate any funds. You wouldn't need to get permission or even inform anyone in the executive branch of the federal government. No one, outside of the handful of people who controlled the secret organization, could tell you what to do, or even influence your decisions by the power of the purse.

It was the ultimate fantasy of the old master spy. As Oliver North later testified, Casey saw it as a potential overseas organization, one that was "self-financing, independent of appropriated monies," and capable of conducting covert operations, including counterterrorism. It was to be, as Casey saw it, "[An] off-the-shelf, self-sustaining, stand-alone entity that could perform certain activities on behalf of the United States."[22]

Stripped to its essentials, what we are talking about here is an organization accountable to no one—not any elected official in the land, no congressmen, no senators, not even the president—no one but its self-appointed masters. As concocted by Casey, Poindexter, and North, this small, superCIA could generate its own funds (secretly), determine what operations it would carry out (secretly), and then, I assume, judge whether or not it did a good job (again secretly). It was to be the ultimate covert activity, accountable to no one, yet all the time able to use the power and to invoke the glory of the United States in carrying out whatever activities it deemed appropriate.

It was also a prescription for disaster. So much power so secretly held could only create arrogance, the kind of arrogance the founding fathers keenly feared when they hammered out a constitution designed to make *all* of the government accountable to the people. Taken to extremes, such a rogue operation could one day even threaten the survival of the republic itself. The superCIA was a very bad idea that fortunately never did get a full-scale test before it was exposed and killed.

Chapter Thirty-One

THE MYSTERY OF THE MISSING MONEY

There are still some mysteries that remain in the Iran-Contra affair, and most of them center around money. Large amounts of money. Satchels full of cash were toted to and fro around the world, hundreds of thousands of dollars were stuffed in White House safes, and tens of millions of dollars flowed through numbered Swiss bank accounts.

One thing history teaches us is that whenever people come into the possession of large amounts of money that no one knows they have, they almost always do one thing—they keep the money. This is especially true if the amount involved is very large, large enough to make a significant change in a person's life. It is relatively easy to be honest and virtuous when everyone is watching. It is more difficult to be good when no one knows.

During the investigation of the Iran-Contra affair, a number of questions were raised about the possible misuse or misappropriation of money by Oliver North, questions that have not been fully answered. They are important questions because their answers will have a significant impact on our understanding of how and why the

Iran-Contra affair happened, and who was at fault, and what should be done in the future to prevent it from ever happening again.

If Oliver North is innocent of the allegations that he, in effect, accepted large sums of money as bribes to influence his decisions in the White House, then we will probably conclude that North was simply a patriotic, high-strung American who was seduced by the powers of the White House, and his desires to serve the president, into an overly zealous pursuit of his duty. An honorable man of good intentions, he perhaps should be censured, but surely not punished. The fault that remains will lie with President Reagan and the organizational structure that led North astray.

On the other hand, if any of the allegations should prove to be correct, that he was in fact involved in an intricate web of payoffs, then we have a very different story. If some of North's decisions were influenced by the prospect of personal monetary gain, we can forget a lot of what we have read about the lofty goals of rescuing American hostages and helping the Freedom Fighters in Nicaragua. And no administrator, no matter how brilliant, no organization, no matter how cleverly structured, can guard against the consequences of betrayal by someone in a critical position who has been corrupted by money.

North is such a central figure to the whole affair that the question of his culpability is critical to our understanding of it. The allegations have been made, the investigations continue, and it may be years before the question is resolved beyond doubt. It may never be resolved to everyone's satisfaction.

Oliver North is an exceptionally likeable person. I never met him personally in my travels in and out of the White House, but I talked to several close friends who knew him well for many years. They all loved the guy. According to them he was friendly and charming, a patriot devoted to his country, a straightforward, decent man who worked terribly long hours and was single-mindedly loyal to President Reagan. He is securely married, has lovely kids, doesn't have affairs with other women, and is a fervent, born-again Christian, a charismatic fundamentalist who deeply believes that God guides him in his work.

The power and depth of this part of North's character blazed brilliantly when he testified before the congressional inquisition, nicely named the Select Committee on Secret Military Assistance to Iran and the Nicaraguan Opposition, in July 1987. The congressmen and senators who sat on the high dais looking down at the normally contrite witnesses had mistakenly delegated much of the questioning to bright, pushy lawyers who had never engaged in verbal combat with a veteran of the back corridors of White House political intrigue. It never seemed to occur to them that there might be some good reason why this young Marine officer, who looked so freshly scrubbed and innocent, was the chief operational officer for the covert activities of the National Security Council. North's testimony was a stunning shock to the staid inquisitors. He looked them straight in the eye and testified, unashamedly and unafraid, for five straight days.

When the congressional hearings were over, Oliver North was, for a while, a new American celebrity. He received approximately 150,000 telegrams of congratulations, and the offers for speaking engagements and book contracts poured in. The American people loved the spectacle of the young Marine officer, proudly wearing his uniform, beribboned with medals for personal bravery and valor under fire, standing up to his aging tormentors. It was classic theater, full of heat and passion.

But there was little light. The spectacle did little to illuminate how and why the Iran-Contra affair came about. North's presence was so intimidating that he literally blew away any sensitive, probing questions raised by the inquisitors.

There were six specific incidents involving North and potential corruption that came to light during the course of the investigations. Any one of them by itself could be plausibly explained, but, in my view, when taken together, they form a disturbing pattern. It becomes especially disturbing when you reflect on how crucial North's role was to the entire Iran-Contra affair. North was the pivot point in the White House. He was the de facto chief of operations. He had a great deal to say about what arms dealers would do the buying, selling, and profiting. He was the switching point for much of the money; first it came to him, and then it went to others. The temptations must have been great. During the time he had this enormous responsibility, and was working so hard, traveling from country to country, and meeting daily with some of the most powerful and wealthy people in the world, he was making less than $60,000 a year—and that was before paying taxes. With four children, two of them close to college age, and his wife not working, he had to watch carefully how he spent his money. One can only speculate what ran through his mind when he sat down to deal with men who could misplace an amount equal to what North could make in a full year and not even notice it was gone.

These are the six incidents involving Oliver North and money:

(1) $175,000 in Travelers Checks and Cash. In the course of carrying out the secret activities, Bill Casey suggested to North that he set up an operational account to handle various expenses. There were two sources of money for the account. Over the course of two years, about $100,000 in travelers checks were given to North by Adolfo Calero, one of the chief Contra leaders who, at the time, was receiving a $7,000 monthly salary directly from North. As much as $75,000 in cash was provided by General Richard Secord, one of the arms dealers working under North's direction.[1]

The entire $175,000 in cash and travelers checks was completely under North's discretionary control. He has freely admitted having the money and spending it. North testified that he "kept a detailed account of every single penny that came into that account and that left that account. All of the transactions were recorded on a ledger that Director Casey gave me for that purpose. . . . I made an enormous amount of travel. The schedule was brutal. Much of it was paid for out of that operational account. There were times when the account was down to zero, no money in it. I didn't have any travelers checks, and I'd handed out all the cash, not to myself, but to others. Under those circumstances I would use my own money, Lieutenant Colonel Oliver North's paycheck money, his own money that he had earned. . . . And the next time I got cash or travelers checks, I would use those checks to reimburse myself."[2]

What an extraordinary setup. A personal expense account that was self-monitored. No expense reports to file for approval by a superior, no records kept for tax purposes; it was all done by the honor code, sort of the ultimate expense account with no accountability to anyone else.

North vehemently denied any wrongdoing in connection with the secret expense account monies, stating flatly under oath that "I never took a penny that didn't belong to me."[3] Unfortunately, he cannot provide any evidence to support his claim. The detailed records he claimed to have kept no longer exist. As North explained it, "The ledger for this operational account was given to me by Director Casey. And when he told me to do so, I destroyed it . . . somewhere between what I would judge to be the 13th of October and the 4th of November (1986), he told me specifically, 'Get rid of things. Get rid of that book because that book has in it the names of everybody, the addresses of everybody. Just get rid of it, and clean things up.' And, I did so."[4]

While the records that could clear North's name are gone, there are a few fragmentary tracks left by the bank's record of the travelers checks North cashed. The committee investigators were able to identify $2,240 worth of travelers checks personally cashed by Colonel North.[5] Most of the travelers checks were cashed at Giant Food stores and other retail establishments. One travelers check for $100 was cashed on November 30, 1985, at National Tire Wholesalers to pay for two snow tires for North's automobile. One was cashed for $20 at Parklane Hosiery to buy leotards for his two little girls. One was cashed for $20 at The American Cafe, a nice restaurant in the Georgetown area of Washington, and a few more were cashed at gas stations, a drugstore, and a dry cleaning establishment.

Oliver North was also generous. When Robert Owen, a young man who did courier work for North got married, North gave the newly married couple a handsome gift of $1,000.[6] The money apparently came from North's stand-alone expense fund. It was surely a nice, thoughtful thing to do. Most of us would feel very good if we could give young, newly married friends $1,000 gifts. But most of us don't have the kind of expense accounts that would allow us to indulge in such personal philanthropy.

(2) The $16,000 Home Security System. In April 1986 North was informed that Abu Nidal threatened to kill him.[7] Abu Nidal is one of the world's most ruthless terrorists and North was understandably concerned for himself and his family. He went to John Poindexter and asked for financial help, money to install a personal home security system to protect his family, and soon learned that the U.S. government does not provide protective services to all officials who receive threats. North then complained bitterly to General Secord. Secord understood and said, "Don't worry about that. I've got a good friend."[8] Shortly thereafter, Glenn Robinette, a former CIA security expert, showed up at North's suburban home in Virginia and installed an extensive $16,000 security system.[9]

North accepted the gift from Secord unhesitatingly and later, when the investigators began to close in, tried to conceal the transaction by writing two phony letters. When North was confronted with the evidence of the $16,000 gift and his attempt to cover it up, he readily admitted guilt saying, "I admit to making a serious, serious, judgment error." But he was defiantly unrepentant and unapologetic, asserting to the congressional investigating committee that if General Secord paid the bill for the security system he just wanted to say, "Thank you, General Secord, and . . . you guys ought to write him a check because the government should have done it to begin with." [10]

Later, months after the hearings were over, it was reported that Oliver North sold a rental house he owned and made $40,000 in May 1986, just about the same time he was pleading poverty and accepting the $16,000 home security system as a gift. [11]

Anyone who has ever felt the injustice of a government bureaucracy can sympathize with North's feelings. But it seems that North was not coerced by lack of funds into accepting that large gift. Apparently he didn't want to use his own money. His actions were the actions of a man who likes to write his own rules, by his own standards. I'm sure he believed with all his heart that the government had an obligation to pay for the protection of his family and that, when it failed to do so, he was justified in accepting a gift. But it was still wrong.

(3) The $200,000 Nest Egg. By early 1986 the American arms dealers—Hakim and Secord—had taken over from the arms dealers from Iran, Israel, and Saudi Arabia. Albert Hakim met Oliver North for the first time in February 1986 in Frankfurt, Germany. During the next months he had only occasional contact with North, but it apparently was enough to develop an intense feeling of friendship and admiration. By April 1986, Hakim testified under oath that he "had become extremely fond of Lieutenant Colonel North," and that "he is an amazing person. . . . I really love this man." [12] Hakim knew North cared very deeply about his family and that he was about to leave on a secret trip to Iran where there was always a risk that he might be taken hostage. Hakim also knew from talking to North that he was worried about the expenses of his children's college education.

Most people might have left it at that, but not Hakim. He was apparently so filled with an overwhelming desire to help North that he decided to establish a special fund for North, so that if anything should happen to him the money would go to his wife and his four children. Hakim then went to his partner, General Secord, and proposed that they take $500,000 from the enterprise for this purpose. Secord was scornful, pointing out to Hakim that he was using his own life-style as a reference point and that Hakim had "no understanding of what a soldier's life is, and that there are benefits that the government provides." [13] Hakim countered and "came up with the figure of $200,000." According to Hakim, "General Secord made no opposition to this. He did not disagree, and yet he did not come right out and say that, fine, go ahead and do it. And I did not pursue this. That is how this was developed." [14]

Hakim was acutely aware that this might be construed as a bribe. North was an employee of the U.S. government in a very sensitive, important position. In that job he was in a position to directly affect how much arms business Mr. Hakim and General Secord received. A "yes" from Ollie North could means millions of dollars in profits to the company Hakim and Secord owned.

Hakim moved with the caution and sophistication of a successful, experienced Middle East businessman. First he engaged the services of a high-powered lawyer, Willard Zucker. Mr. Zucker was not your ordinary lawyer. He owned a company in Geneva, Switzerland, called Compagnie de Services Fiduciares. [15] Zucker's firm provided its clients with a variety of legal and financial services, including setting up offshore corporations and opening numbered Swiss bank accounts. In addition they managed as much as $70 million of their clients' money. In the mid-1970s Hakim established a second home in France, close to Geneva, Switzerland, and became one of Zucker's clients. [16]

During one of Zucker's trips to the United States Hakim asked him to help in getting the $200,000 to Oliver North without, as Hakim put it, "compromising Ollie's position or his family." [17] It was decided that Zucker should meet secretly with Oliver North's wife, Betsy. So Zucker telephoned Mrs. North and on May 1, 1986, Mrs. North boarded a train in Washington, D.C., for the one hour and forty minute ride to Philadelphia, Pennsylvania where she met with lawyer Zucker. [18] Oliver North, who had a special concern for the safety of his family, was well aware that his wife was spending the whole day traveling to Philadelphia and back to meet with Hakim's Swiss lawyer. North later testified that when Hakim "suggested that my wife meet with his lawyer in Philadelphia, I agreed that my wife should do so." [19]

What happened at the meeting has been the subject of much speculation. According to North, "There was no money mentioned, no account mentioned, no will mentioned, no arrangement. The meeting focused on how many children I had, their ages, and a general description of my family." [20] Well, we know North had four children and their ages were seventeen, fifteen, ten, and six, so most of the discussion must have dealt with a general description of his family. Hakim later confirmed that Zucker wanted to meet with Mrs. North to learn about North's family, "to see if he could find a proper way of getting the money in some sort of fashion, which was never determined, through the relatives." [21] Hakim maintains that nothing came of the meeting, but that he persisted and talked with Zucker about arranging a phony job in real estate for Mrs. North that could act as a cover for the money Hakim wanted to give Oliver North. Hakim testified:

> "The idea that we came up with was maybe we could arrange for a part-time job for Mrs. North, and since we did not know what the qualifications of Mrs. North were, we decided that maybe if Mr. Zucker could find someone that could offer that position to her, and even if she did not qualify, we could make use of the button set-aside to cover her salary, and Mr. Zucker told me that he knew of a land real estate developer that he was going to contact and see if he could find a way, approaching the problem that way. And that was the last time that we discussed about this issue, and to the best of my knowledge, no money was sent to North's family and no solution, no proper solution was found." [22]

But something was afoot. On May 20, 1986, less than three weeks after Mrs. North spent a whole day traveling back and forth to Philadelphia to discuss her family structure with Hakim's Swiss lawyer, Hakim transferred $200,000 of his company's money to a special earmarked account, code-named Bellybutton. Bellybutton was the code name Hakim used for Lieutenant Colonel North. [23] And there, in that special bank account, the money sat and waited. According to both Hakim and North, neither North nor his family ever actually received any of the $200,000. But, as Hakim later testified, "I put a wheel into motion and then if North's family wanted to open the door to my motion, they could. If they wanted to close the door to it, they also could do that. I just simply went ahead and put this action into motion and left the rest up to them"[24]

As far as we know, the Norths never withdrew any money and the $200,000 is still in the account. North vehemently denied even knowing about the account, saying, "the very first time I heard these things was as a consequence of these hearings. I was shocked."[25]

(4) The $2 Million Will. At about the same time in 1985 that Hakim set aside $200,000 of the arms company's funds for North's potential use, he executed a special will. Two million dollars of the company's funds were earmarked in another special account and the will specified that if Hakim died, General Richard Secord "would then control the money in the account."[26] When General Secord died all the money, the $2 million would be controlled by—guess who?—Lieutenant Colonel Oliver L. North. The second paragraph of the will specified:

> Should Richard V. Secord, after having qualified to give us instructions concerning this account, die or become disabled or otherwise be unable to communicate with us, a decision we shall make in our best judgment we shall then accept instructions with respect to this account from Oliver North alone, both with respect to the investment of assets and the payment of funds from the account, whether to him or to any third party he shall designate.[27]

The will stated further that,

> Should none of the three individuals named above (Hakim, Secord, North) be alive, then upon receipt of proof of death in form satisfactory to us, we shall divide the then-remaining balance in this account in three equal parts of equal value and hold one such part for the designees of that individual if he shall have left a written designation with us, or if he shall not, we shall pay that part to the properly designated representative of his estate.[28]

Is it possible that North was a silent partner in the arms firm that was selling U.S. weapons to Iran at his direction? North says he was shocked to discover he was in the will. Hakim, hedging slightly, says, "To my knowledge, he [North] was not aware." On the other hand, Hakim seemed to consider North an integral part of the arms selling enterprise. When asked if "this was an enterprise ultimately in which North was at the top," Hakim replied, "That is correct. That was my judgment." [29] But why would Hakim and Secord go to so much trouble? Was it solely because of their admiration and love for North?

Or did they want to keep North happy because he was the one man who could make or break the lucrative arms deal they had going with Iran, the one man who could determine whether or not they could make millions and millions of dollars? Is it reasonable to assume that a man such as Hakim, an international businessman who spent most of his working life in Iran, who has no previous record of spontaneous generosity, would be willing to set aside $500,000 of his own money for North's use, and actually set aside $200,000, and then will $2 million to this man he knew for scarcely two months—and not even tell him about it?

(5) Ross Perot's $300,000. Ever since William Buckley, the high-ranking CIA executive with knowledge of the entire scope of America's anti-terrorism strategy, was kidnapped on March 16, 1984, by Middle East terrorists there had been a frantic U.S. effort to get him back. In early 1985 Oliver North thought he had found a way. According to unnamed informants, the people holding Buckley would let him go and another hostage as well for a payment of $200,000. North called Ross Perot.

Ross Perot is a genuine American hero. Besides making hundreds of millions of dollars in legitimate business activity, he masterminded the daring rescue of two of his own company executives in Iran after the Shah was overthrown. He succeeded where Carter had not, and where Reagan would not. Perot did not like the Iranians much, and he loved his country a lot. So, in May 1985 he handed over $200,000 in cash to Oliver North to pay for the release of Buckley and the other hostage. According to press reports, North sent "a messenger to pay Perot's $200,000 to the informant." The money disappeared. The hostages were never released. In October 1985 the United States learned that Buckley had been killed.

But this did not stop the irrepressible North. In January 1986 he telephoned Perot again and asked for another $100,000. This time it was supposed to be for five hostages who were going to be delivered to the island of Cyprus by boat. Again, no hostages, and the money disappeared.

All told, Perot was out some $300,000 in cash, after taxes. But Perot is a very wealthy man who took it all rather philosophically, saying, "I would rather try and fail than not try."[30]

(6) The $10 Million That Was Mislaid. In the early summer of 1986 the Contra forces in Nicaragua were in serious trouble, desperately short of money. Oliver North was keenly aware of this and beseeched Bill Casey to do something about it. Casey cagily came up with the idea of soliciting the tiny kingdom of Brunei for the princely sum of $10 million, a sum sufficient for the Contras' needs.[31]

Brunei is a fabulously wealthy country located on the northern tip of Borneo, facing the South China Sea. Much of its wealth is centered in the person of the man who rules the country, Sultan Muda Hassanal Bolkiah Muizzaddin Waddaulah. Graduated from the Royal Military Academy in Sandhurst, England, the Sultan has ruled Brunei since his twenty-first birthday.[32] Brunei is also one of the tiniest, most helpless kingdoms on earth, and it sincerely values its friendship with the United States.

So Casey apparently spoke to George Shultz and asked him to solicit the Sultan for $10 million, a variety of international fund raising that was permitted under law. Shultz agreed and delegated the details of the task to his young, aggressive assistant secretary of state for inter-American affairs, Elliott Abrams.[33]

Some thought it would be easy. John Poindexter, for example, told North privately in June 1986 that "They [Brunei] have lots of money and very little to spend it on."[34] Actually it turned out to be fairly difficult to part the Sultan from $10 million in cash, even though he was reputed to be the richest man in the world, worth billions of dollars. On June 24, 1986, the Secretary of State made a special side trip to Brunei and spent three hours with the Sultan.[35] On August 8, 1986, Elliott Abrams flew to London and met secretly with a representative of the Sultan.[36] Finally, on August 19, 1986, the Sultan came through and transferred $10 million into a secret numbered account in the Credit Suisse bank in Geneva.

Back in Washington, D.C., and in the jungles of Nicaragua,

there should have been joy, the champagne should have been broken out, and a great victory toasted. For the first time since the bedraggled efforts of the United States to help the Contras began, they had enough money to buy the supplies of war they needed to fight effectively. Ten million dollars! That was the biggest lump sum bonanza that ever came the way of the Contras. And Oliver North was responsible for it. He should have been very proud. Now the Contras could fight, fully equipped, well-fed, armed to the teeth. Soon victory could be theirs and Nicaragua would be free.

But something went terribly, terribly wrong. The money, all of the $10 million, disappeared. The $10 million in cold cash that the Sultan of Brunei sent to the secret numbered account in the Credit Suisse bank never showed up. The account coffers remained empty.

Then the most curious thing of all happened—nothing. No alarm bells went off. No red alert sounded. No one seemed unduly alarmed that this critical, tremendous amount of help for the Contras, due at this desperately critical time, had not arrived. There is no trace of Lieutenant Colonel Oliver North mounting a massive hunt for the missing funds for his beloved Contras. There is no record of concern on the part of John Poindexter who approved the scheme. There is no hint that Bill Casey or George Shultz or General Secord ever inquired about it. Elliott Abrams did testify that on several occasions he "checked with North to see if the money had been deposited," and was told that "the money had not reached the account."[37]

Not until the Iran-Contra scandal broke open several months later and the FBI started investigating did the fact of the missing $10 million come to light. And then the search for it began with a vengeance. Finally, the $10 million was found in May 1987, almost nine months after it left the Sultan's hands. On May 12, 1987, Senator Inouye proudly announced that the investigating committee he chaired located the money.

The $10 million was deposited, apparently by mistake, in a numbered bank account of a Swiss shipping magnate, whose identity has not been revealed by the Swiss authorities. According to Mark A. Belnick, executive assistant to the chief counsel of the Senate Select Committee investigating this, part of the account number, 386, was reported to Elliott Abrams as 368 by Oliver North. The lucky fellow into whose bank account the $10 million wandered didn't seem to think it was too unusual. He did not report it to anyone. Evidently he had a lot of money flowing in and out of his bank account. However, he was concerned enough not to spend the $10 million or invest it as if it were his own. Instead, as soon as he noticed he had an extra $10 million, he withdrew it and invested the entire amount in a certificate of deposit in another bank, where it sat serenely for all those months, quietly earning $253,000 in interest, safe and secure.[38]

The official explanation for the mislaid $10 million is that the Sultan was given the wrong bank account number. So when he delivered on his part of the bargain he sent the money unknowingly to the wrong numbered account. According to the investigating committee some of the numbers got transposed somewhere along the way. So where did the bank number for the sultan come from? From Elliott Abrams. But where did he get it? That is where the story gets interesting.

As Elliott Abrams embarked on his trek to the land of Brunei in his quest for $10 million, he soon realized he had to have a specific place for the Sultan to send the money. He couldn't very well take a large suitcase and have the Sultan load it up with cash. It would be too heavy.

The volume and weight of $10,000,000 in cash is surprisingly large. Assume you use $100 bills, not brand new ones, but ones a trifle used. It would take a dozen normal sized briefcases to hold all the money, which itself weighs well over two hundred pounds.

So Abrams turned to two possibilities. First, he called the CIA. He contacted Mr. Alan Fiers, the head of the CIA's Central American Task Force, in early August 1986. Fiers suggested that the best way was to get one of the Contras to open a bank account and then have the Sultan deposit the money in that account. Abrams agreed that was a good idea. Fiers had a bank account opened in the Bahama Islands and sent Abrams the account number.[39]

Abrams also turned to Oliver North. According to Abrams' testimony he contacted North the same day and put the same question to him. Soon North provided Abrams with a second bank account.[40] The account number given to Abrams by North was from the Credit Suisse bank in Geneva. So now Abrams had *two* bank accounts and discussed which one he should use with some of his colleagues in the State Department. Unluckily for them they chose the Swiss numbered account. Perhaps if they had chosen the Bahamian bank the $10 million would not have gotten lost. Later, while testifying under oath, Oliver North swore that he "would not have given intentionally a wrong number to Mr. Abrams," and volunteered the opinion that his secretary, Fawn Hall, "made very few errors, and I don't know that she made the error on that card or someone else did, or that that was precisely the card that was carried to the representatives of the Brunei government."[41]

When the high-ranking CIA official, Alan Fiers, heard months later that the money had not gone into his bank account in the Bahama Islands but instead went into a bank account in Switzerland and disappeared, he was astonished. He testified, "That probably left me as speechless as anything in this whole endeavor, that that $10 million which we sorely needed and still do need—I mean, it would be the margin of comfort even in today's operation [1987]—went into a bank account in Geneva and disappeared. It just left me dumbstruck and still does. I still find it hard to believe."[42]

A lot of people still find it hard to believe.

The story is further complicated by some of the secret PROF (Professional Office System) notes that came to light during the investigations. The PROF notes were the private memoranda that members of the National Security Council staff sent back and forth to one another by computer, completely confident that any record of their correspondence was instantly erased when they typed the order to delete. Unknown to them, a large memory storage disc secretly wired to their computers was saving for posterity every last word. The words they wrote were all highly classified so even the few people who knew about the storage never dreamed that someday you and I would be reading them.

On June 10, 1986, very late in the evening, at 11:22 p.m.—almost two months before Abrams contacted Alan Fiers in the CIA about a bank account number—Oliver North sent a computer message to John Poindexter in his office over across the street in the small west wing of the White House. Part of it read, "Elliott [Abrams] called me and asked 'where to send the money.' I told Elliott to do nothing, to send no papers and to talk to no one further about this until he talks to you. He is seeing you privately tomorrow. At this point I need your help. As you know, I have the accounts and the means by which this thing needs to be accomplished."[43]

The next day Poindexter typed a computer reply to North in which he said, "I asked Elliott at lunch. He said he had recommended Brunei where Shultz is going to visit. They have lots of money and very little to spend it on. It seems like a good prospect. Shultz agrees. I asked Elliott how the money could be transferred. He said he thought Shultz could just hand them an account number. I said that was a bad idea, not at all letting on that we had access to accounts. I told Elliott that the best way was for Brunei to direct their embassy here to receive a person that we would designate and the funds could be transferred through him. Don't you think that is best?"[44]

Later that day in a PROF note to a staff member, Poindexter cautioned, "We should not mention Brunei to anybody. Elliott said only Shultz and Hill are aware."[45]

These three small computer messages are perhaps the hardest evidence we have regarding the events that led up to the disappearance of the $10 million. What they show is that two people—North and Poindexter—were intent on keeping knowledge of the impending Brunei contribution to the Contras very closely held. They obviously realized the enormity of what they were dealing with—a secret $10 million cash contribution. Poindexter displayed a great deal of interest in the mechanics of the money transfer, going so far as to suggest that he and North designate a person who would go to the Brunei embassy in Washington and have "the funds transferred through him." That Poindexter idea did not pan out, but if it had, would it have meant that special accounts and wire transfers, not known to the State Department, would have been used; or could it possibly have meant that North and Poindexter would have brought $10 million of cash into their White House offices? Perhaps. North kept at least part of his expense account cash and travelers checks in a safe in his office up on the third floor of the Old Executive Office Building. In any event, it is clear that both North and Poindexter took an unusually intense interest in the details of the upcoming Brunei bonanza. They accorded it their close, personal attention.

And that is why, when the money did not show up in the proper account, ready to be spent on weapons and other supplies for the Contras, it is so puzzling that nobody did anything. Why didn't North scream? Why didn't Poindexter send a computer message to North demanding to know what happened to the money?

Apparently no one ever bothered to tell the Contras that they were about to come into a large amount of money, so they felt no disappointment when the $10 million was mislaid. But why weren't the Contras told the money was coming so they could plan their next series of offensives against the communists? Surely this would have been sound battle strategy.

All in all, the saga of the $10 million is an unbelievable tale.

Chapter Thirty-Two

SOME LESSONS

The Iran-Contra affair rocked the Reagan administration, but it has not undermined the basic agenda of political revolution that has been decades in the making. The scandal passes, the ideas that fuel the revolution remain. But the Iran-Contra affair was instructive.

In the aftermath of any great scandal there are usually two questions. One, are there any lessons to be learned from the affair? And two, is there anything we can do now to prevent something similar from happening again in the future?

The answers are yes and yes. There are clear lessons and there are some specific actions we can take.

The first major lesson of the Iran-Contra affair is the rediscovery that bad ideas are feeble and powerless. The ideas that drove the Iran-Contra affair forward succeeded only as long as they were concealed, only as long as the knowledge of those ideas was limited to a handful of people who either lacked understanding or courage to oppose them. As soon as the bad ideas were exposed to a little public scrutiny, as soon as people, hundreds and thousands of people, began to discuss and debate those ideas, they withered and died almost instantly. And the good ideas, the ones that have survived centuries of debate and discussion, once again triumphed.

The Iran-Contra affair was marked by two sets of ideas in conflict with one another. Both sets of ideas dealt with issues that have been part of civilization for centuries.

The first set revolved around the question of capture and ransom. Seizing innocent people as hostages is a crime of acute injustice. Like kidnaping, it is a cowardly crime, but a very effective means of bringing pressure to bear. It is almost impossible to stop and extremely difficult to counter.

After centuries of experience with the crime, mankind has worked out a basic rule for dealing with it: under no circumstances do you pay ransom, no matter how heart-wrenching the special case, for if you give in to the ransom demands it only encourages more hostage-taking in the future. That is the good idea. The age-old wisdom is to endure the short-term pain and anguish of the few in order to prevent the pain and anguish of many more people in the future.

But of course this is an abstract answer, true in theory and principle. When someone dear and close to the one who must make the decision about paying ransom is the person being held captive and tortured and threatened with death, it is emotionally difficult to do what should be done. And then the bad idea often prevails.

The bad idea in dealing with hostage-taking is to do whatever seems necessary, to pay the ransom demanded, to do anything, absolutely anything, to bring the captive to safety. This powerful emotion is understandable from the viewpoint of an individual who will weight the present pain of the known hostage far greater than the future pain of unknown strangers. But when a government is involved, when decisions must be made affecting all those who consent to be governed, that emotion must be rejected. Paying ransom is always a bad idea for government.

In the Iran-Contra affair this was the cardinal sin President Reagan and his aides committed. Their compassion and concern for the innocent Americans imprisoned in the dark cells of the Middle East blinded them to the far greater horror of the consequences of paying ransom, a horror compounded when that ransom took the form of selling U.S. weapons and spare parts to a pitiless regime ruled by a fanatical enemy of the United States. The only reason the hostage-taking and ransom-paying succeeded for as long as it did was because of the extreme secrecy under which it was conducted. As soon as selling weapons to Iran in an attempt to ransom American hostages was exposed, it stopped. Not within months or years, but immediately.

The second set of ideas in the Iran-Contra affair revolved around the question of when and under what circumstances one is justified in breaking or circumventing the law. Once again the distilled wisdom of the ages is that you do not break the law; you attempt to change the law. That is the good idea. No matter how odious you think the law to be, no matter how it pangs your conscience, no matter how lofty and important the goals it prevents you from reaching, the law must be obeyed as long as free men have the means to persuade their fellow citizens to change it.

In a totalitarian state where the law is a joke, where freedom of speech, freedom of press, freedom of assembly, and free elections do not exist, then there may be times when one is fully justified in disobeying the law. But in a constitutional republic such as the United States, obeying all the laws, willingly, in the full spirit of the purpose of those laws, is fundamental to its preservation. The good idea says that you cannot and must not break or bend the law no matter how pure your goals, no matter how passionate your desire. This is doubly true for government officials, especially those in offices with great responsibilities and authority. They have sworn to uphold those laws and they have a special duty, magnified by their high visibility, to set an example for the entire nation by not only obeying the law scrupulously, but also taking great pains to avoid even the impression of trying to get around the law.

The bad idea, which has been with us for as long as we have had free governments, is the mischievous philosophy that the ends sometimes justify the means, the idea that it is OK to bend and stretch the law, to slyly circumvent it and, if really necessary, to violate the law, to break it if your cause is just and grand enough. In the Iran-Contra affair this was the second cardinal sin that afflicted the Reagan administration. President Reagan never broke the law, but his frustration with the Boland Amendment that forbade aid to the rebels fighting the communist dictatorship of Nicaragua was plain and clear. He wanted that law changed. And when he failed, some of his aides took it upon themselves to achieve what they thought he wanted. In the process they bent the law, they twisted it, they went under it and around it and, every now and then, they just said the hell with it and broke the law.

Reagan was appalled when he learned of some of the things that happened. On December 14, 1986, Secretary of State George Shultz went to the family quarters of the White House and told President Reagan some of the things that were done in his name. Shultz later described the president's reaction: "[He] was astonished. I have never seen him so mad . . . his jaw set, his eyes flashed."[1]

But the president should not have been surprised. For as long as there have been rulers and kings and presidents, ambitious aides have tried to curry favor with their princes by doing, somehow, whatever it was they thought their leader wanted done. When the king of England, Henry II, murmured softly to his aides in the year 1170, "Will no one rid me of this turbulent priest?" few were surprised to learn that the archbishop, Thomas Becket, was murdered shortly thereafter by four of King Henry's knights.[2]

Rulers and kings and presidents must be extremely cautious in their demands and orders and even in their expressions of desire. They must constantly remind and command those who carry out their orders to obey and uphold the law at all times. It is one of the first rules of governing.

The congressional debate on military aid to the Contras in Nicaragua made it crystal clear that U.S. government aid was banned. True, the Boland Amendment did not specifically ban the National Security Council staff from giving such aid, but neither did it ban the Department of Housing and Urban Development from giving aid to the Contras. A narrow, legalistic interpretation of the law could provide a thin justification for what was done, but it was totally against the spirit of the law. What should have been done, instead of spending an enormous amount of time and effort trying to get around the law, was to fight for its repeal, to turn the issue into a major political confrontation between the Democrats and the Republicans. The issue in principle is a simple one. Will the United States support the efforts of people throughout the world who are struggling to achieve the kind of freedom that we ourselves enjoy? Will we provide them with money and weapons in that fight? Or will we sit back and let them fend for themselves? The outcome of that political debate is still unclear, but the Reagan administration would have been far better off if it had fought that fight directly and openly rather than skulking about in the underground wilderness of foreign policy to do secretly what they failed to do openly.

This clash of good ideas and bad ideas was at the heart of the Iran-Contra affair. Among a small group of men close to the president these ideas jousted with one another. On one side of the debate were the ideas of never paying ransom and always obeying the law. The prime proponents of these old, but good ideas were George Shultz and Caspar Weinberger. Arrayed on the other side were the ideas that getting the hostages back justifies the ransom being asked and that we should try to get around the law banning aid to Contras because it is a bad law. The prime proponents of these old, bad ideas were William Casey and Robert McFarlane, and later his successor John Poindexter. In that debate President Reagan and his other two key advisers, Vice President George Bush and Chief of Staff Donald Regan, as far as we know, watched and listened. George Bush and Donald Regan finally succumbed to the arguments that Casey and McFarlane and Poindexter were offering. And then President Reagan himself yielded. It was the most serious mistake he made up to that point in his presidency.

There were many people who came to share the blame for the Iran-Contra fiasco, but the ultimate responsibility must lie with the president. Even when misled, and deceived, and perhaps even lied to in the campaign to persuade him, it was President Reagan in the end who agreed to sell arms to the Iranians and who failed to admonish his aides to scrupulously follow the law with regard to aid to the Contras. As he has often said, "All you have to do is say no." All he had to do was say no to the sale of arms to Iran, no to the payment of any form of ransom, and no to the slightest deviation from embracing the full spirit of the Boland Amendment while it was still the law of the land.

But he didn't. And for a time the bad ideas prevailed.

Something as painful as the Iran-Contra affair usually has some lessons and Americans may be culling them from its wreckage just as we sifted political lessons from the ashes of Watergate in the early 1970s. The lessons of the Iran-Contra affair are quite different from those of Watergate because they are much more deeply involved with the substance of governing a powerful, free society in a dangerous, hostile world. Let's take a look at what some of these lessons might be.

Trust. There is an old German proverb that says "mistrust carries one much further than trust." Trust is a noble quality in a person, but in high government office it can be a dangerous one. Any modern president of the United States must delegate massively. He has no choice. He must allow others to act in his name. But the Iran-Contra affair reaffirmed how important it is to continuously monitor that delegation of authority.

President Reagan's personal trust in people is almost unbounded. He assumes people will tell him the truth, will not lie to him, will not deceive him. He assumes people will not put their personal fortunes above their public trust. It is an endearing quality, but it is unsuitable—in that extreme—to the world of Washington.

During the last few decades the absolute size of government has increased massively, far more than the number of high government officials who run it. One consequence of this growth is that each government official has enormously greater power, and their decisions can have large impacts on the lives and fortunes of many, many individuals. As the stakes involved increase, so do the efforts of those involved to turn decisions in their favor. The temptations can be great.

A president of the United States must govern with a skeptical eye on all that is presented to him, questioning and probing when necessary. If there is any moral to the Iran-Contra affair, it is that the leader who accepts people at their word, even those of long acquaintance, runs a great danger of being betrayed.

Secrecy. The difficulty of decisionmaking on the foreign policy side of government is complicated by the need for secrecy. Many of the decisions made in foreign policy—especially defense and intelligence matters—are based on extremely sensitive information, very secret, highly classified. This is how much of it must be. For if the information were made public it could have serious and damaging consequences to our national security.

Exposing some classified information could make it possible for an enemy to figure out who gave it to us and thus endanger the life of the spy. Spying is serious business; it can sometimes kill. Exposing classified information can also, in some cases, alert the enemy that we know what they are up to, allowing them to conceal those activities from us in the future. And finally, exposing classified information may give to our enemies knowledge they can use to fashion weapons or strategy that threatens our national security. Secrecy is necessary and indispensable in a free society that is only a small part of an unfree world.

Unfortunately, we pay a high price for that secrecy. The more important a piece of information is to the decision-making process, the more critical a piece of information is to swinging the decision one way or the other, the more likely that piece of information will be highly classified. The more highly classified the piece of information, the fewer the people who know about it, and the fewer the people who can be trusted to take part in the decision-making process. The fewer people who are cleared to know about highly classified information, the more important, and busy, those people are likely to be.

The natural end result of this necessary process is that the most important, most critical pieces of intelligence are often restricted to the hands of a very few, very busy people. The unfortunate consequence is that the kind of unlimited, free-ranging, rigorous scrutiny that any major new public policy desperately needs is sharply limited. The same shroud of secrecy that protects us also cripples our capability to make wise decisions. The Iran-Contra affair is a classic case. Secrecy dominated and then controlled the events of the Iran-Contra affair as the circle of discussion and debate narrowed, and fewer and fewer gave advice and counsel, with less and less wisdom and judgment.

There are other costs to secrecy in government. The purpose of secrecy is to deny knowledge to our enemies. It is not the purpose of secrecy to prevent our own citizens from knowing what is going on. It is emphatically not to deny knowledge of public policies to our political opponents, as happened in the Iran-Contra affair. Secrecy is a very powerful, slippery weapon. The very fact of secrecy makes it all too easy to turn it from a legitimate purpose to an illegitimate one.

Secrecy is also a happy breeding ground for incompetence and crookedness. The shield of secrecy that prevents an inquisitive enemy from abroad, with an army of professional spies, from finding out what is going on in the United States can also be used to hide failed policies and corruption from the folks at home. The temptations to hide failure and steal a few dollars are pervasive and sometimes overwhelming.

Secrecy can hide good things also. One of the most difficult things for a person making a career in modern day intelligence work is that his successes can only be recognized and shared by a very small number of people. Much of what some of our spies do cannot even be shared with their spouses or families. Successful spies must be very strong people—smart, capable, willing to encounter danger, and live with the fact that no one will ever know the really important things they did for their country.

But secrecy is important and it is going to stay with us for a long time. The trick is for us to learn how to best live with it, how to keep it controlled and tamed, to remain the master of our secrets. It has not and will not be easy.

There is a delicious power to having secrets. The fewer people who know the secret, the better it tastes. The more tightly guarded the secret, the more important it is. There are few things that make a person feel as important as being handed a bound document, whose stiff cover is boldly stamped with deep red or black or bright green words like TOP SECRET, CODE WORD, and EYES ONLY. I have seen people very carefully leave those documents casually face up on their desk, the same way some people leave expensive magazines on their coffee tables at home.

The privilege of being privy to secrets that only the president of the United States and a few others will ever know is something that is powerfully attractive to most people. Having access to classified material in government is a symbol of status, and acquires a value over and above the content of the classified material. That is one of the reasons why it is so difficult to do what we should do.

What we should do is simple in principle. There is far, far too much classified material and far, far too many people with access to that material. Things are classified that should not be classified. There are so many things classified that it is difficult to properly protect really important secrets. Our scarce counterintelligence resources are spread thinly. As many people have recommended for many years—including in recent years such authorities as Edwin Meese, the attorney general, and Edward Teller, the nuclear physicist—we need to reduce the number of things that are classified, the number of people who are cleared to receive secret material, and then focus our energies on preserving and protecting the important secrets that remain. Easy to say, but it won't be easy to do.

My first encounter with the secrecy classification system of the U.S. government came in 1970 when I was working in the White House as a special assistant to President Nixon. I chaired an interagency task force charged with recommending policy and legislation to eliminate the military draft and establish all-volunteer armed forces. One night while working late on a report I realized that some of the numbers concerning the size of our military forces that I wanted to use came from a report stamped with a big, bold red TOP SECRET. I knew I could not take classified numbers from a top secret report and use them in my report without classifying my report top secret also. And I had to use the numbers or my report would not make any sense. Reasoning right along, that meant I somehow had to classify this version of my report, something I had no idea how to do.

Given the importance of classifying a document top secret, I knew there must be a detailed, formal procedure to follow. I dreaded it, but figured it had to be done. So I called John Court, one of Henry Kissinger's staff members on the National Security Council who had worked closely with me on a segment of the interagency report, and said, "John, I've got a little problem. I have to use some classified military statistics in this report. How do I go about getting it classified top secret?"

He asked, "Do you have a typewriter?"

I said, "Yes."

"OK, then," he said, "first you take the piece of paper you want to classify and roll it into the typewriter."

I cranked the paper into the typewriter.

"All right, I've done that."

"Fine," he continued. "Now type TOP SECRET."

I'm sure there are detailed, formal procedures for classifying material, but that night Court's system seemed to work just fine. Nobody ever questioned the classification and since then I've often wondered how many other documents got classified the same way.

For a total period of more than a decade, I have been cleared for and had access to the most highly classified secrets of the United States. Little of that material seemed to justify the effort and expense of trying to keep it secret. Much of it I read about, or was shortly about to read, in the *New York Times* or the *Washington Post*.

We need to reduce the amount of material classified and focus on keeping secret the precious few things that justify the effort and expense necessary to do it correctly. And then we should provide stiff penalties for those who do reveal the remaining secrets. The shabby, open secret around Washington is that there is no real penalty for revealing classified information.

Outside Advisers. A set of outside advisers in critical policy areas is essential to the successful functioning of a modern-day presidency in the United States. To a president, there is great value in being able to talk directly with independent, private citizens every now and then. He is much more likely to get from them the straight talk he needs to hear, free from any trimming or slanting that is the natural result of an aging administration. After a while, people in government develop vested interests in pursuing certain policies and soon consciously and unconsciously become advocates of their position. Often the hardest thing for a president to get is a full range of options in critical issue areas, with all the pros and cons clearly and concisely set forth. It is a brutal, sometimes painful process, but absolutely necessary if a president is to have a fighting chance to make sound, wise decisions.

At the onset of the Iran-Contra affair, President Reagan's network of outside advisers on the foreign policy side was placed in mothballs, their gun barrels plugged. The President's Foreign Intelligence Advisory Board (PFIAB), which should have been in the forefront of reviewing and checking covert action, was purged, struggling along with an administratively weak chairman who had no close political or strong personal ties to the president. A large PFIAB, well staffed, with leadership the president and other key people in the national security community respected and listened to, could be an effective check against a recurrence of the policy mistakes that happened during the Iran-Contra affair.

The President's Intelligence Oversight Board (PIOB) was misled repeatedly by William Casey, and the tiny three-person board, with one professional staff member and one secretary, was woefully unequipped to ferret out the truth from the intelligence community. While not expected to investigate and discover potential violations of law by the intelligence community, PIOB is responsible for investigating any charges of wrongdoing that are brought to its attention. But even then the board has little power. If someone lies to the board there is no penalty, save the shame of being found out. The PIOB should be given the power to take testimony under oath, as congressional committees do, with all the usual penalties for perjury.

The third presidential advisory board in this area is the President's General Advisory Committee on Arms Control and Disarmament (GAC). While it had nothing to do with the Iran-Contra affair, it is concerned with a vitally important issue. In 1985, the chairman, William Graham, who did a superb job in chairing the committee and providing sound, timely advice to the president, resigned to become the deputy head of the National Aeronautics and Space Administration (NASA), and later science adviser to the president himself. When Graham left in the fall of 1985 he was not replaced for almost two years. The committee fell into disuse, people resigned, and by the fall of 1987 there were eight vacancies. Whether by neglect or deliberate intent, this crucial advisory committee was taken out of action for two full years at a very critical time.

One fear commonly expressed about these three boards is that they are potential security risks, that they have so many members (twenty-one for the old PFIAB, three for PIOB, and fifteen for GAC) that they cannot keep secrets. Nonsense. Over the years the boards have had an extraordinarily good record of keeping secrets. Almost never does anything leak from the advisory boards, although there were a couple of serious leaks from PFIAB when it began operating with its much smaller membership of fourteen in 1986.

The vast majority of leaks of government secrets come from full-time members of the government, usually very high-ranking officials, who operate with almost full impunity. The people they leak to, the press, will not tell who the leakers are and, in the rare instance when the leakers are caught, nothing of any note happens to them. No, the real dislike of outside advisory boards is due to the fact that they are outsiders—with direct access to the president. The outside advisers don't leak many secrets, but they have the background and independence to flatly contradict a foolish policy set forth by inside, full-time employees.

An outside board of advisers, such as PFIAB, should be of ex-

traordinary help in evaluating the desirability and suitability of covert activities. It should be more able to resist the temptation to
support a covert action that is designed primarily to hide its existence from the American public rather than from our enemies. As
a general rule, covert activities should be confined to those activities that, if they were known, would have the overwhelming support of the American people. If you can't make your case politically,
chances are that you don't have a good case.

The existence of a strong and active PFIAB, with full and timely
access to covert activities, would almost certainly guarantee that an
Iran-Contra-style fiasco would not happen again. If any part of the
machinations of the Iran-Contra affair—the sales of arms, the payment of ransom, the diversion of money to the Contras—had come
before my colleagues on the board in 1985, there certainly would
have been a strong, immediate protest to President Reagan—one
I think he would have listened to seriously.

Separation of Intelligence and Policy. Like the separation of church
and state, although not quite so well known, there has been a long
tradition in America of keeping the business of collecting and producing intelligence separate and apart from the policy-making process. For good reason. There is a strong temptation to slant
intelligence reports to support one's policy if you are both a policy
player and simultaneously a producer of intelligence.

That is why no head of the United States intelligence services
ever had cabinet rank before William Casey. It was not that the
services of the head of the CIA were not highly valued, it was just
deemed inappropriate for him to participate in policymaking. His
was an equally important, but very different, role—to provide an
objective set of facts and judgments that would give the policymakers a sound base for their eventual decisions.

President Reagan broke this tradition in 1981. Because of very
unusual circumstances he gave Bill Casey an important role in the
policy-making process—complete with a seat at the cabinet table
and a suite of offices in the White House complex. Most of this
break with tradition was corrected when William Webster replaced
Casey after he died in 1987. Webster was pointedly not given cabinet rank for the express purpose of once again separating intelligence gathering from policymaking. But, like Casey, Webster
maintains an office in the White House complex. If you walked
along the third floor of the Old Executive Office Building in 1988,

and looked very closely at the door of the office in the northwest corner of the building, you saw a small, two-line sign that read, "William Webster, Director of Central Intelligence."

No Military or Intelligence Personnel as NSC Advisers. Another old tradition in the United States is civilian control of the military, stemming from the suspicions of the founding fathers. It is more than a tradition; it is the law. Section 133 of Title 10 of the United States Code proclaims that "a person may not be appointed as Secretary of Defense within 10 years after relief from active duty as a commissioned officer or a regular component of an armed force."

We should now seriously consider whether that same prohibition should apply equally to the national security adviser. When the post of national security adviser was first established in 1947, no one ever dreamed that the position might one day possess the influence and power that Henry Kissinger, for example, wielded. In a very real sense the national security adviser to the president is often superior to the secretary of defense, thus effectively short-circuiting the carefully built-in safeguards that have developed over the years.

Look at the Iran-Contra affair. Robert McFarlane, the national security adviser when the whole business was developing, was a career military man. John Poindexter, who took it upon himself not to tell the president about crucial covert activities, was a career military man. Oliver North was a career military man. North's two top aides were career military men. There was even a high-ranking member of the intelligence community working in the White House. Donald Gregg, who was the Vice President's national security adviser, spent some nineteen years in the higher reaches of the CIA before resigning to join President Carter's National Security Council staff and eventually working his way over to Vice President Bush.

The law that prohibits military officers from assuming the position of secretary of defense, unless they have been retired from active duty for ten years, should now be extended. For the same reasons we do not allow career military people to become secretary of defense, neither should we allow career military people to hold the more sensitive, potentially more powerful job of national security adviser to the president. And while we are seriously considering why we allow military officers a free rein in the White House that is denied to them in the Pentagon, let us also consider the wisdom of allowing career military people to serve as the vice president's national security adviser.

Records of All Cash Transactions. As the size of the federal government expands and the wealth of the world grows, the sums of money handled covertly will grow also. The existence of large amounts of cash or travelers checks or any other valuable untraceable commodity, such as gold for example, is a temptation that almost always leads to corruption. We need to require a thorough, complete system of monitoring every cash or near-cash transaction, a system that will ensure full and timely accountability for all government employees, including those engaged in covert activities. We have a very extensive system now, but as the Iran-Contra affair proved, it is not complete.

The People. The most difficult problem of all is people. Picking people who will not only work hard and be loyal, but who will also be honest and wise and politically astute. At times during the Iran-Contra affair, President Reagan was deceived and misled by some of his closest, most trusted aides. There is no way that he or any other president can guarantee that will never happen again. There is no way to guarantee White House aides and cabinet heads will have wisdom and integrity and display judgment.

We will just have to try.

We live today in the greatest nation that ever existed—the freest, the most prosperous, the most powerful.

This nation is founded on the idea that people are capable of governing themselves, that dictators and rulers and masters of all sorts are not the natural condition of mankind. But that idea is only an assumption, some might say a giant leap of faith. For it assumes that enough of us will take the time, put forth the effort, and dedicate ourselves to the process of governing—of nominating and electing people qualified to represent us, people committed to preserving and protecting our rights.

As far as people go there is one who makes more of a difference than anyone else. The president. We all know that it is the president who picks those top government officials to whom so much power and authority is delegated. We all know that it is the president who makes the final decisions, right or wrong, on critical issues. We all know that it is the character and managing skills of the president that sets the tone of our entire government. And if we move from the economy and domestic programs and scandal into the realm of nuclear weaponry, we begin to realize that the power that rests in the hands of that person is awesome.

We know all that but we usually don't like to think about it. Just the idea of that much power in the hands of one person can seem, well, unseemly. But it is there, and every four years the power grows even greater.

The obvious lesson is that the election of a U.S. president is just as important as we all know it is, perhaps more.

While President Reagan was misled and, in a sense, betrayed by some of his senior aides and advisers in the Iran-Contra affair, it is also true that he, and he alone, made the decisions that led to scandal. It was President Reagan, not William Casey or John Poindexter or Oliver North, that ordered the sale of U.S. weapons to Iran and allowed effective ransom to be paid for American hostages.

In the broad sweep of history the painful saga of the Iran-Contra affair will be at best a small footnote. But if it reminds us once again that our republic is vulnerable, that it does matter who is president, and who the president's men and women are, then it will not have been endured in vain.

Even the ancient Greek gods were not without flaw. Achilles, the son of the king of the Myrmidons and Thetis, the sea nymph, was reputed to be the "bravest, handsomest, and greatest warrior of the army of Agamemnon"[3]—until a small weakness in Achilles' heel eventually led to his mortal wounding by an arrow from Apollo.

Those very qualities of character that made it possible for Reagan to do so much, to rise so swiftly and surely to power, to put us on the path toward the reduction of nuclear weapons, to lead us to the greatest economic expansion in history, were the same qualities that almost destroyed him. The same detached, almost regal manner of managing was, on its other side, a naive trust in aides that bordered on irresponsibility. The same willingness to delegate that helped Reagan produce Star Wars and Reaganomics also brought him the Iran-Contra affair.

But unlike Achilles' wound, Reagan's was not fatal. Not to him nor to the Revolution.

Seven

After Reagan

"What Reagan and his comrades have done is to shape America's policy agenda well into the twenty-first century."

Chapter Thirty-Three

THE REVOLUTIONARIES

Perhaps the most revealing interview Reagan ever gave took place on May 14, 1979, many months before he began to campaign full-time for the presidency. It was a one-hour television interview with Bill Moyers, one of America's most skillful and sensitive reporters. Whether it was his training for the clergy or his long service as a White House aide to President Johnson, Moyers somehow managed to elicit some personal, very private views on the presidency that Reagan never expressed publicly before and, as far as I know, never did again. Right at the end Moyers said, "If you run, it seems to me you're going to be confronted with three accusations. You're too old, you're too reluctant—you're not that hungry enough to pay the price to become president—and third, you're out of touch." Reagan began to respond defensively, but Moyers interrupted:

"Are you *hungry* enough for it?"

Reagan replied:

"Hungry enough for that job? Not in the sense of saying, 'Oh, I want to say I'm president, I want to live in the White House.' But hungry to do the things that I think can be done and at an age where I'm not looking down the road saying, 'How will this affect the votes in the next election?' But to be able from the first day to say: 'I can do this. I can try to do this for the people' . . . you bet I'm hungry to do that."[1]

Well, Reagan is now in his eighth year as president. Did he do what he wanted to do? Did he do something for the people? Or did the revolution fail? Did the Iran-Contra scandal of 1986 and the stock market crash of 1987 reveal the weaknesses of the Reagan administration and its policies? Have the nation's hopes for lasting security and permanent prosperity been left in the wake of these turbulent episodes? Or were these damaging events largely independent of new revolutionary forces at work?

As is always true in politics, we can never be sure about the future. For so much depends on what people do. But there is mounting evidence that suggests that the main element of what became known as the Reagan revolution will continue, that the Iran-Contra affair and the stock market crash were aberrations, caused by events unlikely to repeat themselves. Of course, Reagan himself will no longer be president. His place will be taken by a new leader and thousands of new people will staff the federal government. But whether the new administration in January 1989 is Democrat or Republican, it will be largely irrelevant to the major policy changes that will likely dominate this republic for the next decade or so.

What Reagan and his comrades have done is to shape America's policy agenda well into the twenty-first century. The prospects are nil for sharply progressive tax rates and big, new social welfare programs, some of the former mainstays of the Democrats' domestic policy agenda. Everyone is for a strong national defense, differing only in the degree and quality of it. Massive funding for nuclear missile defense efforts and the turning from arms control to arms reduction will remain high on our foreign policy agenda. By and large the United States has reached a consensus on the big policy items—national defense and the economy—that always dominate the political process.

Of course, many policy problems remain. The large federal deficit and the imbalance in foreign trade will be difficult and unpleasant to solve. There are many other troublesome issues—from abortion to immigration policy to AIDS to agriculture—that, although not as fundamental or critical as national defense and the economy, will continue to demand our talents.

But the course has been altered. We are now following a new path, not drastically different from the one we were following a decade or so ago, but one marked by a heightened appreciation of the need for a strong national defense, the desirability of low tax rates and minimal government regulation, and a greater prosperity and sense of national confidence.

With all our faults the United States has assumed an even stronger role as a model for other countries throughout the world. Virtually everywhere you look you see other countries copying many of our actions, even though they often call it something else. In China and the Soviet Union, in France and New Zealand, and in many other lands, they have changed direction, moving towards more capitalism. True, many of them have not gone very far, but the important thing is not how far they have yet gone, but the fact that they have turned. And, until and unless there is a new intellectual revolution that produces ideas for a society that is more productive and more free than a capitalistic one, these trends will likely continue.

Paradoxically, the greater the growing consensus in the world on the fundamental issues of prosperity and peace, the more likely we are to be in for a time of bitter and confusing politics. For if the tide of the new capitalism continues to rise higher, and if the joint efforts of the United States and the Soviet Union to reduce nuclear weapons are successful, we may enter a new era—an era of peace and capitalism in the world, marked by rapidly growing prosperity. And if that happens, people will be freed from more fundamental concerns and able to focus on other issues. It may be a raucous and messy time politically, but it will be a sign of fundamental achievement of a more stable, more prosperous, safer world.

Already there are signs of political discontent in the United States. At the same time that political consensus is growing on fundamental issues, the political leadership of both parties is fading away. For various reasons the leaders who dominated both parties for the last twenty years will not be running in 1988 and beyond. The old oak trees are gone—Goldwater, Rockefeller, Nixon, Ford, and Reagan for the Republicans, the Kennedys, Johnson, McGovern, Carter, and Mondale for the Democrats. The years after Reagan will be a time for new political leadership. There will be no choice.

At the heart of any revolution are the people who cause it to happen, the prime movers, the thinkers, the political activists, the campaigners. They are the soldiers who topple governments and change the course of history, paving the way for others to govern. They are the revolutionaries.

We know a lot about the famous revolutionaries of our country—those who were involved in its making, Samuel Adams and Thomas Jefferson and George Washington; those who preserved it and expanded freedom, like Abraham Lincoln; and those who fought wars to defend it from aggression, Woodrow Wilson and Franklin Roosevelt.

We know a lot about the major political figures of our time who played key roles in the revolutionary changes of the last twenty-five years—Barry Goldwater, Richard M. Nixon, and Ronald Reagan. We know a lot about the intellectuals who helped drive that revolution, from William F. Buckley, Jr., the editor of *National Review,* to Milton Friedman, the Nobel laureate economist, from Ayn Rand, the novelist and philosopher, to Irving Kristol, the social critic. We even know quite a bit about the early patrons—men like Richard Scaife and David Packard, whose financial support was crucial to the movement's growth.

But we usually neglect the stories, not out of malice but simply because we do not know them, of the thousands of men and women who, while they never achieve fame, also contributed significantly to that ongoing revolution. Most of these people will remain unsung, their exploits known only to family and friends. But their stories are, in their own way, just as important as the adventures of the ones we know.

Whenever we get the chance, we should tell the stories. The three short stories that follow illustrate, with real people and real events, how individuals can and do influence the course of political events in the United States.

The first story is about a man from Rhode Island, Silas Downer, virtually unknown to history, who by his writings and speeches and political activism, helped bring about the revolution of 1776.

The second story is about a man from Montana, Frank Whetstone, who is still active today and who, three times in the past, has played an important role in determining the Republican nominee for president.

The third story is about a man from Idaho, Bill Barlow, a businessman, not engaged in writing or politics, who used the events of his everyday life to reaffirm and strengthen one of our most basic constitutional rights.

Silas Downer

Late one hot summer afternoon well over two hundred years ago a man, self-described as very small in stature, climbed a ladder high into a tall elm tree growing in front of Captain Olney's Tavern in the town square of Providence, Rhode Island, a small colonial city on the East Coast of North America. The date was July 25, 1768, eight years before the Revolutionary War began in America. His name was Silas Downer. Thirty-nine years old. One of thirty men who graduated from Harvard College in the class of 1747. At Harvard he wrote his master's thesis on the sensitive question of political liberty, arguing against the proposition that "each person in all of his own private activities, must look to the advantage of the community."[2] He was a lawyer by training and the town's librarian by profession. Downer was one of a small breed in pre-revolutionary America, a genuine intellectual.

Downer was neither famous nor wealthy. He never ran for public office. On the other hand he had a reputation for being "highly intelligent, widely read, and a talented writer."[3]

He was a settled man, married for ten years to the former Sara Kelton, although there is evidence to suggest he may have been somewhat of a rake in his younger days. While at Harvard he was twice fined for possessing prohibited liquors, and once fined for disturbing a prayer meeting.[4] Just two months after he married, another young colonial lady, Mary Deane, hauled him into a Rhode Island court and charged Downing with "being the father of a female Bastard Child." Silas was acquitted "from being the Reputed father."[5]

This day Silas' mind was on matters of far greater consequence. Today he was thinking about revolution. When he reached the top of the ladder he stepped onto the uneven plank floor of a tree house perched among the shady leaves. From his vantage point high in the old elm tree he could see the large crowd of his fellow citizens assembled in the square below, waiting to hear him speak as advertised in last Saturday's newspaper, the *Providence Gazette* of July 23, 1768.

Downer was a member of the Sons of Liberty, the secret society of men and women who plotted the American Revolution. The Sons of Liberty was formed in the summer of 1765 to oppose the stamp taxes the British levied upon the American colonies and quickly developed into the vehicle of revolution. They borrowed their name from a phrase used in a speech by a member of the British parliament defending the interests of the colonists.

The bells chimed out the time, five o'clock, and Silas Downer began to speak. It was powerful stuff. As Carl Bridenbaugh, a historian who read the original document, said, "The eloquence and unequivocably radical argument of the orator still leap out from the yellowed pages."[6] Downer spoke for well over half an hour, explaining, reasoning, and pleading with his fellow countrymen. The bottom line of his speech was this: "In short, I cannot be persuaded that the parliament of Great-Britain have any lawful right to make *any laws whatsoever* to bind us, because there can be no fountain from whence such right can flow."[7] Downer was preaching treason against the mother country publicly, openly, arguing that Englishmen had no right whatsoever to rule the colonies. It was the intellectual heart of the argument that would soon lead to war. What is truly remarkable about the speech that Silas Downer gave from his tree house that afternoon in late July 1768 is that he spoke of the revolutionary idea—England had no right to govern the colonies—fully *six years before* anyone else dared to express it in public.[8]

In America we honor and revere the men who made our revolution, the minutemen who fought on the battlefield at Concord against the British, the founding fathers who wrote the Constitution, the great patriots of the Revolution, Thomas Paine, Thomas Jefferson, Samuel Adams, John Adams, James Otis, and George Washington. And we should, for these were giants of history, great men who accomplished great things. But few speak of Silas Downer and others like him who played smaller, but still vital roles in securing liberty in the United States.

When reading the basic, more general histories of the United States it is all too easy to get the impression that one dark night in April 1775 the silversmith Paul Revere bounded onto the back of his horse and galloped around the countryside in Massachusetts crying, "The British are coming, the British are coming." And then, as if by magic, farmers grabbed their muskets from the rack on the wall, and hurried off to do battle with the British. Later, after years of hardship and bravery, the unorganized Americans defeated the British military machine and, in a flash of political and philosophical brilliance, wrote the American Constitution. Of course, it did not happen this way.

There was a long period of preparation. Of repeated injustices committed by the British government against the colonies, of complaints and resistance against this treatment, and then of planning and plotting to shake off the English yoke of oppression. The foundations of the American Revolution were laid far back in time, by hundreds, perhaps thousands of men and women who thought and argued, and planned, and then took action. It was not planned and carried out solely by farmers, mechanics, and backwoodsmen. The leaders of the revolution came primarily from intellectuals and craftsmen who lived in the cities, who drew their inspiration from great thinkers like John Locke. Most of those who plotted the Revolution we know little about and never will, for much of what they did was done in secrecy.

At first they met in secret, they traveled in secret, they corresponded secretly, and they wrote under assumed names. They formed secret societies—the most famous and powerful being the Sons of Liberty, that loose association of colonists from New Hampshire to North Carolina, covering the length and breadth of the growing colonies—all dedicated to the cause of a new nation founded on individual liberty, to revolution.

There were even a few chapters of the Daughters of Liberty, unusual because women were not allowed to take part in the normal political life in the eighteenth century. But these women were not bound by convention, and soon were meeting, writing, and conspiring. During the Stamp Act crisis in 1765, when the colonists violently objected to an arbitrary stamp tax imposed by the British parliament, one young Daughters of Liberty chapter "announced that they would accept the attentions of only those young men who were willing to fight against the act 'to the last extremity.' "[9]

Many historians have neglected the intellectual foundations of the American Revolution, concentrating instead on the battles between armies and navies on land and sea, on the marching men and clashing bayonets, and on the solemn drama of writing and ratifying the Constitution. But in recent times it seems that more and more historians have been reviewing the forgotten archives. We know now, for example, that there were organized Sons of Liberty groups in at least fifteen cities, and that some of these groups were "knit into an intercolonial correspondence union," many years before the Committees on Correspondence were formed in 1772.[10] There were, perhaps, more early Sons of Liberty organizations and if we are lucky we shall find them as the historical research continues.

Silas Downer, the man who was one of the political theorists of the American Revolution, perhaps the earliest one, lay virtually unknown in history for almost 200 years until the noted historian Carl Bridenbaugh published a thirty-nine page biography of Downer in 1974. We can argue about the relative significance of Downer as a seminal thinker in the American Revolution, but if we apply the usual standards for crediting originality of ideas—who said it first and, most importantly, who published it first—then Downer's role in the making of our Revolution is significant.

Undoubtedly there are many like Downer, quiet men and women, unnoticed yet by history, who fought passionately and successfully in the battle for liberty. Americans did not ask the British for their liberty, they demanded it, and when it was refused, they took it. But before they took it, they thought and carefully worked out the reasons behind their actions. Downer was one of the thinkers of the American Revolution, one of the first colonists to write down his thoughts, to speak publicly of the reasons for revolution, to publish his political thoughts and conclusions in pamphlets and newspapers.

But how did a handful of intellectuals who believed in the political philosophy of John Locke, aided and abetted by mechanics and backwoodsmen, plan and carry out a successful revolution? How did they defeat Great Britain, the most powerful nation in the world, and snatch from her nervous hands one of the most valuable pieces of real estate in the world? In other words, how did they move from a diverse colony of farmers and merchants in 1765 to a united, ultimately effective fighting force some ten years later, itching and spoiling for war with Great Britain?

They had a campaign. Not exactly like the presidential campaigns we have today. But they did have a campaign, at least if you define a campaign as an activity or process wherein you try to persuade enough people to a certain political point of view that action is taken to change public policy. In that sense, they had a terrific campaign, one that lasted for well over ten years. It was waged privately, by letter and whispered talk, and publicly, rarely in the early years but more and more frequently as the ten-year campaign rolled on, by pamphlets, some no more than a few pages long, printed by private presses, by newspapers, and by speeches at public meetings. The campaign was not to elect any one person to office. The campaign was to persuade enough people in the fledgling country that an armed revolt was necessary, *absolutely necessary*, against Great Britain if they were to preserve and protect the personal liberties they now enjoyed and wished to pass on to their children.

The campaign succeeded brilliantly. When the time came to fire the guns in 1776, the American colonists were largely ready, at least enough of them to ensure a long, determined effort at revolution, enough of them to outlast both the British and their fellow Americans who were not persuaded by the campaign. All through the five hard years of war, to the final victory at Yorktown in 1781, and to a new nation with a constitution in 1787, the Sons and Daughters of Liberty were everywhere, guided perhaps by the closing words of Silas Downer's speech to them in July 1768:

"We do therefore, in the name and on behalf of all the true Sons of Liberty in America, Great-Britain, Ireland, Corsica, or wheresoever they are dispersed throughout the world, dedicate and solemnly devote this tree, to be a tree of liberty. May all our councils and deliberations under its venerable branches be guided by wisdom, and directed to the support and maintenance of that liberty, which our renowned forefathers sought out and found under trees and in the wilderness. May it long flourish, and may the Sons of Liberty often repair hither, to confirm and strengthen each other. When they look towards this sacred Elm, may they be penetrated with a sense of their duty to themselves, their country, and their posterity. And may they, like the house of David, grow stronger and stronger, while their enemies, like the house of Saul, grow weaker and weaker.

"Amen."

Frank Whetstone

November 7, 1986. I got up at 6:30 A.M. and drove to the San Francisco airport. I was flying to Kalispell, a small mountain town in northern Montana, seventy-two miles from the Canadian border, named after the Kalispell Indians who lived there long before white men came to America. From there I was driving to an isolated ranch in the Rocky Mountains. The weather report said that it was snowing and the temperature was expected to fall to five degrees below zero that night.

By the time we landed in Kalispell, the sun had slid behind the mountains. It was bitter cold and the sky was black as I loaded my duffle bags into the four-wheel drive I rented from Hertz. I'd done it before and I didn't know why I was doing it again, for there is nothing so taxing and dangerous as driving on ice-covered, winding mountain roads you have never seen before, at night, in a snowstorm. The ranch I was headed for was called the Double Diamond, named after the design that graced its branding irons. It was run by a personable, highly competent young man named Casey Cunningham, a native of Montana. The ranch was almost 90 miles from the airport and it took me close to four hours to find it. When I stopped in front of the single level, heavy-timbered cabins it was very dark and very cold, with only the warm, yellow glow from the windows indicating life.

From all parts of the country that day, from as far away as Massachusetts and Hawaii, about thirty men were doing the same thing—taking time off from their work, using vacation time, paying all their own expenses—to rendezvous at a snowbound mountain ranch for several days of talking, meeting, and listening. They were all sworn to semi-secrecy. Their families, perhaps their bosses, and a few close friends knew where they were, but no one else, and in particular the national press corps, even knew there was a meeting. If someone observed them slowly driving through the gate on the snow-covered road leading up to the ranch, they would note that individually they were not a terribly distinguished lot—a few lawyers, ranchers, an academician, small businessmen, and perhaps a banker or two.

But taken together they were a very special gathering, engaged in a high risk game with the highest stakes in the world.

Some had played five or six times before. For others it would be the first time. They were the twentieth century equivalent of the Sons of Liberty, the informal, secret bands that plotted and planned the events that led up to the first American Revolution in 1776. These modern Sons of Liberty were now plotting to elect the next president of the United States of America, planning and scheming to determine who would succeed Ronald Reagan to become the most powerful person in the world on January 20, 1989. This was the first time I had been invited.

At first it seemed preposterous. These were not the wealthiest men in the United States, they were not very well known, not celebrities. With a few exceptions they held no high government office, there were no Nobel Prize winners; not one of them, individually, would be considered a powerful man. To an objective observer their quest was at best presumptuous, at worst an arrogant tilting at political windmills. But in the American tradition of the men who flew to the moon, in spite of earlier assurances by some of the finest scientists in the world who said they could not, these men were instrumental before in nominating presidential candidates of the Republican party and then electing them president.

Many of the men in this group played a key and decisive role in nominating Barry Goldwater for president in 1964, although he lost the general election to Lyndon Baines Johnson. They helped nominate and elect Richard Nixon president in 1968. And when Nixon ran for reelection in 1972 they were just quiet, watching and waiting. In 1976 they played a key and decisive role in Ronald Reagan's precedent-shattering, though ultimately unsuccessful, drive against the incumbent president, Gerald R. Ford. Despite Reagan's razor-thin loss to Ford in the 1976 fight for the Republican nomination, they stayed loyal to Reagan and once again played a key and decisive role in his nomination and election in 1980. In 1984, when Reagan ran for reelection, they again relaxed and watched and waited, as they did in 1972, and looked ahead to 1988 and beyond.

Now they were meeting again.

The meetings spread over three days. Nothing very formal. No agenda, except to determine who ought to be the next president of the United States. A lot of private conversations, small group discussions, a couple of full group meetings. Not all the meetings took place inside the cozy, warm log cabins. These were men who felt as comfortable in mountain snow as in a padded chair by the fire—strong environmentalists with a deep reverence for nature. They climbed and hiked and talked in pairs, and in threes and fours, out through the fields and woods. Most of the players had known each other for many, many years. They shared the strong common bond of believing in a political philosophy of limited government, one which maximized individual liberty and economic freedom, backed up by a powerful national defense clearly superior to any in the world. And they trusted each other. While they often disagreed sharply on the best person to embody their political beliefs in the White House, that was only a detail in the complex bond that drew them together.

The group had not remained constant. Old members left or died, new members joined. And I am sure it was not the only group, be it Democrat or Republican, that met secretly to consider the question of who should next be president. This particular group was dominated by men from the far West of the United States. For example, there was Gerald (Jerry) T. Neils who ran a cow-calf ranching operation in Flat Coulee Creek just west of Cut Bank, Montana on the Blackfeet Indian Reservation in the early 1960s. In late 1963 Niels became the cochairman of the Goldwater-for-President organization in Montana. At the Republican convention in July 1964 in San Francisco, Montana gave all of its fourteen delegates to Goldwater in his winning drive for the presidential nomination.

And then there was Anderson (Andy) Carter from New Mexico, a tall, blunt talking rancher and banker who, with his sons, played a significant role in acquiring delegate support in Reagan's rise to power. While unable to attend this particular meeting the Carters were, like so many of the others, back doing what they do best, running their private businesses and thinking about the next revolutionary surprise for political America.

The most distinctive man at the Montana gathering was its chairman and founding father, Frank Whetstone. Whetstone is a big, burly, white-haired man who lives in Cut Bank, a tiny town in northern Montana. If he were a fictional character in a novel about politics in America, he probably would not be believable. But he is real. Whenever a revolution happens we tend to focus all our attention on those who fight in the battles of the revolution. We almost always neglect or forget those who planned the revolution, the ones who thought about where to step before the first steps were taken.

Like many of the people who belonged to the Sons of Liberty

and plotted the first American Revolution, Whetstone did not belong to any special group or class of people. He was just one of a
small band of Americans who felt so strongly about national policy
that he dropped everything he was doing and went out in 1964 and
helped elect Republican delegates in the western mountain states
to go to the Republican convention in 1964 and vote for Barry
Goldwater. Goldwater lost that year, so no one paid serious attention to the people who were instrumental in securing the nomination for him. In 1968 Whetstone was out corralling western
Republican convention delegates, this time for Richard Nixon. Nixon
won. But still no more than a handful of people paid any attention
to Frank and his boys in the Far West.

In 1976 Frank Whetstone went to work for Ronald Reagan and
lined up an almost solid block of western states delegates that nearly
propelled Reagan into the Republican nomination in his first serious run at the presidency. In 1977 Whetstone and many others like
him went back to work, and their decades of effort paid off bigger
than perhaps even they dreamed was possible. In 1980 they helped
elect one of their own, someone who shared their deepest political
values. With the election of Ronald Reagan, their political fantasy
turned into reality.

Where did the power of this rather unlikely group of political
plotters come from? How on earth did these individuals manage to
exert a significant influence on the course of history? It was done
with a combination of keen insight, courage, sacrifice, and decisive
action. They had the insight to understand that the key to electing
a president was first to nominate him, and that the key to nominating a presidential candidate lay in the selection of the delegates
who did the nominating. They had the courage to make up their
own minds as to who they thought would be a distinguished president and to stick with that conviction, publicly and privately, over
a period of many years. They were willing to sacrifice huge hunks
of their personal time, torn from their careers and their families, to
spend their personal fortunes, to study, and travel, and to work
long hours with no guarantees of success. And they were willing to
take decisive action.

The odds of success were overwhelmingly against them, yet
they pressed on, cajoling and persuading, and electing delegates
who would commit to the candidate of their choice. They took

great risks, pouring time, money, and effort into a venture that others shunned. If they failed no one would take notice, and they would lose all they invested, save the satisfaction of having fought in a great cause. When they won, no one took much notice either, as the attention of the national media machine swung to the presidential nominee and what he was saying, hardly noticing how he got there, neglecting the conspiracies that led to his nomination.

The word conspiracy has a bad, undeserved reputation. Derived from the ancient Latin word *spirare*, which means to breathe, conspire literally means to join in a secret agreement either to do an unlawful act *or* to use such means to accomplish a lawful end. Most people seem to use the word conspire to describe unlawful acts, while most people who conspire do so to accomplish lawful ends. Some people don't even believe in conspiracies. I know, I didn't believe in conspiracies until I started engaging in them some twenty-odd years ago.

There are people like Whetstone and Carter and Neils in all the political parties in the United States. They are the true believers, the ones who take action to back up their beliefs. Most of the time they fail, but they never stop trying and some of them do succeed. They are the modern version of the pre-revolutionary Sons of Liberty. They are Democrats and Republicans, liberals and conservatives. They are the new political revolutionaries in America.

These "sons" of Kalispell and others like them, from every political party, are in a very profound way the unsung heroes of modern America. They played a significant role in helping to preserve and protect the liberties and prosperity and security we enjoy today. Let us hope that their example will serve as a model for future generations of Americans. For the future of liberty and justice will depend on the new sons and daughters of Kalispell.

The most important work any man or woman can do is to preserve and protect and, whenever possible, advance the cause of liberty. Father Time rolls on and the sons of Kalispell grow old and die. Whether their passion for liberty will continue to live, or whether it will only be a wonderful, brief interlude in history, will depend on the next generation, on the young men and women who will meet, if not in the mountains of Montana, then in the skyscrapers of New York or on the beaches of California, to plot and plan the next round of the advancement of liberty.

Bill Barlow

For over twenty years I have been actively involved in three very different worlds—in the intellectual world of the universities and think tanks, in the presidential campaign world, and in the policy-making world of the White House. Through these experiences I have been privileged and lucky to know and work with many of the prime movers in these three different worlds, the people who played major roles in the intellectual and political revolution that is still spreading throughout the world.

They are an extraordinary, diverse group of people, and all, almost without exception, unusually capable. They are intelligent, hard-working, persistent, and dedicated, but what seems to set them apart from others is *why* they are involved. Basically, they care. They often go to great lengths not to show it, but they care very deeply about the society they live in, the nature of the government they have, and the kind of lives they and their children live. Their passion for a free society crosses political party lines. Democrats and Republicans may disagree on what should be done, but they all feel strongly about the political principles they believe in.

A story comes to mind that seems to capture the essence of what motivates people like this. It is a story I heard Ronald Reagan tell a number of times during the many hundreds of speeches I listened to him make on the presidential campaign trail.

I first heard him tell it one night in 1979 when he was speaking to several hundred business executives in a midwestern city. This kind of speech is not an easy one to make. It is almost always given, as this speech was, in a hotel conference room, with stark, off-white walls and functional, semi-comfortable furniture. The room was empty of any warmth or charm. The businessmen were there primarily because they had to be, because of their jobs. They just ate a big meal and were getting sleepy, and some had a drink or two, further dulling their interest in hearing some fancy out-of-towner expound on national policy. Getting and holding the attention of this kind of audience is hard to do, but Reagan managed to do it time after time.

The group he talked to this night seemed more jaded and bored than usual. Maybe it was because they all seemed to be middle-level executives, old enough to realize that there wasn't much hope of changing their lives very much. They all just sat there, polite and quiet. Some of them crossed their arms and stared at the back of the fellow in front of them while Reagan talked.

As he neared the end of his speech, Reagan paused and decided to tell them a story, a story that raised his listeners' heads as they sat up straighter in their seats, a story that by the time it was over had one or two of the men trying to unobtrusively wipe away a tear. Slowly Reagan's words began to capture his audience.

"The other day, I said it was possible to fight city hall and even the marble halls in Washington. Here is confirmation of that fact.

"I mentioned a businessman in Idaho, Bill Barlow, who had been encouraged by his Congressman, George Hansen, to stand up to OSHA (Occupational Safety and Health Administration).

"Bill Barlow and his four sons have a plumbing, heating and electrical subcontracting business in Pocatello, Idaho. They have thirty-five employees in their family-owned business. Bill said he knew that OSHA would get around to inspecting him sooner or later. So, in the meantime, he did a lot of studying and thinking. He came to the conclusion that such inspection of private property by government was a violation of a constitutional right under the Fourth Amendment.*

"Incidentally, OSHA bases its right to search without a warrant on Section 8(a) of the Occupational Safety and Health Act.

"Well, when the OSHA inspectors finally reached the Barlow firm, Bill said, 'Not without a warrant.'

"Earlier a lady in New Mexico had done this and was upheld by a federal court. In Bill's case, however, OSHA declined to get a warrant and obtained a court order instead.

"Bill refused to obey the order and was cited for contempt of court. He petitioned for the empaneling of a three-judge court, challenging the constitutionality of Section 8(a) of the OSHA Act.

"On December 30, 1976, the U.S. District Court ruled in his favor, ruled that Section 8(a) is, indeed, unconstitutional and that it 'directly offends against the prohibitions of the 4th Amendment of the Constitution of the United States of America.'

*Article IV, December 15, 1791: The right of the people to be secure in their persons, houses, papers, and effects, against unreasonable searches and seizures, shall not be violated; and no warrants shall issue, but upon probable cause, supported by oath or affirmation, and particularly describing the place to be searched, and the persons or things to be seized.

"Here is a citizen who, like the farmers at Concord Bridge, took a stand for what he believes is right and, thanks to him, freedom is a little more secure for all of us."

Now Reagan had the full, intense attention of every middle-aged businessman in the room, and he continued.

"This may well be a landmark decision. OSHA has announced it will appeal to the U.S. Supreme Court, but, in the meantime, will suspend further inspection in Idaho.

"Powerful forces are rallying to support OSHA and first in line is the AFL-CIO. Bureaucracy itself feels threatened because OSHA isn't the only agency that has been guilty of search-and-find-guilty missions. The AFL-CIO claims that all government inspections are threatened, but this is a scare tactic exaggeration.

"The people should be on the side of Bill Barlow. All that he is asking and all that the District Court upheld is that shop keepers, farmers, and manufacturers should have the same constitutional protection we give to suspected criminals. They can't be searched without a warrant showing probable cause."

And then Reagan finished his story.

"Bill Barlow's long court battle with the federal government took months of his personal time, cost him tens of thousands of dollars, and put him under strong emotional pressure. All of his friends thought it was hopeless. In the 1970s a lone individual just did not challenge the forces of Washington and expect to win.

"But he did win. The judges held that he was right, that the law was unconstitutional, and that the agents of the most powerful government on the face of the earth could not enter his private property.

"Later, when it was all over, someone asked him why he had done it. Why had he sacrificed so much of his own time, his money, and his effort to fight for this principle? He thought for a moment and then answered,

" 'Well, over the years a lot of our young people have risked and even given their lives for our country.

"I just thought it was time one of us old duffers did something.' "

There was total, rapt silence. Then slowly, one by one, they all stood and applauded for a full minute or so. Reagan looked down until the big room was quiet, then raised his head, casually waved goodbye with one hand, and walked off the stage.

There are a lot of "old duffers" out there—men, women, some

not so old. Many of them have in their own special way, often without anyone knowing or caring, done their part to advance the cause of freedom and to protect the rare and unusual degree of personal liberty we enjoy in America today.

EPILOGUE

Twice in my life I directed the research and policy development operation of a successful political campaign for the presidency of the United States—through the presidential primaries, the nominating convention of the Republican party, the presidential campaign itself, and the transition.

Twice in my life I was appointed by a newly elected president to serve as a domestic and economic policy adviser in the White House, first for Richard Nixon in 1968 and then for Ronald Reagan in 1980.

Twice in my life, I resigned my White House post after a year or two and returned to the Hoover Institution at Stanford University in California. From there, I watched each president succeed beyond my fondest hopes.

Twice I returned briefly during their reelection campaigns to help draft the Republican party platform and then went home again to California to watch the incumbent Republican presidents, first Nixon and then Reagan, get reelected by two of the largest political landslides in American history.

And then, twice in my life, I watched these Republican presidencies disintegrate, consumed and preoccupied with scandal. Twice, just at the peak of their power, two brilliant, conservative presidents came crashing down. President Nixon was destroyed politically. President Reagan was wounded.

Looking backward now, it is clear that the lasting legacy of these men, what they achieved in terms of fundamental change in the foreign and domestic policy of this nation, will be what they will be primarily remembered for, not the scandals that marred their time. For in the long run of history, it is towering achievements, not flaws, that mark great political leaders.

The political legacy they helped create is sweeping.

Anyone who is born an American is very lucky. Americans have more individual liberty than any other people in the world. Their country is the wealthiest in the world. And they are defended by the most powerful military force in the world.

All this did not happen by accident.

It did not happen because Americans are superior people. We are not stronger or smarter than other people in the world. The natural resources and the climate of the United States are good, but they are not unmatched. It did not happen because of culture or heritage. Many other countries have had sophisticated civilizations for thousands of years. In terms of culture the United States is just reaching full strength. It has not yet begun to stretch its muscles, to test the limits of its power.

What gave birth to this young, growing giant was the invention of a new political philosophy—just over 200 years ago—a political philosophy that has grown, and changed, and matured over those years.

In its current form it is United States capitalism, very different from most people's idea of the old capitalism. It is a new blend of extraordinary personal freedom, great economic wealth, and overwhelming military power.

As we move relentlessly toward the beginning of the twenty-first century, we enter the age of a new capitalism. That new capitalism is most fully formed in the United States, but elements of it are now spreading rapidly in other countries throughout the world. A new, restless, surging capitalism is on the move.

The new capitalism is a powerful idea but, like all ideas, it is not necessarily permanent. Capitalism is an idea and ideas need constant renewal, to be passed from person to person as the gen-

erations change. Momentum is now on the side of the new capitalists, but the destiny of the new capitalism is not guaranteed. Its
destiny will depend on those to whom this rare torch of liberty has
been passed.

The present citizens of the United States now hold in trust the
future of America and with it the future of the entire free world.
Their fathers and mothers, and theirs before them, produced a great
society—not perfect, just simply the best anyone has created so
far.

What we will do with that heritage is the great question of our
lives.

SOURCES

Chapter One:

1. Philip Taubman, *New York Times*, November 15, 1985, p. 1.
2. Ibid.
3. Peter Duignan and Alvin Rabushka, eds., *The United States in the 1980s* (Stanford, CA: Hoover Press, 1980).
4. Sidney Blumenthal, "Gorbachev's Primer on America," *Washington Post*, November 17, 1985.
5. "Reagan and Past Landslides," *Congressional Quarterly Almanac*, 1984, p. 4B.

Chapter Two:

1. *Time*, November 4, 1985, p. 40.

Chapter Three:

1. *Harper's Magazine*, August 1986, pp. 1–14.
2. Honorable R. O. Douglas, Minister of Finance, Financial statement

made to the New Zealand House of Representatives, July 31, 1986, p. 1.

3. E. J. Dionne, Jr., *New York Times*, March 3, 1985.
4. E. J. Dionne, Jr., *New York Times*, March 24, 1985.
5. *Christian Science Monitor*, August 26, 1986.
6. Ibid.
7. Roger Fontaine, *Washington Times*, August 2, 1985.
8. James Brooke, "Adam Smith Crowds Marx in Angola," *New York Times*, December 29, 1987, p. 4.
9. Barbara Crossette, "Hanoi Loosens Central Economic Reins" *New York Times*, December 29, 1987, p. 5
10. Michael J. Bonafield, "Soviets Give Warning to Satellite Countries on Shifts," *Washington Times*, July 8, 1985.
11. "Gorbachev Speaks on Economic Progress, Planning," *Foreign Broadcast Information Service; USSR National Affairs*, June 12, 1985, p. R3.
12. Ibid., pp. R13–R17.
13. "Soviet Will Let Individuals Provide Some Goods and Services for Profit," *International Herald-Tribune*, November 20, 1986.
14. Mikhail Gorbachev, *Perestroika: New Thinking for Our Country and the World* (New York: Harper & Row, 1987), p. 49.
15. Ibid.
16. Ibid., p. 52.
17. Ibid., p. 58.
18. Ibid.
19. Ibid., p. 100.
20. Ibid., p. 158.
21. Ibid., pp. 36–37.
22. Ibid., p. 19.
23. Ibid., pp. 25–26.
24. Ibid., pp. 51–2.

Chapter Four:

1. Peter L. Berger, *The Capitalist Revolution: Fifty Propositions About Prosperity, Equality, and Liberty* (New York: Basic Books, Inc., 1986), p. 115.

Chapter Five:

1. Peter Hannaford, *The Reagans: A Political Portrait* (New York: Coward-McCann, 1983), p. 107.
2. Ibid.
3. *New York Times*, February 28, 1976.

4. *San Jose Mercury News*, March 18, 1976.
5. *Los Angeles Times*, March 18, 1976.
6. *Washington Post*, March 20, 1976.

Chapter Six:

1. Ronald Reagan with Richard G. Hubler, *Where's the Rest of Me?* (New York: Duell, Sloan and Pearce, 1965), p. 21.
2. Ibid., pp. 28–29.

Chapter Eight:

1. *New York Times*, "Transcript of Reagan's Remarks to the Convention," August 20, 1988, p. A–12.
2. President Ronald Reagan, Address to the Nation, March 23, 1983, *Presidential Documents*, 12:19, March 28, 1983, p. 23.
3. *Pravda*, February 11, 1967. Cited by William T. Lee and Richard F. Staar, *Soviet Military Policy: Since World War II*, Hoover Institution Press, Stanford, California, 1986, p. 200.
4. *New York Times*, December 9, 1987, p. 1.
5. Ibid., p. 7.
6. Ibid.

Chapter Ten:

1. Selected excerpts taken from Martin Anderson, *An Insurance Missile Defense* (Stanford, CA: Hoover Institution Press, 1986); *New York Times*, "For a Limited Missile Defense," Martin Anderson, October 29, 1984; *The Washington Post*, "We Need an Insurance Missile Defense System," Martin Anderson, November 26, 1985; *Wall Street Journal*, "The U.S. Can Build a Pinpoint Strategic Defense Now," Martin Anderson, May 19, 1986.

Chapter Twelve:

1. Jack W. Germond and Jules Witcover, *Chicago Tribune*, "Reagan needs economic plan," September 1, 1980, Section 5, p. 4.
2. *Washington Post*, "Reagan Plan Figures Called Way Off Base," by Caroline Atkinson, September 5, 1980, p. 1.
3. "A Modest Program," *Wall Street Journal*, September 22, 1980.

Chapter Thirteen:

1. Adam Smith, *An Inquiry Into The Nature and Causes of the Wealth of Nations*, Grant Richards, London, 1904, Volume II, pp. 544–545.

2. Robert E. Keleher and William P. Orzechowski, "Supply-Side Fiscal Policy: An Historical Analysis of a Rejuvenated Idea," in *Supply-Side Economics: A Critical Appraisal*, edited by Richard H. Fink, Aletheia Books, University Publications of America, 1982, p. 147.

3. John Maynard Keynes, *The Means of Prosperity*, Harcourt, Brace and Company, New York, 1933, p. 5.

4. *Washington Times*, May 28, 1986, p. B1.

5. Jude Wanniski, *The Way The World Works: How Economies Fail—and Succeed*, Basic Books, Inc., New York, 1978, p. 301.

6. Sidney Blumenthal, *The Rise of the Counter-Establishment*, Time Books, New York, 1986, p. 174.

7. Jude Wanniski, "It's Time to Cut Taxes," *Wall Street Journal*, December 11, 1974.

8. Herbert Stein, *Presidential Economics: The Making of Economic Policy from Roosevelt to Reagan and Beyond*, Simon and Schuster, New York, 1984, p. 241.

9. *Human Events*, June 20, 1987, p. 18.

10. Lawrence B. Lindsey, *Taxpayer Behavior and the Distribution of the 1982 Tax Cut*, Working Paper No. 1760, National Bureau of Economic Research, Inc., Cambridge, Massachusetts, October 1985, p. 35.

11. *Wall Street Journal* editorial, "Supply-Side Results," December 31, 1987, p. 8.

12. Letter from Martin Feldstein, March 24, 1987.

13. Walter S. Salant, *A Critical Look at Supply-Side Theory and a Brief Look at Some of Its International Aspects*, Brookings Institution General Series Reprint 425, Washington, D.C., May 1987, pp. 122–123.

14. Letter from Walter S. Salant, August 18, 1987.

15. Herbert Stein, from foreword to *Reagan and the Economy: The Successes, Failures & Unfinished Agenda* by Michael J. Boskin, ICS Press, San Francisco, 1987, p. xv.

16. Herbert Stein, *Presidential Economics: The Making of Economic Policy from Roosevelt to Reagan and Beyond*, Simon and Schuster, New York, 1984, pp. 258–259.

17. Letter from Jack Kemp to the editor of the *Wall Street Journal*, "Kemp on Stein: 'Are We All Supply-Siders Now?'" April 4, 1980, p. 10.

18. *The Economist*, "Conservative Economics," October 24, 1987, p. 23.

19. Alan S. Blinder, *Hard Heads, Soft Hearts: Tough-Minded Economics for a Just Society* (New York: Addison-Wesley, 1987) p. 87.

20. Ibid., p. 88.

21. Letter from Alan S. Blinder, November 24, 1987.

22. *Economic Policy*, "A European Forum: The Conservative Revolution," Press Syndicate of the University of Cambridge, October 1987, p. 49.

23. Ibid.

24. Ibid., p. 181.
25. Bruce Bartlett, "The Battle for Reagan's Mind," *The Libertarian Review*, July 1980, p. 12.
26. Blumenthal, op. cit., p. 225.

Chapter Fourteen:

1. Anne Edwards, *Early Reagan* (New York: William Morrow, 1987), p. 95.
2. Ibid., p. 112.
3. William E. Simon, *A Time for Truth* (New York: Readers Digest Press, 1978) jacket copy.

Chapter Fifteen:

1. Robert Pear, "Economic Expansion in U.S. Continues into a 59th Month," *New York Times*, October 1, 1987.
2. *Economic Report of the President* (Washington: GPO, 1988), Table B–32: *Population and the labor force,* employment including resident Armed Forces, p. 284.
3. Ibid., Table B–1, p. 244.
4. Ibid.
5. Ibid., Table B–74, p. 332–3.
6. Selected excerpts taken from Martin Anderson, *An Economic Bill of Rights* (Stanford, California: Hoover Institution Press, 1984).
7. Text of Remarks by the President at Independence Day Celebration, The Jefferson Memorial, Washington, D.C., July 3, 1987.
8. Paul L. Ford, ed., *The Writings of Thomas Jefferson* (New York, 1896), vol. 7, p. 310, quoted in Richard E. Wagner et al., eds., *Balanced Budgets, Fiscal Responsibility, and the Constitution* (Washington, D.C.: CATO Institute, 1982), p. 107.

Chapter Sixteen:

1. Richard Nathan, *The Plot That Failed: Nixon and the Administrative Presidency* (New York: John Wiley and Sons, 1975), p. 50.
2. Wallace Earl Walker and Michael R. Reopel, "Strategies for Governance: Transition and Domestic Policymaking in the Reagan Administration," *Presidential Studies Quarterly* 16, no. 4 (Fall 1986): 1.
3. G. Calvin Mackenzie, "The Reaganites Come to Town: Personnel Selection for a Conservative Administration," paper presented at the American Political Science Association Meetings, New York City, September 2, 1981 (revised January 1982), p. 3.

4. *National Journal*, February 21, 1981, p. 302.
5. Mackenzie, p. 15.

Chapter Eighteen:

1. Michael K. Deaver with Mickey Herskowitz, *Behind the Scenes* (New York: William Morrow, 1987), p. 165.
2. Ibid., p. 166.
3. Ibid.
4. Ibid.
5. Ibid., p. 86.
6. Ibid., p. 87.
7. Ibid.
8. Ibid.
9. Ibid.
10. Ibid.
11. Ibid., p. 247.

Chapter Nineteen:

1. Walker and Reopel, p. 735.
2. Letter from Stuart E. Eizenstat, August 20, 1981.

Chapter Twenty:

1. David A. Stockman, *The Triumph of Politics: How the Reagan Revolution Failed* (New York: Harper and Row, 1986), p. 393.
2. Owen Ullmann, *Stockman: The Man, the Myth, the Future* (New York: Donald I. Fine, 1986), p. 70.
3. Stockman, p. 109.

Chapter Twenty-One:

1. William Safire, *New York Times*, January 19, 1987.
2. Stockman, p. 2.
3. John Greenya and Anne Urban, *The Real David Stockman* (New York: St. Martin's Press, 1986), p. 127.
4. Blumenthal, p. 213.
5. Paul Craig Roberts, *The Supply-Side Revolution* (Cambridge: Harvard University Press, 1984), p. 122.
6. Telephone interview with Paul Craig Roberts, June 22, 1987.
7. *U.S. News and World Report*, September 30, 1985, p. 31.

Chapter Twenty-Three:

1. *Fortune*, September 15, 1986, p. 36–37.
2. Richard P. Nathan, "International Change under Reagan," John L. Palmer, ed., *Perspectives on the Reagan Years* (Washington, D.C.: Urban Institute, 1986), p. 141.
3. *Newsweek*, December 1, 1980, p. 30.
4. Ann Reilly Dowd, "What Managers Can Learn from President Reagan," *Fortune*, September 15, 1986, p. 41.
5. Ibid.
6. Meg Greenfield, "How Does Reagan Decide?" *Newsweek*, February 20, 1984, p. 80.
7. Dowd, Ibid.
8. *Christian Science Monitor*, May 15, 1981.
9. Dowd, p. 41.

Chapter Twenty-Four:

1. Bernard Weinraub with Gerald Boyd, "Reagan's Ability to Lead Nation At a Low, Critics and Friends Say," *New York Times*, June 28, 1987.

Chapter Twenty-Five:

1. *The United States Government Manual,*(Washington: GPO, 1986–87).
2. Alexander M. Haig, Jr., *Caveat: Realism, Reagan, and Foreign Policy* (New York: Macmillan, 1984), p. 159–60.
3. *New York Times*, March 11, 1987.
4. *New York Times*, August 1, 1987.

Chapter Twenty-Six:

1. *Wall Street Journal*, February 26, 1987.
2. Joseph E. Persico, *Piercing the Reich: The Penetration of Nazi Germany by American Secret Agents during World War II* (New York: Ballentine, 1979).
3. Ibid., p. 23.
4. Ibid., frontispiece.
5. Ibid., p. 209.
6. Ibid.
7. Ibid., p. 262.
8. Hannaford, p. 229.
9. Executive Order No. 12334, December 4, 1981.
10. Laurence I. Barrett, *Gambling with History; Ronald Reagan in the White House* (New York: Doubleday, 1983), p. 464.

11. Ibid., p. 382.
12. David Hoffman, "Casey Is Cited as Source of Carter Briefing Book," *Washington Post*, June 23, 1983.
13. *New York Times*, July 6, 1983.
14. Rowland Evans and Robert Novak, *Washington Post*, July 11, 1983.

Chapter Twenty-Seven:

1. *Report of the President's Special Review Board,* February 26, 1987, p. B–58.
2. Ibid., p. III–12.
3. *Encyclopedia Britannica*, 15th ed., "convulsions."
4. *New York Times*, December 24, 1986.
5. *Washington Post*, December 24, 1986.
6. *Acta Neurol Scand* 1986, June 1973 (6) p. 602–14.
7. *Journal of Surgical Oncology*, 33, no. 2 (October 1986): 95–102.
8. Eugene A. Quindlen, M.D., "Intracranial Neoplasms," Rex B. Conn, M.D., ed., *Current Diagnosis* (Philadelphia: W. B. Saunders, 1985), p. 965.
9. *Washington Post*, January 14, 1987.
10. Ibid.
11. William Safire, "In From the Cold," *New York Times*, May 7, 1987.
12. William Safire, "Three Blind Mice," *New York Times*, June 11, 1987.
13. Rowland Evans and Robert Novak, "Inside Report," *San Francisco Examiner*, July 8, 1987.

Chapter Twenty-Eight:

1. White House Press Release, November 15, 1981.
2. *The President's Foreign Intelligence Advisory Board (PFIAB)*, Hale Foundation, 1981.
3. Ibid.
4. Ibid., pp. 8–9.
5. Ibid., p. 12.
6. Interview with Robert C. McFarlane, February 2, 1988.
7. Ibid.
8. Peter Kilborn, *New York Times*, November 5, 1985.
9. Interview with Donald Regan, September 29, 1987.
10. Robert C. McFarlane.
11. "Bush Committee Set for White House Bid," *Washington Times*, October 29, 1985.

12. Donald Regan.
13. *Washington Times*, August 12, 1985.

Chapter Twenty-Nine:

1. *San Jose Mercury News*, March 8, 1987, and *Regardie's*, "The Man Who Knew Too Much," John Wallach and Janet Wallach, March 1987, pp. 50–64.
2. Ibid.
3. Ibid.
4. Ibid.
5. Bob Woodward and Lou Cannon, *Report of the President's Special Review Board*, page III–22 and C–4, C–5; *The Washington Post*, "McFarlane Note Told of Saudi Cash," March 19, 1987, p. 1.; Jeff Gerth, " '81 Saudi Deal: Help for Rebels for U.S. Arms," *New York Times*, February 4, 1987, p. 1.
6. *San Jose Mercury News*, March 8, 1987.
7. Ibid.
8. *Report of the President's Special Review Board*, B–11, fn. 5.
9. Ibid.
10. *San Jose Mercury*, March 8, 1987.
11. *Washington Post*, "Lobbyist Deaver Abandoned by Last Foreign Client," Michael Isikoff, March 7, 1987, p. A4.
12. Ibid.
13. Ibid.
14. *Report of the President's Special Review Board*, page B–3.
15. *Jane's Weapons Systems*, 1986–87, pp. 69–79.
16. *Webster's Seventh New Collegiate Dictionary*, s.v. "lobbying."
17. Ibid., s.v. "cabal."
18. *Washington Post*, January 12, 1987.
19. *Washington Post*, February 1, 1987.
20. National Security Archive, *The Chronology* (New York: Warner Books, 1987), p. 491.
21. *Washington Post*, February 1, 1987.
22. *Report of the President's Special Review Board, Washington Post*, January 12, 1987. *Washington Post*, February 1, 1987; *The Chronology*, 92–3; *Chronology*, 98; *Chronology*, 108; "Report," B–17; "Report," B–18; *San Francisco Examiner*, February 18, 1987; "Report," B–26 and B–29; "Report," B–29; "Report," B–29; "Report," B–29; "Report," B–47.
23. *Report*, B–18.
24. Ibid.

25. Ibid., B–10.
26. Ibid., B–9.
27. Ibid., B–18.
28. Ibid., B–14.
29. *New York Times*, June 23, 1987.
30. *Report*, B–3.
31. Michael Ledeen, "How the Iran Initiative Went Wrong," *The Wall Street Journal*, August 10, 1987.
32. *Washington Post*, February 1, 1987.
33. Ledeen, August 10, 1987.
34. *Report*, B–52, B–53.

Chapter Thirty:

1. *Chronology*, pp. 140–141.
2. *Report of the President's Special Review Board*, B–19, B–20.
3. *Chronology*, p. 245.
4. George Carver, "Covert Operations," *Washington Times*, August 17, 1987.
5. Statement by Arthur Liman during Oliver North's testimony before the Select Committee on Secret Military Assistance to Iran and the Nicaraguan Opposition, July 10, 1987.
6. *Time*, July 13, 1987, pp. 29–30.
7. *The New Republic*, February 16, 1987, p. 13.
8. *New York Times*, "Pentagon Aides Say North Spent 10 Days in Hospital in 1974," Keith Schneider, December 24, 1986, p. A6.
9. Ibid.
10. *Time*, July 13, 1987, p. 30.
11. "The Story of Lieutenant Colonel Oliver North," *U.S. News & World Report*, 1987, p. 10.
12. Ibid., pp. 15–17.
13. *Washington Post*, Glenn Frankel, December 27, 1986, and January 12, 1987, *Chronology*, p. 235.
14. Ibid.
15. North's testimony, July 14, 1987.
16. *New York Times*, July 11, 1987.
17. *New York Times*, July 9, 1987, page 6, North's testimony of July 8, 1987.
18. Poindexter's testimony, July 15, 1987.
19. *New York Times*, July 9, 1987.
20. *New York Times*, July 16, 1987.
21. Ibid.

22. *Taking the Stand: The Testimony of Lieutenant Colonel Oliver L. North* (New York: Pocket Books, 1987) p. 443.

Chapter Thirty-One:

1. *Taking the Stand: The Testimony of Lieutenant Colonel Oliver L. North,* with an introduction by Daniel Schorr (New York: Pocket Books, 1987), p. 189.
2. Ibid., pp. 190–191.
3. Ibid.
4. Ibid., pp. 190 and 193.
5. *New York Times*, May 21, 1987.
6. Transcript of Robert Owen's testimony, May 19, 1987, lines 588–596.
7. North's testimony, p. 181.
8. North's testimony, p. 182.
9. *Wall Street Journal*, July 7, 1987.
10. North's testimony, p. 186.
11. "Sale of North Town House Reportedly Investigated," *San Jose Mercury News*, September 21, 1987.
12. Transcript of Hakim's testimony, June 3, 1987, lines 1368–89.
13. Ibid., lines 1399 to 1401.
14. Ibid., lines 1401–05.
15. *Chronology*, p. 639.
16. Hakim's testimony, lines 204–07 and 316–46.
17. Ibid., line 1438.
18. "Story of Lieutenant Colonel North," p. 115.
19. North's testimony, 195.
20. Ibid.
21. Hakim's testimony, lines 1461–64.
22. Ibid., lines 1469–82.
23. Ibid., lines 1345–59.
24. Ibid., lines 1509–14.
25. North's testimony, 197.
26. Hakim's testimony, lines 1642–43.
27. Ibid., lines 1645–53.
28. Ibid., lines 1749–56.
29. Ibid., lines 1673–75.
30. *Time*, June 8, 1987, 25.
31. Secord's testimony, May 5, 1987, lines 1952–2024.
32. *International Who's Who*, 1986–87 ed.
33. *Report of the President's Special Review Board*, B–24.

34. Ibid.
35. *Chronology*, p. 403.
36. Ibid., p. 453.
37. Ibid., p. 463.
38. *New York Times*, May 13, 1987.
39. *Chronology*, pp. 446–449.
40. Ibid.
41. North's testimony, p. 459.
42. *Chronology*, 448–49.
43. *Report*, B–124.
44. Ibid., B–124.
45. Ibid., B–125.

Chapter Thirty-Two:

1. *New York Times*, July 24, 1987.
2. W. L. Warren, *Henry II* (Berkeley, CA: University of California Press, 1973) p. 508; and Richard Barber, *Henry Plantagenet* (London: Barrie and Rockliff, Ltd., 1964), p. 144.
3. *Encyclopedia Brittanica*, Micropedia, Vol. 1, pp. 58–59.

Chapter Thirty-Three:

1. Transcript of "A Conversation with Ronald Reagan," *Bill Moyers' Journal*, Show #415, air date: May 14, 1979, pp. 16 and 17.
2. Carl Bridenbaugh, *Silas Downer: Forgotten Patriot* (Providence, RI: Rhode Island Bicentennial Foundation, 1974), 2, note 2; 3.
3. Ibid., p. 3.
4. Sibley's Harvard Grads, Massachusetts Historical Society, Boston, 1961, Volume 12, pp. 129–131.
5. Bridenbaugh, pp. 3–4.
6. Ibid., p. 33.
7. Ibid., p. 34.
8. Ibid., p. 35.
9. Franklin Folsom, *Give Me Liberty: America's Colonial Heritage* (Chicago: Rand McNally, 1974), p. 168.
10. Edward Countryman, *The American Revolution* (New York: Hill and Wang, 1985), p. 98.

Index